Jury Duty

This book provides the reader with an introduction to the jury system in the United States. It provides a brief historical account of the origins of juries and compares juries in the federal versus state court systems, and a grand jury versus a trial jury. The text offers answers to the most frequently asked questions that prospective jurors and students have about the steps of jury duty, from receiving the juror summons to rendering a final verdict. Through this easy-to-digest overview, the reader will gain an appreciation for the intended purpose of the American jury and develop a better understanding of how shifting social norms, over the past 250 years, have impacted the decision-making powers granted to the jury. Each chapter features contemporary research findings about juries, learning objectives, review and discussion questions, ethical considerations, summary tables, and features focusing on news, fun facts, court decisions, and reflections from working professionals. The book is written for students in the social and behavioral sciences, including criminal justice and administrative justice, law, policy and society, psychology, psychology and law, race and gender studies, political science, sociology, social work, and prelaw courses; for legal professionals and law students, who frequent courthouses and prepare legal documents, briefs, trial evidence, and defendant or victim testimonies for litigation; and, of course, this book will appeal to prospective and former jurors.

Michael E. Antonio is Professor of Criminal Justice at West Chester University in Pennsylvania. He earned his Bachelor of Science degree in Psychology from Ursinus College and his Ph.D. in Law, Policy, and Society from Northeastern University. He served as the Lead Research Scientist on the Capital Jury Project with Dr. William J. Bowers from 2001 to 2005. Some of his publications related to juries appeared in *Wash. & Lee L. Rev.*, *Boston University L. Rev.*, *Judicature*, *Behavioral Sciences & the Law*, and *Justice System Journal*.

Paula Hannaford-Agor was director of the Center for Jury Studies at the National Center for State Courts from 2006 to 2025. In that capacity, she regularly conducted research and provided technical assistance and education to judges, court staff, and lawyers on the topics of jury system management and jury trial procedures. She has authored or contributed to numerous books and articles on the American jury, including *Jury Trial Innovations* (2nd edition, 2006), *The Promise and Challenges of Jury System Technology* (NCSC 2003), and *Managing Notorious Trials* (1998). She received her law degree and a Master of Public Policy degree from the College of William & Mary in 1995 and her Bachelor of Arts in Government & Politics from George Mason University in 1991.

Jury Duty

An Introduction

Michael E. Antonio and
Paula Hannaford-Agor

Routledge
Taylor & Francis Group
NEW YORK AND LONDON

Designed cover image: Getty Images

First published 2027
by Routledge
605 Third Avenue, New York, NY 10158

and by Routledge
4 Park Square, Milton Park, Abingdon, Oxon, OX14 4RN

Routledge is an imprint of the Taylor & Francis Group, an informa business

Library of Congress Cataloging-in-Publication Data
Names: Antonio, Michael E. author | Hannaford-Agor, Paula author
Title: Jury duty : an introduction / Michael E. Antonio and Paula Hannaford-Agor.
Description: Abingdon, Oxon [UK]; New York, NY : Routledge, 2026. |
Includes bibliographical references and index. Identifiers: LCCN 2026005591 (print) |
LCCN 2026005592 (ebook) | ISBN 9781041151111 paperback |
ISBN 9781041151128 hardback | ISBN 9781003677796 ebook
Subjects: LCSH: Jury—United States | Jurors—United States—Decision making
Classification: LCC KF8972.A93 2026 (print) | LCC KF8972 (ebook)
LC record available at https://lccn.loc.gov/2026005591
LC ebook record available at https://lccn.loc.gov/2026005592

ISBN: 978-1-041-15112-8 (hbk)
ISBN: 978-1-041-15111-1 (pbk)
ISBN: 978-1-003-67779-6 (ebk)

DOI: 10.4324/9781003677796

Typeset in Galliard
by codeMantra

Access the Support Material: www.routledge.com/9781041151111

For every American.

Michael E. Antonio

For Tom Munsterman, who nurtured me after I was first bitten by "the jury bug."

Paula Hannaford-Agor

Contents

Preface

There are two kinds of citizens living in America today, those who were previously summoned to jury service and those who may be summoned in the future. All citizens, regardless of occupation, economic status, race, national origin, ethnic group identification, religion, sex, sexual orientation, color, or disability may be summoned and may qualify for jury service. Qualified jurors may be asked to report to the courthouse on a given day and time. This summons is not a suggestion but a legal mandate that all qualified citizens are expected to follow. This book, therefore, is relevant to all citizens who may be summoned and qualify to fulfill their civic responsibility to their community, state, or country.

Many prospective jurors may report to the courthouse on their assigned day but have no functional or operational understanding about the jury system. The jury deliberation process and the manner for how juries reach a verdict has been popularized in several classic Hollywood movies, such as *Twelve Angry Men*, *To Kill a Mockingbird*. More recently, jury antics were portrayed in the mockumentary series *Jury Duty*. Clearly, media portrayal of juries on television may either be skewed or outright wrong. Also, few prospective jurors may be aware of the intent of the Founding Fathers for explicitly including language and sentiment about "trial by jury" into the very documents that define American citizens' rights to liberty and freedom. Arguably, the American jury system could be greatly improved if citizens knew more about the power and purpose of the jury.

Goals

There are only so many goals that can be achieved in one textbook about the American jury system. Within the confines of these pages, we have a few broad aims in mind.

First, juries have the power to shape society. This text was written to excite common citizens (including students) about jury service and for them to see that jury service offers a unique opportunity to directly impact their local community, state, and, possibly, country, if called to serve as a grand juror or trial juror.

Second, we hope the readers will better appreciate the intended purpose of the American jury and better understand how shifting social norms over the past 250 years have impacted the decision-making powers granted to the jury.

Many books on juries are written in complex legalese and focus only on very specific aspects of the jury system (e.g., voir dire, deliberation, etc.). This book is intended for multiple audiences, including undergraduate and graduate students from any college major. Students who study the social or behavioral sciences, like criminal justice and criminology, public policy and public administration, psychology, political science, social work, sociology, and race and gender studies, will have a particular interest.

This text was also written with university instructors in mind. Each chapter includes test bank questions (categorized as easy, moderate, or difficult in intensity) and PowerPoint slides that follow chapter content. Also, each chapter's endnotes were written following American Psychological Association format to conform with standards used by many social scientists.

Chapter Features

"What Do You Think" questions and answers. Unique to this text, each chapter opens with a series of true/false questions designed to stimulate the reader's thinking about a specific aspect of the jury system or jury service. Answers to these questions are provided at the end of each chapter.

Learning Objectives. Objectives describe what the reader will be able to do after reading the chapter material. Meeting these objectives will result in readers being able to describe, explain, list, compare, etc., information related to the American jury system.

"Box" segments. Each chapter includes box segments that provide supplemental information about the issue being addressed. Box segments may include a specific example, details about a court case, juries in the news, or fun facts. This information is intended to engage the reader.

Summary tables. Some chapters describe a significant amount of information related to U.S. Supreme Court decisions, trial procedures, trial outcomes in notorious cases, etc. Summary tables in many chapters organize and briefly summarize main points.

"From the Field" segments. Each chapter features a current or former academic or practitioner who had some involvement with juries or jury service. Some of the individuals worked as court administrators, judges, professors, trial attorneys, and trial consultants.

Conclusion. The chapter material ends in the conclusion section. A transitional sentence or paragraph is included that ties the current chapter that that that that to the topic that will be addressed in the next chapter.

Summary. Each chapter ends with a summary of the main points discussed in the order they were addressed in the chapter.

Discussion Questions. Multiple discussion questions are posed to spur critical thinking about chapter material. Unique to this text, some of the questions are identified as an "ethical consideration" and encourage a response involving critical thinking.

Review Questions. Several review questions are posed at the end of each chapter that correspond with the learning objectives. Readers can assess their understanding and reexamine chapter content where needed.

Key Terms. These terms emphasize important material related to the chapter's content. Each term is shown in bold font.

Acknowledgments

We are deeply grateful to the Founding Fathers, the Framers of the U.S. Constitution, for their visionary courage and wisdom for establishing a government where power ultimately resides with the people. Their trust in ordinary citizens to shape the laws governing their lives, rather than relying on a centralized authority to dictate the community's moral compass, laid the foundation for this work. Without their enduring legacy, this text would not exist.

This project also owes its depth and breadth to the generous contributions of others. Many individuals provided invaluable support by sharing contemporary jury research, court documents, practitioner insights, and feedback on earlier drafts. We extend my heartfelt thanks to Sara Boches, Giovanni Campbell, Nina Chernoff, John Choi, Lucretia Clemons, Elizabeth Dumond, Richard Gabriel, Pamela Gates, Dave Golberg, Patrick Martin, Barbara McDermott, Thomas J. McSweeney, Shuaiyb Newton, Julie Pfaff, Matt Pierlott, Susan R. Shutt, Christopher Stangl, Stella M. Tsai, Nicole Waters, and Paul Wilson, for their time, expertise, and dedication. Your contributions were instrumental to the success of this text.

—M.E.A. & P.H.A

PART I

Purpose—Origin, Intention, and Implementation

This section of the text examines the historical evolution and contemporary challenges of the jury trial system in the United States. The origins of jury trials trace back to Ancient Athens around 500 BCE, with medieval England formalizing the system under monarchs like King Henry II and through the Magna Carta, which laid the groundwork for modern practices. English traditions, including specialized juries, were adopted by American colonists, with early trials recorded in Jamestown and Plymouth. The U.S. Constitution and Bill of Rights, influenced by these principles, enshrined jury trials in Article III and in the Sixth and Seventh Amendments to ensure impartial justice and citizen participation. However, historical exclusion of racial minorities and women from jury service reveals persistent inequalities, despite reforms reducing overt discrimination. The federal jury system includes grand juries, which assess probable cause for indictments but face criticism for prosecutorial control and secrecy, and trial juries, which handle criminal and civil cases with distinct evidentiary standards. State jury systems, shaped by federalism, vary in size, eligibility, and procedures, with grand juries often criticized for lacking accountability, particularly in cases involving police misconduct. Ongoing debates highlight the need for reforms to enhance transparency, reduce prosecutorial influence, and ensure fair representation, underscoring the jury system's critical role in upholding justice and democratic governance.

DOI: 10.4324/9781003677796-1

1 The Seeds of Trial by Jury

What Do You Think?

Before reviewing the concepts addressed in this chapter, answer True or False to each of the following questions or statements. Correct answers can be found at the end of Chapter 1.

1. In England, trials by ordeal were enacted after a trial by jury.
2. King Henry II of England is credited with establishing the first grand jury in the Middle Ages.
3. The Magna Carta laid the critical groundwork for jury trials practiced in medieval England and later adopted by the United States.
4. In 17th century England, a Gentlemen Jury was comprised of jurors who were of a similar race and had a shared culture with the defendant.
5. The first jury trial in America occurred in the Plymouth Colony.
6. In the first known murder trial in the American colonies, John White was charged with the killing of John Newcomin.
7. A grand jury refused to charge publisher John Peter Zenger with seditious libel for printing comments critical of Governor William Crosby.

Learning Objectives

After reading this chapter, you will be able to:

1. Describe the types and purpose of "trials by ordeal" used in medieval England.
2. Discuss how King Henry II is associated with the first grand jury.
3. Recognize the importance of the Assize of Clarendon on the evolution of trial by jury.
4. Explain the association among barons, English nobility, King James, and the Magna Carta.
5. Discuss the importance of the first English expeditions to the New World.
6. Explain how the first English legal traditions and customs were adopted in colonial America.

Introduction

The purpose of this chapter is to inform the reader about antecedents to the contemporary American jury system, including the turbulent beginnings the Founding Fathers faced when attempting to develop a national identity that eliminated all resonance of oppression and abuse experienced by the early American colonists at the hands of the English monarchy in the 18th century. The noble ideals of a jury system that protected the freedoms of

DOI: 10.4324/9781003677796-2

average citizens and dispensed justice in a fair and impartial manner were unique features that emerged from this struggle.

The jury system that was conceived during the infancy of the newly formed nation evolved over centuries as American society and culture matured and developed. Truthfully, the American jury system is still evolving today among calls for reform from legal scholars and the public alike. Contemporary problems related to the dismissal of prospective jurors based on gender or race and to grand juries that fail to indict law enforcement officers who use lethal force are among the leading concerns of opponents who criticize the jury system. Any discussion about the current problems of the American jury is meaningless without a clear and thorough description of the origins, history, and evolution of trial by jury from medieval England.

This chapter highlights several important historical events and people who resided in medieval England from the 7th to the 13th centuries. This information is important to better understand the development and evolution of English common law, which heavily influenced legal practices and tradition in colonial America. The brief history provided in this chapter relates to the reigns of several English monarchs and the sensational events surrounding the signing of the Magna Carta. A review of this material is by no means a complete picture about the important happenings in medieval England or a full explanation for how these complex events informed and influenced the Founding Fathers of the United States. Indeed, research about how and in what ways England's common law shaped the origins and intent of the U.S. Constitution will uncover vast arguments, criticisms, and debates among even the most informed and learned historians in this area. Given this disclaimer, let us begin.

In This Chapter

This chapter describes specific aspects of the American jury system. Material relates to: 1) the origins of trials by ordeal; 2) English monarchs' influence on the development of legal traditions and customs; 3) events surrounding the development of the Magna Carta; and 4) the adoption of English laws and customs by the original American colonists.

Ancient Athens

Trial by jury first emerged in Ancient Athens around 500 BCE. Under the leadership of Cleisthenes (570–508 BCE) and later Pericles (495–429 BCE), male citizens over the age of 30 volunteered to hear disputes about civil, criminal, and political matters.[1] Unlike modern times, these juries were large, consisting of 200 to 500 members randomly selected from the thousands who volunteered to serve. Each member was permitted to cast an anonymous vote to determine the outcome of the case. The majority verdict determined the winning side. With such large juries, majority rule deterred the use of bribery and other illicit efforts to influence the jury's decision and may have facilitated inclusion of citizens from many classes of Athens' society. Also, Pericles instigated a juror compensation system that further ensured representation by poorer citizens. The Athenian jury system may have been the first attempt to empanel a fair and representative jury.

The procedures governing juries in Athens were unique compared to today's standards. First, plaintiffs and defendants represented themselves and gave impassioned speeches during the trial. Judges and attorneys were removed from the process, and the empaneled jurors did not engage in a deliberation process but rather cast independent votes for guilt or innocence.[2] The outcome of the trial, based on the majority vote, could not be appealed. The Athenian system empowered common citizens to make decisions about important matters facing their society. These are the basic ideals comprising a democratic system of government. In Athens, as in modern democratic jury trials, jurors' emotions and feelings could actively influence trial outcomes.[3] Box 1.1 describes this possibility in a high-profile case involving Greek philosopher Socrates in 399 BCE. Box 1.2 features a practitioner who provides additional insight about the influence of Greek philosophy on the American jury system.

Box 1.1: Trial of Socrates

Athenian teacher and philosopher Socrates was tried on multiple charges in an Athenian court in 501 BCE. One charge was for undermining traditional religious practices by failing to acknowledge the Athenian gods. A second charge was for corrupting his young students by encouraging them to question authority and traditional values of Athenian society, and for instilling anti-democratic sentiments within Athens' youth.[4] His student, Plato, wrote in the *Apology* about how Socrates' relentless questioning of social and political traditions enraged Athens' ruling class.

At his trial, Socrates actively defended himself, boldly asserting his dedication to truth and moral inquiry. He argued that his questioning invigorated Athens by sparking critical thought. Despite his passionate defense speech, the jury of 501 Athenians narrowly convicted him of the charges. Socrates firmly rejected exile, steadfastly upholding his philosophical mission even in the face of death. The court sentenced him to die by drinking a cup of hemlock.[5] The trial vividly highlighted tensions between individual free thought and societal conformity, with Socrates' execution solidifying his legacy as a martyr for philosophy. His students, including Plato, later enshrined his ideas, profoundly shaping Western thought.

Box 1.2: From the Field

Name: Matthew Pierlott

Position: Professor of Philosophy

How long have you been in this position?

I have taught since 2006.

What was the significance of the Athenian jury system to the foundations of your field?

Plato's *Apology* depicts the trial of his teacher, Socrates, and in it we see an implicit critique of the system. The character of Socrates alleges the jury has been biased by rumors spread about him for years and asks them to pretend he is a stranger they know nothing about. He also alleges that his three accusers are insincere in their charges, motivated by their own sense of being embarrassed by Socrates' previous public challenges to their views. While the large number of citizens serving on the jury helped protect them from bribery, these juries were still very vulnerable to gossip and rhetoric. This fact likely influenced much of Plato's work, since many of his early dialogues focused on exposing the superiority of his teacher's philosophical method over the rhetoric of the "sophists," like the three accusers. Additionally, the fact that they convicted Socrates likely led to many of Plato's suspicions about whether a direct democracy could achieve justice. In his *Republic*, Plato argued democracy pursues freedom at the expense of what is true, good, and just. He views citizens in a democracy as too occupied with their own private desires and vulnerable to manipulation because of it. It is easy to imagine that his experience of Socrates' trial and death is at the heart of these critical conclusions.

How did you think this has shaped the way we understand the proper functioning of juries today?

While our system is very different than the Athenian system, we do worry about prior prejudice. We think it is extremely important that a jury of our fellow citizens play a role in the administration of justice and the protection of innocence. Nonetheless, we allow attorneys to question jurors to weed out bias during the selection process, and we sometimes require sequestration to prevent bias from potentially misleading information circulating in the media and society.

What is your advice to someone interested in philosophy and its connection to the criminal justice system?

Philosophy is a wonderful field to help prepare anyone interested in law school. Philosophy majors perform very well on LSATs, consistently outcompeting many other majors, and the discipline is great training for the critical and analytical thinking needed to succeed in law school. It also is a great major or minor to enhance one's learning in Criminal Justice or Political Science majors. We have had several of our undergraduate majors go on to successful careers in law. Indeed, some of our graduate students transition to law school and report their preparation in philosophy helped them adjust and thrive in law school more easily than their peers.

The Middle Ages

Civilized societies throughout human history have developed many ways to punish disruptive and criminal behavior committed by individuals against other persons or property. Arguably, some of these punishments were far more severe than the actual behavior committed, or allegedly committed, by the accused.[6] Social norms change over time. Sometimes these changes occur quickly, and other times changes progress slowly over the centuries. What society perceives as fair and just punishment at one point in time may be determined to be cruel and inappropriate by later generations, and vice versa.

A good starting point for a discussion about changes in society can be found by reviewing the medieval history of England, a period referred to as the Middle Ages.[7] Scholars have debated the exact years that mark the official start and end dates for this period in history. For purposes here, it can be estimated that the range of years for the Middle Ages is from 450 through 1500.[8,9] The events that occurred during these years were as important as they were nuanced. Many of the historical details pertaining to this period fall beyond the scope of the jury; however, the seeds for the jury system practiced in the United States today were formed during several centuries of disputes among church leaders, common Englishmen, less powerful nobility (referred to as **barons**), and reigning monarchs of the Middle Ages.

Historians have written extensive reviews of English medieval history, explaining how many of the laws currently governing the United Kingdom were formulated during these important centuries.[10] The actual laws of the United Kingdom are not codified into one formal document but rather comprised of laws and rules that govern state institutions and how the state interacts with its citizens.[11] The U.S. Constitution and individual Amendments, including the Bill of Rights, are a unique departure from this, as the laws and regulations binding the central government in the United States are written and publicly available for all citizens to understand and use. The **Founding Fathers** clearly wanted American citizens to be aware of their basic rights and guarantees to freedom and protection against abuse and tyranny.

Trials by Ordeal

Trials by jury in England did not develop overnight. For centuries, disputes about innocence and methods for determining guilt were decided through **trials by ordeal**.[12] During the period between the 6th and 12th centuries, often the guilt or innocence of the accused was not disputed in front of either a judge or jury. Instead, the accused would undergo a test, an ordeal, which often involved great emotional and physical suffering, including torture.[13]

Several types of trials by ordeal were used. A common type involved **trial by water**.[14] In this trial, the accused was lowered into a body of water, typically a stream, pond, lake, river, or pool. Their arms and legs were bound to prevent swimming and to restrict other bodily movements. The act of sinking signified they were innocent of the crime. If the accused floated, they were found guilty of their crime and would receive a punishment for the alleged wrongdoing.[15] A specific type of trial by water, referred to as the **swimming test**, was used in Salem, Massachusetts in 1692.[16] Table 1.1 describes other common trials by ordeal used during this period, including fire, cauldron, combat, host, and blood. As the table indicates, evidence that determined the guilt or innocence of the accused was often subjective in nature. For example, the degree of injury incurred through trials by ordeal and the speed of recovery and healing from those injuries could be interpreted in specific ways to invoke a desired result.

> While the United States never practiced formal trials by ordeal, as seen in medieval England, during colonial America submersion in water was used to test someone accused of witchcraft.

For some trials by ordeal, the method for determining the guilt of the accused was left in divine hands. The facts of the case were not discussed during these trials; rather, the sinking or floating (innocence or guilt, respectively) of the accused in a trial by water, for example, was viewed as an act of God. The conscience of the community during the Middle Ages trusted that God would ensure an innocent person would be saved from punishment.[22] Trial by ordeal was a punishment not reserved for the poor or property-less people exclusively. Box 1.3 provides an example of a trial by fire imposed on a member of the ruling class during the Middle Ages. Box 1.4 provides comments from a law professor about trials by ordeal.

Table 1.1 Trials by Ordeal Used in the Middle Ages

Trial	*Method*
Fire[17]	The accused was made to walk approximately three meters while holding a hot iron in their hands. The speed and completeness by which the wound healed determined the truth of the accusation.
Cauldron[18]	In France, if someone was accused of contempt in court, they were required to insert their hand into a boiling cauldron to retrieve an object submerged in the scalding hot liquid. The degree of injury and speed of healing would determine innocence.
Combat[19]	Many rules were involved in such ordeals, including when the battle began and ended, what weapons could be used, how the fighting could be stopped, and how victory was determined. Innocence was determined through injury, death, or yielding (shouting "Craven!"). Craven is a term that means cowardly.
Host[20]	A priest was made to pray publicly by an alter and consume the Holy Eucharist. If he physically choked or could not swallow the host, it was seen as a sign he was guilty of the accusation.
Blood[21]	Someone accused of committing a murder would be made to circle the deceased body and touch the victim's wounds. If the body showed any sign of movement or further bleeding, the accused would be found guilty of the murder.

Box 1.3: Trial by Ordeal, Not Just for Commoners

One incident involving trial by fire received much attention, not due to the method for determining guilt, but rather for the status of the accused. The incident involved Queen Emma of Normandy. Emma was accused of engaging in adultery with the Bishop of Winchester.[23] This was a truly scandalous act during medieval times. The veracity of the claim has been debated; some historians questioned whether the Queen's own son, King Edward the Confessor, out of desire to strengthen his own political power, started the shocking rumor. Emma was forced to endure a trial by fire to determine her true innocence of alleged adultery. Her ordeal involved walking over red-hot plowshares, which were sharp, steel blades used to dig or cut into the soil to prepare the ground for planting crops.

Some accounts about Emma's ordeal indicated prayers were offered to St. Swithin asking for protection during of the trial itself.[24] She successfully completed the ordeal with minimal injuries or discomfort. It was believed that divine intervention contributed to her passing the trial; therefore, she was deemed innocent from the accusation of committing adultery. The earliest documentation for this event arose in the 13th century, two hundred years after her death; however, the legend persists.

Box 1.4: From the Field

Name: Thomas J. McSweeney

Position: Professor of Law

Why did medieval societies rely for so long on ordeals like fire, water, or combat to decide guilt, and what does this tell us about how people thought about justice at the time?

This is a big question, and one that historians have spent a lot of time debating. They have come up with a lot of different answers. But one way to think of it is this: many procedures in England during the 11th and 12th centuries relied on oath helpers. The accused would be required to take an oath that they had not committed the wrong and find a certain number of people (the number often depended on the seriousness of the wrong and the accused's status) to swear along with him. The person who could not find any oath-helpers or who was of too low a status to be thought worthy of that process was not completely out of luck, however; they could take God as their witness. I think the ordeal, particularly as used in the early common law, makes the most sense when we think of it as the accused's last chance. In the early common law, the procedure laid out in the Assize of Clarendon of 1166 was that those accused of certain serious crimes would go to the ordeal only if the jury of the local hundred (a subdivision of a county) and of the four nearest villas said they were suspected of the crime (although it is a bit more subtle than that). At that point, a lot of people had said they thought the accused had probably done it. The ordeal was that person's last shot to appeal to God. It was, in some ways, a procedural safeguard for the accused. And ordeals led to very high acquittal rates.

Many ordeals and early trials relied on the belief that God would reveal the truth. How did religion influence medieval ideas of guilt and innocence, and do you see any echoes of that influence in today's courtrooms?

Religion played a big role in the early common law. We owe the trial jury to a decision by the Church. In 1215, the Fourth Lateran Council prohibited clerics from participating in ordeals. The king's courts in England were not sure what to do, since ordeals were the ordinary way of trying accused felons and a priest was generally required to bless the implements. The courts experimented with different things before, around 1221, they decided on the trial jury as the replacement for the ordeal.

But religion entered into the administration of the common law in more personal ways, too. To give just one example, Elizabeth Papp Kamali's excellent book, *Felony and the Guilty Mind in Medieval England*, looks at new ideas about culpability, which placed heavy emphasis on the actor's intent, which were developing in the fields of theology and canon law in the 12th and

13th centuries. These ideas were being disseminated broadly, particularly through the Church's requirement, again laid out in the canons of the Fourth Lateran Council, that the laity confess their sins every year. Through confession, people in England were learning to think not just about what they had done, but also the intention with which they had done it. Kamali finds evidence that those ideas were influencing juries when they made decisions. That focus on intent as something that can make an act more or less culpable is still with us today!

Origins of Trial by Jury in England

King Henry II

As English society evolved, including changes to its traditions, customs, and laws, there was a desire to move away from disputes decided by the will of God to a system dependent more on human decision-making and reasoning. England needed strong leaders to implement these changes and develop a **common law** to unite the splintering kingdom. King Henry II reigned during the middle to late part of the 12th century (1154–1189) when England was enmeshed in war.[25] Additionally, the King was facing pressures from the Church, whose leaders claimed authority to accuse individuals of a crime and dispense harsh punishments for such alleged behavior.[26] Church leaders rarely explained the reasons for their decisions or justified their actions; they often operated under a shroud of secrecy.

The kingdom's nobility, the barons, urged their King to intervene. In 1166, Henry issued a ruling, an assize,[27] historically referred to as the **Assize of Clarendon** because the document was drafted at the King's royal hunting grounds at the Clarendon Palace located in Wiltshire, England. This ruling impacted the administration of many English laws and practices of that time, the full scope of which are quite complex and beyond the discussion here related to juries.[28] Overall, the assize authorized community leaders, not the Church, to make complaints and accusations of criminal behavior against individuals.

The legal reforms of King Henry II, particularly the Assize of Clarendon (1166), established that 12 freemen or knights from various regions of the kingdom would meet publicly as a jury of presentment to report accusations of serious crimes, such as robbery, murder, or theft. These men, connected to the local community, served as accusers or witnesses, not as judges or executioners. If they reported a suspected crime, the accused would be brought before a royal judge, and their guilt or innocence was often determined by a trial by ordeal, such as trial by fire or water, until such practices began to decline after 1215 when trial by jury gradually emerged.

Assize (pronounced as·size, ə-ˈsīz)

- An action to be decided by such a judicial inquest, the writ for instituting it, or the verdict or finding rendered by the jury
- The time or place of holding such a court, the court itself, or a session of it

Henry's innovative decision about how to resolve disputes imposed much needed control in the kingdom and was a first step for reorganizing English common law. Historians have hailed this assembly of 12 men as the first grand jury[29] and other decisions of the assize as the initial steps toward developing a trial by jury in which one's guilt and punishment would rest in the hands of the people.[30]

King John

England in the early part of the 13th century was under the rule of King John (1199–1216). This was a period of great strife for England. King John lacked military strategy on the battlefield. He waged wars with members of his own household, fought with the Church over naming an Archbishop, and seized religious property from the Church in retaliation for its opposition to him.[31] He was unpopular among the religious English commoners, who resented his disputes with the Church, and was at odds with the kingdom's barons because he expensed numerous and long-lasting wars by levying heavy taxes and taking property from them.[32]

The barons eventually tired of the heavy taxation and extended wars. They banded together to put pressure on King John to reform his treacherous ways. They even threatened to withhold paying their portion of the required taxes, despite attempts by the King to seize their land and force imprisonment upon them. In 1215, the barons laid siege to Runnymede, the King's stronghold, and the two groups met to discuss an end to the hostilities.[33] The resulting agreement produced from those negotiations was a document called the **Magna Carta.** The Magna Carta established laws that everyone, including the King, had to follow and limited the King's power in medieval England by 1) establishing the rule of law, 2) forming a representative government, and 3) instituting trial by jury.[34] Centuries later, these three ideals were the founding principles for the Framers of the American government and judicial system.

Magna Carta

The true impact of the Magna Carta on English law and traditions has been debated by scholars. The language, including individual clauses, served the purposes of the barons, who were concerned with how taxes were levied and collected, and how land and other property seized by the King were returned and distributed.[35] The Magna Carta addressed many issues pertaining to customs and rights specifically affecting the nobility of medieval England, and the overall purpose was to restrict the powers of the King.

The document also provided additional safeguards and protections for the rights of the accused and increased the fairness for persons accused of crimes. Grand jury proceedings in medieval England were held in secret, meaning the jury's decision to accuse someone of a criminal act was not influenced by the King, judge, or prosecutor. This was a significant development and showed that future conflicts could be addressed through legal means. The Framers of the U.S. Constitution included the grand jury proceeding in the **American jury system**. As we will see in Chapter 2, some 500 years after the signing of the Magna Carta, the Founding Fathers used these concepts of judgment by one's peers when drafting the Declaration of Independence, the Constitution, and the Bill of Rights.

Shortly after signing the Magna Carta, King John renounced the document, claiming he was coerced by the barons at the time and therefore the language was nonbinding.[36] Regardless of its immediate impact, the ideas associated with juries, especially grand juries, that were started under King Henry II in the 12th century took hold and began to develop in England after 1215. Many historians agree that the document influenced the Founding Fathers to include the notion of **trial by peers** that is the underpinning of the contemporary American jury system. These origins can be seen in the language of the Magna Carta. For example, **Clause 39**, while important, only applied to free men living in England at that time, so common citizens, those who were poor and without property, were not afforded these promises.

Clause 39[39]

No free man shall be seized or imprisoned, or stripped of his rights or possessions, or outlawed or exiled, or deprived of his standing in any other way, nor will we proceed with force against him, or send others to do so, except by the lawful judgement of his equals or by the law of the land.

Moreover, some historians have argued that the phrase **"judgment of his equals"** had limitations and meant "men, regardless of rank, could not be tried by those who ranked below (or above) them in the feudal hierarchy, and that freemen could not be tried by the unfree."[37] Other historians have emphasized the language in the Magna Carta only referred to a "trial by peers" and that the emergence of a trial by jury did not result for nearly another century in England.[38]

Regardless of these limitations, the ideas described in this document addressed concerns of the commoners and nobility in the Middle Ages. The changes the English monarchs made to the common law and customs because of the Magna Carta continued to evolve for centuries in England. Initially, jury trials were used to solve disputes between complainants that were not serious in nature, but rather problems associated with violating common laws. On one side was the defendant or the person (or organization) accused of a crime, and the other side was the plaintiff or person who brought a complaint of wrongdoing or harm against another person or entity.

Early English tradition for jury selection included identifying individuals who lived in the area where the dispute occurred, who witnessed the actual incident, and/or who knew the parties involved. These jurors would testify under oath during the trial about their knowledge of the events, then collectively the jury would reach a decision about guilt or innocence. Over the centuries, English traditions for trial by jury gradually changed. By the 1600s, individuals were no longer asked to serve the dual role of witness and juror. The jury system transformed into its contemporary model in which observers of the criminal wrongdoing served as witnesses during the trial and individuals who were unfamiliar with the incident served the exclusive role as a juror and decider of fact.[40]

Specialized Juries

Several types of **specialized juries** evolved in 17th century England. One type of early English jury was comprised of wealthy, property-owning men whose status in society permitted them to serve on grand juries in which issues of national importance were decided. These were called **Gentlemen Juries**.[41] These jurors also were empaneled to investigate homicides or suspicious deaths[42] and asked to settle disputes over local customs and those between tenants and landlords.[43] A second type of trial allowed for **Party Juries**. These juries were comprised of individuals who understood the language, culture, and nationality of non-English or foreign defendants.[44] Occasionally, women were empaneled to determine whether a female defendant was pregnant, especially in death penalty cases where the woman faced execution. While not an issue involving language or nationality, these "jury of matrons" were a specialized group of women selected from the community and tasked with reaching a decision that significant legal and social repercussions.[45] A third type of specialized jury was the **Professional Jury.** These individuals were educated men who had training and possessed special knowledge in specific areas, such as medicine, trade, or religion.[46] Both trial attorneys had to agree to empanel an individual on a Professional Jury. Jurors were chosen specifically because their expertise related to the issue of law being considered during the trial. Table 1.2 summarizes the evolution of specialized juries in England during the 17th century.

Supporters of Professional Juries typically criticized the traditional system of jury selection that randomly gathered residents from the local community. They claimed ordinary citizens were incapable of understanding evidence presented in complex or technical cases.[47] Special juror lists, therefore, were developed that contained only the names of highly trained and educated professionals from the community who would better understand the evidence presented during complex trials. A jury that was empaneled using this method was referred to as a **blue-ribbon jury.**[48] Criticisms about whether Professional Juries reflect a fair cross-section of the community are discussed in Chapter 10. Box 1.5 describes a brief history of the blue-ribbon jury selection method used in the state of New York in the early 1900s, and the U.S. Supreme Court's response to a challenge that this jury selection process violated litigants' constitutional rights to a fair and impartial jury.

Table 1.2 Evolution of Specialized Juries in England in the 17th Century

Jury Type	*Explanation*
Gentlemen	Wealthy men who owned property. Served on a grand jury proceeding related to issues about national importance.
Party	Individuals who had similar nationality, race, or shared culture with the defendant.
Professional	Highly educated individuals with specialized knowledge or training in a specific field or profession.

Box 1.5: Blue-Ribbon Jury Selection in New York State

In 1946, two vice-presidents of labor unions from New York state were arrested and charged with criminal conspiracy and the extortion of money.[49] The jury convicted both men of all charges. On appeal, the petitioners claimed the jurors who were empaneled represented higher socioeconomic statuses while no laborers and few women comprised the jury. They argued the jury was not a representative sample from the community, but rather disproportionately contained groups traditionally hostile to labor unions. Moreover, they claimed empaneling such "blue-ribbon" juries was a violation of their rights to equal protection of the law and to due process. The petitioners appealed their cases to the U.S. Supreme Court (see, *Fay v. People of State of New York*[50]).

The U.S. Supreme Court found the lower trial court did not violate state laws for selecting jurors because in New York at that time, statutory qualifications allowed for empaneling specialized or blue-ribbon juries.[51] Moreover, the Court found the petitioners' claims about a violation of due process "must stand or fall on a showing that these defendants have had a trial so unfair as to amount to a taking of their liberty without due process of law. On this record we think that showing has not been made."[52] Essentially, the U.S. Supreme Court upheld New York's blue-ribbon standard as not violating a litigant's constitutional rights.

In 1965, Governor Nelson Rockefeller signed legislation that abolished blue-ribbon juries in New York following persistent claims from "civil liberties groups, bar associations and the state Democratic party" that these juries did not represent the communities where the trial was held.[53]

Jury Trials in the New World

Failed Expeditions

For three centuries after the signing of the Magna Carta, English rulers expanded and lost territories in seemingly endless wars, conflicts, and marital arrangements. In the 1580s, England was an isolated island nation that had few prospects for expanding landownership beyond its immediate borders and currently occupied lands. Neighboring countries, such as the Netherlands, Portugal, Spain, and Sweden, built sturdy, sea-faring vessels and had already colonized distant plots of land in various continents throughout the world, including Africa and South America. Out of a desire to increase their presence in the world and motivated to increase their own wealth and political influence, England doubled its efforts to develop ships and to launch new expeditions to distant lands.

England's earliest expeditions were met with little success. In 1585, British explorer Sir Walter Raleigh set sail for a previously uncharted and unclaimed land in what they called the New World. Raleigh and his men, who were soldiers of the Crown, crossed the Atlantic Ocean and landed on an obscure island along the coast of present-day North Carolina. They named this place Roanoke. England's attempt to be the first to colonize this land resulted in a dismal failure. From the outset, the colony was battered by famine and attacks from Native American populations. Many of the men died from starvation and injuries sustained during skirmishes with the indigenous people. The expedition returned to England approximately one year after arriving in Roanoke, with only a few dozen soldiers remaining behind.

Undeterred, England launched a second expedition to the New World and Roanoke in 1587. The nation was resolute to establish Roanoke as the first, permanent English settlement. This expedition, led by John White, included three ships loaded with supplies and over 100 men, women, and children who were going to make the new colony their home. This attempt at colonization, however, befell the same fate as the previous one. Due to food shortage, poor planning, and insufficient time to cultivate life-sustaining crops, White was forced to return to England within a few months after his initial arrival at Roanoke to procure additional supplies to help sustain the colony. His return to Roanoke was delayed for several years due to increased tension and war with neighboring Spain. When White finally returned with supplies in 1590, to his surprise, the colony and its inhabitants were gone. The mysterious fate and disappearance of the Roanoke colony is still pondered and debated among historians today.[54]

First Permanent Settlement

A third attempt at colonizing the New World was made in 1607. Captain Christopher Newport led an expedition from England that landed in the region now known as the Chesapeake in the state of Virginia.[55] The colony established there was called **Jamestown**, and was located near a vital water source, a river the colonists named the James River. These namesakes were given in honor of the reigning monarch of England, King James (1603–1625).[56] The leaders of the Jamestown settlement, who were associated with the Virginia Company, initially were more successful with forming friendships with the Native American populations than were the settlers from Roanoke. This facilitated opportunities for trading goods and understanding cultural differences; however, the harsh winter months took their toll on the colonists.[57] Reportedly, the inhabitants suffered much like the settlers who colonized Roanoke. In Jamestown, the inhabitants once again struggled with famine and resorted to eating their own farm animals, local vermin, and snakes, and may have engaged in cannibalism to survive. While over 500 settlers arrived in Jamestown in 1607, only 60 remained by the year 1610.[58]

In addition to being the first permanent English colony in America, the Jamestown settlement was also the location of the first documented jury trial. The trial was conducted in 1607 under the Virginia Company's governing council and followed the common law traditions of England. The dispute was over a civil matter involving two plaintiffs, Jesu Johnson and Captain John Smith, who sued the ousted President of the Virginia Company, Edward Maria Wingfield, for slander.[59]

Jurors were selected from the surviving Jamestown settlers. It is likely the common settlers were passed by and those empaneled had higher social standing in the community. After both sides presented their evidence, the jury members deliberated and found in favor of the two plaintiffs. Overall, Johnson was awarded 100 pounds sterling and Smith was awarded 200 pounds sterling in damages.[60] This was a significant amount in the early 1600s. The awards showed the harm and severity of Wingfield's crime in the eyes of the jury but also demonstrated the early Jamestown colonist's determination to follow legal tradition and precedent established through English common law.

The harsh living conditions in Jamestown and the threats and confrontations among native populations overall, severely limited the civil liberties enjoyed by the first settlers. Martial law dominated the political environment of the settlement during its early years, simply to ensure its survival. This decision suspended future jury trials for over a decade. While the initial years living in the Jamestown settlement were challenging, the inhabitants endured. Starting in 1610, additional resources, supplies, and people were sent to the colony from England. Over the next decade, trade among native populations continued and crops, including tobacco, were planted and harvested for sale. The new colony was beginning to become profitable. England's foothold in America was established with the success of the colonists in the settlement at Jamestown.

Growing American Colonies

The history of colonial America shows that new settlements were being established throughout the eastern coastline for decades during and after the colonization of the Jamestown settlement. English traditions, laws, and regulations were enforced among those colonists living in America. Among such traditions was the expanded English concept of trial by jury. In 1620, the **Plymouth Colony** was established, and within three years, a charter was created that described "twelve honest men" must be empaneled to resolve issues of criminal wrongdoing. It took only a few years before the colonists were placed in a position that required empaneling a jury to consider the innocence or guilt of a colonist accused of first-degree murder, the most serious crime against another person. Now as a historical note, the Plymouth Colony is recognized for holding the **first murder trial** in America in 1630.[61] **John Billington** was tried and convicted of killing fellow colonist John Newcomin.[62] Box 1.6 provides some details about this infamous case from American history.

Box 1.6: America's First Murder Trial[63]

In 1620, an English ship, the *Mayflower*, set sail for America. Many of the passengers were practicing Puritans who sought resettlement to escape religious persecution in England. Virginia was the original destination for these colonists, but the ship was diverted unexpectedly and landed in Plymouth Rock instead. Like many of the early settlements of the New World, the colonists struggled in the first few months, losing half of the original 100 colonists. The survivors, including

John Billington and his family, were considered the original settlers of the Plymouth Colony in Massachusetts.

Allegedly, Billington and his sons were a disruptive force and caused several issues while en route to America. After landing, Billington was reprimanded multiple times by settlement leaders for challenging the colonists' conservative practices and lifestyle. In 1630, an altercation with fellow colonist, John Newcomin, forever associated John Billington as the first American colonist convicted of murder. The specific details are debated, but allegedly the two men had a long history of personal disagreements with one another. After an intense argument with Billington, Newcomin was found dead, lying in a field near the colony. An examination of the body showed Newcomin was shot in the back. According to the Plymouth charter, a jury was assembled. The jury found Billington guilty of the murder, and he was hanged in the fall of 1630. His death marked the first public execution in colonial America.

The revenue generated from the newly developing colonies in America, such as Jamestown and Plymouth, was returned to England, and the King and his noblemen retained much of the political power and decision-making over the inhabitants of North America. These practices contributed to frustration among the early American colonists; however, the colonies still adopted English law and customs, including the well-established tradition of the grand jury. In 1735, English loyalist Governor William Cosby demanded that a grand jury charge a colonial newspaper publisher, John Peter Zenger, of seditious libel for printing content that publicly criticized him in his role as a community leader. Seditious libel refers to publishing comments of an inflammatory or provocative nature. The independent-thinking grand jury comprised of American colonists refused to find evidence that a crime was committed and did not charge Zenger of seditious libel.[64] This infamous case had great implications for the jury deliberation process and will be discussed in Chapter 8.

The staunch control imposed by loyal English subjects only further enraged the American colonists. The pressure that Governor Cosby tried to impose upon the grand jury to charge Zenger only added to the growing frustrations many colonists had with their English overseers related to heavy taxation and impingement upon other freedoms. Collectively, these and other events[65] contributed to the American Revolutionary War in 1775 in which Americans fought for and won their independence from England in 1783.[66]

The American Jury

Each chapter included in this text about the American jury system presents findings from many sources. This approach was used to provide a broad overview of the structure, operation, and function of juries in the federal and state court systems. Arguably, the importance of studying juries and conducting research with individual jurors began in the mid-1950s with the development of the Chicago Jury Project from the Chicago School of Law. The methodological techniques for evaluating juries in this research initiative included both data collection strategies used by social scientists (e.g., interviews, questionnaires, and observations) and practical application and expertise about juries from legal professionals. Borrowing from the Chicago Jury Project methodology, the chapters presented in this text cite current research from various social science and legal sources about the American jury. Box 1.7 describes further details about the origins of the Chicago Jury Project and its wide impact on the study and understanding of juries today.

Box 1.7: Chicago Jury Project

The Chicago Jury Project was funded by the Ford Foundation in 1952. The project has a long and interesting history from its purpose-driven origins to its long-lasting impact for integrating legal research with empirically-driven social science evidence.[67] Briefly, in the mid-part of the 20th century, the Chicago School of Law was looking for its identity. While multiple focuses were discussed, jury research was selected as an area of interest because little extensive empirical legal research had been conducted in the area previously.[68] Harry Kalven and Hans Zeisel were among the lead researchers selected for the project.

The project offered a unique view about juries that were not previously achieved on such a wide scale, and in doing so cemented innovative collaborations among social scientists, attorneys, and judges. Researchers gathered data using numerous methodological approaches. For example, they "observed trials, interviewed jurors, surveyed judges and jurors, gathered public opinion about the jury through questionnaires, and conducted mock-jury experiments using recorded transcripts of trials," all for the stated goals of "examining jury behavior and decision-making."[69] Arguably, the most controversial aspect of the Chicago Jury Project occurred from the decision to secretly record actual deliberations in jury trials in Wichita, Kansas. While few trial attorneys or legal professionals reacted harshly to this data collection method, the news media launched protests that spawned scandal and eventually a congressional hearing in front of a U.S. Senate Subcommittee. Also, federal and state statutes were passed during this time that forbid taping jury deliberations. The reaction may have been so intense because it was during the time of McCarthy Era politics when the media and the American public were concerned about threats against the democratic process. Releasing information that jurors were secretly recorded during their deliberation (a traditionally closed-door practice) fueled preexisting tensions of the day.[70]

Today, human subject protocols would never allow such a practice to secretly record an interview or deliberation, but in the mid-1950s when the jury project data was gathered, there were no such guidelines or restrictions. Indeed, the invention of a tape-recorded interview was a new method that scientists were using in their research. It would take another 10 to 20 years for the research community to organize and develop specific protocols that would guide the ethical practices of researchers who collected data with human subjects. Unfortunately, these restrictions did not come until many people were harmed (physically and emotionally) because of participating in various social science research projects.[71]

In recent decades, allowances were made to film or record jury deliberations. Major news networks have studied juries for the purpose of understanding what goes on inside a jury room; other jury research projects have requested, and have been granted permission by courts, to record actual deliberations with real jurors.[72] Clearly, the media do not see recording jury deliberations as a threat as it once did in the mid-1950s. It is possible that new human subject protocols, including that jurors must be informed they are being recorded, are not perceived as diminishing the jury system or the public's trust.

Despite early setbacks, the Chicago Jury Project made significant and lasting contributions to the field of legal research. Overall, the data gathered from the project resulted in numerous publications, including the book, *The American Jury*.[73] This work was unique for its time because it used empirical research to describe a judgment reached by a jury versus a judge, and in doing so was the first research to focus on the impact of the jury on the "operation of the legal system."[74] Other contributions included greater numbers of legal professionals studying and recognizing the significance of social science evidence for legal research and for the creation and design of other major research studies that examined real juries, including the Arizona Jury Project[75] and the Capital Jury Project.[76]

In many ways, the Chicago Jury Project initiated interest and generated a more thorough and rigorous examination of the American jury system by academic scholars and legal professionals alike. These substantial research endeavors over the previous 75 years facilitated the writing of a jury text of this scope and nature. Also, many of the improvements made to the contemporary jury system, related to jury selection, impartiality, etc., were set in motion through the initial efforts of researchers from the Chicago Jury Project.

Conclusion

Many, but not all, English traditions and legal customs imposed on the American colonists by British loyalists were adopted when leaders developed their own constitution for governing the newly formed nation. The tradition of grand juries had been firmly established in the American colonies for generations. The Founding Fathers included it in the Bill of Rights. The Fifth Amendment of the United States Constitution states that, "no person shall be held to answer for a capital, or otherwise infamous crime unless on a presentment or indictment of a Grand Jury."[77]

The Founding Fathers were adamant that basic individual rights and freedoms to life and liberty would be firmly established and maintained for all Americans. Who "all" Americans refers to has been fiercely debated over the past 250 years. This text addresses this complex issue as it relates to the American jury system. The right to a trial by jury is among the most fundamental rights granted to American citizens. This guarantee of a jury trial is described in multiple passages throughout the original documents that define the unique hallmarks of the government of the United States of America.

Chapter 2 describes the fiery efforts of the Founding Fathers to create a government that protected the basic freedoms and liberties of all American citizens. It was their intention that citizens' rights be protected against the abuses and oppression of a centralized government. The Constitution and Bill of Rights comprise the founding documents that describe how these rights are to be protected and extended to all citizens. The language comprising these Articles and Amendments clearly shows the Founding Fathers believed common citizens should hold the power to govern themselves and that active participation in government through jury service and other activities was essential for Americans to share their voice about the laws that impact their everyday lives. These issues and the specific Amendments that guarantee the right to a jury trial are also discussed in the next chapter.

Summary

This chapter described many important concepts about the origins of trial by jury that emerged in Ancient Athens around 500 BCE. The practices of trials by ordeal (fire, water, combat, etc.) that emerged later persisted for centuries before the practices of a trial by jury gradually took shape. The early medieval history of England showed how several monarchs

(King Henry II and King John) initiated jury trials to address complaints by commoners and nobility about unfair treatment and abuse of power. The signing of the Magna Carta established the rule of law and the creation of a formal trial by jury that we are familiar with today. Over the centuries, the evolution of jury trials in England led to specializations including Party, Gentlemen, and Professional Juries.

The tradition of a trial by jury was carried to the New World by the earliest American colonists. The first trial by jury occurred in the Jamestown settlement, while the first murder trial occurred in the Plymouth Colony. America's desire for independence from England and subsequent victory in the Revolutionary War broke the stronghold the monarchy had over the colonies. The Founding Fathers were tasked with writing their own rules and laws that shaped the newly formed nation. Many legal traditions and customs from England were adopted when constructing the founding documents of the country. For example, the Magna Carta, which laid the foundation for jury trials, heavily influenced the Framers of the U.S. Constitution and the Bill of Rights.

Discussion Questions

1. Ethical consideration. Legal scholars and laypersons today may view the use of trial by ordeal in the Middle Ages (690–1216) as misguided or inappropriate for determining the innocence or guilt of the accused. How do you think individuals living one thousand years in the future will judge the current practices of the American judicial system? Is it likely future generations will perceive the justice system, based on judges and juries, as misguided or inappropriate? What could be available to determine innocence or guilt in the future that is not readily available today? Also, how will future generations judge current punishment practices or the punishment practices from the recent past, such as chain gangs, mandatory minimum sentences, long prison sentences, and capital punishment?
2. In the 13th century, the English legal system moved away from having cases decided by the will of God to adopting a system based on observed facts and human judgment. Is there any aspect of religion or spirituality remaining in the American courtroom or jury service today? Do you think personal religious beliefs or Church doctrine impacts who is selected for jury service or the type and severity of punishment reached during an average jury trial? (Hint: If you are struggling to answer these questions, you may want to further research the jury swearing-in process and the sentencing outcomes reached by individual jurors of various religious backgrounds who served on capital cases.)
3. The influences of the Magna Carta and the evolution of juries in the Middle Ages impacted the traditions and customs brought to America by the early colonists. What features of the American jury system do you think are the most important remnants of the old English system and why? Your answer may depend upon your personal knowledge of the jury system and your firsthand experiences with the U.S. court system. It is fine if you are struggling to answer this question. As you read each chapter in this text, you should begin to develop a better understanding of the American jury system and its purpose, structure, and operations. Soon you will be able to answer, and refine, what you think is the most important feature of the jury system and why.

Review Questions

1. How was guilt or innocence of criminal wrongdoing determined during the Middle Ages? What was the deciding factor and who was the ultimate decision-maker?

2. Which English monarchs played a pivotal role in the development of trial by jury? What was the specific influence of each?
3. What is meant by specialized juries? What types of specialized juries were used in the English legal system?
4. How were the Founding Fathers of the United States influenced by the Magna Carta? What specific language of the Constitution and Bill of Rights demonstrate this?
5. Describe how English laws and traditions were used among the earliest settlements in colonial America. What "firsts" occurred in the settlements at Jamestown and Plymouth Rock related to jury trials?

Answers to Chapter 1 "What Do You Think?" Questions

1. False. Trials by ordeal were practiced for centuries in England and elsewhere before jury trials.
2. True. In 1166, King Henry II assembled men from 12 local communities throughout the English kingdom to represent the first grand jury.
3. True. The Magna Carta concerned trial by peers but is viewed as a critical first step for the creation of juries and was influential for the Founding Fathers of America.
4. False. Jurors of a Party Jury had similar background characteristics, while jurors of a Gentlemen Jury were wealthy men, owned property, and made decisions that affected the national government.
5. False. The first jury trial in the American colonies occurred in the Jamestown settlement.
6. False. In the first murder trial in the American colonies, John Billington was charged with the first-degree murder of John Newcomin.
7. True. Despite pressure, the grand jury did not charge Zenger with seditious libel. Such coercion enraged American colonists against abuse and oppression by British loyalists.

Key Terms

American jury system
Assize of Clarendon
barons
Billington, John
blue-ribbon jury
Clause 39
common law
first murder trial
Founding Fathers
Gentlemen Juries
Jamestown
judgment of his equals
Magna Carta
Party Juries
Plymouth Colony
Professional Jury
specialized juries
swimming test
trial by blood

trial by cauldron
trial by combat
trial by fire
trial by host
trial by peers
trial by water
trials by ordeal

References

1 Monoson, S.S. (1993). *Plato and Athenian democracy* (Vols. 1–2). Princeton University Press.
2 Whittaker, A.M. (2012). Jury justice from the classic Greeks. *The Corinthian*, *13*(1), 10.
3 Schwartzberg, M. (2010). Shouts, murmurs and votes: Acclamation and aggregation in ancient Greece. *Journal of Political Philosophy*, *18*(4), 448–468.
4 Gatton, M. (2024). *The shadows of Socrates: The heresy, war, and treachery behind the trial of Socrates*. Simon & Schuster.
5 Gatton, M. (2024). *The shadows of Socrates: The heresy, war, and treachery behind the trial of Socrates*. Simon & Schuster.
6 Andrews, W. (2013). *Medieval punishments: An illustrated history of torture*. Skyhorse Publishing.
7 Snell, M. (2023, April 5). *The early, high and late Middle Ages*. ThoughtCo. https://www.thoughtco.com/defining-the-middle-ages-part-6–1788883
8 Snell, M. (2023, April 5). *The early, high and late Middle Ages*. ThoughtCo. https://www.thoughtco.com/defining-the-middle-ages-part-6–1788883
9 Snell, M. (2023, April 5). *The early, high and late Middle Ages*. ThoughtCo. https://www.thoughtco.com/defining-the-middle-ages-part-6–1788883
10 Lester, A. (1976). Fundamental rights in the United Kingdom: The law and the British Constitution. *University of Pennsylvania Law Review*, *125*(2), 337–363.
11 Mackie, S. (2017). Brexit and the trouble with an uncodified constitution: *R (Miller) v. Secretary of state for exiting the European Union. Vermont Law Review*, *42*(2), 297–343.
12 The Untold Past. (2020, July 8). *Trial by ordeal—brutal medieval justice* [Video]. YouTube. https://www.youtube.com/watch?v=RHc1haeckOs
13 The Untold Past. (2020, July 8). *Trial by ordeal—brutal medieval justice* [Video]. YouTube. https://www.youtube.com/watch?v=RHc1haeckOs
14 Leatherale, D. (2019, February 9). *Trial by ordeal: When fire and water determined guilt*. BBC News. https://www.bbc.com/news/uk-45799443
15 Leatherale, D. (2019, February 9). *Trial by ordeal: When fire and water determined guilt*. BBC News. https://www.bbc.com/news/uk-45799443
16 Andrew, E. (2023, July 18). *7 bizarre witch trial tests*. History. https://www.history.com/news/7-bizarre-witch-trial-tests
17 The Untold Past. (2020, July 8). *Trial by ordeal—brutal medieval justice* [Video]. YouTube. https://www.youtube.com/watch?v=RHc1haeckOs
18 The Untold Past. (2020, July 8). *Trial by ordeal—brutal medieval justice* [Video]. YouTube. https://www.youtube.com/watch?v=RHc1haeckOs
19 The Untold Past. (2020, July 8). *Trial by ordeal—brutal medieval justice* [Video]. YouTube. https://www.youtube.com/watch?v=RHc1haeckOs
20 Medieval Madness. (2022, June 24). *Trial by ordeal and trial by combat: A totally fair way of dealing out justice* [Video]. YouTube. https://www.youtube.com/watch?v=FQRAxpPMygM
21 Medieval Madness. (2022, June 24). *Trial by ordeal and trial by combat: A totally fair way of dealing out justice* [Video]. YouTube. https://www.youtube.com/watch?v=FQRAxpPMygM
22 Leatherale, D. (2019, February 9). *Trial by ordeal: When fire and water determined guilt*. BBC News. https://www.bbc.com/news/uk-45799443
23 O'Brien, H. (2005) *Queen Emma and the Vikings: A history of power, love and greed in 11th-century England*. Bloomsbury.
24 Cracknell, M. (2017, July 15). *St. Swithin and Queen Emma*. LinkedIn. https://www.linkedin.com/pulse/st-swithin-queen-emma-michelle-cracknell

25 Mayer, H.E. (1982). Henry II of England and the Holy Land. *The English Historical Review*, *97*(385), 721–739. https://doi.org/10.1093/ehr/XCVII.CCCLXXXV.721
26 Mayer, H.E. (1982). Henry II of England and the Holy Land. *The English Historical Review*, *97*(385), 721–739. https://doi.org/10.1093/ehr/XCVII.CCCLXXXV.721
27 Merriam-Webster. (2023). Assize. In *Merriam-Webster.com dictionary*. https://www.merriam-webster.com/dictionary/assize
28 Hurnard, N.D. (1941). The jury of presentment and the Assize of Clarendon. *The English Historical Review*, *56*(223), 374–410.
29 Helmholz, R.H. (1983). The early history of the grand jury and the canon law. *The University of Chicago Law Review*, *50*(2), 613–627.
30 Helmholz, R.H. (1983). The early history of the grand jury and the canon law. *The University of Chicago Law Review*, *50*(2), 613–627.
31 Bressler, R. (2018). *The thirteenth century: A world history*. McFarland & Company.
32 Bressler, R. (2018). *The thirteenth century: A world history*. McFarland & Company.
33 Shoenberger, A. (2015). Magna Carta, the Charter of the Forest, and the origin of the jury system. *Nottingham Law Journal*, *24*, 156–162.
34 Magna Carta 1215.
35 Bressler, R. (2018). *The thirteenth century: A world history*. McFarland & Company.
36 Shoenberger, A. (2015). Magna Carta, the Charter of the Forest, and the origin of the jury system. *Nottingham Law Journal*, *24*, 156–162.
37 Tate, J.C. (2016). Magna Carta and the fundamental right to due process. *Frontiers of Law in China*, *11*(2), 236–242. https://doi.org/10.3868/s050–005–016-0014–6
38 Bressler, R. (2018). *The thirteenth century: A world history*. McFarland & Company.
39 Magna Carta. (1215). Clause 39.
40 Bertelsen, K. L. (1998). From specialized courts to specialized juries: Calling for professional juries in complex civil litigation. *Suffolk Journal of Trial & Appellate Advocacy*, *3*, 1–35.
41 Bertelsen, K L. (1998). From specialized courts to specialized juries: Calling for professional juries in complex civil litigation. *Suffolk Journal of Trial & Appellate Advocacy*, *3*, 1–35.
42 Gunn, S., & Gromelski, T. (2022). Coroners' inquest juries in sixteenth-century England. *Continuity and Change*, *37*(3), 365–388.
43 Waddell, B. (2012). Governing England through the Manor Courts, 1550–1850. *The Historical Journal*, *55*(2), 279–315.
44 Oldham, J. (1998). The history of the special (struck) jury in the United States and its relation to voir dire practices, the reasonable cross-section requirement, and peremptory challenges. *William & Mary Bill of Rights Journal*, *6*(3), 623–675. https://scholarship.law.wm.edu/cgi/viewcontent.cgi?article=1434&context=wmborj
45 Rotenstein, V.N., & Hans, V.P. (2022). Gentlewomen of the jury. *Michigan Journal of Gender & Law*, *29*(2), 243–274.
46 Oldham, J. (1998). The history of the special (struck) jury in the United States and its relation to voir dire practices, the reasonable cross-section requirement, and peremptory challenges. *William & Mary Bill of Rights Journal*, *6*(3), 623–675. https://scholarship.law.wm.edu/cgi/viewcontent.cgi?article=1434&context=wmborj
47 Rhee, W., & Sellers, C.F. (2023). Retooling blue-ribbon advisory committees for a post-fact world. *West Virginia Law Review*, *125*(2), 451–540. https://researchrepository.wvu.edu/cgi/viewcontent.cgi?article=6390&context=wvlr
48 Ketler, D.W. (1947). The constitutionality of blue-ribbon juries. *Journal of Criminal Law and Criminology*, *38*(4), 369–375. https://doi.org/10.2307/1138013
49 *People v. Fay*, 296 N.Y. 510, 68 N. E.2d 453 (1946).
50 *Fay v. People of State of New York*, 332 U.S. 261 (1947).
51 N.Y. Special Jurors in Certain Counties Law § 749-aa (4)
52 *Fay v. People of State of New York*, 332 U.S. 261 (1947).
53 Schanberg, S H. (1965, July 16). *Blue-ribbon jury barred in state; Governor signs measure to abolish panels fought by rights groups and bar*. The New York Times, 29. https://www.nytimes.com/1965/07/16/archives/blueribbon-jury-barred-in-state-governor-signs-measure-to-abolish.html
54 Miller, L. (Director). (2023, February 20). The lost colony of Roanoke (Season 4, Episode 4) [TV series episode]. In *America's Hidden Stories*. Arcade Publishing.

55 Quinn, D.B. (1952). Christopher Newport in 1590. *The North Carolina Historical Review*, *29*(3), 305–316.
56 Quinn, D.B. (1952). Christopher Newport in 1590. *The North Carolina Historical Review*, *29*(3), 305–316.
57 LaCombe, M.A. (2010). "A continuall and dayly table for gentlemen of fashion": Humanism, food, and authority at Jamestown, 1607–1609. *The American Historical Review*, *115*(3), 669–687. https://doi.org/10.1086/ahr.115.3.669
58 Gundersen, J.R. (2002). Secrets of the dead II: Death at Jamestown. *The Journal of American History*, *89*(3), 1157–1158. https://doi.org/10.2307/3092510
59 Price, D. (2005). *Love and hate in Jamestown: John Smith, Pocahontas, and the heart of a new nation* (1st Vintage Books ed.). Vintage Books.
60 Price, D. (2005). *Love and hate in Jamestown: John Smith, Pocahontas, and the heart of a new nation* (1st Vintage Books ed.). Vintage Books.
61 Office of Jury Commissioner. (2023, November 14). The early days of the jury system. *Mass.gov*. https://www.mass.gov/info-details/learn-about-the-history-of-the-jury-system#the-early-days-of-the-jury-system-
62 Office of Jury Commissioner. (2023, November 14). *The early days of the jury system*. Mass.gov. https://www.mass.gov/info-details/learn-about-the-history-of-the-jury-system#the-early-days-of-the-jury-system-
63 Bulla, C.R., & Burchard, P. (1956). *John Billington, friend of Squanto*. Crowell.
64 Administrative Office of the United States Courts. (2012, April). *Handbook for federal grand jurors*. https://www.uscourts.gov/sites/default/files/grand-handbook.pdf
65 Zobel, H.B. (1970). *The Boston Massacre*. W.W. Norton & Company.
66 Greene, J.P. (2010). *The constitutional origins of the American Revolution*. Cambridge University Press.
67 Zimring, F.E. (2003). *The American Jury Project and the Chicago Law School*. Fulton Lectures 2003.
68 Ferguson, G.W. (1955). Legal research on trial. *Journal of the American Judicature Society*, *39*, 78–103.
69 Cornwell, E.Y. (2010). Opening and closing the jury room door: A sociohistorical consideration of the 1955 Chicago Jury Project scandal. *The Justice System Journal*, *31*(1), 49–73.
70 Cornwell, E.Y. (2010). Opening and closing the jury room door: A sociohistorical consideration of the 1955 Chicago Jury Project scandal. *The Justice System Journal*, *31*(1), 49–73.
71 Wenglinsky, M. (2018). Obedience to authority: An experimental view. *Contemporary Sociology*, *47*(4), 423–428. https://doi.org/10.1177/0094306118779813a
72 Diamond, S.S., Vidmar, N., Rose, M., Ellis, L., & Murphy, B. (2003). Juror discussions during civil trials: Studying an Arizona innovation. *Arizona Law Review*, *45*(1), 1–81.
73 Kalven, H., & Zeisel, H. (1966). *The American Jury*. Little, Brown and Company.
74 Ferguson, G.W. (1955). Legal research on trial. *Journal of the American Judicature Society*, *39*, 78–103.
75 Diamond, S.S., Vidmar, N., Rose, M., Ellis, L., & Murphy, B. (2003). Juror discussions during civil trials: Studying an Arizona innovation. *Arizona Law Review*, *45*(1), 1–81.
76 Bowers, W.J. (1995). The Capital Jury Project: Rationale, design, and preview of early findings. *Indiana Law Journal (Bloomington)*, *70*(4), 1043–1102.
77 U.S. Const. amend. V

2 It's in the Constitution

What Do You Think?

Before reviewing the concepts addressed in this chapter, answer True or False to each of the following questions or statements. Correct answers can be found at the end of Chapter 2.

1. The articles of the U.S. Constitution and the Bill of Rights were ratified in 1788.
2. The right to a jury trial in civil cases is guaranteed in the Sixth Amendment.
3. The right to a jury trial in criminal cases is guaranteed in the Seventh Amendment.
4. The Federal Judiciary Act of 1789 grants authority to the states to develop procedures for jury selection.
5. Every American citizen has been encouraged to serve on either a criminal or civil trial since the Constitution was ratified.
6. A state statute in Georgia once forbade African Americas from serving on jury trials.
7. California was the first state to allow females to serve on jury trials.
8. Texas was the last state to allow females to serve on jury trials.

Learning Objectives

After reading this chapter, you will be able to:

1. Describe the articles of the U.S. Constitution and Amendments of the Bill of Rights that pertain to juries and jury trials.
2. Explain the debate between the Federalists and the Anti-Federalists over the power and authority of a centralized government.
3. Discuss what motivated the Founding Fathers to create a participatory government for American citizens.
4. Identify U.S. Supreme Court decisions related to racial and gender inequality for jury selection.

Introduction

This chapter explains the constitutional guarantees to a trial by jury for every American citizen and describes several criticisms about the jury selection process itself. The original documents that led to the break with the English monarchy and those that specified the unique laws and structure of government in this country, including the Declaration of Independence, the articles of the Constitution, and the amendments comprising the Bill of Rights,

DOI: 10.4324/9781003677796-3

collectively described the inalienable right for a trial by jury to resolve a dispute of a criminal or civil matter. A central government cannot deny citizens this right.

The information shared in this chapter serves as an introduction to many legal terms, court procedures, and constitutional principles described in greater detail throughout this text. More importantly, the purpose of this chapter is to inspire the reader to become more excited about jury service and the amazing opportunity that jury service in America provides for the common citizen to get involved and actively participate in government. These were the fundamental interests of the Framers of the U.S. Constitution, referred to as our Founding Fathers. They wanted American citizens to hold the power that shaped their government, rather than be shaped by an oppressive government that stripped away individual liberties and freedoms.[1]

In This Chapter

This chapter describes specific aspects of the American jury system. Here information is provided about: 1) where language about the right to a trial by jury is guaranteed in the U.S. Constitution; 2) the quarrels that occurred between the Federalists and the Anti-Federalists; 3) the motivation for creating a participatory government; 4) the principles for equality in jury selection; and 5) the struggle for racial and gender representation in the contemporary American jury system.

The Founding Documents

The guarantee to a **trial by jury** was enjoyed by the earliest colonists and was written into the founding Charter of the first English settlement established in Jamestown in 1607. The American colonies grew and flourished over the next 150 years, but times were not easy. The earliest American colonists suffered significant physical challenges, philosophical dilemmas, and losses.[2] During these decades, the colonies were under control of the English monarchy, which developed and enforced laws, conducted military courts, oversaw commerce, and levied taxes. The period from 1607 to 1775 represented an ever-increasing uneasiness between the American colonists, who were given little or no participatory power in government, and their British administrators who were loyal to the crown.[3]

By the mid-1700s, the British monarchy utilized Admiralty Courts to address disputes about maritime and trade laws in the American colonies. Specifically, the courts heard claims about robbery or violence occurring on the seas (piracy) and smuggling goods. These courts, however, did not empanel local citizens to serve as jurors to decide these disputes; rather, a trial judge, who was appointed by the British monarchy, reached a decision that often favored the monarchy over the interests of the colonists.

The reliance on Admiralty Courts increased through the 1760s and beyond. The passage of laws like the Sugar Act (1764) and Stamp Act (1765) put more pressure on the colonists, while those who ignored the British laws were harshly prosecuted. The Loyalists, those colonial citizens who supported British rule, viewed the courts as a mechanism for maintaining order and consistency for how laws were administered; however, many colonists openly criticized the courts for being biased against their interests and for denying them their rights to common law traditions, including trial by their peers.

The early colonists were also frustrated with the British practice of holding trials in England. The Treason Act (1543), which was applied to the American colonies, allowed for the transport of all colonists accused of treason or other serious misconduct to a court in England to be tried for their crimes. The colonists strongly condemned this practice because it denied the accused the ability to devise a proper defense, it limited the accused from submitting favorable eyewitness testimony, and it deprived the accused the right of a jury of their peers.

The American colonists were frustrated that the monarchy controlled nearly every aspect of their lives. Their grievances, 27 in total, were publicly shared in one of the most important documents in American history, the **Declaration of Independence**. In 1776, Thomas Jefferson documented numerous complaints against the reigning monarch, King George III, and the English government, including one grievance related to the use of Admiralty Courts, which deprived the colonists of their right to a trial by jury ("For depriving us in many cases, of the benefits of Trial by Jury") and one related to transporting citizens across the ocean to be tried in an English court of law ("For transporting us beyond Seas to be tried for pretended offences").[4] Box 2.1 lists some of the other grievances included in the Declaration of Independence about the abuse of power and oppression the English monarchy imposed on the colonies.

Box 2.1: Declaration of Independence[5]

Numerous charges were brought against the "King of Great Britain" for "repeated injuries and usurpations, all having in direct object the establishment of an absolute Tyranny over these States." Some of the grievances included in the Declaration of Independence (July 4, 1776) are shown below:

- He has refused his Assent to Laws, the most wholesome and necessary for the public good.
- He has refused to pass other Laws for the accommodation of large districts of people, unless those people would relinquish the right of Representation in the Legislature, a right inestimable to them and formidable to tyrants only.
- He has dissolved Representative Houses repeatedly, for opposing with manly firmness his invasions on the rights of the people.
- He has refused for a long time, after such dissolutions, to cause others to be elected; whereby the Legislative powers, incapable of Annihilation, have returned to the People at large for their exercise; the State remaining in the meantime exposed to all the dangers of invasion from without, and convulsions within.
- He has made Judges dependent on his Will alone, for the tenure of their offices, and the amount and payment of their salaries.
- He has erected a multitude of New Offices, and sent hither swarms of Officers to harass our people, and eat out their substance.
- For imposing Taxes on us without our Consent.
- For depriving us in many cases, of the benefits of Trial by Jury.
- For transporting us beyond Seas to be tried for pretended offences.
- For taking away our Charters, abolishing our most valuable Laws, and altering fundamentally the Forms of our Governments.
- He has plundered our seas, ravaged our Coasts, burnt our towns, and destroyed the lives of our people.

Americans entered an inevitable war with Great Britain in 1775. Seven years later, the Americans emerged victorious.[6] During the early years of the conflict, the Founding Fathers began drafting the structure and laws of the newly formed United States of America. Their first attempt was the **Articles of Confederation**. This was adopted in 1777 and ratified in 1781 and could be considered the first Constitution. These articles created a loose confederation of states with a weak central government to coordinate collective needs like defense and trade. The Articles of Confederation ultimately failed because the weak central government lacked the power to tax, regulate commerce, or enforce laws effectively. Overall, this contributed to economic instability and disunity among the states. This prompted the Founders to propose a stronger framework for the federal government, which ultimately became the U.S. Constitution.

Alexander Hamilton, John Jay, and James Madison collectively wrote *The Federalist Papers*, a series of 85 articles and essays that promoted ratification of the U.S. Constitution.[7] The Framers of the Constitution disagreed about whether the document went far enough to limit the power assigned to a centralized government. Supporters of the Constitution, the **Federalists**, believed the language sufficiently limited the government's power and, despite opposition, the U.S. Constitution was ratified in 1788 and contained seven articles that established the structure of the government and placed decision-making power in the hands of the nation's citizens.[8] One of the articles pertained to a citizen's right to a trial by jury. The preamble to the Constitution, beginning with the famous opening line, "We, the People ..." clearly suggested the decision-making power of citizens was prominent in the Framer's thinking.[9] **Article III,** section 2 states:

> The Trial of all Crimes, except in Cases of Impeachment, *shall be by Jury*; and such Trial shall be held in the State where the said Crimes shall have been committed; but when not committed within any State, the Trial shall be at such Place or Places as the Congress may by Law have directed.[10] (emphasis added)

The **Bill of Rights**, with which many Americans are familiar today, was not included with the original Articles ratified in the Constitution. Historians described the contention among the Framers about including such language; however, the decision was made not to insert the Amendments into the original document.[11] This decision was vigorously objected to by prominent **Anti-Federalists** of the day. Box 2.2 provides more details about the ideology of the Anti-Federalist movement, including supporters' efforts to insert language that better protected an individual's rights and freedoms.

> [A] bill of rights is what the people are entitled to against every government on earth, general or particular, and what no just government should refuse.
>
> —Thomas Jefferson, Founding Father
> Letter to James Madison (1787)

Due Process of Law

A means to ensure the fairness of the legal system by requiring the government to follow certain procedures before limiting citizens of their lives, liberties, and property.

Several states that ratified the original Constitution did so under the condition that the Bill of Rights would soon be added. The Bill of Rights, which included the first 10 Amendments of the U.S. Constitution, documented the freedoms granted to every American, including freedoms of assembly, religion, speech, and due process of law.[12] The Anti-Federalists insisted such language be included in the founding documents of the nation to ensure that the rights of common citizens would be protected against the abuses of a powerful and oppressive government. In 1791, the Bill of Rights was ratified to the U.S. Constitution, which included several Amendments pertaining to a citizen's rights and protections associated with a trial by jury.[13] Box 2.3 lists aspects of the Bill of Rights determined to be essential freedoms for all Americans by the American Civil Liberties Union. Box 2.4 features insights from an expert on Constitutional Law about the influences of the Anti-Federalists and the Magna Carta on the development of the Bill of Rights and the structure of the central government.

Those who deny the right of a jury to protect an individual in resisting an unjust law of the government, deny him all defense whatsoever against oppression.

—Lysander Spooner, American Jurist, Philosopher, and Abolitionist (1808–1887)
An Essay on the Trial by Jury (1852)

Box 2.2: Anti-Federalist Ideals

The Anti-Federalists represented a political movement in the late 18th century that was concerned with shifting power from the federal government and reallocating it to state and local governments and the citizens. Contrary to the label, the Anti-Federalists were patriotic Americans. Some of the supporters were Patrick Henry (Virginia), Samuel Adams (Massachusetts), and Samuel Bryan (Pennsylvania). The Anti-Federalists believed the articles of the Constitution were not restrictive enough to limit the power of the federal government, including limiting judicial powers while protecting individual liberties. James Madison (a Federalist) drafted the original Amendments that addressed these concerns. Because of the Anti-Federalists' opposition, Americans today have the safety and protections specified in the Bill of Rights.

Give me liberty or give me death!

—Patrick Henry, Founding Father
Second Virginia Convention (March 23, 1775)

Box 2.3: American Civil Liberties Union

The American Civil Liberties Union (ACLU) described the importance of the Bill of Rights, indicating the Founding Fathers believed certain rights were granted to all human beings by nature.[14] The Bill of Rights was designed to protect these natural rights from being oppressed by a central government:[15]

Freedom of Religion:

- The right to exercise ones own religion, or no religion, free from any government influence or compulsion.

Freedom of Speech, Press, Petition, and Assembly:

- Even unpopular expressions are protected from government suppression or censorship.

Privacy:

- The right to be free of unwarranted and unwanted government intrusion into ones personal and private affairs, papers, and possessions.

Due Process of Law:

- The right to be treated fairly by the government whenever the loss of liberty or property is at stake.

Equality Before the Law:

- The right to be treated equally before the law, regardless of social status.

Box 2.4: From the Field

Name: Christopher Stangl

Position: Professor of Political Science

How long have you worked in this position?
I have been a professor since 2006.

Why were the Anti-Federalists so insistent on including the Bill of Rights in the founding documents of the U.S.?
The Anti-Federalists were not a single group. There were regional differences and differences over the importances of various issues. Also, they differed in the intensity of their views and their willingness to compromise. Some quickly came to support the Constitution once a Bill of Rights was promised. Others never made their peace with this increase in centralized government authority. That issue, though, more than any other, drove Anti-Federalist opposition to a U.S. Constitution that lacked a Bill of Rights. There simply was no trust that, once empowered, what today we call the "federal" government would check itself. As famous as the arguments presented by James Madison in *Federalist #10* and *Federalist #51* are today, the Anti-Federalists generally did not agree and did not think the protections alluded to by Madison were enough. In many respects, the very quick emergence of political parties demonstrates that the Anti-Federalists might have had a point.

What concept(s) drafted in the Magna Carta had the greatest influence on the Founding Fathers of the U.S.?
The concept that a king would have to negotiate his power and potentially compromise with other interests. Sometimes the Magna Carta is presented as if a bunch of large-scale landowners compelled the king to respect property rights, but that is a misunderstanding. The barons *were*

major property owners, and they certainly had an interest in protecting their holdings against royal appropriation, especially to fund wars they opposed. But it was also *because* they were major property owners that asserted other rights that the king was expected to honor. There is clearly an element of hierarchy to the conditions around the Magna Carta that was still largely present among the Framers.

Juries and Jury Trials in the Constitution

The founding documents of this country were created for the purpose of ensuring fairness. The Declaration of Independence was an ultimatum by the American colonists to be treated fairly by the English monarchy. The Articles and Amendments of the Constitution continued this certitude that the newly formed central government of the United States would be respectful of its citizens by ensuring fair treatment of every American. The words liberty and justice are synonymous with the words freedom and fairness. But who were the Founding Fathers referring to when they wrote about freedom and fairness for *all or every* American?

Fifth Amendment[24]

No person shall be held to answer for a capital, or otherwise infamous crime, unless on a *presentment or indictment of a Grand Jury*, except in cases arising in the land or naval forces, or in the Militia, when in actual service in time of War or public danger; *nor shall any person be subject for the same offense to be twice put in jeopardy of life or limb*; nor shall be compelled in any criminal case to be a witness against himself, *nor be deprived of life, liberty, or property, without due process of law*; nor shall private property be taken for public use, without just compensation. (emphasis added)

Sixth Amendment[25]

In all criminal prosecutions, the accused shall enjoy the right to a speedy and public trial, *by an impartial jury of the State and district wherein the crime shall have been committed*, which district shall have been previously ascertained by law, and to be informed of the nature and cause of the accusation; to be confronted with the witnesses against him; to have compulsory process for obtaining witnesses in his favor, and to have the Assistance of Counsel for his defense. (emphasis added)

At the insistence of the Anti-Federalists, the original U.S. Constitution was amended to include language that protected the basic freedoms and liberties Americans enjoy today.[16] Three of the first 10 Amendments added to the Constitution address a citizen's right to a federal grand jury proceeding and a federal jury trial in both criminal and civil matters. For example, the **Fifth Amendment** addresses a citizen's right to fair treatment,[17] specifically protecting a citizen from being charged with a crime(s) arbitrarily by the central government. Under this Amendment, a federal grand jury must first recommend charging the accused of a crime. After an indictment, a term meaning to formally charge or to accuse of a serious crime, the individual is placed on trial. The Fifth Amendment also established the finality of a jury's verdict. If a jury acquits the accused, the State cannot pursue further action or review.[18] There are some exceptions to the finality of a jury verdict, however. These issues will be addressed in Chapter 9 when considering invalidating a jury's verdict based on exceptions to the no-impeachment rule.[19]

The **Sixth Amendment** in the Bill of Rights addresses a citizen's right to a trial by an **impartial jury** in serious criminal matters only, including felony offenses. But what does the phrase "impartial jury" mean and how can a defendant's right to an impartial jury be violated? There are two important interpretations of an impartial jury. For example, one explanation refers to empaneling jury members who can judge the case objectively and fairly. That is, their decision-making is not discriminatory, prejudiced, or biased against the defendant. The courts have mechanisms embedded into the jury selection process where a trial attorney and judge screen prospective jurors to determine they have no conflict of interest or personal bias against either party. Any individuals deemed unable to meet the standards of a fair and impartial juror are removed.

An impartial jury also has a second meaning. It is one that is selected from a jury pool that reflects a fair cross-section of the community; that is, the community or region where the crime occurred and where the trial is to take place. A jury pool comprised of eligible citizens reflects the community when it is demographically representative of the community.[20] The jurors who are empaneled do "not have to represent an exact proportion of a community's racial, ethnic, or gender makeup" to ensure impartiality.[21]

> The Sixth Amendment secures to persons charged with crime the right to be tried by an impartial jury reflecting a fair cross-section of the community.
>
> —Ruth Bader Ginsburg
> U.S. Supreme Court Justice (1993–2020)

Box 2.5: Civil Jury Project

The New York University School of Law serves as host to the Civil Jury Project (CJP). The purpose of the CJP, which began in 2015, was to examine the changing role of civil juries in the American jury system from what the Founding Fathers intended and wrote in the Constitution centuries ago. Another purpose of the CJP was to develop a better understanding about why civil juries are seldom used in federal and state court systems today and to examine the impact this has had on other legal institutions and citizens' rights to a fair and speedy trial in civil matters.

One broad goal of the CJP, beyond developing a better understanding of its operation, was to strengthen the civil jury system itself. It meets this goal through gathering former civil jurors and trial attorneys to share their collective experiences about their jury service. The CJP also sponsors separate workshops with judges to allow them to discuss personal experiences and situations with jurors who served on civil trials. These initiatives facilitate transferring knowledge and experiences among all courtroom actors (judges, trial attorneys, and jurors) related to trial proceedings in civil cases.

The CJP shares findings about civil jury research projects through its social media platforms and monthly newsletter, *Jury Matters*, and through an established network of professionals in the field. For example, the CJP collaborated with over 300 federal and state judges who presided over civil trials, 70 academics scholars who researched jury issues, and 40 jury consultant advisors.

Finally, the **Seventh Amendment** in the Bill of Rights guarantees the right to a civil jury trial in federal court. Juries are used in civil cases to decide whether a civil defendant is responsible for physically or economically harming another person and, if so, awarding monetary compensation for that harm. However, civil matters related to family and probate issues concern issues of equity (fairness and justice) and typically are not eligible for jury trials. The same standards required for criminal juries, including impartiality, fairness, representativeness, and finality of the jury verdict apply to civil juries. This Amendment was inserted at the insistence of the Anti-Federalists, in large part because Article III, section 2 of the ratified Constitution, did not address a citizen's right to protection by a civil jury.[22] Several states that ratified the original articles of the Constitution did so only under the promise that civil trial protections would be added to the founding documents later. The Anti-Federalists' persistence facilitated the inclusion of civil jury trials into the Bill of Rights, which added an important level of protection for fairness, freedom, and liberty.[23] Box 2.5 describes the Civil Jury Project, established around 2015, which has engaged in research and gathered data from many legal professionals and jurors who served on civil trials. Overall, the Sixth and Seventh Amendments to the Constitution grant citizens, not the State, with ultimate power to reach judgment about potential guilt or harm in criminal or civil matters, respectively.

Seventh Amendment[26]

In Suits at common law, where the value in controversy shall exceed twenty dollars, ***the right of trial by jury shall be preserved***, and no fact tried by a jury, shall be otherwise re-examined in any Court of the United States, than according to the rules of the common law. (emphasis added)

> What many of those who oppose the use of juries in civil trials seem to ignore is that the founders of our Nation considered the right of trial by jury in civil cases an important bulwark against tyranny and corruption, a safeguard too precious to be left to the whim of the sovereign, or, it might be added, to that of the judiciary.
>
> —William Rehnquist, U.S. Supreme Court Justice (1986–2005)
> *Parklane Hosiery Co., Inc. v. Shore*, 439 U.S. 322 (1979)

Fourteenth Amendment

The Bill of Rights, comprised of the first 10 Amendments of the U.S. Constitution, established the "rules for due process of law and reserves all powers not delegated to the Federal Government to the people or the States."[27] Initially, the purpose of the Bill of Rights was to curb abuses from a federal or central government; however, the Due Process Clause of the **Fourteenth Amendment**, ratified in 1868, allowed the U.S. Supreme Court to apply or "incorporate" certain protections from the Bill of Rights to state governments. The **Incorporation Doctrine** was an evolving legal principle in which the U.S. Supreme Court ruled that certain provisions of the Bill of Rights applied equally to state governments.[28] For example, it was not until 1968 that the Court ruled in *Duncan v. Louisiana* that the Sixth Amendment's right to a trial by jury for serious crimes (e.g., where imprisonment could exceed six months, if found guilty) was so "fundamental to the American scheme of justice" that it applied to the states through the Due Process Clause.

Fourteenth Amendment[29]

No State shall make or enforce any law which shall abridge the privileges or immunities of citizens of the United States; ***nor shall any State deprive any person of life, liberty, or property, without due process of law***; nor deny to any person within its jurisdiction the ***equal protection of the laws***. (emphasis added)

Not all provisions from the Bill of Rights have been incorporated against the states, however. To date, the Court has not applied the Fifth Amendment's grand jury provision to the states. As described in Chapter 3, many states do not require a grand jury indictment to pursue a criminal prosecution. Nor has the Court incorporated the Seventh Amendment's right to a civil jury trial to state government. Rather, civil juries in most states are protected either by state constitutions or state statutes. The U.S. Supreme Court has heard numerous claims from petitioners during the past 250 years that individual rights to an impartial jury, at the state level, had been violated as guaranteed through the "due process" and "equal protection" clauses of the Fourteenth Amendment. Several important cases arguing such claims, along with the Court's findings in those cases, are reviewed throughout this text. Box 2.6 features comments from a legal professional about the powers given to juries and why it is important for juries to be the ultimate decision-makers at trial.

Box 2.6: From the Field

Name: Nina Chernoff

Position: Attorney and Professor of Law

What do you think the Framers got right about protecting the role of juries in criminal trials?

The Framers were right about the need for restraints on government power; they knew regular Americans must be able to prevent powerful people in government from abusing their power. The criminal jury is a tool to do just that: it allows regular people to make decisions about when and how government authorities can enforce criminal laws. For example, the legislature could pass an unfair law, and a corrupt prosecutor could unjustly charge someone with breaking that law, and a biased judge could allow the trial to proceed unfairly, but the jury has the power to prevent a conviction from being imposed. In that sense, the jury stands between a criminal defendant and the government officials who want to prosecute and says: "you have to go through us first."

What did the Framers get wrong about protecting the role of juries?

The Framers were wrong about who should *count* as a member of the community. Although the Framers were clear that they wanted the legal process to be informed by the voices of community members, they defined that community too narrowly by limiting jury eligibility to only White, male property owners. As our nation's understanding of community has evolved, however, the legal system has similarly recognized that the jury pool must include a fair cross-section of the *full* community, which includes people of all races, ethnicities, genders, and income levels.

What is one major difference between the role of the jury at the time of the Framers and the role of the jury today?

At the time of the Framers, juries determined both the facts and law. That meant if Congress passed a law that community members felt was unfair (for example, a law against reading books), the jury was allowed to openly reach a verdict that said yes, the defendant engaged in the prohibited conduct (he read a book), but we refuse to convict him because we think this law is unjust. Today the jury's role is limited—at least officially—to just deciding the facts. So today, if the same law was passed that banned reading, and the jury concluded that the defendant had read a book, the jury's role would be to convict.

Yet as a practical matter, juries *still* have the power to refuse to convict when they think a law is unfair. This is because judges are not allowed to undo a "not guilty" verdict, even if the jury reached that verdict for the wrong reasons. For example, imagine a jury is considering a case where the defendant is charged with possessing marijuana, and the evidence is clear that the defendant *did* possess marijuana, but the jury members feel it is wrong to criminalize drug possession. In that situation, the jury could decide to acquit the defendant, even though the evidence demonstrates he was guilty. This is referred to as jury "nullification," where the jury does not officially assert that it is declining to enforce a particular law, but chooses not to convict despite the evidence. People disagree about whether jury nullification should be encouraged or discouraged, but it remains a part of the jury's role in the legal process.

How important do you think juries are today?

Juries are still essential, and they become even more important when other branches of government assume more power or when people have concerns about how the government is exercising its power. Consider one of the largest protests that followed the shooting of Michael Brown by police officer Darren Wilson in Ferguson, Missouri. After it was announced that Officer Wilson would not be prosecuted for the shooting, hundreds of protesters held a mock trial where they "tried" Wilson for murder. That type of protest powerfully illustrates the idea that a legal outcome is unfair if the community's judgment is excluded from the process.

One way to evaluate the importance of juries today is to imagine you are accused of doing something wrong, but you are innocent. Now picture two groups of people. One group is all the people who are in power where you live: the police, the prosecutors, the judges, and elected officials. The other group consists of your peers: your classmates, neighbors, and people in your community. Which group do you want to decide your fate? Most of us want our peers to make that decision, and that is why the jury exists.

Participatory Government

The Founding Fathers wanted common citizens to be involved in the administration of government. This desire likely developed from their feelings of being oppressed for generations by the English monarchy. The Constitution, therefore, describes the rights, protections, and expectations for Americans to participate actively in government. For example, the

Constitution establishes patterns for when citizens can vote in general elections, the privacy for how to submit their vote, and who is eligible to vote.[30] The Founders of this country understood the power of free elections and wanted the American people to decide who should hold office and how legal matters should be resolved. Unfortunately, while Americans have the right to participate in government through elections, too often many citizens do not take advantage of the opportunity given to them.[31] For example, the Pew Research Center revealed only 37 percent of eligible voters cast a vote in the three major national elections (including two midterm elections and one Presidential election) between 2018 and 2022.[32] This percentage seems small but represents a significant increase in voter registration and turnout for American political elections in recent decades. What would the Founding Fathers think about this today?

The Constitution allows citizens to become active participants in their government in other ways, such as participating in government through the public assembly of groups. The Constitution allows for and protects citizens' rights to gather and organize rallies about political matters. Americans' First Amendment rights to free speech and freedom of the press were given to foster public participation in government and minimize government intrusion and control.[33] The First Amendment is discussed in Chapter 8 in relation to jury nullification. Finally, the Founding Fathers allowed for the private assembly of groups to practice religious freedoms based on their own set of beliefs. Religious freedom was granted to all Americans through the Constitution. This includes freedom to participate in religious organizations of their choice. Citizens are not forced to follow a national church or religious ideology.

> The wisdom of our ages and the blood of our heroes has been devoted to the attainment of trial by jury. It should be the creed of our political faith.
>
> —Thomas Jefferson, Founding Father
> Letter to Thomas Paine (1789)

The **participatory government** the Founding Fathers created for Americans is unique; however, a citizen's involvement in such activities is not required. For example, Americans are not required to vote[34] or participate in political rallies or engage in private religious activities of any kind. The participatory nature and language of the Constitution offer convincing evidence that the Framers believed all Americans *should* be actively involved; however, participation is *not* mandatory.

Serving as a member of a jury, however, is different from the other types of government participation described above. Participating in a trial by jury is one of the few requirements of citizenship. Participating in jury service is not a choice for Americans but is an obligation built into the founding documents of this country. This point bears repeating. A written summons to appear for jury service does not come with an option to consider serving, or to ignore the notification altogether. The jury summons is a requirement of citizenship.

The goal of the Founding Fathers was to design a government that puts power into the hands of its citizens. Having achieved this goal, why do so many Americans react to jury service with loathing and frustration? An answer to this question may be because the act of jury service itself can impact Americans financially and disrupt normal routines, such as work and family responsibilities, social activities, and vacations.[35] Another reason for an unenthusiastic reaction to a juror summons could be that contemporary Americans have never been under the control of an abusive and oppressive monarchy like the individual Founding Fathers were.[36] This lack of experience to have one's basic freedoms suppressed may cause some

Americans to underappreciate or simply misunderstand the struggles the colonists endured so we can be free today. Regardless, jury duty is a civic responsibility, no matter how one feels about it. Every American who receives a jury summons is obligated to participate.

It is important for Americans to remember that jury service enables them to shape government, impact laws, and hold unjust leaders accountable for their actions. American citizens should reevaluate the benefits of jury service in their lives, including the fact that serving on a jury trial can be an educational experience. Many jurors, without training in law or government, may not know how the justice system operates in society. Their knowledge may be limited to television crime dramas and Hollywood depictions of the adversarial process at work inside the courtroom during trial proceedings.[37] They may have heard phrases such as "equal protection of law," "jury of one's peers," or "peremptory challenges," but do not understand the constitutional principles that underlie these terms. This is when jury service can provide a remarkable education, enlightening many Americans about their legal rights and the power granted to them in the founding documents of the United States.

The educational experience of jury duty is intertwined with a juror's active involvement and decision-making, as described in the Constitution. For many Americans, jury service might be the only time, other than voting in a national or local election, they participate in the government process. Ideally, jurors will leave their jury experience feeling educated and empowered that their involvement helped resolve a civic matter based on their unique experiences and the conscience of the community they represent. Research findings are described in later chapters that show citizens are generally satisfied with their jury experience and report an increased knowledge about the government process.[38]

> I vote and I do jury duty.
>
> —Christopher Hitchens
> Author and Journalist

Every American

The phrase "every American" implies equality. Equality in jury service can be examined in several ways. First, equality can be measured during the jury deliberation process itself. For example, *every* juror on the panel, regardless of whether there are six or 12, is equal. *Every* juror hears the same facts and evidence presented at trial; *every* juror is responsible for considering the evidence that was presented; *every* juror must reach a verdict or decision about an outcome in a case; *every* juror comprising the jury is necessary and equal; *every* juror is challenged to share their own ideas and make their voice be heard during the deliberation; and *every* juror is equally equipped to listen, debate, and disagree about trial facts and differences of opinions.

The Administrative Office of the United States Courts described the importance of jury service for *every* American, stating:

> The performance of jury service is the fulfillment of a high civic obligation. Conscientious service brings its own reward in the satisfaction of an important task well done. There is no more valuable work that the average citizen can perform in support of our government than the full and honest discharge of jury duty.[39]

There are instances when litigants would prefer not to have their case tried by a jury. When this occurs, they can opt for a bench trial instead. Box 2.7 describes these circumstances in greater detail.

Box 2.7: Non-Jury Trials

Non-jury trials, as the name suggests, are trial proceedings that do not utilize individuals selected randomly from the community to serve as jurors. These trials are referred to as bench trials or trials by judges because a judge assumes all responsibilities normally assigned to jurors in a trial by jury. These responsibilities include determining the facts of the case based on the evidence presented at trial. In a bench trial, the judge applies the law to the evidence, then renders a judgment. One advantage of a bench trial is that it saves time and resources from having to empanel a full jury, which includes jury selection, instruction on the law, and deliberation with fellow jurors.

A criminal defendant can waive their right to a jury trial and request a bench trial if they believe there is an advantage for doing so. For example, this may occur in a civil case in which the laws can be quite complex or in a criminal case in which heinous and vicious behaviors might bias the jury against the defendant.[40] In many states, the prosecuting attorney would have to agree to allow a case to be tried as a bench trial.[41]

The Seventh Amendment of the U.S. Constitution guarantees citizens the right to a trial by jury in civil cases in which monetary awards are determined. As noted above, however, the Seventh Amendment does not apply to the states, and many states restrict the right to a civil jury trial to cases involving more substantial monetary claims. For example, bench trials are commonly used for disputes over small claim violations, potentially involving a few hundred dollars, although the exact amount is set by the individual jurisdiction. Judges can consider and settle small claim disputes more quickly and efficiently compared to empaneling a jury of one's peers.

An individual's social background characteristics, including employment status or education level, do not distinguish one juror's civic responsibilities from another juror during jury service. Diverse life experience, however, may facilitate discussion and enlighten fellow jurors' thinking and perspective about facts presented during the trial proceeding.[42] Jurors should be instructed before the deliberation begins to approach the task and their fellow jurors as equals, and to respect each other's viewpoints. Research has shown that juries with diverse makeups deliberate longer and more accurately evaluate trial evidence.[43]

A second way to measure equality in the American jury system has more to do with who is considered eligible for jury service and the jury selection process, rather than how jurors approach and interact with one another during the deliberation. The history of the United States, before and after the creation of the Constitution and the Bill of Rights, illustrates explicit acts of discrimination and exclusion of various people from participating in the government process. Findings from the U.S. Supreme Court over the generations since the ratification of the Constitution have demonstrated clear violations of a petitioner's right to fairness, equality, and justice as described in the founding documents of this nation.

Equality and Jury Service

Every qualified American is obligated to participate in jury service, if summoned. In federal courts and in most state courts, these qualifications include U.S. citizenship, residency in the geographic area served by the court, minimum age of 18 (19 or 21 in some states), English fluency, and the absence of any legal disqualifications (usually felony conviction or mental incompetence). The jury selection process that is practiced today, however, is very different to how jurors were selected for jury service several generations ago. For example, after the Constitution was ratified, and before the Bill of Rights was included, the newly formed government passed the **Federal Judiciary Act of 1789**.[44] This Act established the federal court system but also recognized the states retained authority for determining their own method for selecting individual jurors.

America's earliest practices for selecting jurors were borrowed from traditions used in England during the Middle Ages. The sheriffs, court officials, and municipal officers often lived and worked in the very communities where the crimes occurred, and the jury trials were held.[45] In this capacity, the law enforcement and the court staff had very close ties with individual community members and their families. Residents of small, non-industrialized towns or villages were tight-knit communities. Community members, including court officials, shopped in the same stores, ate at the same restaurants, worshipped in the same churches, and educated their children in the same schools.[46] When it became necessary to conduct a local trial, naturally the court officials relied on their personal knowledge of community members to select and empanel a jury. Juries that were assembled in this fashion were referred to as a key-man jury.[47]

Key-man jury systems were used in colonial America and continued in the federal courts and in most states until the 1960s. In this system, the jury commissioner, who was a locally elected or appointed official, was responsible for soliciting nominations from "key men" in the community, including local government officials, business leaders, clergy, and other prominent community leaders. Each nominee would be interviewed to confirm that they were "of fair character, of approved integrity, well-informed, and of sound judgment."[48] Prospective jurors would serve trials in the upcoming term of court, which could include a 1 to 2-year commitment. The names of jurors who were deemed qualified were given to the local Clerk of Court to be summoned as needed for jury trials.

The landscape of colonial America in the 18th century through the early part of the 20th century facilitated the use of key-man juries. For example, judges in early America often **rode circuit** and were not necessarily familiar with local community values. The jury commissioner's role was explicitly a check on the judicial branch to ensure that judges could not select jurors who did not reflect community values. One criticism of the key-man system was that it excluded racial minorities, women, and people of lower socioeconomic classes. In some instances, this exclusion was intentional; but in many locations, it was unintentional because the key men and the jury commissioners rarely interacted with minorities or with people who were from lower socioeconomic statuses in their communities. Key-man jury systems were abandoned in the late 1960s and early 1970s as states adopted random selection from broad-based lists and objective qualification criteria.

Rode Circuit[49]

Historically, judges traveled by horseback or carriage ("rode") to different regions or circuits to hear cases that arose in the local community.

> The great thing about our system of democracy is when they call you for jury duty, you have to come … It's an honor and a privilege. I was called and I've got to be here.
>
> —Antonio Villaraigosa
> Mayor of Los Angeles (2005–2013)

Racial Inequality

The key-man system of jury selection is one example of a practice that undermines the representational ideal of a diverse jury pool. A review of the history of the American jury system, however, yields many other examples of discriminatory practices that further called into question whether every qualified American citizen could be called to jury service. For example, the right to vote was not granted to formerly enslaved African Americans until 1870. The U.S. Supreme Court found in the highly cited *Dred Scott* case (1857) that enslaved African Americans and descendants of enslaved African Americans could not be citizens of the United States.[50] The denial of citizenship precluded African Americans from participating in government and enjoying basic rights and protections guaranteed by the Constitution. Moreover, denying citizenship disqualified African Americans the ability to serve on a jury trial, testify in court, or be included in trial proceedings.[51]

It was not until the ratification of the Fourteenth Amendment that African Americans were granted U.S. citizenship in 1868. Section 1 of the Amendment states: "All persons born or naturalized in the United States, and subject to the jurisdiction thereof, are citizens of the United States and of the State wherein they reside." This addition to the Constitution granted U.S.-born African Americans certain rights enjoyed by White citizens and equal protection under the law; however, full exercise of these rights faced significant obstacles for decades due to discriminatory practices.

Citizenship was only one of the barriers blocking racial minority representation in trial juries. For example, until the late 19th century, some states, including West Virginia, allowed only White, male citizens to serve on a jury. A specific West Virginia statute indicated, "all white male persons who are twenty-one years of age and who are citizens of this State shall be liable to serve as jurors."[52] This statute was enforced for decades before it was challenged and considered by the U.S. Supreme Court in ***Strauder v. West Virginia***[53] in 1880. The main issue at stake in *Strauder* was structural racism and how prospective jurors were drawn from the community under the West Virginia statute. The U.S. Supreme Court needed to decide whether the jury pool must be representative of the community and free from racial exclusion. Because the West Virginia statute expressly limited jury eligibility to White males, the Court found in *Strauder* that West Virgina's statute was unconstitutional, and that racial discrimination denied the petitioner the right to "equal protection of the law" guaranteed by the Fourteenth Amendment.

The statutory exclusion of races other than White was the key to the holding in *Strauder*. In ***Virginia v. Rives***, a companion case to *Strauder*, the Court made it clear that the Equal Protection Clause of the Fourteenth Amendment could not address factors out of government control, such as socioeconomic conditions, that kept Blacks from participating in jury service.[54] In *Virginia v. Rives,* two Black men were charged with murder in Patrick County, Virginia. Both the grand jury and the jury pool from which the venire was selected consisted entirely of White males, although there was no explanation for the exclusion of Blacks from the jury pool. The defendants first petitioned the state court to modify its jury selection procedures to ensure that one-third of the jury pool consist of Black men. The court denied the petition on grounds that the jurors were properly selected according to state law and that the court had no authority to deviate from that procedure. The defendants then tried to remove their case to federal court, arguing that the state's jury selection procedures violated their equal protection rights. The case eventually made it to the U.S. Supreme Court. In the absence of evidence that the state's jury procedures explicitly excluded Blacks from jury service, the Court found that the defendants' equal protection rights were not violated, and they had no right to have their case heard in federal court.

This distinction between official state action and private action of individuals outside government control continues today. In 1979, the U.S. Supreme Court decided ***Duren v. Missouri***, a case that involved the exclusion of women from the jury pool but which applies equally to racial and ethnic minorities.[55] In its opinion, the Court articulated a three-prong test to determine whether a defendant's right to a jury selected from a fair cross section of the community has been violated: (1) the group excluded from the jury pool is a "distinctive group" in the community; (2) the group's representation in the jury pool is not fair and reasonable given their representation in the community; and (3) the underrepresentation is due to systematic exclusion. The term "systematic exclusion" encompasses factors over which the state has control, including statutes and court rules, but excludes socioeconomic factors that affect individuals' eligibility or willingness to participate in jury service. Chapter 5 discusses how different jury selection procedures can either erect or remove barriers to jury service that affect demographic representation in jury pools.

U.S. Supreme Court decisions concerning the exclusion of racial and ethnic minorities did not focus exclusively on the creation of jury pools. Despite the Court's finding in 1880 to make the jury selection process more inclusive of African Americans from the community, racially discriminatory practices continued for generations. ***Swain v. Alabama*** (1965) addressed concerns about overt racially discriminatory practices within the courtroom setting during the jury selection process.[56] The U.S. Supreme Court needed to decide whether removing Black jurors from a venire represented discriminatory intentions that violated the Equal Protection Clause of the Fourteenth Amendment. Overall, the Court conceded removing jurors based solely on race was an abuse of an attorney's power; however, the defendant needed to show a pattern of such practices across multiple cases, not just in the present circumstance. Essentially, the U.S. Supreme Court's finding in *Swain* allowed courts and trial attorneys in Alabama and in other states to use race to exclude minority jurors from being selected and empaneled on jury trials.

With the passing of the **Jury Selection and Service Act (1968)**, the government attempted to end racial inequality at the federal level. Jury selection procedures were required to be randomized rather than relying on court officials handpicking jurors based on knowledge of an individual's characteristics or accomplishments. The states followed suit and adopted a more randomized process for identifying and determining juror eligibility. It took the U.S. Supreme Court another 20 years, however, to right the wrong in *Swain v. Alabama* that allowed trial attorneys to use racial characteristics to exclude community members from a jury. The Court's decision in *Batson v. Kentucky*[57] in 1986 addressed a petitioner's claim that his constitutional right to a fair and impartial jury was impeded because racial minorities were excluded from the jury. *Batson* and racial discrimination during the jury selection process are described in Chapter 6. Box 2.8 provides more details about the *Strauder*, *Duran*, and *Swain* cases in which racial discriminatory practices were overturned (West Virgina and Missouri) or affirmed (Alabama) by the U.S. Supreme Court.

Box 2.8: Exclusion from Jury Service Based on Race

Strauder v. West Virginia[58]

Taylor Strauder, an African American, was convicted for the murder of his wife and sentenced to death by an all-White jury in West Virginia in 1874. Strauder challenged the conviction, claiming his Fourteenth Amendment right to "equal protection under the law" was violated because the all-White jury deprived him of a fair and impartial trial.[59] The U.S. Supreme Court addressed this claim directly and stated the purpose of the Amendment was to apply all civil rights enjoyed by White persons to people of any race and to grant all people "protection of general government should it be denied by the States."[60] The Court's finding in *Strauder* was an important first step for eliminating racial discrimination from the process for how jurors are selected and empaneled in the American jury system; however, the states found other ways to minimize the impact of decision-making relating to racial minorities on trial verdicts.[61]

Duren v. Missouri[62]

In 1973, William ("Billy") Duren was charged with first-degree murder in the Circuit Court of Jackson County, Missouri. At the time, the county population was 54 percent female and 46 percent male. Although juror selection procedures did not differ based on gender, Missouri did allow women to claim an exemption from jury service (essentially allowing women to "opt out") that was not available to men. Approximately half of women who were mailed a qualification questionnaire claimed the exemption, resulting in a qualified juror list with only 26 percent women. To make matters worse, if a man failed to appear for service after receiving a jury summons, the sheriff was dispatched to arrest him and bring him to explain why he should not be held in contempt of court; however, when a woman failed to appear, the jury commissioner assumed that she had intended to claim the exemption and did not send the sheriff to enforce the summons. Only 17 percent of the jurors who reported for service for Billy Duren's trial were women.

On appeal to the U.S. Supreme Court, Duren argued that Missouri's exemption for women resulted in a jury pool that underrepresented women, violating his right to a jury selected from a fair cross section of the community. In response, Missouri argued that the exemption was necessary for women to safeguard the role of women in home and family life. In its opinion, the Court explained that states are permitted "to prescribe relevant qualifications for jurors, and to provide reasonable exemptions [from jury service]" but found that exempting all women from jury service was overbroad because not all women had domestic responsibilities that would be burdened by jury service.[63]

Swain v. Alabama[64]

On February 7, 1962, Robert Swain, an African American, forcibly entered a residential home located in Talladega County, Alabama. He proceeded to assault and rape a 17-year-old White girl who was present in the residence. The victim identified the assailant later that day at the Talladega County jail. He was indicted and later convicted of rape and sentenced to death by a trial jury from the Circuit Court of Talladega County. Swain appealed the indictment and conviction on constitutional grounds, including a violation of the Equal Protection Clause of the Fourteenth Amendment. In 1963, the Supreme Court of Alabama heard his claims.[65] First, Swain argued that only two African American jurors comprised the grand jury that indicted him of the crime, and no African Americans were empaneled on the trial jury that found him guilty and imposed a death sentence. During the jury selection process, six African Americans were removed by the prosecuting attorney through use of peremptory challenges. Swain's appeal was based on the demographic characteristics of Talladega County in the 1960s that showed approximately one-quarter of the population was African American.

The Supreme Court of Alabama denied Swain's claims on several grounds. First, the Alabama Court denied claims that the jury selection process to qualify jurors based on 1) good character and sound judgment obtained from city municipal records, 2) voter registration lists, and

3) church enrollment records resulted in more White community members being empaneled than African Americans. Second, the Alabama Supreme Court also denied that removal of six prospective African American jurors violated equal protection guarantees under the law. Specifically, the Court reasoned that a history of removing African Americans must first be established over a period of time to substantiate claims of racially discriminatory practices. The Alabama Court reached this decision despite evidence that no African American served on a jury in Talladega County since approximately 1950. In 1965, Swain appealed his case the U.S. Supreme Court to no avail. The highest court in the land affirmed the Alabama Supreme Court's finding that Swain's Fourteenth Amendment right to equal protection under the law was not violated.[66]

Table 2.1: Summary of Cases about Racial Inequality in Jury Selection

Case	*Decided*	*Opinion*
Strauder v. West Virginia[67] 100 U.S. 303	March 1, 1880	Statutes that exclude prospective jurors from jury service based on racial characteristics are unconstitutional and in violation of the Fourteenth Amendment of the Bill of Rights.
Virginia v. Rives[68] 100 U.S. 313	March 1, 1880	Court made it clear that the Equal Protection Clause of the Fourteenth Amendment could not address factors out of government control, such as socioeconomic conditions, that kept Blacks from participating in jury service.
Duren v. Missouri[69] 439 U.S. 357	January 9, 1979	The Court declared a three-prong test related to jury selection, including the group excluded is a "distinctive group" in the community; group's representation in the jury pool is not fair and reasonable; and underrepresentation is due to systematic exclusion.
Swain v. Alabama[70] 380 U.S. 202	March 8, 1965	A history of systematic racial discrimination for excluding jurors from jury service must be established for a petitioner to claim his guaranteed right to "equal protection under the law" was violated.

Gender Inequality

Juror eligibility for jury selection was further restricted beyond citizenship and racial requirements. For example, while the Court in ***Strauder*** indicated it was unconstitutional to deny African Americans the ability to serve on a state jury, the ruling still limited membership to male jurors only. In 1869, the Wyoming territory, before it became an official state, allowed women to serve on jury trials.[71] Wyoming's reasoning may be questionable, however, as there is a belief this status was granted to women in large part to facilitate more women to relocate to the region. In 1895, Utah was the first official state to grant women the right to serve on a jury.[72]

Nineteenth Amendment

The right of citizens of the United States to vote shall not be denied or abridged by the United States or by any state on account of sex.

Female access to the participatory government, encouraged by the Founding Fathers, was limited for generations after the ratification of the Constitution and the Bill of Rights. For example, the government only recognized a woman's right to vote in 1920 with ratification of the Nineteenth Amendment. Although only seven states permitted women to serve as trial jurors before 1920, ratification of the Nineteenth Amendment spurred many states to amend their juror qualification criteria to permit women. By 1930, an additional 16 states permitted women to serve, and by 1950 a total of 37 states did so (out of 48—Alaska and Hawaii did not become states until 1959).

U.S. Supreme Court decisions followed this trend. One of its earliest decisions to allow women to serve on juries came in ***Ballard v. United States*** (1946), in which the Court found it unconstitutional to block women from the federal district courts in California.[73] The passing of the **Civil Rights Act of 1957** allowed women to serve as jurors in federal courts. Their participation was allowed even in states that prohibited female juror eligibility. This change ensured uniformity within the federal court system and increased the number of citizens eligible for jury service. All but three states had amended their jury statutes to permit women by 1957. In 1968, Mississippi became the last state to change its legal statute to allow females to serve on a jury.[74]

A second decision about female eligibility for jury service was made by the U.S. Supreme Court in ***Taylor v. Louisiana*** in 1975.[75] This ruling is important for several reasons, including the recency of the decision. The year 1975 is not that long ago considering the long history of juries in America. Briefly, the U.S. Supreme Court found in *Taylor* that a Louisiana statute requiring women (and not men) to register for jury service violated the petitioner's right to a fair trial represented by a fair cross-section of the community. The Court's finding held that a written declaration from women who resided in Louisiana to be considered eligible for jury service, but not from men, was an unfair burden and denied the petitioner his right to an impartial jury. Four years later, the Court decided *Duren v. Missouri*, invalidating an exemption for women from jury service that was not available to men. The Court found the standards for jury selection must be the same for both female and male residents.[76] Box 2.9 provides more details about these cases and gender eligibility for jury service.

Box 2.9: Exclusion from Jury Service Based on Gender

Ballard v. United States[77]

Edna W. Ballard was tried and convicted of using, and conspiring to use, the U.S. mail to defraud the government. She was tried and convicted in the Southern District Court of California by a jury of 12 men. In the 1940s, a statute for the state of California allowed women to be eligible to serve on a jury trial; however, the state's practice was to not summons women to serve. Federal law at the time required federal district courts (in which Ballard was originally convicted) to follow the practices of the highest state court of law. Under these conditions, no women were selected by the district court at Ballard's original trial. The U.S. Supreme Court overturned Ballard's conviction, citing that federal statute relating to juries required membership to reflect a fair cross-section of the community. Moreover, the Court found since California allowed women to be eligible for jury service, the state recognized women as members of the community and therefore an all-male jury was inconsistent with the state's ideals for a fair and impartial jury.[78]

Taylor v. Louisiana[79]

In 1972, a grand jury recommended indicting Billy J. Taylor for aggravated kidnapping. The proceeding was held in St. Tammany Parish, Louisiana, a community whose population was 53 percent female. The jury selection procedure for the criminal trial included a venire of 175 persons. All the individuals were male. Taylor's attorney requested to "quash the venire"[80] because a jury panel of all males denied the defendant his right to a fair and impartial jury. Specifically, Taylor claimed having female citizens, and not males, formally register to serve on a jury trial created a biased jury. The 22nd Judicial District of Louisiana denied his request and a trial jury convicted Taylor and sentenced him to death for his crime.

Taylor appealed his conviction to the Supreme Court of Louisiana and later challenged the constitutionality of Louisiana's jury selection *process* to the U.S. Supreme Court. The Court found in *Taylor v. Louisiana*, "we impose no requirement that petit juries actually chosen must mirror the community…but the jury wheels, pools of names, or venires from which juries are drawn must not systematically exclude distinctive groups in the community."[81] Essentially, the Court found Louisiana's practice to require females to formally register for jury service but not holding males to such standards violated the Sixth Amendment's guarantee to an impartial jury. The Court struck down Louisiana's law stating that jury pools must represent a fair cross-section of the community, including both genders.

Table 2.2: Summary of Cases about Gender Inequality in Jury Selection

Case	*Decided*	*Opinion*
Ballard v. United States[82] 329 U.S. 187	December 9, 1946	Jury selection practices of federal district courts must follow the same standards for determining juror eligibility established by the state and local community. Overall, females cannot be excluded from federal jury service in California.
Taylor v. Louisiana[83] 419 U.S. 522	January 21, 1975	Legal statutes and protocols that determine standards for juror selection and eligibility (including demanding a written declaration) must be the same for female and male residents.

Conclusion

It has been a long and slow-moving process for the American jury system to recognize the importance of representative jury pools. The jury selection practices from the 19th through mid-20th centuries that resulted in jury panels that were all-White, male, property owners, neighbors, eyewitnesses, etc. have gradually changed or been eliminated. Today, race and gender no longer serve as constitutionally justifiable reasons to remove eligible jurors from a jury pool. However, claims are made today that the American jury still does not represent a cross-section of the community. Criticism about trial attorneys' inappropriate use of peremptory challenges to remove jurors based on race[84] is described in another chapter.

The next chapter explores the structure and function of grand juries in state and federal courts. The right to a grand jury proceeding described in the Fifth Amendment directly applies to accusations made against individuals for committing federal crimes. The Founding Fathers were motivated to ensure that no individual could be charged with a crime by a central government unless a grand jury found probable cause that the accused had committed the crime. The Fifth Amendment requires the use of grand juries in all federal courts but does not apply to state courts. Connecticut and Pennsylvania do not use grand juries to issue indictments at all, and only 15 states require a grand jury indictment to initiate felony cases. In the remaining states, the use of a grand jury is optional or is required only for capital cases.

Summary

This chapter focused on the Founding Fathers' attempts to create a new nation based on principles of freedom and justice for all citizens. The struggles among the Framers of the Constitution showed how difficult this task was for all involved. One source of agreement was that all individuals should have a right to a trial by jury for criminal disputes. The motivation for this development was that all people would have the protection of their peers from wrongful imprisonment and unwarranted accusations of criminal misconduct. The Founding Fathers believed that the consensus of citizens from the community in which the crime was committed would yield an outcome that was just and impartial, and beyond the power, authority, and decision-making of a centralized government.

The structure of the United States government was designed to give decision-making powers to the citizens. This authority was described in the Bills of Rights. For example, the Sixth Amendment guaranteed individuals the right to trial by jury in all criminal matters, while the Seventh Amendment provided this guarantee in civil disputes. These inalienable rights cannot be taken away from American citizens.

The Founding Fathers also intended for American citizens to be actively involved and participate in their government. This enthusiasm may have been lost over the generations since the American colonists suffered abuse and oppression at the hands of the English monarchy. Without such active participation in jury service, the juries empaneled might not represent a fair cross-section and diverse community intended by the Framers of the Constitution. A jury verdict based on fairness and impartiality is the only way to ensure that an individual's right to equal protection of the law and due process is fully achieved.

Arguably, the Founding Fathers' intentions for equal protection of the law for everyone has not been met. The sad reality is this equal protection, and the constitutional guarantees to a fair and impartial jury, have been denied to a vast number of Americans for many generations. Indeed, racial minority groups and female citizens were denied access to jury service and their petitions to the U.S. Supreme Court about violations of basic Constitutional rights were often ignored. Today, the American jury system is less tolerant of blatant discriminatory practices; however, critics still point to many contemporary examples of discrimination and inequality for jury selection that affect case outcomes.

Discussion Questions

1. History indicates the Founding Fathers argued about many issues while designing the structure and operations of the U.S. government. The Anti-Federalists vigorously sought more checks on the powers of a centralized government, while the Federalists believed the Constitution addressed these concerns sufficiently. One issue both sides agreed upon was creating a secure jury system that empaneled American citizens to be the finders of fact based solely on the evidence presented at trial. Why do you think all the Founding Fathers were in unison on this issue specifically? How did their collective experience living under British rule unify them?

What problems did the Framers of the Constitution foresee for the newly formed nation that necessitated a trial by jury to protect its citizens? What does this tell you about their beliefs and hopes for the American jury and its future?

2. Ethical consideration. The American jury system has been criticized for numerous discriminatory practices, including summoning or excluding jurors for jury duty, for not empaneling women or racially diverse jurors, and for harshly punishing defendants based on racial characteristics. Several important U.S. Supreme Court decisions related to racial and gender inequality were issued in the 1970s and 1980s. This is recent when considering that the right to "trial by jury" was granted approximately 250 years ago.

   What does this tell you about the lingering effects of race and gender discrimination in both the jury system and in American society today? What other issues might the U.S. Supreme Court need to address concerning inequality and the American jury system in the future?

Review Questions

1. As described in this chapter, what was the main disagreement between the Federalists and the Anti-Federalists in the late 18th century?
2. The Bill of Rights granted basic freedoms that all American citizens enjoy today. What inalienable freedoms does this include?
3. The Founding Fathers intended for Americans to participate in the government process. In what ways can Americans do this?
4. Describe several historical U.S. Supreme Court decisions related to racial and gender discrimination in the American jury system. What did the Court find and what was its decision based on specifically; that is, what constitutionally guaranteed right was protected or denied?

Answers to Chapter 2 "What Do You Think?" Questions

1. False. The articles of the U.S. Constitution were ratified in 1788, but the Bill of Rights were not ratified until 1791.
2. False. The right to a jury trial in *criminal* cases is guaranteed in the Sixth Amendment.
3. False. The right to a jury trial in *civil* cases is guaranteed in the Seventh Amendment.
4. False. The Federal Judiciary Act of 1789 established the federal court system but was not intended to displace the predominant role of state courts within the federalist system of governance. The Act recognized the inherent authority of state courts to determine procedures for jury selection and other features associated with juries.
5. False. For many generations prospective jurors were excluded from jury service based on race and gender.
6. False. A West Virgina statute in the 19th century specifically excluded African Americans from jury service.
7. False. Utah was the first state to allow females to serve on jury trials.
8. False. Mississippi was the last state to allow females to serve on jury trials.

Key Terms

Anti-Federalists
Article III, section 2

Articles of Confederation
Ballard v. United States
Bill of Rights
Civil Rights Act of 1957
Declaration of Independence
Duren v. Missouri
Federal Judiciary Act of 1789
Federalists
Fifth Amendment
Fourteenth Amendment
impartial jury
Incorporation Doctrine
Jury Selection and Service Act (1968)
key-man jury
participatory government
rode circuit
Seventh Amendment
Sixth Amendment
Strauder v. West Virginia
Swain v. Alabama
Taylor v. Louisiana
trial by jury
Virginia v. Rives

References

1 Levy, L.W. (1999). *Origins of the Bill of Rights*. Yale University Press. https://doi.org/10.12987/9780300129021
2 Baker, C.R. (2019). What can Thomas Jefferson's accounting records tell us about plantation management, slavery, and enlightenment philosophy in colonial America? *Accounting History*, *24*(2), 236–252. https://doi.org/10.1177/1032373218772589
3 Galiani, S., & Torrens, G. (2019). Why not taxation and representation? British politics and the American Revolution. *Journal of Economic Behavior & Organization*, *166*, 28–52. https://doi.org/10.1016/j.jebo.2019.08.024
4 Declaration of Independence. (1776). https://www.archives.gov/founding-docs/declaration-transcript
5 Declaration of Independence. (1776). https://www.archives.gov/founding-docs/declaration-transcript
6 Shankman, A. (2017). Toward a social history of Federalism: The state and capitalism to and from the American Revolution. *Journal of the Early Republic*, *37*(4), 615–653. https://doi.org/10.1353/jer.2017.0066
7 Frank, J. (2008). "Unauthorized propositions": "The Federalist Papers" and constituent power. *Diacritics*, *37*(2/3), 103–120. https://doi.org/10.1353/dia.0.0030
8 Wilson, J.L. (2022). Constitutional majoritarianism against popular "regulation" in the Federalist. *Political Theory*, *50*(3), 449–476. https://doi.org/10.1177/00905917211043796
9 Ferguson, A.G. (2012). *Why jury duty matters: A citizen's guide to constitutional action*. New York University Press. http://ebookcentral.proquest.com
10 U.S. Const. art. III, § 2
11 Amar, A.R. (1991). The Bill of Rights as a Constitution. *The Yale Law Journal*, *100*(5), 1131–1210. https://doi.org/10.2307/796690
12 U.S. Const. amend. I–X
13 Ketcham, R. (Ed.). (1986). *The Anti-Federalist papers and the constitutional convention debates*. New American Library.

14 Barth, J. (2023). "Liberty of conscience is every man's natural right": Historical background of the First Amendment. *Journal of Policy History*, *35*(4), 435–453. https://doi.org/10.1017/S0898030623000234
15 American Civil Liberties Union. (2002, March 4). *The Bill of Rights: A brief history*. https://www.aclu.org/documents/bill-rights-brief-history
16 Frank, J. (2008). "Unauthorized propositions": "The Federalist Papers" and constituent power. *Diacritics*, *37*(2/3), 103–120. https://doi.org/10.1353/dia.0.0030
17 Ferguson, A.G. (2012). *Why jury duty matters: A citizen's guide to constitutional action*. New York University Press. http://ebookcentral.proquest.com
18 U.S. Const. amend. V
19 Fed. R. Evid. 606(b)
20 National Center for State Courts. (2010). *Jury managers' toolbox: A primer on fair cross-section jurisprudence*. https://www.ncsc-jurystudies.org/__data/assets/pdf_file/0026/7478/a-primer-on-fair-cross-section.pdf
21 Martz, C. (2021). Jury of your peers. *Bill of Rights in Action*, *36*(4), 1–4. https://www.crf-usa.org/images/pdf/a-jury-of-your-peers.pdf
22 Landsman, S. (1999). The civil jury in America. *Law and Contemporary Problems*, *62*(2), 285–304. https://doi.org/10.2307/1192260
23 Landsman, S. (1999). The civil jury in America. *Law and Contemporary Problems*, *62*(2), 285–304. https://doi.org/10.2307/1192260
24 U.S. Const. amend. V
25 U.S. Const. amend. VI
26 U.S. Const. amend. VII
27 U.S. National Archives and Records Administration (2024, January 11). *The Bill of Rights: What does it say?* https://www.archives.gov/founding-docs/bill-of-rights/what-does-it-say
28 Lash, K.T. (2022). Respeaking the Bill of Rights: A new doctrine of incorporation. *Indiana Law Journal*, *97*(4), 1439–1486.
29 U.S. Const. amend. XIV
30 U.S. Const. amend. VII
31 Shaw, D., & Petrocik, J. (2020). *The turnout myth: Voting rates and partisan outcomes in American national elections*. Oxford University Press. https://doi.org/10.1093/oso/9780190089450.001.0001
32 Pew Research Center. (2023, July). *Republican gains in 2022 midterms driven mostly by turnout advantage*. https://www.pewresearch.org/wp-content/uploads/sites/20/2023/07/PP_2023.07.12_validated-voters_REPORT.pdf
33 Barth, J. (2023). "Liberty of conscience is every man's natural right": Historical background of the First Amendment. *Journal of Policy History*, *35*(4), 435–453. https://doi.org/10.1017/S0898030623000234
34 Putnam, R. (2000). *Bowling alone: The collapse and revival of American community*. Simon & Schuster.
35 Keller, J. (2024, January 13). *Confessions of a juror: How mandatory jury duty impacts Americans*. Bar Prep Hero. https://barprephero.com/confessions-of-a-juror/
36 Barth, J. (2023). "Liberty of conscience is every man's natural right": Historical background of the First Amendment. *Journal of Policy History*, *35*(4), 435–453. https://doi.org/10.1017/S0898030623000234
37 Klentz, B.A., Winters, G.M., & Chapman, J.E. (2020). The CSI effect and the impact of DNA evidence on mock jurors and jury deliberations. *Psychology, Crime & Law*, *26*(6), 552–570. https://doi.org/10.1080/1068316X.2019.1708353
38 Administrative Office of the U.S. Courts. (2024, January 15). *Juror experiences*. https://www.uscourts.gov/services-forms/jury-service/learn-about-jury-service/juror-experiences
39 Administrative Office of the U.S. Courts. (2024, February 21). *Handbook for trial jurors serving in the United States district courts*. https://www.uscourts.gov/sites/default/files/trial-handbook.pdf
40 Winfree, T.L., Mays, L.G., & Alarid, L.F. (2022). *Introduction to criminal justice: The essentials* (3rd ed.). Aspen Publishing.
41 Martz, C. (2021). Jury of your peers. *Bill of Rights in Action*, *36*(4), 1–4. https://www.crf-usa.org/images/pdf/a-jury-of-your-peers.pdf
42 Sommer, S.R. (2006). On racial diversity and group decision making: Identifying multiple effects of racial composition on jury deliberations. *Journal of Personality and Social Psychology*, *90*(4), 597–612. https://doi.org/10.1037/0022-3514.90.4.597

43 Diamond, S.S., Rose, M.R., & Murphy, B. (2006). Revisiting the unanimity requirement: The behavior of the non-unanimous civil jury. *Northwestern University Law Review*, *100*(1–2), 201–230.
44 Judiciary Act of 1789. (1989). *The foundation of the federal judicial system*. National Archives and Records Administration. https://www.archives.gov/milestone-documents/federal-judiciary-act#:~:text=The%20First%20Congress%20decided%20that,for%20in%20the%20Constitution%2C%20and
45 Ferguson, A.G. (2012). *Why jury duty matters: A citizen's guide to constitutional action*. New York University Press.
46 Ferguson, A.G. (2012). *Why jury duty matters: A citizen's guide to constitutional action*. New York University Press.
47 Albritton, E.M. (2003). Race-conscious grand juror selection: The equal protection clause and strict scrutiny. *American Journal of Criminal Law*, *31*(1), 175–210.
48 Illinois Jury Act 705 ILCS 305
49 Legal Information Institute. (n.d.). Circuit riding. *Cornell Law School*. https://www.law.cornell.edu/wex/circuit_riding
50 *Dred Scott v. Sandford*, 60 U.S. 393 (1857).
51 Smith, S.L. (2018). Dred Scott on the pacific: African Americans, citizenship, and subjecthood in the North American West. *Southern California Quarterly*, *100*(1), 44–68. https://doi.org/10.1525/scq.2018.100.1.44
52 W. Va. Acts 102 (1872–73).
53 *Strauder v. West Virginia*, 100 U.S. 303 (1880).
54 *Virginia v. Rives*, 100 U.S. 313 (1880).
55 *Duren v. Missouri*, 439 U.S. 357 (1979).
56 *Swain v. Alabama*, 380 U.S. 202 (1965).
57 *Batson v. Kentucky*, 476 U.S. 79 (1986).
58 *Strauder v. West Virginia*, 100 U.S. 303 (1880).
59 *Strauder v. West Virginia*, 100 U.S. 303, 304 (1880).
60 *Strauder v. West Virginia*, 100 U.S. 303, 306 (1880).
61 *Batson v. Kentucky*, 476 U.S. 79 (1986).
62 *Duren v. Missouri*, 439 U.S. 357 (1979).
63 *Duren v. Missouri*, 439 U.S. 357 (1979).
64 *Swain v. Alabama*, 380 U.S. 202 (1965).
65 *Swain v. State*, 156 So. 2d 368 (1963).
66 *Swain v. Alabama*, 380 U.S. 202 (1965).
67 *Strauder v. West Virginia*, 100 U.S. 303 (1880).
68 *Virginia v. Rives*, 100 U.S. 313 (1880).
69 *Duren v. Missouri*, 439 U.S. 357 (1979).
70 *Swain v. Alabama*, 380 U.S. 202 (1965).
71 Wyoming Historical Society (2024, February 18). *Women's suffrage and women's rights*. https://www.wyohistory.org/encyclopedia/topics/womens-suffrage-and-womens-rights
72 Utah State Legislature. (2024, February 18). Article IV, section 1. [Equal political rights]. https://le.utah.gov/xcode/ArticleIV/Article_IV,_Section_1.html
73 *Ballard v. United States*, 329 U.S. 187 (1946).
74 Preston, D. (2020, November 17). Beyond the trivia—Women on juries. KRCG. https://krcgtv.com/features/beyond-the-trivia/beyond-the-trivia-women-on-juries
75 *Taylor v. Louisiana*, 419 U.S. 522 (1975).
76 *Taylor v. Louisiana*, 419 U.S. 522 (1975).
77 *Ballard v. United States*, 329 U.S. 187 (1946).
78 *Ballard v. United States*, 329 U.S. 187, 197 (1946).
79 *Taylor v. Louisiana*, 419 U.S. 522 (1975).
80 *Taylor v. Louisiana*, 419 U.S. 522, 524 (1975).
81 *Taylor v. Louisiana*, 419 U.S. 522, 538 (1975).
82 *Ballard v. United States*, 329 U.S. 187 (1946).
83 *Taylor v. Louisiana*, 419 U.S. 522 (1975).
84 Ogletree, C.J. (1994). Just say no! A proposal to eliminate racially discriminatory uses of peremptory challenges. *American Criminal Law Review*, *31*(4), 1099–1151.

3 Grand Juries in Federal and State Courts

What Do You Think?

Before reviewing the concepts addressed in this chapter, answer True or False to each of the following questions or statements. Correct answers can be found at the end of Chapter 3.

1. Grand jury proceedings are held in the first tier of the federal court system.
2. Federal and state grand jurors must determine the guilt or innocence of a defendant based on the facts presented at trial.
3. Defense attorneys bear the full responsibility for presenting evidence during a grand jury proceeding.
4. Federal grand jurors must reach a unanimous vote to issue an indictment.
5. Oklahoma allows for empaneling the fewest number of grand jurors among all the states.
6. Grand jurors have been criticized for recommendations reached in police use of lethal force incidents.

Learning Objectives

After reading this chapter, you will be able to:

1. Identify where federal grand juries fit within the three branches of the U.S. government.
2. Describe the role of the prosecutor, defense attorney, and jurors in federal and state grand jury proceedings.
3. Explain the criticisms voiced against federal and state grand juries.
4. Define the burden of proof, explain the meaning of an indictment, and identify specific provisions of the Bill of Rights that pertain to grand jury proceedings.
5. List the challenges prosecutors face in police lethal use of force incidents.
6. Describe the arguments and reasons for reforming state grand jury proceedings.

Introduction

The U.S. Constitution, ratified in 1788, set forth the new structure of the federal government. Among its features were numerous checks and balances to decrease the likelihood that any one person or political party could achieve ultimate control and decision-making power over the citizens of the newly formed nation. It has been hailed for its ingenuity and intentional design to mitigate perceived failings of the English monarchy that were addressed in Chapter 1.

DOI: 10.4324/9781003677796-4

Disputes between the Federalists and Anti-Federalists occurred openly during the infancy of the United States. The arguments included, among other things, further limiting the powers of a national government. The Anti-Federalists were concerned about a centralized government impeding the rights of individuals, much like the English monarchy did to the early American colonists. They wanted to remove power from the national government and place it in the hands of the states. The creation and ratification of the Fifth Amendment in the Bill of Rights extended the protection of a grand jury to individuals accused of serious crimes. This right was granted to anyone accused of committing a federal crime. Grand juries have been empaneled for the past 250 years. In recent decades, however, grand jury proceedings have been highly criticized, and opponents have called for reforming the grand jury system or minimizing its use. How would the Founding Fathers respond to such criticisms today?

In This Chapter

This chapter examines grand juries in the federal and state court systems. Information addressed in this chapter includes: 1) the organization of the federal and state courts; 2) the prosecutor's role and the jury's responsibility in federal and state grand jury proceedings; 3) the main criticisms voiced against federal and state grand juries; and 4) critics' suggestions for change and reform to grand jury proceedings.

Organization of Federal and State Judicial Systems

The three branches of the government may be addressed in American history and government classes in many middle or high school classrooms in the United States educational system. These branches include the legislative (Congress which makes the laws), the executive (President who implements and enforces the laws), and the judicial (courts that determine the constitutionality of laws). This basic structure of three branches of government exists at the federal level and at the state level in each of the 50 states and the five federal territories (District of Columbia, Puerto Rico, U.S. Virgin Islands, Guam, and the Northern Mariana Islands). This text focuses on the judicial branch, which involves trial and appellate courts, grand jury proceedings, trial juries, and individual jurors.

Federal District Courts

Federal courts are structured into a three-tiered system: the 94 **Federal District Courts** (also referred to as trial courts), 12 regional circuit Courts of Appeals and one federal circuit court (which hears appeals over certain categories of cases), and the Supreme Court of the United States (which hears and makes the final decision about issues of law).[1] Only the district courts empanel jurors to serve on either grand jury proceedings or trial juries.

Table 3.1 shows the structure of the federal judiciary in the U.S. court system. The Federal Judiciary Act of 1789, one of the first legislative Acts passed by Congress, created the **federal court system**. These are called Constitutional Courts and were described under Article III of the Constitution. ("The judicial Power of the United States shall be vested in one supreme Court, and in such inferior Courts as the Congress may from time to time ordain and establish."[2]) Article III indicates that the Supreme Court was the only court required under the Constitution. As shown in Table 3.1, other types of federal courts were created by Congress to address specific issues that are beyond the scope of this textbook.

The district courts, or inferior courts, make up the first level of the federal court system. There are 94 district courts dispersed throughout the 50 states and the federal territories.[3] Each state has at least one district court, and many states have multiple district courts. For example, Pennsylvania has three district courts. Box 3.1 shows how each county comprising the Commonwealth of Pennsylvania is associated with one of the three Federal District Courts. The number of district courts assigned per state is determined by population density.[4] Each district court is located geographically within one of the 12 regional circuits that comprise the U.S. Court of Appeals.

Table 3.1: The Federal Judicial System

U.S. Supreme Court			
↑	↑	↑	↑
Foreign Intelligence Surveillance Court of Review	Court of Military Appeals	Courts of Appeals for Federal Circuit	U.S. Federal Court of Appeals (12)
↑	↑	↑	↑
Foreign Intelligence Surveillance Court	Military Courts	Court of International Trade Court of Veterans Appeals Claims Court	Federal District Courts (94)

Box 3.1: District Courts of Pennsylvania and Affiliated Counties[5]

Eastern District

(a) The Eastern District comprises the counties of Berks, Bucks, Chester, Delaware, Lancaster, Lehigh, Montgomery, Northampton, and Philadelphia.

Courts for the Eastern District are found in Allentown, Easton, Lancaster, Reading, and Philadelphia.

Middle District

(b) The Middle District comprises the counties of Adams, Bradford, Cameron, Carbon, Centre, Clinton, Columbia, Cumberland, Dauphin, Franklin, Fulton, Huntingdon, Juniata, Lackawanna, Lebanon, Luzerne, Lycoming, Mifflin, Monroe, Montour, Northumberland, Perry, Pike, Potter, Schuylkill, Snyder, Sullivan, Susquehanna, Tioga, Union, Wayne, Wyoming, and York.

Courts for the Middle District are found in Harrisburg, Lewisburg, Scranton, Wilkes-Barre, and Williamsport.

Western District

(c) The Western District comprises the counties of Allegheny, Armstrong, Beaver, Bedford, Blair, Butler, Cambria, Clarion, Clearfield, Crawford, Elk, Erie, Fayette, Forest, Greene, Indiana, Jefferson, Lawrence, McKean, Mercer, Somerset, Venango, Warren, Washington, and Westmoreland.

Courts for the Western District are found in Erie, Johnstown, and Pittsburgh.

Three features mark the Anglo-American system as different from all other is the extent to which our law is formed in litigation. Another feature is the way we conduct these cases: we pit antagonists against each other, to cast up from their struggles the material of decisions. A third—and largest in the public consciousness—is the trial by jury.

—Charles Rembar, American Attorney *The Law of the Land: The Evolution of Our Legal System* (1980)

All federal District Courts follow the same criminal procedures. Generally, federal courts will hear cases involving disputes about "the United States Government, the U.S. Constitution, or other federal laws."[7] The federal courts will also consider disputes related to diversity of citizenship; that is, arguments between "two parties not from the same state or country"[8] and where the monetary value of disputes is $75,000 or more. Rulings reached by federal courts of appeal often become precedent that federal district courts will follow when considering a case with similar circumstances. This is referred in the courts as stare decisis or "let the decision stand." Decisions issued by the U.S. Supreme Court and the federal circuit courts have precedential value for Federal District Courts within their respective jurisdictions, but not necessarily for state courts. Establishing precedent provides direction and continuity for how cases will be resolved. Laws and social practices change over time; therefore, a long-standing precedent might be overturned or updated as patterns in social norms and perceptions of acceptable behavior evolve in a society.

Precedent (pronounced pres.ɪ.dənt)[6]

- An adjudged case or decision of a court of justice, considered as furnishing an example or authority for an identical or similar case afterwards arising or a similar question of law.
- A draught of a conveyance, settlement, will, pleading, bill, or other legal instrument, which is considered worthy to serve as a pattern for future instruments of the same nature.

Each state and federal territory also has its own judicial branch to manage criminal and civil cases. One of the differences between the federal judicial branch and state judicial branches is the structure of the court systems themselves, including the number and level of courts where cases can be filed and tried. State court organizational structures are the culmination of each state's unique legal history and its efforts to improve the administration of justice. Accordingly, state court organizational structures can be as unique as the constituencies they serve. Only five states and the five U.S. territories resemble the federal court system with a single level of trial court.[9] Regardless of whether the case involves civil claims or criminal charges, it is processed within the same court system. The remaining 45 states have a multi-tiered trial court consisting of at least one general jurisdiction court that has authority to hear major crimes and cases involving complex legal issues arising within the geographic boundaries served by the court (usually the county) and one or more limited jurisdiction courts. As the name implies, limited jurisdiction courts are restricted to hearing a limited range of cases. These often include less serious crimes (misdemeanors) and civil cases, and traffic offenses. Many of these limited jurisdiction courts serve smaller geographic areas within the county, such as cities, towns, or other political subdivisions.[10] In addition to differences at the trial court level, eight states and four federal territories have only a single court

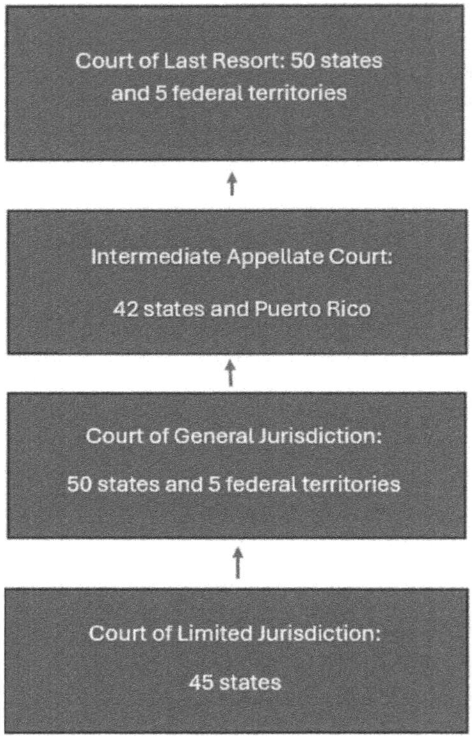

Figure 3.1: State Court Systems in the United States

of last resort, rather than an intermediate court of appeals. Figure 3.1 summarizes variations in state court systems.

Grand Juries in Federal and State Courts

There are two types of juries in the American justice system: the grand jury and the **petit jury** (better known as the **trial jury**). These terms were introduced to England prior to the contributions of King Henry II in the 12th century (described in Chapter 1). Briefly, the Norman conquest of England, led by William the Conqueror in the Battle of Hastings in 1066, stimulated legal reforms, including the development of the jury system. William established legal practices where a group of local countrymen (referred to as an inquest) provided information to the King in exchange for favors including land acquisition and tax relief. These inquests evolved into the first grand jury or "large jury," consisting of 23 members. In contrast, a petit jury or "small jury" consists of 6–12 members. Typically, the phrase "trial jury" is used in place of petit jury because it most aptly describes the jury's role to adjudicate trials; the phrase "trial jury" will be used in this textbook. In the federal court system, grand jury proceedings and jury trials are only conducted in the district courts. This chapter focuses on grand juries from the federal and state court systems, while Chapter 4 examines the trial jury in both systems.

The Founding Fathers intended for grand juries to operate separately from the executive branch of government. Indeed, the use of grand juries to determine whether sufficient evidence existed to charge someone of a crime was so firmly established in the American colonies that the nation's Founders included them in the Bill of Rights to "help protect the rights of citizens and uphold the laws of the land." The Fifth Amendment of the United States Constitution reads, in part, that "no person shall be held to answer for a capital, or otherwise infamous crime unless on a presentment or indictment of a Grand Jury."[12] The phrase "**infamous crime**" is broad and has been interpreted to mean felony offenses. Felonies may be related to arson, assault, burglary, drug/narcotics use, homicide, kidnapping of minors, larceny, rape, robbery, stolen goods or property, etc.[13] and may have a minimum one-year prison sentence, if found guilty of such charges. The Fifth Amendment, therefore, requires that a grand jury review evidence and determine whether charges may be brought against a defendant related to a felony offense. However, an individual suspected of committing the crime may waive a grand jury proceeding altogether and agree to be prosecuted without an **indictment**. When this occurs, the prosecutor makes a written charge of the crime, referred to as **information**. An information is a formal criminal charge brought by a prosecutor to start a criminal proceeding.

Indictment (pronounced in-ˈdīt-mənt)[11]

A formal written statement framed by a prosecuting authority and found by a jury (such as a grand jury) charging a person with an offense.

As discussed in the previous chapter, the Fifth Amendment to the U.S. Constitution require an indictment by grand jury before the federal government can pursue criminal charges against criminal defendants; however, the U.S. Supreme Court has not incorporated the Fifth Amendment against the states. Consequently, how the criminal process begins in state courts, including whether a grand jury indictment is required, is a matter of state constitutional and statutory law. Box 3.2 describes the U.S. Supreme Court's finding in *Hurtado v. California*, which allowed states to indict an accused without empaneling a grand jury.

Box 3.2: *Hurtado v. California*[14]

Joseph Hurtado was arrested in California for the fatal shooting of Jose Antonio Estuardo. The shooting was motivated by an illicit affair between Estuardo and Hurtado's wife. The prosecuting attorney decided not to hold a grand jury proceeding to obtain an indictment, but instead filed an information formally accusing Hurtado of murder and seeking court approval to prosecute him.

The Constitution of the State of California, adopted in 1879,[15] in Article I, section 8, states: "Offenses heretofore required to be prosecuted by indictment shall be prosecuted by information, after examination and commitment by a Magistrate"

A judge accepted the prosecutor's information and in 1882 Hurtado was tried for murder in front of a California jury. The jury convicted Hurtado of murder and sentenced him to death. Hurtado appealed the decision to the Supreme Court of California claiming his prosecution based on information denied him his right to a grand jury proceeding under the Fourteenth Amendment's due process clause. The California Court denied his claim in 1883.

Next, Hurtado appealed to the U.S. Supreme Court in 1884 claiming his right to a grand jury proceeding, guaranteed in the Fifth Amendment and applied to the states though the due process clause of the Fourteenth Amendment, was violated. The Court affirmed the lower court's finding that individual states are not bound by a grand jury's indictment recommendation to officially charge an individual of a felony offense.

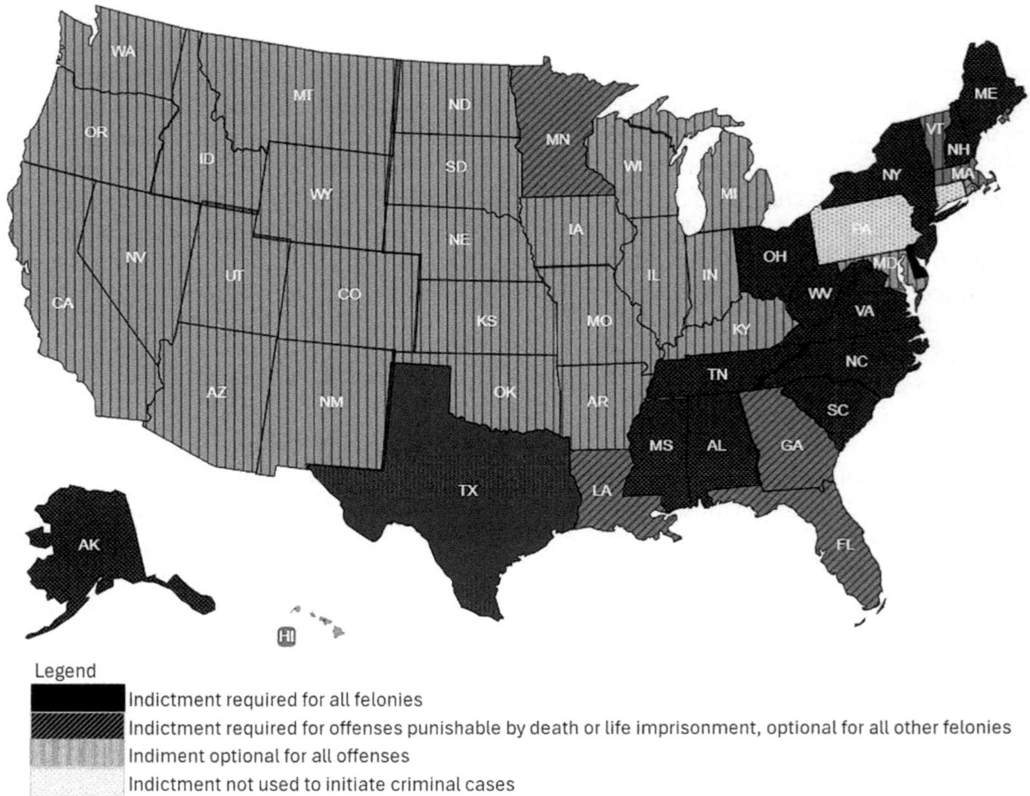

Figure 3.2: Indictment Requirements for Felony Offenses

(*Source:* Hannaford-Agor et al., 2019. *Reforming the grand jury process: Recent efforts to improve public confidence in cases involving police use of lethal force* at p. 4.)

Every state, except Pennsylvania and Connecticut, authorizes the use of grand juries to issue indictments.[16] Only 15 states follow federal standards by requiring all felony cases to be brought to a grand jury, which must first recommend an indictment before proceeding to a jury trial. In most states, prosecutors have the option to initiate felony proceedings either through a grand jury indictment or through an information in state court. Five states require empaneling a grand jury only for cases where punishment could result in a death sentence or life imprisonment. Figure 3.2 illustrates state variations for indictment requirements. Except in cases involving great public controversy, most prosecutors forego the grand jury process. An example of such cases could be law enforcement officers using lethal force, which is addressed later in this chapter.

As in the federal justice system, grand juries in state courts are used for criminal investigations and, when authorized to do so, issuing indictments. In many states, they also serve other functions, including investigating misconduct or incompetence by government officials (13 states); investigating the condition of jails, prisons, and other detention facilities (13 states); examining public buildings (three states); examining public records (three states); examining election fraud or rules violations (two states); and other special duties.[17]

The Prosecutor

Federal and state trial courts are responsible for summoning individuals for grand jury service, confirming their eligibility, administering the oath of service, and managing administrative tasks. Once grand jurors are empaneled, however, a **prosecutor** takes the lead in presenting evidence and securing indictments against people accused of crimes.[18] The purpose of a grand jury is to ensure that the government cannot prosecute an individual without showing probable cause that they committed a serious crime. Jurors must first provide an impartial review of relevant facts against the accused. In this sense, a grand jury protects or shields individuals from an oppressive government and one that abuses its power, but a grand jury proceeding also gives the government power and authority to prosecute its own citizens suspected of committing crimes.[19] This power may be abused by prosecutors to aggressively seek an indictment in some cases, while providing intentionally weak evidence to a grand jury in other cases, making an indictment less likely. In recent decades, critics increasingly argue that prosecutors present purposively weak evidence in cases involving police use of deadly force.[20] Box 3.3 features comments from a former prosecutor about his experiences and interactions with federal grand jurors.

Box 3.3: From the Field

Name: Shuaiyb Newton

Position: Assistant District Attorney, Delaware County District Attorney's Office; former Federal Prosecuting Attorney, Eastern District of Pennsylvania

Serving as a grand juror is a significant time commitment. Research shows this may result in a grand jury comprised of jurors who are older, retired, self-employed, etc. How does the composition of a grand jury impact the constitutional guarantee to a fair and impartial jury?

First, we commonly have fair and impartial jurors from a variety of backgrounds. I do not believe if we eliminate a large swath of workforce employees that we will sacrifice a fair and impartial jury. That said, any jury service tends to pose a hardship to individuals who are gainfully employed. Due to the length of grand jury service, that hardship is magnified, which likely has the effect of eliminating workforce employees (and there is likely an age correlation that comes with this).

Second, there are two types of grand juries in Pennsylvania: (1) investigating grand jury, and (2) indicting grand jury. Neither of those grand juries is responsible for convicting someone. So, you always have the prophylactic of additional due process after the decisions of either type of grand jury, i.e. you can have a jury trial. (An investigating grand jury is pre-arrest and can be thought of as prosecution working with and/or substituting efforts of law enforcement. An indicting grand jury is a post-arrest process that substitutes a preliminary hearing where a sufficient basis has been made for witness intimidation.)

Prosecutors exclusively determine what evidence gets presented to a grand jury. What type of evidence is most critical to share and what evidence are federal prosecutors less willing to present?

You only want to present the least amount of evidence possible to meet the burden of proof. At a grand jury hearing, the burden is very low—more likely than not the crime occurred, and the defendant committed the crime. Whatever evidence identifies the defendant as the person who committed the crime—eyewitness or circumstantial—must be presented to the grand jury. You do not want to present your entire case or expert testimony that may confuse the grand jury.

Grand jurors are permitted to request additional witness testimony or evidence to aid their decision-making before recommending an indictment. Under what circumstances could a federal prosecutor deny such a request?

The prosecutor has complete discretion on what evidence the grand jury hears. If the grand jury wants clarification, it is in the prosecutor's best interest to make sure they understand the evidence. The prosecutor can recall witnesses and ask clarifying questions. If the grand jury wants to know about the defendant's history or possible defenses, for example, the prosecutor must inform the grand jury the requested information is irrelevant to their decision. The prosecutor is presenting their case to the grand jury, so they are presenting the evidence they believe will achieve an indictment.

The Jurors

In federal court, the grand jury consists of 16 to 23 citizens selected at random from the population. The number of jurors was established from English common law during the Middle Ages.[21] The individuals selected for a grand jury must reside within the federal district where the court is physically and geographically located. Having such a large pool of eligible jurors to choose from may ensure inclusivity of individuals who reside in small or large communities, and urban, rural, or suburban settings. Casting a wide net to identify a vast number of eligible jurors also may increase representativeness of community members on the jury[22] and randomly selecting from individuals in this jury pool is the best way to achieve a representative grand jury.

A **federal grand jury** proceeding has several unique features compared to a federal jury trial. At least 16 of the 23 jurors must be present for the federal grand jury proceeding to occur. This number constitutes a **quorum**. A federal grand jury proceeding will not be held when fewer than 16 jurors are in attendance. Federal grand juries do not need to be **unanimous** in their decision to indict. The decision to indict is official if at least 16 grand jurors are present for the vote and at least 12 of them agree to go forward with an indictment.[23]

Chapter 5 describes the source lists from which the names of eligible jurors are randomly selected for jury service. For now, once a grand jury is selected and seated, the court will appoint a jury foreperson and deputy foreperson.[24] One or both forepersons must be present during each day of the grand jury proceeding. Next, all seated jurors will be sworn in by a judge or court clerk and take an oath to uphold the rules binding the court and its procedures.[25] Finally, before the proceedings begin, the district judge will **charge the jury**. This means the judge will provide instructions about the roles, duties, and obligations expected during grand jury proceedings and after the proceedings end.

Grand juries in state courts differ from their federal counterparts with respect to size and indictment requirements. The largest grand jury size is 23, which is possible in 13 states and the District of Columbia. Many of the remaining states permit smaller grand juries, empaneling fewer than 20 jurors. California is unique and bases the size of the grand jury on the number of residents living in the county where the proceeding is to be held.[26]

Generally, states that do not require a grand jury indictment tend to have smaller-sized juries than do states that require an indictment.[27] Overall, many states require 12 jurors to indict, which ironically is the most common size of petit juries in felony trials. The average proportion of grand jurors required to issue an indictment across the states allowing grand jury proceedings is 65 percent.[28] Other states have a minimum number of grand jurors who must agree to issue a true bill, and that number always reflects at least the majority of the grand jurors. Figure 3.4 relates to state variations in grand jury size and the number of jurors

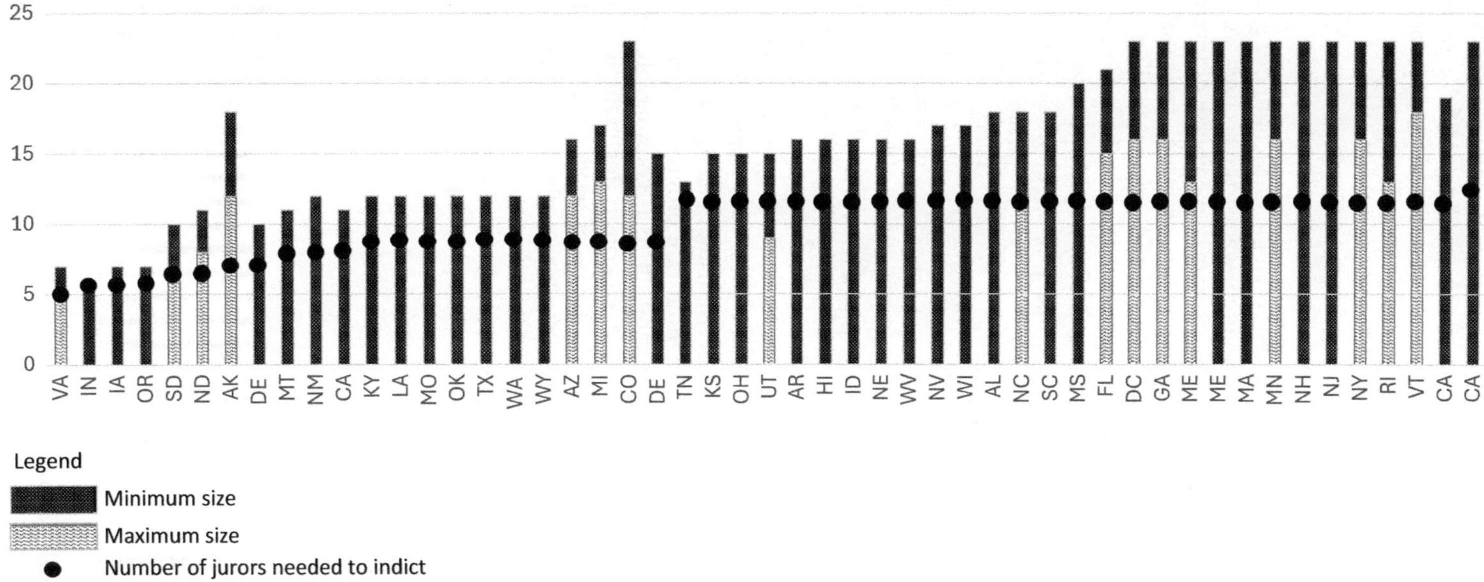

Figure 3.4: Number of Jurors Needed to Indict

(*Source:* Hannaford-Agor et al., 2019. *Reforming the grand jury process: Recent efforts to improve public confidence in cases involving police use of lethal force* at p. 5.)

needed to indict.[29] States that empanel larger number of grand jurors (between 15 and 23) tend to require 12 jurors to recommend an indictment. This is like the guidelines for the federal grand jury. States that allow for a smaller number of total grand jurors to be empaneled (12 or fewer) require nine or fewer jurors to indict.

Term of Service for Grand Juries

Grand jury proceedings differ in other ways. For example, the length of a grand jury proceeding is based on the amount of evidence presented against the accused. A prosecutor's presentation of evidence can be made in a few hours or over the course of several days, but some cases might take multiple weeks or months to present a thorough review of relevant evidence and facts against the accused.[31] The length of a grand jury proceeding is also determined by the level of complexity of the case, the detailed nature of the evidence, and the number of witnesses called to testify. In general, the statutory requirement for length of service requires federal grand juries to be seated for terms up to 18 months. This does not mean the jurors report to the courthouse every day for terms 18 months. The exact schedule varies and depends upon the availability of witnesses to testify, the prosecutor's schedule, and other administrative issues. Jurors on grand juries may meet one day per week or several consecutive days per month until all evidence is presented, and they have reached a decision about an indictment.[32] The actual length of service may be extended an additional six months, if ordered by a judge.[33]

Federal Grand Jury[30]

Type of jury composed of up to 23 citizens. The jury decides if evidence is strong enough to bring an accused to trial for the specified crime.

In state courts, the term of service for grand jurors is considerably less than for federal courts, as Figure 3.5 shows. In Kentucky and Wisconsin, for example, the term of service is only one month. A total of 19 states have terms of service less than 12 months. Only two states—South Carolina and Tennessee—have terms of service longer than federal courts (24 months).

A grand jury must be empaneled to review evidence and issue indictments in federal court and in 13 states for *all* felony cases before they can proceed to a jury trial. During these long

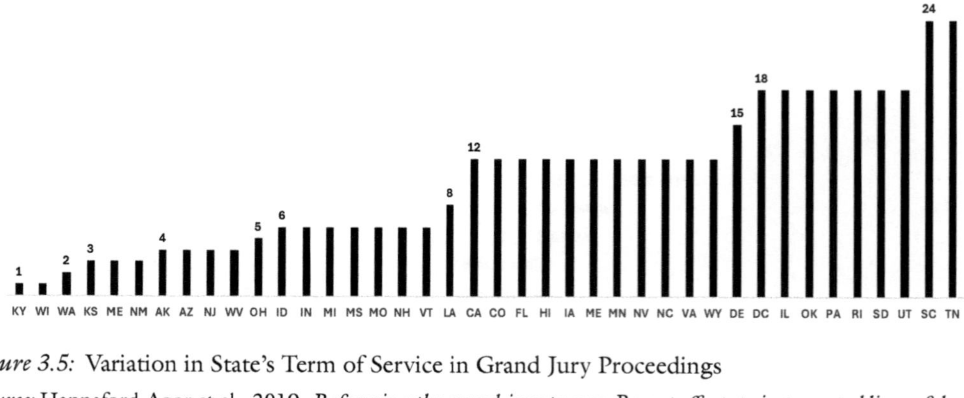

Figure 3.5: Variation in State's Term of Service in Grand Jury Proceedings

(*Source:* Hannaford-Agor et al., 2019. *Reforming the grand jury process: Recent efforts to improve public confidence in cases involving police use of lethal force* at 5.)

terms of commitment, grand jurors may consider dozens or even hundreds of separate and unrelated cases where they are asked to determine whether an indictment is appropriate for multiple individuals accused of various crimes.[34] If the grand jury is not able to issue an indictment by the time the term of service expires (12–18 months), the prosecutor must begin presenting evidence of the crime to the next grand jury. Participating in multiple grand jury proceedings is a major time commitment for average citizens. These demanding expectations may limit the jury pool to older citizens who are retired or to citizens who have more flexibility in the workplace or even work from home.[35]

As mentioned, the prosecutor may include in their presentation of evidence individual testimonies from witnesses. The witnesses will be asked questions directly by prosecutors and possibly by the jurors in federal grand jury proceedings. Indeed, grand jurors are permitted special authority and power not usually available to trial jurors.[36] Also, the witnesses providing testimony during a grand jury proceeding may not be represented by their own attorneys or have legal counsel present. The witness may stop their testimony during the proceeding and consult with their own attorney, who may stay outside of the courtroom, but is not permitted inside the courtroom during the grand jury proceeding and presentation of evidence. Also, grand jurors may request additional information from the prosecutor if they believe it will be helpful when determining whether to indict the accused. For example, jurors may ask for additional physical evidence or documentation to be presented inside the courtroom, or for additional witnesses to be called, if available.[37] Such requests are referred to as ***Subpoena ad testificandum*** and ***Subpoena duces tecum***. Box 3.4 describes these forms of subpoenas and the power of grand jurors in more detail.

It is permissible that the prosecuting attorney allows witness testimony and evidence that is favorable to the defense side;[40] however, it is not typical that the individual(s) being accused of the crime appears before the actual grand jury to testify on their own behalf. The accused might not be aware that a grand jury has been convened to discuss potential charges against them. Grand jurors are instructed that the lack of testimony by the suspected individual and an absence of defense witnesses should not be used against the accused when deciding whether to recommend an indictment.

Box 3.4: Unique Role of Grand Jurors

Grand juries are allowed to play an investigative role when deciding whether the accused should be indicted. The authority that jurors have during a grand jury proceeding exceeds the powers granted to trial jurors. Grand juries are allowed to issue subpoenas to gather additional evidence that will determine whether to recommend charges be brought against the accused or to not recommend charges because the evidence was not compelling enough to do so.
Grand jurors have the power to issue two types of subpoenas:

1. *Subpoena ad testificandum* (witness) is a grand jury's demand for a person or a representative to provide testimony during the proceeding because it believes the testimony may be relevant to a decision to indict.[38]
2. *Subpoena duces tecum* ("you shall bring with you") is a grand jury's demand for a document, file, record, or other physical evidence to be submitted during the proceeding that could be used to determine whether charges should be brought against the accused.[39]

Deliberation and Indictment

Grand jurors begin their deliberation in isolation after the prosecutor has presented all the evidence about the alleged criminal act and the witnesses were allowed to provide their testimony. The individual jurors must discuss the evidence presented during the grand jury proceeding and determine whether there is **probable cause** that the individual being accused committed the crime. This means that, based on the facts and circumstances presented, a reasonable person believes there is sufficient evidence that the accused committed a crime and that criminal proceedings should be initiated.[41] Probable cause, as a burden of proof, is a far lower standard than proof beyond a reasonable doubt set for trial juries in criminal cases and lower than the preponderance of the evidence standard set for civil juries.

A decision to indict is referred to as a "**true bill**." If this occurs, the accused is then referred to as the defendant. The prosecutor will prepare the formal written indictment for the grand jury's consideration. The prosecuting attorney or assistant prosecutor is not required to sign the indictment received by the grand jury. If a grand jury concludes that no probable cause exists that the accused has committed a crime, it will deliver a "**no-bill**" or "**not a true bill**" vote.[42] If the accused is incarcerated at the time of the grand jury proceeding, they must "be released from jail or freed from bail."[43] The prosecutor could pursue additional legal action against the accused if the grand jury decided not to indict. For example, the prosecutor still has an option to bring misdemeanor charges against the accused through a preliminary hearing or bring a separate civil lawsuit. Also, federal prosecutors have the authority to present the same or additional evidence to a new grand jury, if a previous grand jury has delivered a no bill. The likelihood of this occurring is rare; however, any charges the prosecutor filed against the accused typically are dropped or dismissed if the grand jury does not recommend an indictment.

A grand jury's obligation has been fulfilled when a decision is reached and shared with the prosecutor and the judge. If the jury indicts the accused, a criminal trial will be scheduled, but with a new panel of jurors. The grand jurors who issued the indictment will not be recalled or seated as trial jurors on the criminal trial. Jurors are provided with clear instructions that nothing they heard during the grand jury proceeding can be shared outside the courtroom or deliberation room. This includes discussions with the media and their own families. Jurors may not even share information from the deliberation discussion or the voting patterns of individual jurors with the prosecuting attorney.[44] This shroud of **secrecy** surrounding a grand jury's decision has been lifted in some cases that have garnered national attention and the public's demand for justice. Box 3.5 describes special circumstances when the prosecuting attorney can release evidence and transcripts from a grand jury proceeding.

Box 3.5: Limitations to Secrecy

Rule 6 of the Federal Rules of Criminal Procedure pertains to the grand jury. The federal rules clearly indicate that any matter occurring before a grand jury cannot be disclosed outside of the courtroom. This rule of secrecy applies to grand jurors, an interpreter, a court reporter, an operator of a recording device, a person who transcribes recorded testimony, and an attorney for the government.[45]

There are exceptions to this rule of secrecy and nondisclosure. The exceptions, however, provide additional allowances for sharing details of a grand jury proceeding for the federal prosecutor only. For example, disclosure of grand jury proceedings may be made to "an attorney for the government for use in performing that attorney's duty" and for "any government personnel—including those of a state, state subdivision, Indian tribe, or foreign government—that an attorney for the government considers necessary to assist in performing that attorney's duty to enforce federal criminal law."[46]

The idea that the grand jury operates in total secrecy, therefore, is not entirely truthful. Secrecy must be maintained by everyone, except the federal prosecutor who can share details of the proceedings under multiple circumstances. Notwithstanding these exceptions, strict rules for secrecy and nondisclosure still apply to what was discussed during the grand jury's deliberation and to the voting decision reached by individual jurors.[47] Critics have argued that releasing the pre-deliberation instructions provided to grand jurors by the prosecutor might aid the defendant if the case goes to trial. For example, if the juror instructions omitted elements of the crime or misrepresented evidence, the defense can request the indictment be dismissed.[48]

The **secrecy** employed during a grand jury proceeding has some advantages,[49] although critics may argue otherwise. The secrecy of a grand jury proceeding allows witnesses to respond fully without fear that their testimony will be shared publicly[50] and the secrecy minimizes the chances that witnesses could be coerced or intimidated by others. Also, the closed-door proceeding may protect individuals, who were not charged ("no-bill") with a crime from unwarranted and undeserved public scrutiny, judgment, and prejudice.[51] Also, the secrecy may prevent a person, who is under consideration for an indictment, from escaping or fleeing prior to the jury's decision.[52] Finally, the strict limitations on sharing details about a grand jury proceeding and the decision-making among fellow jurors may encourage more open and honest discussions during the deliberation process.

Criticism of the Grand Jury

Officially, grand jury proceedings are supervised by a judge, who charges the jurors, but the prosecutor is almost entirely in control of the process.[53] The only individuals present, in addition to the prosecutor, are the jurors, the witness(es), a stenographer, a court reporter, and interpreter (if necessary).[54] The grand jury proceeding, therefore, allows the prosecutor free reign inside the grand jury room. No defense attorneys are permitted in the grand jury room or have any involvement in deciding what evidence is presented. The proceeding is also performed without the involvement of a judge.[55] Critics have observed that "there is no other instance in which a public servant is given such freedom from scrutiny."[56]

Some have argued that prosecutors, who are part of the executive branch, have been permitted more control in grand jury proceedings over the generations while still maintaining privacy and secrecy originally granted to jurors.[57] Legal scholars and practitioners have complained that because grand jury proceedings are so skewed for the federal prosecutor's side, an indictment is easy and is often expected. Research findings support these claims, revealing that 99 percent of grand jury proceedings end with a jury indicting the accused.[58] The Bureau of Justice Statistics reported findings from over 30,000 cases where U.S. attorneys declined to prosecute individuals suspected of criminal matters. In only 11 incidents was the reason related to a grand jury's decision not to indict ("no true bill").[59] Sol Wachtler, former Associate Judge of the New York State Court of Appeals (1973–1984), is often cited for his observation that a prosecutor could convince a grand jury to indict a ham sandwich.[60]

Rules of Evidence

Critics also voice concern about the types of evidence allowed to be presented inside the courtroom during a grand jury proceeding. First, critics objected to the use of **hearsay evidence** allowed during grand jury proceedings. Hearsay evidence is an out-of-court statement offered to prove the truth of whatever it asserts.[61] An example of hearsay evidence is when a witness testifies that they heard someone else say something, such as "Samantha told me she saw the defendant at the scene of the crime." However, Samantha is not the witness, so she cannot be cross-examined to test the veracity of this statement.[62] The testimony relies on the credibility of Samantha and therefore is considered a weak and unreliable form of evidence to present during a grand jury proceeding. Hearsay evidence is generally not admissible during jury trials, although there are few exceptions.[63] The U.S. Supreme Court found in *Costello v. United States* (1956)[64] that hearsay evidence was admissible by prosecutors during a grand jury proceeding. Prosecutors, however, should make every effort to inform the grand jurors what testimony is based on hearsay and not the personal, direct experience of the witness.[65]

Critics voice concerns about other types of evidence that are admissible during grand jury proceedings that are not allowed during jury trials. The U.S. Supreme Court found in *U.S. v. Williams* (1992)[66] that a prosecutor is not required to disclose exculpatory evidence that casts doubt about whether the accused committed a crime. Such evidence might include eyewitness testimony, documents, files, or video footage that is favorable to the defendant.[67]

Critics have argued that withholding exculpatory evidence from a grand jury "will undermine its ability to do its job."[68] While they are not prohibited from presenting exculpatory evidence, prosecutors, who want to get an indictment in a grand jury proceeding, will focus on inculpatory evidence to present to the jury that goes against the accused. If the grand jury issued an indictment, federal prosecutors are obligated to share any exculpatory evidence with the defendant's attorneys, regardless of whether it was presented to the grand jury.[69]

Finally, the prosecutor is advantaged in another way regarding evidence that is admissible in a grand jury proceeding but not in a jury trial. For example, the exclusionary rule concerns evidence that was gathered in violation of the **Fourth Amendment** and its guarantee against unlawful search and seizure practices. Such evidence is inadmissible during jury trials; however, the U.S. Supreme Court found in *U.S. v. Calandra* (1974)[70] that the exclusionary rule does not apply to a prosecutor who is presenting evidence to a grand jury. The Court explained that the exclusionary rule was designed to guard against police officer misconduct and should not be used to interfere with the decision-making ability of a grand jury to indict or decline to indict an individual accused of a crime. Table 3.2 summarizes these decisions by the U.S. Supreme Court about what evidence is admissible during a grand jury proceeding.

Fourth Amendment

The right of the people to be secure in their persons, houses, papers, and effects, ***against unreasonable searches and seizures, shall not be violated***, and no Warrants shall issue, but upon probable cause, supported by Oath or affirmation, and particularly describing the place to be searched, and the persons or things to be seized. (emphasis added)

Why would the U.S. Supreme Court relax important safeguards and protections described in the Constitution and the Federal Rules of Evidence? Why are hearsay and

Table 3.2: Summary of Court Decisions about Evidence in Grand Jury Proceedings

Case	*Decided*	*Opinion*
Costello v. U.S. 350 U.S. 359	March 5, 1956	The Court affirmed that the use of hearsay evidence during a grand jury proceeding does not violate Fifth Amendment protections and denied establishing procedures to facilitate supervisory oversight of a grand jury's decision to issue an indictment in criminal cases.
U.S. v. Calandra 414 U.S. 338	January 8, 1974	The Court found that the exclusionary rule to bar trial evidence gathered in violation of the Fourth Amendment's protection against illegal search and seizure practices does not apply to a grand jury proceeding; exclusionary evidence is admissible by the prosecutor.
U.S. v. Williams 504 U.S. 36	May 4, 1992	The Court found that the prosecutor does not have to present exculpatory evidence during a grand jury proceeding; such evidence is favorable to the defense (e.g., testimony, video footage) and may indicate the individual is innocent of the crime(s) for which they are being accused.

exculpatory evidence, and evidence gathered through illegal search and seizures, admissible in grand jury proceedings? The answer may be found among the rights and privileges bestowed upon the grand jury itself. In *U.S. v. Williams* (1992), the Court found that grand juries operate independently from the judicial branch of government and are allowed their own **investigative powers** to determine whether to indict.[71] This independence places the grand jury outside the normal control and supervisory role undertaken by the Supreme Court in other legal proceedings and matters occurring in lower courts.[72] This means that the Court will not interfere with the valid recommendation made by a grand jury to indict the accused, even if exculpatory evidence was withheld by the prosecutor. Overall, the Court in *Williams* found the grand jury as a unique body of decision-makers which it could not limit or control procedurally.[73]

A particularly potent criticism is prosecutor use of grand juries in cases involving police use of lethal force. Widespread publicity about incidents involving police use of lethal force has led to increased public concern that police are not being held adequately accountable by the criminal justice system, beginning with the failure of grand juries to return indictments against police officers suspected of using excessive force.

The death of Freddie Gray, a 25-year-old African American male from Baltimore, Maryland[74] may serve as an example. In 2015, six officers, three White officers and three Black officers, were indicted in Gray's death on multiple charges, including second degree murder. The prosecutor performed her duties to present evidence to a grand jury that the officers should be indicted for criminal charges. The grand jury recommended an indictment for all six officers involved with Gray's death. During their individual bench or jury trials, however, the first four officers were either acquitted or the case resulted in a mistrial. The Baltimore prosecutor chose to dismiss the charges on the other officers without taking the cases to trial.[75] In this situation, the Baltimore prosecutor was responding to the conscience of the community by seeking an indictment for the officers involved in the death of Freddie Gray. In some cases that involve police use of lethal force, the evidence may not be compelling enough to convince a trial jury of a defendant's guilt because the burden of proof is much stronger. As mentioned, grand juries must find probable cause, while a trial jury in criminal cases must meet a higher standard, namely, guilt beyond a reasonable doubt.

While there are no official statistics about how often police use deadly force, a *Washington Post* investigation found that since 2015, police have fatally shot around 4,400 people, with 6 percent of those victims being unarmed.[76] The failure of grand juries to indict police officers in controversial killings, especially when the victims are racial or ethnic minorities, has sparked widespread protests. The killings of Michael Brown (Ferguson, Missouri) and Eric Garner (Staten Island, New York), for example, contributed, in part, to the creation of the Black Lives Matter movement.[77]

There have been multiple cases since 2010 in which prosecutors were unable to secure indictments from state grand juries for incidents involving police use of lethal force. Table 3.3 lists and briefly describes several high-profile cases involving law enforcement officers who use deadly force and a grand jury's recommendation *not* to indict the police officer(s)

Table 3.3: High-Profile Cases

Incident	*No True Bill Decisions by Grand Juries*
Eric Garner **Staten Island, New York** **July 17, 2014**	Officers from the New York Police Department responded to a citizen complaint about a physical altercation in a Staten Island neighborhood. Upon arriving, the fight was over, but officers confronted Eric Garner, 43, African American, about illegally selling cigarettes near a public transportation terminal in the neighborhood.[79] Words were exchanged between the parties and Officer Daniel Pantaleo subdued Garner by use of a choke hold, applying significant pressure to his chest and neck that contributed to his suffocation and death. A grand jury reviewed evidence about the incident and acquitted Pantaleo of criminal homicide charges and determined that the officer's actions were justifiable. Four other NYPD officers were given immunity by the county prosecutor and could not be criminally prosecuted.[80]
Michael Brown **Ferguson, Missouri** **August 9, 2014**	In 2014, Michael Brown, 18, Black, was killed by a White police officer, Darren Wilson, in Ferguson, Missouri. After considering evidence presented during a grand jury proceeding, the jury decided not to recommend indicting Wilson on criminal charges in the death of Brown. Their decision sparked violent protests in both the Ferguson community and on a national level. In an unusual response, the prosecutor released evidence presented during the grand jury proceeding, including testimony provided by individual witnesses and Officer Wilson himself.[81] The jury was presented with conflicting statements about whether Brown surrendered at the time he was fatally shot or whether he was approaching the officer, who fired in self-defense.[82]
Tamir Rice **Cleveland, Ohio** **November 22, 2014**	Two officers from the Cleveland Division of Police (Frank Garmback and Timothy Loehmann) arrived at the Cudell Park Recreation Center after a resident called 911 to report an individual ("probably a juvenile") was brandishing a weapon ("probably a fake") and was pointing it at people on a playground. Upon arriving at the playground, the officers located Rice, 12, whose height was 5'7" and who weighed 195 pounds. Rice approached the officers and, according to the officer's testimony, made movements toward his waste. Officer Loehmann, fearing Rice was reaching for a gun, fired two shots that fatally wounded the youth. Police learned later that Rice's weapon was a toy, a pellet gun. A grand jury reviewed evidence and acquitted both officers of criminal charges in the shooting,[83] deeming the officers' actions were reasonable under the circumstances. Rice's family pursued further charges against violations of their federal civil rights. The Department of Justice failed to find sufficient evidence of any violations of civil rights upon review of the case.[84]

of criminal wrongdoing. In many instances, where the grand jury did not recommend indicting the officer(s), the prosecutor was openly criticized for intentionally putting on a weak case. To address these concerns, like criticisms of grand juries in the federal jury system, several states are considering various reform efforts, including improved citizen access to grand juries, removing grand jury secrecy requirements, and using independent prosecutors or special counsel to conduct grand jury proceedings.[78] Box 3.6 features comments from an attorney about grand jury proceedings, including the evidence presented, public confidence, and ways for improvement.

Box 3.6 From the Field

Name: John Choi

Position: County Attorney for Ramsey County, Minnesota

How long have you worked in this position?
I have served in this position since 2011.

When you bring a case to a grand jury, how do you see your role as a prosecutor?
I think the proper role for the prosecutor is to be the legal advisor for the grand jury. Lay people are not necessarily trained in the law, and they are not necessarily trained as investigators. The judge will instruct them about their role and responsibilities, and the role of the prosecutor. But the reality is the prosecutor will have more influence about how grand jury proceedings are organized, what questions are asked of witnesses, and what evidence is presented. The prosecutor does not tell the grand jurors to issue an indictment, but the prosecutor has influence over the process, which may steer the jury toward an outcome.

Grand juries can hear types of evidence, like hearsay, that trial jurors cannot. So how do you decide what evidence to share and how do you explain it to the grand jurors?
It is important for grand jurors to have the benefit of all the information, even if some of it may not be admissible at trial, because the prosecutor would have the benefit of this information if they were making the charging decision. It should be noted, however, that in some jurisdictions inadmissible evidence cannot be considered by the grand jurors. Regardless, the bottom line is a prosecutor should not indict somebody unless they have a good-faith belief that they can prove guilt beyond a reasonable doubt, a much higher standard than probable cause for an arrest. Although in some places it is appropriate to make sure grand jurors are aware that some information might not be used in court, we do not want people to be charged with crimes just because something happened that is outrageous or infuriating or we are just mad at that person. Even though prosecutors have extraordinary influence in grand jury proceedings, we do not want to see the criminal justice system weaponized or politicized in any way.

Grand jury proceedings are secret. From your point of view, what is the main reason for the secrecy? And what kind of issues does that secrecy raise for public trust and confidence?

The secrecy of grand jury proceedings and public trust are kind of at odds in some ways. There is certainly a legitimate public interest in wanting to protect the investigative process, to protect the safety and public reputation of witnesses, and to encourage witnesses to give complete and honest evidence. However, in modern times, that level of secrecy comes at a cost. Today, public transparency is important, especially as there are growing numbers of people who do not have faith in the decision-making of our courts and our legal processes. It is very difficult to get a judge to permit public disclosure of grand jury questions, witness testimony, and deliberations. But if a prosecutor decides not to move forward on a criminal complaint, they can make their evidence public, so that everyone can make up their own mind about whether the prosecutor made the right call.

Are there other things that you can think of that would make the grand jury process better for the justice system and better for grand jurors?

It is probably a good thing that the country is reckoning with this tension between grand jury secrecy and transparency about charging decisions. We may need to change state statutes and court rules to allow for greater public input or at least greater transparency into grand jury proceedings. But, at the end of the day, I think that the solution is to stop using grand juries entirely. We have set up the American system so that the vast majority of local district attorneys make those decisions, and they stand for elections. If citizens do not like the prosecutor's decision, they can hold them accountable at the next election.

Calls for Reform

In 2023, the United States was just one of two countries worldwide that held grand jury proceedings; the other country was Liberia.[85] All other industrialized nations have abolished the practice of a grand jury. The criticisms described in this text about grand juries in the federal and state court systems may explain why such practices were abandoned in justice systems throughout the world. It is unlikely the United States will eliminate grand juries altogether because the Fifth Amendment firmly establishes grand juries to protect citizens' rights to liberty and justice from an oppressive government. Critics strongly urge, however, reforming current practices to allow more transparency about how grand juries operate and how they decide to indict the accused of certain crimes.[86]

The original intent of the grand jury was consistent with the Founding Fathers' principles that a central government should not impede or oppress the freedoms of its citizens. Grand jurors were granted the power and authority to determine whether the accused was being rightfully charged with a crime and not being mistreated by the government. Critics argued that the grand jury lost this noble intent in the generations after ratifying the Bill of Rights. Now, opponents claim grand juries overwhelmingly serve the will of the prosecutor to get the outcome they want and do so under secrecy that conceals evidence presented during the proceeding. The way the grand jury operates today, and some decisions reached by grand juries in recent decades, have caused distrust.

Critics suggest several reforms to the grand jury. First, some have argued for more reliance on preliminary hearings where evidence is presented in a public setting, the defense is available and given an opportunity to ask questions, and a legally trained judge makes the ultimate decision whether to indict.[87] The format of a preliminary hearing addresses critics' concerns about grand jury secrecy. Other suggested reforms include better mechanisms for releasing transcripts of proceedings[88] and excluding certain cases from being considered by grand juries, including police use of lethal force. The state of California has already banned assembling a grand jury for police-involved incidents resulting in a fatality.[89]

Other suggestions for improving the grand jury have included sharing the prosecutor's control and authority to convene a grand jury with the public. Six states currently allow citizens to petition to hold a grand jury proceeding in certain circumstances.[90] If the public can gather a specified number of signatures from registered voters in a jurisdiction, then the state court may allow a grand jury proceeding to occur. Finally, another reform proposed in several states was to appoint a special prosecutor in incidents where police used lethal force. The prosecutor would be separate and independent from the jurisdiction where the crime happened and where the proceeding was scheduled to occur. House bills were introduced in many states to select special prosecutors for grand jury proceedings, but many of these attempts failed to receive the required number of votes needed to be signed into law.[91]

Conclusion

The Founders created a legal system that heavily emphasizes citizen involvement before an individual can be convicted of a serious criminal act. Although there are variations between federal and state grand jury proceedings, a grand jury is designed to allow jurors, and not a centralized government, to consider whether evidence exists to accuse someone of a crime before a trial jury can be convened. Grand juries operate independently from the judicial branch of government and have distinct investigative powers to determine whether to indict. U.S. Supreme Court opinions permit practices in grand jury proceedings that are not allowed in jury trials. Overall, grand jurors are granted unique powers, which the Supreme Court does not limit or control procedurally.

Grand jury proceedings, however, are not without criticism. Critics have voiced opposition that the type and amount of evidence to be presented during a grand jury proceeding contributes to the overwhelmingly high number of indictments recommended, as prosecutors can paint a narrative that best leads to an indictment.[92] Critics call for changes and reform to eliminate the skewedness, secrecy, and advantages that favor the prosecutor. Moreover, critics urge restoring the balance of the grand jury proceeding to better reflect the original intent of the Founding Fathers and to better protect citizens from being wrongfully charged of crimes and criminal wrongdoing.[93]

The next chapter addresses the use of trial juries in the federal and state court systems. A comparison will be drawn about the structure and operations of trial juries in federal and state courts, including eligibility requirements (e.g., citizenship, age, criminal background), unanimity rules, and jury size.

Summary

The focus of this chapter was on the structure and function of grand juries in the federal and state court systems. A grand jury proceeding is convened and coordinated exclusively by a federal or state prosecutor, or, more typically, an assistant prosecutor. The jurors need only determine whether there was a probable cause that an individual committed a crime to issue an indictment. When the jury reaches a true bill decision, the accused is formally charged with a crime and a trial jury is assembled to reach a verdict about guilt or innocence. Both the federal and state court systems operate similarly in this manner. Federal grand juries are comprised of 16–23 jurors, and 12 jurors must agree on the verdict to indict the accused of a crime. The size and rules governing individual state grand jury proceedings vary considerably.

The structure and operation of grand jury proceedings have been highly criticized. Critics argue that a grand jury proceeding allows the prosecutor too much power and control and the proceedings relax important evidentiary safeguards. For example, grand jury proceedings, unlike jury trials, allow hearsay evidence and evidence in violation of the exclusionary rule, and the prosecutor is allowed full discretion to present or ignore exculpatory evidence that is favorable to the defendant. Based on this skewed presentation of evidence, many critics have argued it is common for a grand jury to issue indictments in most cases. Another criticism of grand juries is that they operate in secrecy. The courtroom is closed to the public and the evidence and transcripts of the proceedings are rarely shared. There are a few exceptions when evidence presented during a grand jury proceeding can be shared, but jurors are sworn to secrecy and cannot discuss the proceeding with media or their own family. Critics have argued that grand jury proceedings should be made more transparent and have greater public involvement. Such changes may restore the public's faith in the federal grand jury process.

While almost all states authorize grand juries, only a few require them for all felony indictments. Also, grand juries vary in size and function, with some conducting criminal investigations and others tasked with oversight of public institutions. Like the federal system, criticisms have been voiced against the structure and proceedings of state grand juries. A major concern raised is the perceived lack of accountability in cases involving police use of lethal force, where grand juries often fail to indict officers, particularly in cases involving racial minority victims. The chapter explored how state prosecutors wield significant authority in grand jury proceedings (just like federal prosecutors), which, combined with the secrecy surrounding these proceedings, undermine public trust. Various reform efforts were described, which are aimed at increasing transparency, limiting prosecutorial control, and restoring the grand jury's intended role as a safeguard against government abuse.

Discussion Questions

1. The federal grand jury operates differently than does a federal trial jury. Why do you think the Framers of the Constitution allowed jurors and the federal prosecutor so many privileges during a grand jury proceeding? What advantages do you see the defense attorney having in a grand jury proceeding?
2. Ethical consideration. How do you feel about allowing hearsay evidence and evidence not allowed under the exclusionary rule to be used by a federal grand jury when determining whether to recommend indicting a person(s) of a crime? If you do not support this, are there any special circumstances when you may feel such evidence would be acceptable and valuable for a grand jury to hear when reaching a decision to indict? Why do you think the Federal Rules of Evidence allow such information during a grand jury proceeding, but ban such evidence from being presented during criminal or civil cases where a trial jury must reach a decision about guilt or harm?
3. Ethical consideration. What do you think about a prosecutor's decision to let a grand jury recommend whether someone should be charged with a crime? Does this meet with the

Founding Fathers' intentions to protect citizens from abuse and oppression of a central government, or does this simply provide the prosecutor with an easy way out? Does the status of the individual involved in an incident (e.g., police officer or public official) change your opinion or support about prosecutorial discretion in lethal force cases?

4. Grand juries are rarely used in other legal systems throughout the world. Now that you are familiar with the structure and operation of federal and state grand juries in the American jury system, do you support the continued use of grand juries? What are the main advantages of grand juries that influence your decision to continue them, or what are the main criticisms of grand juries that make you want to disband them? Regardless of whether you want to continue them or remove them, what types of reforms would most likely address proponents' criticisms?

Review Questions

1. Describe the three-tiered federal judicial system and where grand juries reside in it.
2. How does grand jury size and number of jurors required to indict vary between the federal and state court systems? What does a quorum refer to?
3. Describe the burden of proof required for federal and state grand jurors and what it means to issue an indictment.
4. What are the criticisms of federal and state grand juries related to secrecy, prosecutorial decision-making, and presentation of evidence?
5. What reforms have been suggested to address critics' concerns about grand jury proceedings?

Answers to Chapter 3 "What Do You Think?" Questions

1. True. The first tier of the three-tiered federal judicial system includes the district courts which are where grand jury proceedings are held.
2. False. Federal grand jurors can only indict or decline to indict based on evidence presented at a grand jury proceeding.
3. False. A federal prosecutor or assistant prosecutor has full responsibility for presenting evidence during a grand jury proceeding.
4. False. In federal court at least 16 grand jurors must be present for the vote, and 12 or more must agree to indict.
5. False. Virginia allows for the fewest number of grand jurors, as few as five jurors, with four needed to indict.
6. True. Grand juries have been criticized when failing to indict police officers involved in fatal shootings and other lethal use of force incidents.

Key Terms

charge the jury
federal court system
Federal District Courts
federal grand jury
hearsay evidence
indictment
infamous crime

information
investigative powers
no-bill or not a true bill
petit jury or trial jury
probable cause
prosecutor
quorum
secrecy
subpoena ad testificandum
subpoena duces tecum
true bill
unanimous

References

1 Administrative Office of the U.S. Courts. (2024, January 20). *About the U.S. court of appeals.* https://www.uscourts.gov/about-federal-courts/court-role-and-structure/about-us-courts-appeals
2 U.S. Const. art. III, § 1
3 Administrative Office of the U.S. Courts. (2024, January 20). *About the U.S. court of appeals.* https://www.uscourts.gov/about-federal-courts/court-role-and-structure/about-us-courts-appeals
4 Administrative Office of the U.S. Courts. (2025, July 25). *About the U.S. District Courts.* https://www.uscourts.gov/about-federal-courts/court-role-and-structure/about-us-district-courts
5 Legal Information Institute. (2024, January 28). *28 U.S. Code § 118.* Cornell Law School. https://www.law.cornell.edu/uscode/text/28/118
6 *Black's Law Dictionary. (2023, November 23). Precedent. In Black's Law Dictionary (2nd ed.).* https://thelawdictionary.org/precedent
7 Administrative Office of the U.S. Courts. (2023, November 25). *Types of cases.* https://www.uscourts.gov/about-federal-courts/types-cases
8 Administrative Office of the U.S. Courts. (2023, November 25). *Types of cases.* https://www.uscourts.gov/about-federal-courts/types-cases
9 Court Statistics Project. (2025). *Understanding State Court Jurisdictions.* https://www.ncsc.org/resources-courts/understanding-state-court-jurisdictions
10 Court Statistics Project. (2025). *Understanding State Court Jurisdictions.* https://www.ncsc.org/resources-courts/understanding-state-court-jurisdictions
11 Merriam-Webster. (2023, November 23). Indictment. In *Merriam-Webster.com dictionary.* https://www.merriam-webster.com/dictionary/indictment.
12 U.S. Const., amend. V
13 New York State Courts. (2015, May 4). *Grand jury service: An empowering experience.* [Video]. YouTube. https://www.youtube.com/watch?v=A4HIZzNvsOk
14 *Hurtado v. California*, 110 U.S. 516 (1884).
15 Constitution of the State of California. (1880). *The Statutes of California.* https://archives.cdn.sos.ca.gov/collections/1879/archive/1879-constitution.pdf
16 Hannaford-Agor, P.L., Royer, C., Williams, M., & Trochesset, A. (2019). *Reforming the grand jury indictment process: Recent efforts to improve public confidence in cases involving police use of lethal force.* National Center for State Courts. https://ncsc.contentdm.oclc.org/digital/collection/juries/id/318
17 Hannaford-Agor, P.L., Royer, C., Williams, M., & Trochesset, A. (2019). *Reforming the grand jury indictment process: Recent efforts to improve public confidence in cases involving police use of lethal force.* National Center for State Courts. https://ncsc.contentdm.oclc.org/digital/collection/juries/id/318
18 U.S. Department of Justice. (2024, May 5). 9–11.000—Grand jury. *Justice Manual.* https://www.justice.gov/jm/jm-9-11000-grand-jury
19 Administrative Office of the U.S. Courts. (2012) (2023, November 22). *Handbook for federal grand jurors.* https://www.uscourts.gov/sites/default/files/grand-handbook.pdf

20 Simmons, R. (2017). The role of the prosecutor and the grand jury in police use of deadly force cases: Restoring the grand jury to its original purpose. *Cleveland State Law Review*, *65*(4), 519–534.
21 Hurnard, N.D. (1941). The jury of presentment and the Assize of Clarendon. *The English Historical Review*, *56*(223), 374–410.
22 Administrative Office of the U.S. Courts. (2019) (2024, May 5) *Courts seek to increase jury diversity.* https://www.uscourts.gov/news/2019/05/09/courts-seek-increase-jury-diversity
23 Administrative Office of the U.S. Courts. (1999). (2023, November 22). *Handbook for federal grand jurors.* https://www.moed.uscourts.gov/sites/moed/files/documents/Jury_Handbook-GrandJurors.pdf
24 Administrative Office of the U.S. Courts. (2012) (2023, November 22). *Handbook for federal grand jurors.* https://www.uscourts.gov/sites/default/files/grand-handbook.pdf
25 Administrative Office of the U.S. Courts. (2012) (2023, November 26). *Handbook for trial jurors serving in the United States district courts.* https://www.uscourts.gov/services-forms/jury-service
26 Bureau of Justice Statistics. (1998). *State court organization 1998.* U.S. Department of Justice. https://bjs.ojp.gov/content/pub/pdf/sco9806.pdf
27 Hannaford-Agor, P.L., Royer, C., Williams, M., & Trochesset, A. (2019). *Reforming the grand jury indictment process: Recent efforts to improve public confidence in cases involving police use of lethal force.* National Center for State Courts. https://ncsc.contentdm.oclc.org/digital/collection/juries/id/318
28 Hannaford-Agor, P.L., Royer, C., Williams, M., & Trochesset, A. (2019 *Reforming the grand jury indictment process: Recent efforts to improve public confidence in cases involving police use of lethal force.* National Center for State Courts. https://ncsc.contentdm.oclc.org/digital/collection/juries/id/318
29 Bureau of Justice Statistics. (2006). *State court organization 2004. Tbl 38 Grand juries: Composition and function.* https://bjs.ojp.gov/content/pub/pdf/sco04.pdf
30 Black's Law Dictionary. (2023, November 23). Grand jury. In *Black's Law Dictionary* (2nd ed.). https://thelawdictionary.org/grand-jury
31 New York State Courts. (2015, May 4). *Grand jury service: An empowering experience.* [Video]. YouTube. https://www.youtube.com/watch?v=A4HIZzNvsOk
32 Administrative Office of the U.S. Courts. (2024, January 24). *Types of juries.* https://www.moed.uscourts.gov/sites/moed/files/documents/Jury_HandbookGrandJurors.pdf
33 Administrative Office of the U.S. Courts. (2023, November 22). *Reporting on criminal cases—Journalist's guide.* https://www.uscourts.gov/statistics-reports/reporting-criminal-cases-journalists-guide#:~:text=Grand%20juries%20are%20formally%20supervised,of%20the%20U.S.%20attorney's%20office
34 Simmons, R. (2017). The role of the prosecutor and the grand jury in police use of deadly force cases: Restoring the grand jury to its original purpose. *Cleveland State Law Review*, *65*(4), 519–534.
35 Price, S. (2014) (2024, January 24). *A crash course in the American grand jury system.* Poole-Shaffery. https://www.pooleshaffery.com/news/2014/december/a-crash-course-in-the-american-grand-jury-system/
36 Rosenberg, B.E. (2020). Indictments, grand juries, and criminal justice reform. *American Journal of Criminal Law*, *48*(1), 81–135.
37 Administrative Office of the U.S. Courts. (1999) (2023, November 22). *Handbook for federal grand jurors.* https://www.moed.uscourts.gov/sites/moed/files/documents/Jury_Handbook-GrandJurors.pdf
38 Freeman, M. (2006). Subpoena power. In *Truth Commissions and Procedural Fairness* (pp. 188–204). Cambridge University Press. https://doi.org/10.1017/CBO9780511584473.006
39 Freeman, M. (2006). Subpoena power. In *Truth Commissions and Procedural Fairness* (pp. 188–204). Cambridge University Press. https://doi.org/10.1017/CBO9780511584473.006
40 Shapiro, E. (2015, December 28). *Grand jury declines to indict officers in Tamir Rice case, prosecutor says.* ABC News. http://abcnews.go.com/US/prosecutor-make-announcement-tamir-rice- grand-jury-investigation/story?id=35977877
41 Kuckes, N. (2006). The democratic prosecutor: Explaining the constitutional function of the federal grand jury. *The Georgetown Law Journal*, *94*(5), 1265–1318.
42 Administrative Office of the U.S. Courts. (1999). (2023, November 22). *Handbook for federal grand jurors.* https://www.moed.uscourts.gov/sites/moed/files/documents/Jury_Handbook-GrandJurors.pdf

43 Administrative Office of the U.S. Courts. (1999) (2023, November 22). *Handbook for federal grand jurors.* https://www.moed.uscourts.gov/sites/moed/files/documents/Jury_Handbook-GrandJurors.pdfhttps://www.moed.uscourts.gov/sites/moed/files/documents/Jury_HandbookGrandJurors.pdf
44 Administrative Office of the U.S. Courts. (1999) (2023, November 22). *Handbook for federal grand jurors.* https://www.moed.uscourts.gov/sites/moed/files/documents/Jury_Handbook-GrandJurors.pdf
45 Fed. R. Crim. P. 6(e)(2)(B)
46 Fed. R. Crim. P. 6(e)(3)(A)
47 Fed. R. Crim. P. 6(e)(3)(A)
48 Rosenberg, B.E. (2020). Indictments, grand juries, and criminal justice reform. *American Journal of Criminal Law*, *48*(1), 81–135.
49 Administrative Office of the U.S. Courts. (1999) (2023, November 22). *Handbook for federal grand jurors.* https://www.moed.uscourts.gov/sites/moed/files/documents/Jury_HandbookGrandJurors.pdf
50 Rosenberg, B.E. (2020). Indictments, grand juries, and criminal justice reform. *American Journal of Criminal Law*, *48*(1), 81–135.
51 Simmons, R. (2017). The role of the prosecutor and the grand jury in police use of deadly force cases: Restoring the grand jury to its original purpose. *Cleveland State Law Review*, *65*(4), 519–534.
52 Rosenberg, B.E. (2020). Indictments, grand juries, and criminal justice reform. *American Journal of Criminal Law*, *48*(1), 81–135.
53 Administrative Office of the U.S. Courts. (2023, November 22). *Reporting on criminal cases—Journalist's guide.* https://www.uscourts.gov/statistics-reports/reporting-criminal-cases-journalists-guide#:~:text=Grand%20juries%20are%20formally%20supervised,of%20the%20U.S.%20attorney's%20office
54 Administrative Office of the U.S. Courts. (1999) (2023, November 22). *Handbook for federal grand jurors.* https://www.moed.uscourts.gov/sites/moed/files/documents/Jury_Handbook-GrandJurors.pdf
55 Shapiro, C., & Clark, J. (2023, September 27). It's time to abolish grand juries once and for all. *The Nation.* https://www.thenation.com/article/activism/abolish-grand-juries-cop-city-trump
56 Rosenberg, B.E. (2020). Indictments, grand juries, and criminal justice reform. *American Journal of Criminal Law*, *48*(1), 81–135.
57 Calki, R. (1967). The fading myth of grand jury secrecy. *John Marshall Journal of Practice and Procedure*, *18*, 17–36. https://repository.law.uic.edu/lawreview/vol1/iss1/2
58 Hoffmeister, T. (2008). The grand jury legal advisor: Resurrecting the grand jury's shield. *The Journal of Criminal Law & Criminology*, *98*(4), 1171–1230.
59 Bureau of Justice Statistics. (2013). *Federal justice statistics 2010—Statistical tables.* U.S. Department of Justice. Office of Justice Programs. https://bjs.ojp.gov/content/pub/pdf/fjs10st.pdf
60 Gould, D. (2024, February 9). *Sol Wachtler.* Historical Society of the New York Courts. https://history.nycourts.gov/biography/sol-wachtler
61 Fed. R. Evid. 801(c)
62 Fed. R. Evid. 801(c)
63 Fed. R. Evid. 804(b)
64 *Costello v. United States*, 350 U.S. 359 (1956).
65 U.S. Department of Justice. (2024, February 5). 9–11.232—Use of hearsay in a grand jury proceeding. *Justice Manual.* https://www.justice.gov/jm/jm-9-11000-grand-jury#9-11.232
66 *United States v. Williams*, 504 U.S. 36 (1992).
67 Shein, M. (2021, September 14). *What is exculpatory evidence and why does it matter to your post-conviction appeal?* Federal Criminal Law Center. https://federalcriminallawcenter.com/2021/09/what-is-exculpatory-evidence-and-why-does-it-matter-to-your-post-conviction-appeal
68 Rosenberg, B.E. (2020). Indictments, grand juries, and criminal justice reform. *American Journal of Criminal Law*, *48*(1), 81–135.
69 *Brady v. Maryland*, 373 U.S. 83 (1963).
70 *United States v. Calandra,* 414 U.S. 338 (1974).
71 *United States v. Williams*, 504 U.S. 36, 45 (1992).
72 *United States v. Williams*, 504 U.S. 36, 48 (1992).
73 *United States v. Williams*, 504 U.S. 36 (1992).

74 White, C., Weisburd, D., & Wire, S. (2018). Examining the impact of the Freddie Gray unrest on perceptions of the police: Freddie Gray unrest. *Criminology & Public Policy, 17*, 829–858. https://doi.org/10.1111/1745-9133.12404
75 Domonoske, C. (2016, July 27). *Prosecutors drop all remaining charges against officers in Freddie Gray's death.* National Public Radio. https://www.npr.org/sections/thetwo-way/2016/07/27/487606743/prosecutors-drop-all-remaining-charges-against-officers-in-freddie-grays-death
76 Fox, J., Blanco, A., Jenkins, J., Tate, J., & Lowery, W. (2019). *What we've learned about police shootings 5 years after Ferguson.* Washington Post, 9. https://www.washingtonpost.com/nation/2019/08/09/what-weve-learned-about-police-shootings-years- after-ferguson/?arc404=true
77 Dunivin, Z.O., Yan, H.Y., Ince, J., & Rojas, F. (2022). Black Lives Matter protests shift public discourse. *Proceedings of the National Academy of Sciences, 119*(10), e2117320119. https://doi.org/10.1073/pnas.2117320119
78 Hannaford-Agor, P.L., Royer, C., Williams, M., & Trochesset, A. (2019). *Reforming the grand jury indictment process: Recent efforts to improve public confidence in cases involving police use of lethal force.* National Center for State Courts. https://ncsc.contentdm.oclc.org/digital/collection/juries/id/318
79 History.com. (2020, July 15). *Eric Garner dies in NYPD chokehold.* A&E Television Networks. https://www.history.com/this-day-in-history/eric-garner-dies-nypd-chokehold
80 Fagan, J., & Harcourt, B.E. (2014, November 26). *Fact sheet in Richmond County (Staten Island) grand jury in Eric Garner homicide.* Columbia Law School. https://www.law.columbia.edu/news/archive/fact-sheet-richmond-county-staten-island-grand-jury-eric-garner-homicide
81 Hector, M. (2015). Grand juries in the spotlight. *Illinois Bar Journal, 103*(2), 15.
82 Peralta, E. & Calamur, K. (2014, November 25). *Ferguson documents: How the grand jury reached a decision.* National Public Radio. https://www.npr.org/sections/thetwo-way/2014/11/25/366507379/ferguson-docs-how-the-grand-jury-reached-a-decision
83 Siemaszko, C., Silva, D., & Fieldstadt, E. (2015, December 28). *Grand jury declines to indict officers in Tamir Rice case.* NBC News. https://www.nbcnews.com/news/us-news/grand-jury- declines-indict-officers-tamir-rice-case-n486876
84 U.S. Department of Justice. (2020 December 29). *Justice Department announces closing of investigation into 2014 Officer involved shooting in Cleveland, Ohio.* Office of Public Affairs. https://www.justice.gov/opa/pr/justice-department-announces-closing-investigation-2014-officer-involved-shooting-cleveland
85 Shapiro, C., & Clark, J. (2023, September 27). *It's time to abolish grand juries once and for all.* The Nation. https://www.thenation.com/article/activism/abolish-grand-juries-cop-city-trump/
86 Simmons, R. (2017). The role of the prosecutor and the grand jury in police use of deadly force cases: Restoring the grand jury to its original purpose. *Cleveland State Law Review, 65*(4), 519–534.
87 Shapiro, C., & Clark, J. (2023, September 27). *It's time to abolish grand juries once and for all.* The Nation. https://www.thenation.com/article/activism/abolish-grand-juries-cop-city-trump/
88 Simmons, R. (2017). The role of the prosecutor and the grand jury in police use of deadly force cases: Restoring the grand jury to its original purpose. *Cleveland State Law Review, 65*(4), 519–534.
89 Hannaford-Agor, P.L., Royer, C., Williams, M., & Trochesset, A. (2019). *Reforming the grand jury indictment process: Recent efforts to improve public confidence in cases involving police use of lethal force.* National Center for State Courts. https://ncsc.contentdm.oclc.org/digital/collection/juries/id/318
90 Hannaford-Agor, P.L., Royer, C., Williams, M., & Trochesset, A. (2019). *Reforming the grand jury indictment process: Recent efforts to improve public confidence in cases involving police use of lethal force.* National Center for State Courts. https://ncsc.contentdm.oclc.org/digital/collection/juries/id/318
91 Hotujac, M. (2020). The jury is still out: Should Kansas continue to allow its citizens to initiate grand juries? *Kansas Journal of Law & Public Policy, 29*(1), 72–93.
92 Nelson, C. (2016). *With BCA investigation over, what's next in Castile case?* Minnesota Public Radio. https://www.mprnews.org/story/2016/09/28/grand-jury-process-controversy-explained-philando-castile
93 Rosenberg, B.E. (2020). Indictments, grand juries, and criminal justice reform. *American Journal of Criminal Law, 48*(1), 81–135.

4 Trial Juries in the Federal and State Court Systems

What Do You Think?

Before reviewing the concepts addressed in this chapter, answer True or False to each of the following questions or statements. Correct answers can be found at the end of Chapter 4.

1. The Supreme Court's finding in *Duncan v. Louisiana* extended the right to a trial jury in all criminal and civil cases.
2. The burden of proof that must be determined by trial jurors in criminal cases is a preponderance of evidence.
3. There are no limits to the types of civil cases that can be filed in federal courts.
4. Federal courts adjudicate more cases than state courts.
5. Between six and 12 jurors must be empaneled in federal criminal trials.
6. All states follow the federal courts' practice by setting a minimum age of jury service at 18.
7. Nonunanimous jury verdicts are allowed in civil cases in both the federal and state court systems.

Learning Objectives

After reading this chapter, you will be able to:

1. List the type of cases that can be brought to a jury in federal and state court systems.
2. Explain the burden of proof associated with criminal and civil cases.
3. Describe the number of cases filed annually in state trial courts compared to federal trial courts.
4. Explain how state trial juries vary in eligibility requirements for citizenship, age, language, and criminal record.
5. Describe U.S. Supreme Court decisions related to jury size and unanimous verdicts.

Introduction

Most Americans are more familiar with trial jury proceedings than with grand jury proceedings. They likely understand that the jury's role is to reach a verdict, that is, to find someone guilty or innocent or at fault for causing harm. The role that trial jurors have may be far more complicated than grand jurors, however. This is especially true when considering the burden of proof to meet when reaching a verdict at trial. The standards required in jury trials are stricter than simply finding there is probable cause that a crime was committed.

DOI: 10.4324/9781003677796-5

Like grand jury proceedings described in the previous chapter, trial juries differ between the federal and state court systems, and among the state court systems. Each state is its own sovereign, meaning it possesses independent authority to govern itself, enact its own laws, and manage its internal affairs within the framework of the U.S. Constitution. States have the inherent authority to decide how the branches share power and administer government on behalf of the people residing in their states. While state governments have many similarities, each has unique characteristics that reflect the collective values of the state residents, including the structure and procedures of juries and jury trials within each state court system. While federal and state juries share many characteristics, many state jury systems have unique characteristics that reflect differing state priorities and policy preferences.

In This Chapter

This chapter describes trial juries in the federal and state court systems. Here material addresses: 1) the right to a trial by jury in criminal and civil cases; 2) requirements for burdens of proof by juries; 3) variations in eligibility requirements related to citizenship, age, language, etc.; and 4) judicial decisions governing jury size and the unanimity rule in the federal and state court systems.

The Right to Trial by Jury

As discussed in Chapter 1, the first settlers in the American colonies brought the practice of juries and jury trials to the New World from England. Even at that time, however, not all cases were eligible for trial by jury. Each of the American colonies, and later the original states, had their own rules concerning the types of cases that could be decided by a jury. Most states followed the common law practice that jury trials were appropriate in cases involving factual disputes (e.g., Did the defendant murder the victim?), but not in cases involving purely legal disputes (e.g., Under what circumstances is it a crime to kill someone?). Cases involving claims of equity, that is, cases in which a purely mechanical application of rules might result in an unfair outcome (e.g., How should a decedent's property be distributed, if they failed to record a last will and testament?), were not jury-eligible. Instead, equity cases were typically decided by the judge without a jury.[1]

Broadly speaking, two types of cases—criminal and civil—can be tried by juries. In criminal cases, the jury must determine whether the prosecutor has proven **beyond a reasonable doubt** that the defendant committed the crime with which they were accused. This standard is high and forces the prosecutor to clearly describe all charges and show all evidence against the defendant. The penalty in criminal cases may involve imprisonment or restricting the freedoms of an individual; therefore, the highest standard of proof is required. A guilty verdict indicates all members of the jury were firmly convinced the defendant committed the crime(s).[2] Overall, federal (and state) law is reluctant to use precise terminology to define the phrase beyond a reasonable doubt, as leaving the phrase broad and somewhat ambiguous preserves context-specific and unique details of individual cases. This also protects a defendant's right to due process. Most jury instructions leave it to the jurors themselves to decide what the standard means.

The prosecuting attorney represents the government in criminal cases, and a defense attorney represents the defendant, who is the person accused of committing a crime. Juries act as finders of fact and decide whether the evidence indicates the defendant is innocent or guilty. If the jury finds the defendant guilty, the trial judge in most states decides the sentence to impose.[3] Capital trials are an exception to this general rule. In capital trials, also referred to as death penalty cases, a jury first deliberates about the defendant's guilt of a capital crime. If jurors unanimously find the defendant guilty beyond a reasonable doubt, then the trial enters the punishment phase. In this phase of the trial, the jury determines the sentence to be imposed, including whether the defendant should be sentenced to death for their crime.

Although percentages vary from year to year, more than half of federal jury trials[4] and up to three-quarters of state jury trials involve criminal cases.[5] The specific types of criminal cases differ in federal versus state courts. In federal courts, only defendants charged with crimes punishable by imprisonment of six months or more are heard. The Sixth Amendment to the Constitution guarantees the right to a jury trial for serious crimes.[6]

It is important to note that federal courts can only hear cases alleging violations of federal law. Federal crimes are those which Congress enacted to address either criminal activity perpetrated against the federal government or crimes that typically traverse state boundaries, making it difficult for any one state to prosecute effectively. Examples of federal criminal charges include violations of the federal income tax law, narcotics/drug laws, mail theft, terroristic threats, human trafficking, social security fraud, and counterfeiting.[7] Criminal cases in state courts, in contrast, involve more familiar charges, such as homicide (murder and manslaughter), criminal assault/battery, sex offenses, domestic violence, theft, sale and possession of illegal drugs, weapons offenses, and criminal traffic offenses, including driving under the influence.

It was not until 1968 that the U.S. Supreme Court ruled that the Sixth Amendment guarantees criminal defendants the right to a jury trial in state court cases involving serious crimes. In *Duncan v. Louisiana*, the Court reasoned that trial by jury in criminal cases was fundamental to the American justice system.[8] Therefore, the Due Process Clause of the Fourteenth Amendment ensures states cannot deny individuals the right to a jury trial in criminal cases where a federal court would be required to provide one under the Sixth Amendment. It should be noted, however, the Court has not extended the right to a trial jury in misdemeanor cases. Consequently, any rights of defendants to a jury trial in misdemeanor cases, if they exist at all, are found in state constitutions or statutes. Box 4.1 provides more details about the *Duncan* decision.

A criminal case can be filed in federal court after an indictment from a grand jury or, in limited circumstances, by a formal written charge filed by a federal prosecutor. Congress passed the Speedy Trial Act of 1974 that set parameters for the Sixth Amendment's phrase "right to a speedy trial." Under this Act, Congress allowed federal prosecutors 100 days from the time of an individual's arrest until they must appear in front of a trial jury or have

Box 4.1: *Duncan v. Louisiana*[9]

In 1968, the U.S. Supreme Court reiterated that the right to a jury trial in criminal cases was guaranteed by the Sixth Amendment and applied to the states through the Fourteenth Amendment. In *Duncan*, however, the Court interpreted this right as not guaranteed for defendants who were charged with crimes where the maximum penalty was less than six months imprisonment. If the criminal behavior carried a sentence of imprisonment for six months or longer, the Court found in *Duncan* that the defendant should be given an option for a trial by jury.

the charges dismissed altogether.[10] Within that 100-day timeframe, the defendant must be arraigned, which means they will appear in open court and be advised of the charges being brought against them. The defendant must then enter a plea of guilty or not guilty. If a not guilty plea is entered, the case can proceed to trial.

In *Klopfer v. North Carolina*, the U.S. Supreme Court held the guarantee of a speedy trial also applies to state courts, but did not specify a specific number of days in which to bring the case to trial.[11] Instead, the Court explained in *Barker v. Wingo* that a defendant's constitutional right to a speedy trial can only be determined after considering the length of delay, the reason for the delay, the defendant's assertion of the right, and the prejudice to the defendant.[12] State statutes enacted in the 1960s and 1970s clarified when the speedy trial requirement begins and the timeframe in which trials must take place.[13] Each state established its own guidelines for meeting the speedy trial requirement.

Civil cases are the second type of case that can be brought to trial juries. Examples of civil claims include breaking a personal or business contract, seeking damages for a personal or work-related injury or property damage, or collecting on an unpaid debt.[14] To initiate a civil case, the plaintiff files a complaint describing the basis for the claim, and the defendant responds with the answer either contesting the claim or providing additional facts or legal theories as a defense. In civil disputes, two parties argue their respective side in open court.[15] Unlike criminal cases, jurors do not determine guilt in civil cases; rather they must consider whether the evidence shows the defendant is responsible or at fault for harming the plaintiff. In the federal district court system, the jury also must reach a unanimous decision; however, the burden of proof in civil cases is a **preponderance of the evidence**, which is considerably less than beyond a reasonable doubt. In such cases, jurors must determine that "more likely than not" or there was a greater than 50 percent chance the defendant caused the harm.[16] If the defendant is found responsible, then the jury may be asked to determine a monetary amount the plaintiff should be awarded.

> The object of any tyrant would be to overthrow or diminish trial by jury, for it is the lamp that shows that freedom lives.
>
> —Patrick Arthur Devlin, British Judge
> *Trial by Jury* (1956)

The Seventh Amendment guarantees individuals the right to a jury trial for civil cases filed in federal court. Specifically, it states, "In suits at common law, where the value in controversy shall exceed twenty dollars, the right of trial by jury shall be preserved."[17] However, not all civil cases can be filed in federal court. Only cases involving civil rights protected by federal law can be filed in federal court and decided by a federal jury (e.g., wage and working conditions, financial securities) or cases in which the plaintiff and defendant are from different states or countries and the value in controversy is $75,000 or more.[18] Cases that do not meet these criteria must be filed in state courts and decided according to state law and procedure. Unlike the Sixth Amendment, the Seventh Amendment right to a jury trial in civil cases does not apply to the states.

Like misdemeanor cases, the right to a jury trial in a civil case depends on state law, which differs dramatically from state to state. Some states are considerably more protective of civil jury trial rights than the U.S. Constitution. Texas, for example, extends the right to jury trials in cases involving equitable rather than legal disputes, including property distribution in divorce cases,[19] challenges to a decedent's last will and testament in probate cases,[20] and misdemeanor traffic offenses.[21] Box 4.2 features comments from a trial attorney about his experiences and interactions with trial jurors.

Box 4.2: From the Field

Name: David Golberg

Position: Former Assistant District Attorney

How long did you work as a prosecuting attorney?
I was a prosecutor from 2001 to 2014.

What are prosecuting attorneys most concerned with related to jurors and a trial by jury?
We have a few concerns. Our paramount concern is to make sure we find jurors who harbor no bias, ill-will, or distrust towards the criminal justice system or those who work in it. We also need to ensure that the jurors have no preconceived notions towards the guilt or innocence of the accused. Another concern is ensuring that we find jurors who are comfortable taking or defending a converse or minority view in scenarios where peer pressure may be very significant.

Do jurors typically understand their roles and responsibilities as "finders of fact" when they deliberate about guilt or fault?
This issue is one of the biggest challenges. Jurors quite often misunderstand their roles as the factfinder. This can take form in many ways. First, jurors often feel that they can become "investigators" themselves and look into factual issues and happenings on their own. This is a huge concern, as jurors are only supposed to consider the evidence presented to them by trial witnesses and evidence. This evidence is typically curated very carefully to not poison the jury against the accused with information they are not supposed to know (for example, the prior record of the accused, a news article that has unsavory information about the accused or mentions evidence that may have been suppressed for legal reasons). Also, another issue is when jurors try to study the law that applies to their case. This is strictly forbidden. The trial judge is the judge of the law, and the jurors are the judges of the facts. Unfortunately, criminal law can be extremely complicated and nuanced; a juror trying to study it in the confines of a single case can be very prejudicial to the accused. The remedy for these two scenarios is a jury instruction(s) that cautions jurors to avoid this.

Jury Trials in Federal and State Courts

As discussed in Chapter 2, the Framers of the U.S. Constitution strengthened the powers of the federal government to address various shortcomings in the Articles of Confederation. Yet many citizens, especially Anti-Federalists, were still wary of entrusting the federal government with too much power. The first nine amendments to the Constitution protected individual rights. The Tenth Amendment, in contrast, protected states from federal encroachment. **Federalism** is the fundamental principle that government

Tenth Amendment

The powers not delegated to the United States by the Constitution, nor prohibited by it to the States, are reserved to the States respectively, or to the people.

Box 4.3: By the Numbers

In 2024, the Administrative Office of the U.S. Courts reported that federal district courts closed 76,734 criminal cases and 268,242 civil cases, of which only a small proportion were resolved by jury trial (1,537 criminal trials and 1,145 civil trials).[22] Most cases are resolved by plea agreement or settlement. The number of cases filed in federal courts in 2024 represented approximately 5 percent of all case filings in the U.S.[23] State court caseloads are 20 times greater than those of the federal court system.

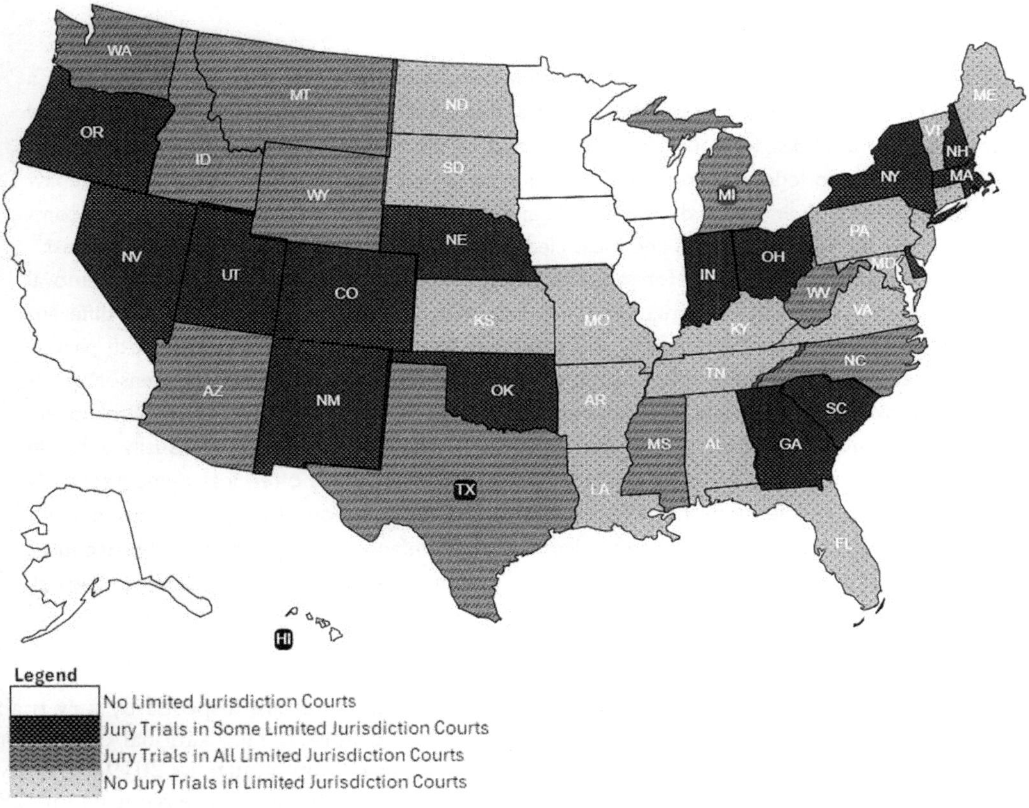

Figure 4.2: Jury trials in Limited Jurisdiction Courts
(*Source:* National Center for State Courts.[24])

authority should be distributed across local, state, and federal levels. The Framers believed that state governments were best situated to enact and enforce their own criminal and civil laws. Box 4.3 describes how today most cases are filed in state courts.

In Chapter 3, we explained that the federal judicial branch consists of three tiers, the first of which includes district courts that have original jurisdiction to hear both criminal and civil cases. In addition to convening federal grand juries, district courts conduct petit jury trials in the federal court system. In state courts, jury trials are conducted in all general jurisdiction trial courts and in limited jurisdiction courts in 27 states. For example, in New Mexico, jury trials are allowed in the District Courts (general jurisdiction) and in the Bernalillo County Metropolitan Court and the Magistrates Courts (limited jurisdiction), but not in the Municipal or Probate Courts (also limited jurisdiction). The remaining 23 states do not permit jury trials in the courts of limited jurisdiction but instead rely on a bench trial as described in Chapter 2. Figure 4.2 displays a map of the United States reported by the National Center for State Courts that illustrates where jury trials are permitted in state limited jurisdiction courts.

The Uniform Code of Military Justice provides for enlisted service personnel and officers to be tried by jurors (called "members") rather than a military judge in a general or special court-martial.[25] While the procedure is similar in many respects to a jury trial in civilian courts, there are key differences that are beyond the scope of this textbook.[26]

Box 4.4: Removal to Federal Court

A defendant might have the ability to move their case from state court to federal court under a limited number of circumstances.[29] Removal is a defendant's right to transfer a case filed in state court to a federal district court. Federal removal of criminal cases is extraordinarily rare and is only available to federal government officials who are charged with a violation(s) of state law while performing their federal duties. A civil defendant has 30 days after receiving the initial complaint to file a notice of removal and must clearly state the grounds for making such a request.

Several reasons may be given for requesting removal in civil cases. First, the basis for removal is almost always diversity of citizenship, meaning that the parties are citizens from different states. The justification for removing the case to federal court is to ensure that both parties are treated equally and that neither has an unfair "home field" advantage. Another reason to request removal is to obtain a different demographic composition of the jury pool. Federal courts typically summon jurors from a wider geographic area than state courts, which usually summon from a single county. As a result, the jury pool in federal court is often less demographically diverse, which the defense might believe is strategically advantageous. Finally, many civil defendants believe that federal district court judges are more defense-friendly and federal procedures governing civil pleadings and summary judgment motions are favorable to the defense. Overall, they may be hoping to avoid going to trial at all.

As in federal courts, only a very small percentage of state cases are disposed by jury trial; most cases are resolved by plea agreement, settlement, or dismissal. The National Center for State Courts estimates that 125,222 jury trials took place in state courts in 2019.[27] Nearly three-quarters (72 percent) of the jury trials involved criminal charges (44 percent felony, 28 percent misdemeanor), 21 percent involved civil claims, and the remaining 7 percent involved other case types, including domestic relations, mental health, and probate cases in a few states. Due to the COVID-19 pandemic, the number of jury trials plummeted to less than 34,000 in 2020 as social distancing and other public health precautions discouraged the types of large public gatherings that would be needed for jury selection. As of 2021, the most recent year in which data is available, the number of jury trials has increased to 48,764, less than half of pre-pandemic totals.[28] Box 4.4 describes the rare circumstance when a case can be transferred or removed from state court to be tried in a district court in the federal court system.

> A right to jury trial is granted to criminal defendants in order to prevent oppression by the Government.
>
> —Byron White, former U.S. Supreme Court Justice (1962–1993)
> *Duncan v. Louisiana* (1968)

Eligibility for Jury Service

Just as not all cases are eligible for jury trials, not all individuals are eligible for jury service. During the Colonial Era and immediately following the American Revolution, only White men who owned real property were permitted to serve as trial jurors. After the Civil War and ratification of the Fourteenth Amendment, the U.S. Supreme Court ruled that formerly enslaved Black men could not legally be excluded from jury service.[30] Although women secured the right to vote in 1920, it was not until the 1940s that a majority of states made women eligible for jury service.[31] The federal courts eventually caught up, allowing women to serve after passage of the Civil Rights Act of 1957.[32] The U.S. Supreme Court finally weighed in on the question of women jurors in 1975, holding in *Taylor v. Louisiana* that states cannot exclude women from jury service.[33]

In the late 1960s and early 1970s, federal and state courts replaced key-man jury systems with random selection of prospective jurors from broad-based lists. In the process, they also adopted objective criteria for jury service. In the federal courts, these criteria were codified in the Jury Service and Selection Act of 1968.[34] This Act guaranteed that grand and petit juries would be selected at random from a fair cross section of the community and that citizens could not be excluded from jury service on the basis of race, color, religion, sex, national origin, or economic status.[35] Although *Duncan v. Louisiana* extended the right to trial by jury in criminal cases in state courts, it did not require state courts to adopt federal eligibility criteria for jury service. Instead, the U.S. Supreme Court has written repeatedly that states retain tremendous discretion to determine qualification criteria for jury service.[36] As such, qualifications for jury service in state courts differ in some respects from those of federal court and each other.

The right to participate as a trial or grand juror in the American justice system is often framed as a privilege and a responsibility of citizenship. Eligibility criteria for jury service also ensure that the individuals who are empaneled in these roles are intellectually, emotionally, and culturally competent to make informed decisions about the merits of the cases they are asked to judge. In the federal courts, these criteria include U.S. citizenship, residency in community served by the court, age 18 or older, sufficiently fluent in English to understand the testimony presented during trial, and not subject to a legal disqualification, such as a previous felony conviction or an adjudication of mental incompetence. In legal challenges to state and local jury systems, the U.S. Supreme Court has repeatedly held that States have broad discretion to determine eligibility and exemption criteria for jury service.[37]

Citizenship and Residency

The federal courts and all but one state (Connecticut) require jurors be citizens of the United States. All courts require that jurors be residents in the community served by the court, which may include the entire state for some federal district courts. Ostensibly, citizenship establishes a presumption that jurors are sufficiently familiar with the American justice system through their upbringing and education, or through the naturalization process, to understand the role that jurors play in the justice system. Individuals who are not citizens may come from countries that do not permit laypeople to participate in the justice system and may not understand the role played by jurors in the American justice system. Similarly, residency assumes that the juror is sufficiently knowledgeable about their community to reflect community values when serving as a juror. In many communities in the United States, the **citizenship** requirement disproportionately excludes people of color, especially Hispanics and Asians, which undermines the ideal of a demographically representative jury pool. In 2013, the California legislature passed a statute allowing all legal residents, regardless of citizenship, to serve as trial jurors; Governor Jerry Brown subsequently vetoed the bill on grounds that jury service is a civic duty that should be exclusive to citizens.[38] More recently, Connecticut granted noncitizen legal residents the right to serve on state trial juries.[39] Residency requirements vary from state to state. Set by statute, they range from a simple intention to remain in the community to residing in the community for a minimum of six months. Federal jurors must have resided in the district or division where the case is to be tried for at least one year.

Age

The minimum **age** at which people can serve as trial or grand jurors also differs from state to state. Most states set the minimum age at 18, the same as in federal courts. Mississippi and Missouri, however, require that trial or grand jurors be 21 years or older, ostensibly because jury service requires greater maturity than voting or other activities in which people can engage beginning at age 18.[40] In Alabama and Nebraska, the minimum jury age is 19.[41]

English Proficiency

The rationale for requiring jurors be fluent in English is primarily practical: in most states, trial and grand jury proceedings are conducted in English and the official record of the trial is in English. For jurors to fulfill their role, they must be able to understand the testimony presented and to communicate effectively with other jurors. When New Mexico was admitted as a state, however, its constitution included an explicit provision that the right to serve on a jury "shall never be restricted, abridged or impaired on account of… [the] inability to speak, read, or write the English or Spanish languages."[42] The New Mexico judicial branch provides foreign language interpreters to translate trial proceedings for jurors with **limited English proficiency** and to communicate with jurors during deliberations. Although Puerto Rico is a U.S. territory, the dominant language is Spanish, and trial proceedings are conducted in that language rather than English. Consequently, jurors serving in the Judicial Branch of Puerto Rico must be fluent in Spanish, rather than English.[43]

Criminal Background

Possibly the greatest variability in juror qualification criteria involves **criminal background**. For most of the nation's history, locally elected or appointed jury commissioners were tasked with identifying prospective jurors "of fair character, of approved integrity, well-informed, and of sound judgment."[44] These were referred to as key-man juries in Chapter 2. Although jury system reforms enacted in the 1960s eliminated these subjective criteria, the absence of criminal history as an objective measure of "fair character and approved integrity" was still considered important for jury service. Today, the federal courts and most states disqualify individuals with a prior felony conviction from jury service unless their civil rights have been restored. However, Colorado, Illinois, Michigan, and Rhode Island do not disqualify persons convicted of a felony from jury service, if they have completed their sentence. Connecticut, the District of Columbia, Kansas, and Massachusetts disqualify convicted felons from jury service for a statutorily defined period following completion of their sentence; and Alabama, Maine, Mississippi, Nevada, and Tennessee only disqualify persons convicted of certain types of felony crimes.[45] Maintaining updated findings and statistics about the various constitutional and statutory changes among the individual states and U.S. territories is a constant challenge. Box 4.5 describes the National Center for State Courts and how the organization works with state court systems to provide information and assistance related to the daily operations of juries.

Box 4.5: The National Center for State Courts

The National Center for State Courts (NCSC), located in Williamsburg, Virginia, was created in 1971 to promote the rule of law and improve the administration of justice in state courts and in courts around the world.[46] The NCSC Center for Jury Studies is one of its oldest operational centers. It functions as an interdivisional hub within the organization to conduct research and provide technical assistance and education to judges, court administrators, and trial lawyers about effective jury system management and trial procedure.[47]

State laws that ban or restrict eligibility for jury service based on criminal history impact segments of the population differently. Most notable is the effects these restrictions have on communities of color. It has been estimated that states that have strict laws forbidding jury service for individuals with previous criminal histories "bar more than twenty million people from jury service, reduce jury diversity by disproportionately excluding Black and Latinx people, and actually cause juries to deliberate less effectively."[48] Empirical findings about demographic and social background characteristics of a prison population illustrate the extent of this problem. For example, prison statistics from 2023 showed that 12 percent of the general population in the U.S. were Black, while 38 percent of inmates housed in U.S. prisons or jails were Black.[49] Black citizens, who were former inmates and who took residence in states with harsh jury eligibility requirements related to incarceration history, will be excluded from the jury pool. This may adversely impact the diversity of a jury in certain communities and detract from empaneling a trial jury that reflects both a fair cross-section of the community members and adequately represents the conscience of the community.

Jury Size

For nearly 200 years, the U.S. Supreme Court defined the "jury" according to the traditional English model of the common law jury.[50] It had three main features: (1) it was composed of 12 jurors; (2) a trial judge advised the jurors; and (3) the jury's verdict was unanimous.[51] The Court required a 12-member jury in all federal criminal cases, including those conducted in federal territories;[52] however, the number of jurors required to be empaneled in criminal or civil jury trials is not specified in the U.S. Constitution.

In keeping with the understanding that the U.S. Constitution governed the operation of the federal government, but not necessarily state governments, many state legislatures adopted statutes and court rules setting a lower number of jurors. Although most states have 12-person juries for felony cases, a few states use smaller juries except for capital felony cases. Arizona and Utah, for example, employ eight-person juries in noncapital felony trials, while Florida and Connecticut employ six-person juries. Figure 4.3, developed by the National Center for State Courts, illustrates **jury size** for noncapital felony, misdemeanor, and civil cases in state general jurisdiction courts.

Williams v. Florida

Florida reduced the size of its noncapital felony juries from 12 to six jurors in 1877, but objections to the constitutionality of a six-person jury was not addressed by the U.S. Supreme Court until 1970 in ***Williams v. Florida***.[53] Briefly, the petitioner, Johnny Williams, a citizen of Florida, was arrested and charged with robbery. During a pretrial meeting at his original trial, his attorney requested a 12-member jury, instead of the six-member jury traditionally seated in Florida. The trial judge denied his request. Upon his conviction, Williams appealed the decision on several grounds, including that his Sixth Amendment right to a trial by jury was violated when he was denied a 12-member jury. The appellate court that considered Williams' claim upheld the trial court's ruling that "the appellant was entitled, under Florida law, to a jury consisting of only six persons; the state contends that the trial court was correct in this ruling."[54] The U.S. Supreme Court heard the case in 1970 and found that smaller juries were permissible under the Constitution. The Court wrote:

> We do not pretend to be able to divine precisely what the word "jury" imported to the Framers, the First Congress, or the States in 1789. It may well be that the usual expectation was that the jury would consist of 12 ... But there is absolutely no indication in "the intent of the Framers" of an explicit decision to equate the constitutional and common-law characteristics of the jury ... the 12-man requirement cannot be regarded as an indispensable component of the Sixth Amendment.[55]

The Court explained that

> while, sometime in the 14th century, the size of the jury at common law came to be fixed generally at 12, that particular feature of the jury system appears to have been an historical accident, unrelated to the great purposes which gave rise to the jury in the first place.[56]

Given that "great purpose" was to prevent the government from oppressing its citizens, the Court concluded that the number of jurors sitting on a jury did not impede that essential function. The justices reasoned that "the number should probably be large enough to promote group deliberation ... and to provide a fair possibility for obtaining a representative cross-section of the community." The Court opined "the reliability of the jury as a factfinder hardly seems likely to be a function of its size" and that it was up to "Congress and the States" to decide the number of jurors to be empaneled as the Sixth Amendment left this issue open.[57]

Colgrove v. Battin

Following the *Williams* decision, it was not long before similar claims were made about the number of jurors allowed by the Constitution in civil cases. In 1973, the Supreme Court held in ***Colgrove v. Battin***[58] that six-member juries were permissible for federal civil trials. The Court found "a jury of six satisfies the Seventh Amendment's guarantee of trial by jury in civil cases."[59] The reasoning was the same as stated in *Williams* that fewer numbers of jurors would not disrupt the function and goals of the jury to guard citizens from an oppressive government.

Ballew v. Georgia

The issue of jury size was taken up by the Court again a few years later in a case from Georgia. Briefly, the petitioner, Claude Davis Ballew, the manager of the Paris Adult Theatre in Atlanta, GA in 1973 was

> first arrested for showing the film [*Behind the Green Door*] on November 9, and the film was seized under [a] search warrant ... Subsequently, the accused was arrested on another warrant for showing the same picture, from another copy of the film.[60]

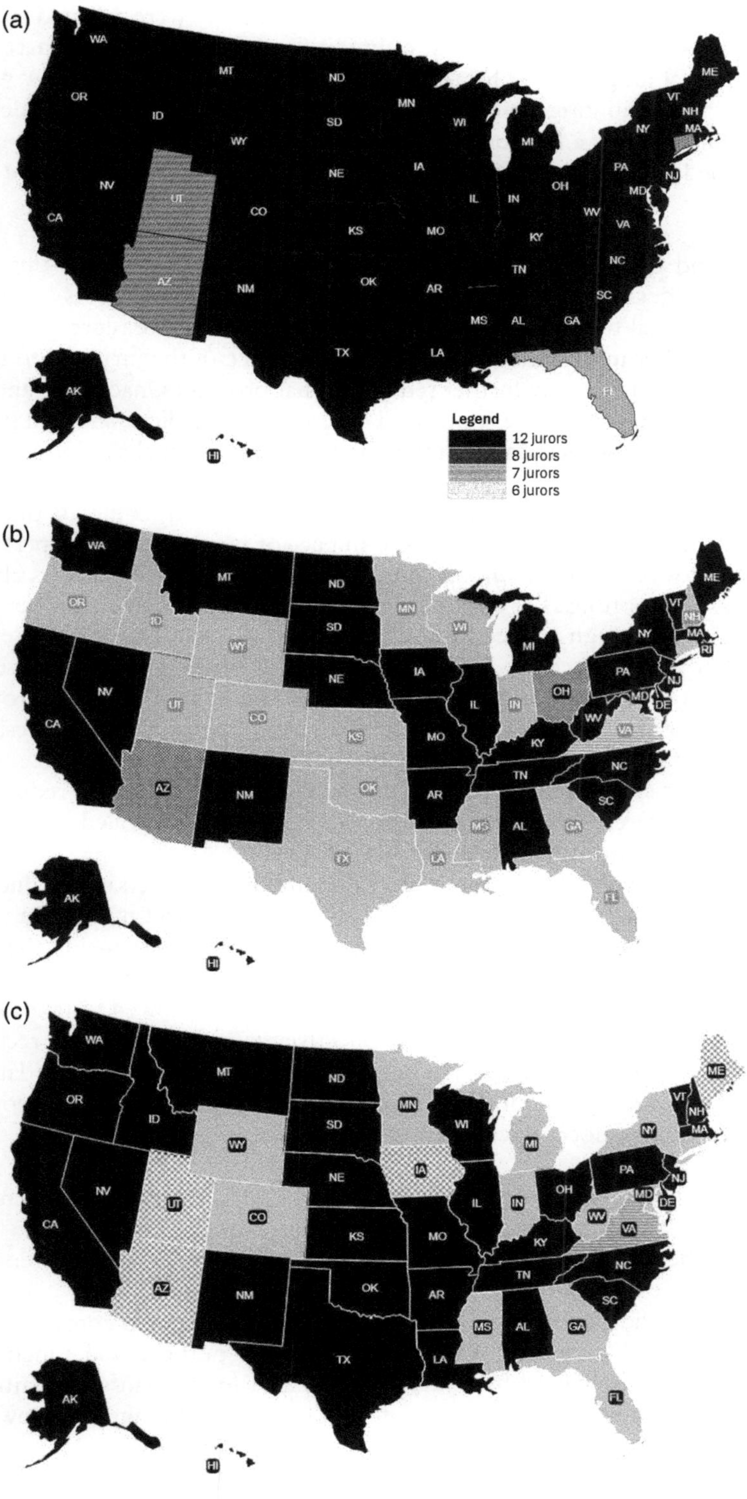

Figure 4.3: State Variation in Jury Size. a) Felony Jury Size, b) Misdemeanor Jury Size, c) Civil Jury Size.

(*Source:* Hannaford-Agor & Moffett, 2024. *2023 State-of-the-states survey of jury improvement efforts.*)

When the case went to trial, five citizens from the community were selected to serve on the jury. Ballew requested a 12-member jury, claiming five jurors were inadequate for a case of this nature. The trial judge denied his request. In September of 1974, Ballew was convicted "on two counts of distributing obscene materials in violation of Criminal Code § 26–2101" in a Georgia courtroom by a five-member jury.[61]

Ballew appealed the ruling to the U.S. Supreme Court. In ***Ballew v. Georgia*** (1978)[62] the Court found:

> the purpose and functioning of the jury in a criminal trial is seriously impaired, and to a constitutional degree, by a reduction in size to below six members ... the assembled data raise substantial doubt about the reliability and appropriate representation of panels smaller than six. Because of the fundamental importance of the jury trial to the American system of criminal justice, any further reduction that promotes inaccurate and possibly biased decision making, that causes untoward differences in verdicts, and that prevents juries from truly representing their communities, attains constitutional significance.

In prohibiting states from conducting jury trials with fewer than six jurors, the Court noted that a great deal of empirical research on the impact of jury size on jury performance was undertaken in the wake of the *Williams* case. Many of the research findings challenged the Court's previous assumptions. For example, it was accepted that requiring fewer jurors would lead to cost savings through reduced juror compensation fees. This can be seen when the number of jurors was reduced from 12 to six; however, the Court did not see significant cost savings from reducing the number of jurors from six to five. Research from the 1990s conducted in California confirmed the state could save 40 percent on jury fees, staff administrative costs, and first-class mailing of jury summonses, if it reduced the size of juries from 12 to six, and would save about 29 percent on the same measures with a reduction from 12 to eight jurors.[63] Research conducted after the Court's decision revealed smaller juries saved negligible amounts of time during voir dire.[64]

The *Ballew* Court also called into question the amount of time savings due to selecting a jury of five instead of six. As attorneys often question and select jurors in a group setting during the voir dire process, little time would be saved by further reducing the jury's size to five. In addition to cost savings, the Court also acknowledged the impact of reduced jury size on juror decision-making, including that most juries were not allowed to take notes during a trial, and decreasing jury size may impact the collective memory of a jury for recalling specific facts and evidence presented at trial. The Court also recognized statistical data that raised concerns about making Type I or Type II errors[65]—that is, smaller juries could be more prone to convicting an innocent person or to letting a guilty person go free.

> The smaller the group, the less likely it is to overcome the biases of its members to obtain an accurate result ... the counterbalancing of various biases is critical to the accurate application of the common sense of the community to the facts of any given case.[66]

Although the Court did not reverse its previous decision about the constitutionality of juries with fewer than 12 members, it concluded that the purpose and functioning of the jury would be seriously impaired by a jury comprised of fewer than six members. Box 4.6 describes decisions made in some states to empanel fewer than five jurors in lower-value civil cases that would be ineligible for a trial jury and therefore would only be eligible for a bench trial or other non-trial procedure.

As the U.S. Supreme Court noted in *Ballew v. Georgia*, its decision in *Williams* generated a great deal of empirical research on the relationship between jury size and jury performance. The broad consensus of this research, which continues to this day, is that six-person juries do not perform as well as 12-person juries on several criteria. Specifically, six-person juries are less representative of community demographic characteristics than 12-person juries, and their verdicts are more variable and unpredictable. Twelve-person juries deliberate longer and demonstrate greater recall of evidence presented at trial.[70] In 2005, the American Bar Association cited this body of research in its endorsement of 12-person juries in its publication *Principles for Juries and Jury Trials*.[71]

Box 4.6: Jury Size in Civil Cases

Although the *Ballew v. Georgia* decision held that five-person juries violated the Sixth Amendment right to trial by jury in criminal cases, some states have created rules allowing juries as small as four members in some types of civil cases, especially lower-value cases that would otherwise be ineligible for jury trials. In 1997, the Superior Court of Arizona in Maricopa County piloted its Short Trial Program, featuring four-person juries, as an alternative for cases that were otherwise required to undergo mandatory arbitration.[67] The Eight Judicial District Court in Nevada implemented a similar program in 2000.[68] Although there are no specific findings about the outcomes of Short Trial Programs, advocates reported the courts saved money by not requiring the presence of "bailiffs, court reporters, or court clerks" during the trials and the fast (one-day) resolution of cases.[69]

Unanimous and Nonunanimous Verdicts

As with jury size, the rules governing how many jurors must agree to reach a verdict raise fundamental questions about the fairness and legitimacy of jury trials. The U.S. Supreme Court has long held that the Sixth Amendment requires unanimity for jury verdicts in federal courts, but until recently it had declined to extend that requirement to the states. For

Table 4.1: Summary of Supreme Court Rulings about Jury Size

Case	*Decided*	*Opinion*
Williams v. Florida 399 U.S. 78	June 22, 1970	Permitted juries of fewer than 12 members in state *criminal* cases
Colgrove v. Battin 413 U.S. 149	June 21, 1973	Permitted juries of fewer than 12 members in state and federal *civil* cases
Ballew v. Georgia 435 U.S. 149	March 21, 1978	Prohibited juries of only five members in state and federal courts; a six-member jury or more is required

decades, all states except Louisiana and Oregon required unanimity in criminal cases, while about half the states permitted nonunanimous verdicts in civil trials. In those states, the rule always required a supermajority—ranging from the strict five-sixths standard (for example, 10 out of 12 jurors or five out of six) to the more lenient two-thirds threshold of eight out of 12 jurors allowed in Montana. Over the past decade, however, the impact of nonunanimous verdicts has attracted renewed scrutiny, culminating in a Supreme Court ruling in 2020 that reaffirmed unanimity as a fundamental constitutional requirement for criminal juries in state courts. To understand how the Court arrived at that conclusion, it is useful to begin with the unique history of Louisiana and Oregon.

Louisiana and Oregon allowed for nonunanimous jury verdicts in criminal trials into the early part of the 21st century. Why was this practice allowed and how did the states' legislatures garner support for nonunanimous jury verdicts in criminal cases? The long history of nonunanimous verdicts in Louisiana originated during a Constitutional Convention that was held in New Orleans in 1898. A public goal of the convention, as documents of the event described, was to establish white supremacy.[72] One avenue the state found for establishing and maintaining control was through jury deliberation and trial verdicts. For example, jury verdicts in criminal cases in Louisiana were altered to allow nonunanimous votes, where ten of 12 jurors would have to agree to a verdict to convict. The decision to allow nonunanimous verdicts was made because the jury composition in Louisiana would rarely exceed one or two racial minority members per jury panel. Essentially, this decision stripped away any racial minority or dissenting vote from acquitting the accused or having the trial result in a hung jury.

The social and political climate in Oregon also shaped perceptions about nonunanimous jury verdicts in criminal trials. By the 1930s, large numbers of immigrants were drawn to the state of Oregon. This included religious groups from the Jewish and Catholic faiths. This period in American history also coincided with the rise of hate groups, including the Ku Klux Klan.[73] These events set the stage for discriminatory trial practices to occur in Oregon and elsewhere. Briefly, in 1934, Jacob Silverman, a Jewish hotel owner, was arrested and tried for first degree murder. A jury trial was held and the jury hung, 11 to 1, on the first-degree murder charge, but ultimately reached a compromise verdict for manslaughter. Public outrage about the less severe verdict led local news media outlets to openly criticize immigrants entering Oregon from Eastern Europe. In the next election cycle, community residents voted by ballot to disband unanimous jury decisions. The community supported nonunanimous jury verdicts, allowing verdicts of 10 to two, to convict the accused during a criminal trial.

Surprisingly, nonunanimous jury practices persisted in both Louisiana and Oregon for decades. The constitutionality of nonunanimous verdicts were appealed to the U.S. Supreme Court in 1972. Petitioners claimed in ***Johnson v. Louisiana*** (1972)[74] and in ***Apodaca v. Oregon*** (1972)[75] that their Sixth and Fourteenth Amendment rights, which guaranteed a unanimous jury decision, were violated. In a 5–4 split decision, the Court affirmed in *Johnson* that nonunanimous jury verdicts did not violate their Constitutional rights to a fair and impartial jury trial.

The Court's confused reasoning has long baffled legal professionals. For example, the justices recognized the Sixth Amendment required unanimous jury verdicts in federal criminal cases, but indicated the protection was not guaranteed to the states through the Fourteenth Amendment.[76] The justices also, generally, pointed out there were no prior research findings that showed "majority jurors simply ignore the reasonable doubts of their colleagues or otherwise act irresponsibly in casting their votes in favor of conviction."[77] The Court found in *Johnson* that the "Louisiana statutory scheme serves a rational purpose and is not subject to constitutional challenge."[78]

The Court made a similar finding in *Apodaca v. Oregon*. The petitioner claimed that nonunanimous verdicts violated his guarantee of a representative jury that reflects a cross-section of the community. The Court dispensed with the petitioner's claim that a nonunanimous jury may limit the contributions of racial minority jurors, stating, "it does not follow that their views will not be just as rationally considered by the other jury members as would be the case under a unanimity rule."[79] Moreover, the Court, commenting about the function of unanimous juries, noted, "we perceive no difference between juries required to act unanimously and those permitted to convict or acquit by votes of 10 to two or 11 to one."[80] The Court affirmed Oregon's nonunanimous verdicts in criminal trials.

Unanimous Verdicts Revisited

The U.S. Supreme Court readdressed the issue of unanimous jury verdicts in ***Ramos v. Louisiana***.[81] The petitioner, Evangelisto Ramos, was tried and convicted of a serious crime by a criminal jury; the jury's vote was 10 to two for conviction. Ramos claimed his conviction, under a nonunanimous jury verdict, violated his Sixth Amendment right to an impartial jury.

In 2020, the Court overturned the petitioner's trial conviction and found nonunanimous jury verdicts do violate the Sixth and Fourteenth Amendments of the Constitution. The Court's finding in *Ramos* relied heavily on the historical interpretation of the Sixth Amendment requiring a jury to reach a unanimous verdict for serious crimes. Specifically, it found that unanimous verdicts were consistent with common law traditions dating back to England in the 14th century. It was written among the English common laws that to find a person guilty of a serious crime the decision had to be confirmed by a unanimous jury of 12.[82] Second, legal professionals, the states, and the courts have insisted that unanimity was implied both in the Sixth Amendment and in Article III of the Constitution. The language of a "trial by an impartial jury" carries with it some meaning, including the right to unanimity for accusations of serious criminal behavior.[83] Some of the first colonies, including Delaware,[84] Maryland,[85] North Carolina,[86] Pennsylvania,[87] Vermont,[88] and Virginia,[89] adopted the unanimity standards into their state constitutions in 1776. Since the late 19th Century, the U.S. Supreme Court consistently held the Sixth Amendment requires unanimous verdicts in criminal trials.

Although criminal jury verdicts in both state and federal court are now required to be unanimous, the *Ramos* decision did not apply to civil jury verdicts. Significant variation exists among the states related to unanimity rules for reaching verdicts in civil cases. As shown in

Table 4.2: Summary of Supreme Court Findings about Unanimity

Case	*Decided*	*Opinion*
Johnson v. Louisiana 406 U.S. 356	May 22, 1972	Upheld Louisiana's nonunanimous jury verdicts in criminal trials (9–3 majority)
Apodaca v. Oregon 406 U.S. 404	May 22, 1972	Upheld Oregon's nonunanimous jury verdicts in criminal trials (10–2 majority)
Ramos v. Louisiana 590 U.S. 83	April 20, 2020	Overturned Louisiana's nonunanimous jury verdicts in criminal trials as unconstitutional; violated the Sixth and Fourteenth Amendments

Figure 4.4, 26 states permit nonunanimous verdicts in civil cases. Thirteen states employ a **5/6 rule**, meaning five of six jurors (or 10 of 12) must agree on the verdict. Twelve states employ a **3/4 rule** (six of eight or nine of 12), while Montana employs a **2/3 rule** (four of six or six of nine).[90]

The existence of nonunanimous verdicts in state civil trials provides a rare opportunity to study how different decision rules affect juror behavior. A 2002 National Center for State Courts study reported hung jury rates of about 3 percent in federal criminal trials and less than 1 percent in federal civil trials.[91] Comparable state statistics are harder to obtain but are likely similar to the low federal rates. Previous empirical research found that unanimity promotes more thorough deliberations and greater juror satisfaction.[92]

Arizona provides the clearest evidence for how nonunanimous rules operate in practice. For example, in Pima County an eight-person civil jury may reach a verdict with six votes. Researchers studying 50 civil trials found that one-third of the verdicts were nonunanimous and one jury hung.[93] Videotaped deliberations revealed how jurors' awareness of the unanimity rule often shaped their discussions. In some cases, jurors pressed for consensus despite unanimity not being required, while in other cases majority members dismissed minority voices once the six-vote threshold was reached. Importantly, holdout jurors were not irrational. They offered reasoned arguments about trial evidence, credibility of witnesses, and the meaning of the jury instructions, and they did not consistently favor either plaintiffs or defendants.

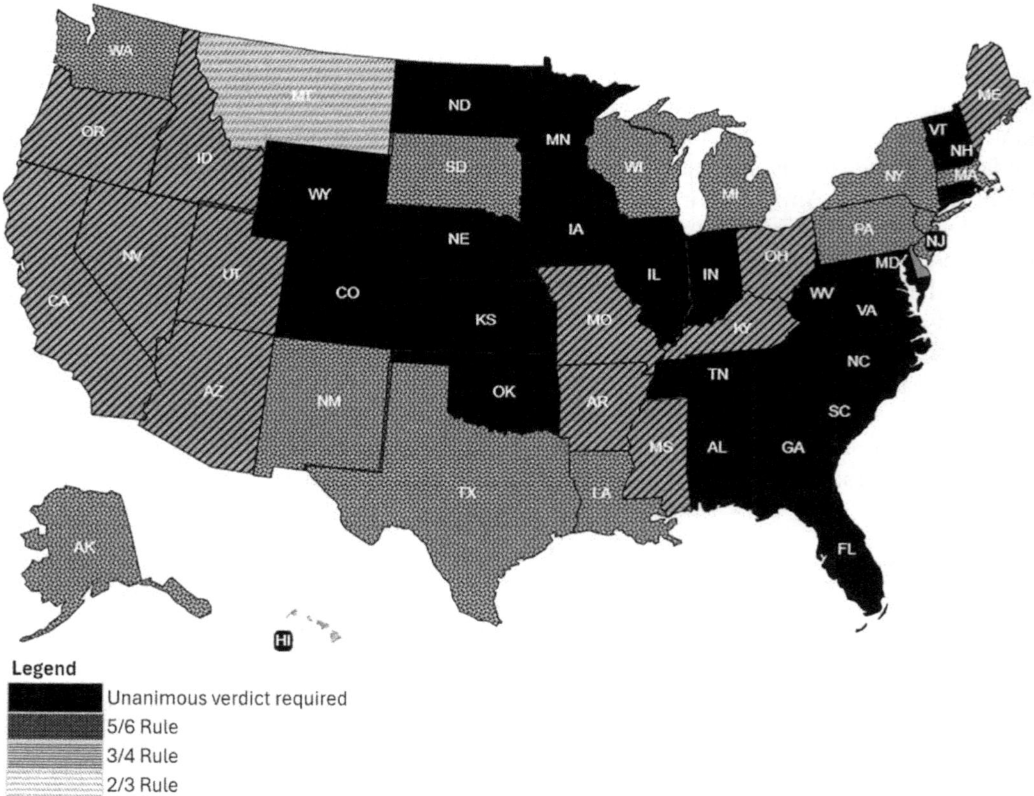

Figure 4.4: Civil Verdict Decision Rules in State Courts

Judges sometimes agreed with minority jurors, underscoring the plausibility of their views. The study concluded that while nonunanimous verdicts reduce hung juries, they risk weakening deliberations by marginalizing dissenting jurors. By contrast, unanimity encourages more thorough debate, consensus-building, and stronger juror confidence in the verdict.

Juror Oaths

The swearing-in process involves jurors taking an oath to uphold the rules of the court for considering evidence and facts truthfully and without prejudice, and for following accepted practices for appropriate conduct inside the courthouse, courtroom, and deliberation room.[95] The jurors may be asked to raise their right hands as they say the oath and/or a Bible might be used during the swearing-in process. A juror may refuse to take the oath for personal reasons and simply affirm that they are aware of their roles and duties as a juror for the court.[96] After the jury is sworn in, the trial proceeding begins. Members of the trial jury will hear opening arguments from both trial attorneys, listen to witness testimony, and view physical evidence admitted during the trial. After the attorneys give their closing arguments, the judge will instruct the jury about the law that is to be applied, and the burden of proof (standard) required for determining guilt or fault. Also, the judge may emphasize that their decision must be made solely based on the evidence presented during the trial.[97]

> **Swearing In[94]**
>
> A formal ceremony for a person or persons to make an official promise to act properly, respectfully, honestly, etc.

The verdict reached by the trial jury is final. Except in very rare circumstances, discussed in Chapter 9, a trial judge cannot invalidate the jury's guilty verdict in a criminal case. In civil cases, the judge is authorized to enter a judgment in favor of the party that lost at trial if they find that no reasonable jury could have reached the verdict given the evidence admitted at trial. This is a very high standard, however. Federal appellate courts have repeatedly held the Seventh Amendment prohibits judges from substituting their own preference about the trial outcome for the jury's collective decision.[98]

Criminal defendants and both parties in civil cases have the right to ask the federal court of appeals to review the case, including the jury's verdict, for legal errors or procedural problems that occurred during the trial or in the original investigation, including fact-gathering by law enforcement. There are limitations on the remedies that courts of appeals can provide, however. In criminal cases, the constitutional prohibition on double jeopardy prevents the prosecution from retrying a defendant for the same crime after an acquittal. In an appeal from a conviction, or in civil cases, appellate judges will only overturn the jury's verdict if they find that the trial judge made an obvious legal mistake (plain error standard) or acted unreasonably or arbitrarily (abuse of discretion standard). Moreover, the court of appeals cannot simply change the verdict in the case. Instead, it must remand the case back to the trial court for a new trial or other remedial measures.

Conclusion

The importance of federalism to the structure of the American government explains many differences between state and federal jury systems. The federal government has constitutional requirements for trial jury proceedings. However, each state has the inherent authority to design its own jury system that reflects its residents' preferences and policies. Although the Sixth Amendment guarantees the right to trial by jury in serious criminal cases, and requires that criminal jury verdicts be unanimous, it does not require that less serious criminal cases or civil cases be eligible for trial by jury. The Constitution also does not specify the qualifications for individuals to be eligible for jury service, the size of the trial jury, or the rules governing verdicts that are reached. These details are left to the states to decide.

Overall, the first section of the text, including Chapters 1–4, established the fundamental reasons and purpose for including trial by jury in the American jury system. These chapters described the Amendments to the Constitution concerning grand juries and trial juries and explained how they operate within the federal and state court systems today. Descriptions about how state jury systems differ from their federal counterparts and from each other provide a useful context for the next section of this text, which relates to the process of jury service, from receiving a summons to deliberating about a verdict. Chapter 5 begins this discussion by examining how operational practices for the jury system vary not only from state to state, but even from court to court within states.

Summary

This chapter described trial juries in the federal and state court systems. Trial juries, like grand juries, occur in the first tier of the federal court system, the district courts. There are 94 district courts located within the U.S. Court of Appeals. Trial juries can hear criminal or civil cases in the federal court system, although the burden of proof that must be established varies depending upon the nature of the case. Criminal cases require a stricter standard for determining guilt, including beyond a reasonable doubt, while civil cases require a verdict based on a preponderance of the evidence. The reason for this difference is because a criminal conviction results in imprisonment, which is a severe restriction on an individual's freedom. Also, the size of the jury in a federal criminal case must be 12 jurors, while the size of the jury in a federal civil case may range between six and 12 jurors, with the size being agreed upon by both trial attorneys. The verdict reached by federal juries in either criminal or civil disputes must be unanimous.

There are variations among the procedures and structure of jury trials in the state court systems. This chapter provided a detailed overview of how state-level juries function within the broader American legal framework due to federalism, which allows each state to establish its own jury practices and legal traditions. It outlined the differences between state and federal jury systems, including eligibility criteria, jury size, and rules for unanimity. For example, while most states use 12-person juries for felony cases, some states permit smaller juries in noncapital, misdemeanor, or civil cases. Eligibility for jury service also varies, especially regarding age, citizenship, language fluency, and criminal background. The chapter highlighted how state court structures differ, with some states allowing jury trials in limited jurisdiction courts and others restricting them to general jurisdiction courts. Additionally, it noted that despite the large number of cases filed in state courts annually, only a small fraction are resolved through jury trials.

Discussion Questions

1. Jury trials are held in the 94 district courts that comprise the U.S. federal court system. In the American jury system, jurors must consider separate burdens of proof in criminal

versus civil cases. In a criminal case the standard is beyond a reasonable doubt, while the standard in a civil case is a preponderance of the evidence. Do these different standards align with the Founding Fathers' intentions, described in the Bill of Rights, to protect citizens' rights to freedom and justice? Do these standards go against the original intentions?
2. As described, trial juries in state court systems operate differently from one another. This discretion was permitted by the Federal Judiciary Act of 1789. Do you have any concerns that variations are allowed among the states and that juries may differ based on size, unanimity rule, criminal history, etc.? Does lack of uniformity among the states influence the concepts of fairness, impartiality, and justice that are guaranteed and protected by the U.S. Constitution and Bill of Rights?
3. If you were the accused and were standing trial in either a criminal or civil case, would it matter to you whether the jury verdict was reached by a six-, eight-, or 12-member jury? Are there specific types of crimes when larger juries are preferred? Explain your answer.
4. Why do you think it took the U.S. Supreme Court approximately 250 years to find that unanimous verdicts in criminal cases were required under the Constitution? What factors or conditions might exist in society today that influenced the Supreme Court's recent decision in *Ramos v. Louisiana* that were not present or influential in the past?

Review Questions

1. How do the number of cases adjudicated in the federal system differ from the state court systems?
2. What standards of proof are required for trial juries in federal and state courts systems related to criminal and civil cases? How does this differ from the standards of proof for grand juries described in the previous chapter?
3. How do state trial juries vary by requirements for citizenship, age, English proficiency, and criminal background?
4. Describe relevant decisions by the U.S. Supreme Court related to jury size. What size (number of jurors) are permitted in criminal and civil trials tried in the federal and state court systems?
5. Describe relevant decisions by the U.S. Supreme Court related to the unanimity rule. What was revealed about reaching unanimous verdicts with the quality of the deliberation and dissenters' levels of satisfaction with the deliberation process?

Answers to Chapter 4 "What Do You Think?" Questions

1. False. The Court's decision in *Duncan v. Louisiana* did not extend the right to a trial jury in misdemeanor or civil cases.
2. False. The standard that must be met in criminal cases is guilt beyond a reasonable doubt.
3. False. Only cases violating protected rights, disputes between states or countries, and when disputes exceed $75,000 can be filed.
4. False. State courts handle approximately 95 percent of all cases adjudicated in the United States.
5. False. In federal court, criminal cases must include a 12-member jury panel, and the verdict reached must be unanimous.
6. False. Many states set 18 as the minimum age; however, in several states jurors must be a minimum of 19 or even 21.
7. True. Both federal and state court systems allow for unanimous verdicts in civil cases.

Key Terms

2/3 rule
3/4 rule
5/6 rule
age
Apodaca v. Oregon
Ballew v. Georgia
beyond a reasonable doubt
citizenship
Colgrove v. Battin
criminal background
Federalism
Johnson v. Louisiana
jury size
limited English proficiency
preponderance of the evidence
Ramos v. Louisiana
Williams v. Florida

References

1 *Parsons v. Bedford*, 28 U.S. (3 Pet.) 433, 446–447 (1830).
2 Newman, J.O. (2019). Taking "beyond a reasonable doubt" seriously. *Judicature*, *103*(2), 32–41.
3 Office of the United States Attorneys. (2024, March 9). *Steps in the federal criminal process (Sentencing)*. U.S. Department of Justice. https://www.justice.gov/usao/justice-101/sentencing
4 U.S. Administrative Office of the Courts. Table T-1—U.S. District Courts—Trial Statistical Tables for the Federal Judiciary. https://www.uscourts.gov/data-news/data-tables/2024/12/31/statistical-tables-federal-judiciary/t-1
5 Hannaford-Agor, P.L, & Moffett, M. (2024). *2023 State-of-the-states survey of jury improvement efforts: The volume and frequency of jury trials in state courts*. National Center for State Courts. https://cdm16501.contentdm.oclc.org/digital/collection/juries/id/365
6 U.S. Const., amend. VI
7 Administrative Office of the U.S. Courts. (2012) (2023, November 26). *Handbook for trial jurors serving in the United States district courts*. https://www.uscourts.gov/services-forms/jury-service
8 *Duncan v. Louisiana*, 391 U.S. 145 (1968).
9 *Duncan v. Louisiana*, 391 U.S. 145 (1968).
10 18 U.S.C. Chapter 208
11 *Klopfer v. North Carolina*, 386 U.S. 213, 222–223 (1967).
12 *Barker v. Wingo*, 407 U.S. 514 (1972).
13 Hannaford-Agor, P.L. (2009). Jury News: Tales of "tales" juries. *Court Manager*, *23*, 27–29.
14 Administrative Office of the U.S. Courts. (2012) (2023, November 26). *Handbook for trial jurors serving in the United States district courts*. https://www.uscourts.gov/services-forms/jury-service
15 Administrative Office of the U.S. Courts. (2012) (2023, November 26). *Handbook for trial jurors serving in the United States district courts*. https://www.uscourts.gov/services-forms/jury-service
16 Seltzer, R., Canan, R.F., Cannon, M., & Hansberry, H. (2016). Legal standards by the numbers: Quantifying burdens of proof or a search for fool's gold? *Judicature*, *100*(1), 56–66.
17 U.S. Const., amend. VII
18 28 USC 1332. https://uscode.house.gov/view.xhtml?req=granuleid:USC-1994-title28-section1332&num=0&edition=1994
19 Texas Family Code §§ 6.703, 9.005. https://statutes.capitol.texas.gov/Docs/FA/htm/FA.6.htm#6.703

20 Texas Estates Code § 55.001. https://statutes.capitol.texas.gov/Docs/ES/htm/ES.55.htm
21 Texas Code of Criminal Procedure § 45A.156. https://statutes.capitol.texas.gov/Docs/CR/htm/CR.45A.htm
22 Administrative Office of the U.S. Courts. (2022) *U.S. district courts—Judicial business 2022.* https://www.uscourts.gov/statistics-reports/us-district-courts-judicial-business-2022
23 National Center for State Courts. (2022). *State of the state courts: 2022 poll.* https://www.ncsc.org/__data/assets/pdf_file/0019/85204/SSC_2022_Presentation.pdf
24 Center for Jury Studies. (2025). *Jury trials by court type.* https://www.ncsc.org/resources-courts/jury-data-dashboard
25 10 USC § 816. https://uscode.house.gov/view.xhtml?path=%2Fprelim%40title10%2FsubtitleA%2Fpart2%2Fchapter47&edition=prelim
26 Bray, C. (2016). *Court-martial: How military justice shaped America from the revolution to 9/11 and beyond.* W.W. Norton & Co.
27 Hannaford-Agor, P.L., & Moffett, M. (2024). *2023 State-of-the-states survey of jury improvement efforts.* National Center for State Courts. https://ncsc.contentdm.oclc.org/digital/collection/juries/id/365/rec/17
28 Hannaford-Agor, P.L., & Moffett, M. (2024). *2023 State-of-the-states survey of jury improvement efforts.* National Center for State Courts. https://ncsc.contentdm.oclc.org/digital/collection/juries/id/365/rec/17
29 28 U.S. Code § 1442
30 *Strauder v. West Virginia*, 100 U.S. 303 (1880); *Virginia v. Rives*, 100 U.S. 303 (1880).
31 Abramson, J. (1994). *We, the jury: The jury system and the ideal of democracy.* Harper Collins Publishers.
32 Civil Rights Act of 1957 § 1861. https://www.congress.gov/bill/85th-congress/house-bill/6127/text.
33 *Taylor v. Louisiana*, 419 U.S. 522 (1975).
34 28 U.S. Code § 1861
35 28 US Code § 1862
36 *Duren v. Missouri*, 439 U.S. 537 (1979).
37 *Berguis v. Smith*, 130 S. Ct. 1383 (2010).
38 McGreevy, P., & Mason, M. (2013, Oct). *Gov. Jerry Brown vetoes measure allowing noncitizens on juries.* Los Angeles Times. https://www.latimes.com/local/la-xpm-2013-oct-07-la-me-1008-brown-bills-20131008-story.html
39 Conn. Gen. Stat. § 51–217
40 JuryDuty101. (2025, July). *Missouri—Jury duty laws, jury selection, juror qualification.* https://www.juryduty101.com/states/missouri
41 Nebraska Judicial Branch. (2025). *Jury service.* https://supremecourt.nebraska.gov/administration/public/jury-service
42 New Mexico Compilation Commission. (2025). *Article VII, Section 3.* https://www.sos.nm.gov/wp-content/uploads/2025/01/NM_Constitution_-2025-for-SOS.pdf
43 Judicial Branch of Puerto Rico. (2025, July). *Jury.* https://poderjudicial.pr/eng/community-education/legal-topics/criminal-cases/jury/
44 Illinois Jury Act. (2025, July). *705 ILCS 305/2.* https://www.ilga.gov/Legislation/ILCS/Chapters#:~:text=(b)%20Except%20as%20otherwise%20specifically,sexual%20orientation%2C%20or%20economic%20status
45 Rottman, D.B., & Strictland, S. (2006). *State court organization (2004),* table 39. https://bjs.ojp.gov/content/pub/pdf/sco04.pdf
46 National Center for State Courts. (2024, January 20). *About us.* https://www.ncsc.org/about-us
47 National Center for State Courts. (2025, Sept. 11). *Center for Jury Studies.* https://www.ncsc.org/our-centers-projects/center-jury-studies
48 Jackson-Gleich, G. (2021). *Rigging the jury: How each state reduces jury diversity by excluding people with criminal records.* Prison Policy Initiative. https://www.prisonpolicy.org/reports/juryexclusion.html
49 Sawyer, W., & Wagner, P. (2023, March 14). *Mass incarceration: The whole pie 2023.* Prison Policy Initiative. https://www.prisonpolicy.org/reports/pie2023.html

50 Morris, T.E. (1970). Florida's six-member criminal juries: Constitutional, but are they fair? *Florida Law Review*, *23*(2), 402–409. https://scholarship.law.ufl.edu/flr/vol23/iss2/12
51 *Patton v. United States*, 281 U.S. 276, 288 (1930).
52 *Thompson v. Utah*, 170 U.S. 343 (1898).
53 *Williams v. Florida*, 399 US 78 (1970).
54 *Williams v. State*, 224 So.2d 406 (1969).
55 *Williams v. Florida*, 399 U.S. 78, 100 (1970).
56 *Williams v. Florida*, 399 U.S. 78, 100 (1970).
57 *Williams v. Florida*, 399 U.S. 78, 101 (1970).
58 *Colgrove v. Battin*, 413 U.S. 149 (1973).
59 *Colgrove v. Battin*, 413 U.S. 149 (1973).
60 *Ballew v. State*, 138 Ga. App. 530 (1976); 227 S.E.2d 65.
61 *Ballew v. State*, 138 Ga. App. 530 (1976); 227 S.E.2d 65.
62 *Ballew v. Georgia*, 435 U.S. 223 (1978).
63 Munsterman, G.T. (1996). *Jury system management*. National Center for State Courts. https://www.ncsc-jurystudies.org/__data/assets/pdf_file/0029/6599/jury-system-management.pdf
64 Sperlich, P.W. (1980). And then there were six: The declining of the American jury. *Judicature*, *62*, 262–276.
65 Panik, M.J. (2005). *Advanced statistics from an elementary point of view* (1st ed.). Elsevier/Academic Press.
66 *Ballew v. Georgia*, 435 U.S. 223 (1978).
67 Superior Court of the State of Arizona. (2025, July 26). *Civil short trial*. https://superiorcourt.maricopa.gov/court-resources/services/adr/civil-short-trial/
68 Hannaford-Agor, P.L., & Waters, N.L. (2012). *Short, summary & expedited: The evolution of civil jury trials*. National Center for State Courts. https://cal-abota.org/pdf/expedited%20jury%20trials/historical%20background%20&%20studies%20on%20ejt/03.%20short,%20summary%20and%20expedited%20the%20evolution%20of%20civil%20jury%20trials.pdf
69 Nevada Short Trial Program. (2025, July 26). *Nevada short trial program*. https://lasvegaspersonalinjuryexperts.com/blog/nevada-short-trial-program/
70 Boyce, E. (2021). *Time to reflect: Has the research changed regarding the importance of jury size?* National Center for State Courts. https://www.ncsc.org/resources-courts/jury-data-dashboard
71 American Bar Association. (2005). *Principles for juries and jury trials, principle 3*. https://www.uscourts.gov/sites/default/files/aba_principles_for_juries_and_jury_trials_2005.pdf
72 Kates, G. (2021, May 17). *Supreme Court rejects challenge to convictions under "racist Jim Crow" jury laws*. CBS News. https://www.cbsnews.com/news/supreme-court-rejects-challenge-convictions-racist-jim-crow-jury-laws/
73 Newton, M. (2007). *The Ku Klux Klan: History, organization, language, influence and activities of America's most notorious secret society*. McFarland & Co.
74 *Johnson v. Louisiana*, 406 U.S. 356 (1972).
75 *Apodaca v. Oregon*, 406 U.S. 404 (1972).
76 *Johnson v. Louisiana*, 406 U.S. 356 at 373 (1972).
77 *Johnson v. Louisiana*, 406 U. S. 356 at 362 (1972).
78 *Johnson v. Louisiana*, 406 U.S. 356 at 364 (1972).
79 *Apodaca v. Oregon*, 406 U.S. 404 at 410 (1972).
80 *Apodaca v. Oregon*, 406 U.S. 404 at 411 (1972).
81 *Ramos v. Louisiana*, 590 U.S. 83 (2020).
82 Blackstone, W., & Christian, E. (1807). *Commentaries on the laws of England*. Thomas B. Wait & Co.
83 *Ramos v. Louisiana*, 590 U.S. ____ (2020).
84 Delaware Declaration of Rights §XIV (1776)
85 Maryland Declaration of Rights §XIX
86 North Carolina Declaration of Rights §IX (1776)
87 Pennsylvania Declaration of Rights §IX (1776)
88 Vermont Declaration of Rights, ch. I, §XI (1786)
89 Virginia Declaration of Rights §VIII (1776)
90 Hannaford-Agor, P.L., Bell, B., & Moffett, M. (2024). *2023 State-of-the-states survey of jury improvement efforts: Civil jury trials*. National Center for State Courts. https://cdm16501.contentdm.oclc.org/digital/collection/juries/id/393

91 Hannaford-Agor, P.L., Hans, V.P., & Munsterman, G.T. (1999). How much justice hangs in the balance? A new look at hung jury rates. *Judicature*, *83*(2), 59–67. https://scholarship.law.cornell.edu/facpub/404/.
92 American Bar Association. (2005). *Principles for juries and jury trials, principle 4.* https://www.uscourts.gov/sites/default/files/aba_principles_for_juries_and_jury_trials_2005.pdf
93 Diamond, S.S., Rose, M.R., & Murphy, B. (2006). Revisiting the unanimity requirement: The behavior of the non-unanimous civil Jury. *Northwestern University Law Review*, *100*(1), 201–230. https://www.americanbarfoundation.org/resources/revisiting-the-unanimity-requirement-the-behavior-of-the-non-unanimous-civil-jury/
94 Merriam-Webster. (2024, September 8). Swearing In. In *Merriam-Webster.com dictionary.* https://www.merriam-webster.com/dictionary/swearingin.
95 Knudsen, K.M. (2016). The juror's sacred oath: Is there constitutional right to properly sworn jury. *Touro Law Review*, *32*(3), 489–534.
96 Administrative Office of the U.S. Courts. (2012) (2024, November 26). *Handbook for trial jurors serving in the United States district courts.* https://www.uscourts.gov/services-forms/jury-service
97 Knudsen, K.M. (2016). The juror's sacred oath: Is there constitutional right to properly sworn jury. *Touro Law Review*, *32*(3), 489–534.
98 *Dimick v. Schiedt*, 293 U.S. 474 (1935).

PART II

Structure—Reporting, Selecting, Instructing, and Deliberating

This section explores the multifaceted jury system, tracing its evolution from community-based selection to modern, database-driven processes that ensure a representative cross-section of citizens. It details the journey of prospective jurors, from receiving a summons and completing qualification questionnaires to navigating voir dire, where attorneys and judges assess biases to select impartial jurors. The use of jury consultants, challenges for cause, and peremptory challenges—despite restrictions to prevent discriminatory practices—highlights the complexities of forming a fair jury. The narrative delves into juror decision-making, emphasizing a preference for constructing stories from evidence over analytical methods, with alignment to judicial verdicts in approximately 80 percent of cases. Challenges such as complex legal jargon and implicit biases underscore the need for clear, standardized jury instructions, as seen in efforts like the California *Book of Approved Jury Instructions.* Finally, the deliberation process reveals the influence of evidence weight, jury demographics, and conformity on verdict outcomes, alongside the controversial role of jury nullification in shaping legal precedents. Together, these elements illustrate the dynamic interplay of civic duty, legal frameworks, and human factors in achieving equitable trial outcomes.

DOI: 10.4324/9781003677796-6

5 Jury Eligibility and the Summons Process

What Do You Think?

Before reviewing the concepts addressed in this chapter, answer True or False to each of the following questions or statements. Correct answers can be found at the end of Chapter 5.

1. The Administrative Office of the U.S. Courts oversees all aspects of jury service in state courts from jury selection to debriefing sessions following a verdict.
2. A master list contains information about community residents who may be randomly selected for jury service.
3. Publicly elected officials, who currently are in the office, do not have to serve jury duty in the federal court system.
4. A jury summons is sent to prospective jurors using both their personal and work-related email addresses.
5. A juror qualification questionnaire assists court staff to determine eligibility for jury service.
6. A fixed flat rate approach compensates individuals for jury service in smaller amounts for the first few days, then increases the amount if the trial continues past a specific number of days.
7. Citizens cannot be punished or sanctioned by a judge if they ignore a jury summons.

Learning Objectives

After reading this chapter, you will be able to:

1. Describe how source lists and a master jury list relate to juror eligibility and selection.
2. Explain what individuals do when they receive a jury summons at their home address.
3. Differentiate between the two approaches used to compensate jurors for their jury service.
4. Identify several frequently asked questions that prospective jurors ask when they are summoned to jury duty.
5. Describe the circumstances when a prospective juror is excused from jury service and when they are exempt from it.
6. List the punishments judges may issue against prospective jurors who ignore their summons to serve jury duty.

Introduction

Few people enjoy receiving junk mail delivered to their homes. Most of the time we dispose of it without giving it a second thought. But on a few occasions, something "official" is

DOI: 10.4324/9781003677796-7

delivered to our mailbox that catches our attention. You open this mysterious letter and read the words, "You are hereby summoned to serve as a juror ..."

Ideally, people will react favorably when they are summoned to jury duty. For example, they may be excited to have an opportunity to serve their community and fulfill their civic responsibilities. They also may be eager and enthusiastic to learn what type of case they may serve on in the future. However, some recipients may be discouraged by receiving the jury summons. They may have a sense of fear or anxiety due to not knowing what to expect from the experience. They may immediately wonder how serving on jury duty will impact their work obligations, their responsibilities for young children, or their efforts to care for elderly family members. They may be concerned that jury service will affect pre-planned vacations and other social activities. There may be legitimate reasons why prospective jurors should be temporarily or permanently excused from jury service. Put yourself in their shoes. How would you react if you received a summons for jury duty today? If you were previously called for jury service, think back. How did you react when you first opened the jury summons?

As discussed in Chapter 4, individuals may be ineligible for jury service, or they may be exempt. Prospective jurors are given an opportunity to state in writing their reasons for not being able to serve. The courts review the prospective jurors' reason(s) to be excused, and a judge or court administrator makes the ultimate decision whether to grant or deny the request. Finally, a perennial challenge for state and federal courts are prospective jurors who simply fail to respond to their jury summons at all. In some instances, the jury summons was never delivered to the prospective juror due to inaccurate or out-of-date mailing addresses. Other reasons for juror nonresponse are more speculative, including the extent to which institutional barriers, such as inadequate juror compensation, and jurors' general anxiety about the conditions of jury service inhibit jurors from responding to their summons. Especially the loss of privacy, personal safety risks, or even apprehension about having to deliberate with other jurors on contentious issues in today's polarized social climate can discourage citizens from serving. Regardless of the juror's intent, summons nonresponse and failure to appear rates often undermine the demographic diversity of the jury pool and the efficiency of jury operations.[1]

In This Chapter

This chapter focuses on the initial steps of the jury process, that is, juror summoning and qualification. Information addressed in this chapter includes: 1) the process for identifying, selecting, qualifying, excusing, and exempting prospective jurors from jury service; 2) the duties citizens have after receiving a jury summons, 3) a review of frequently asked questions prospective jurors have about jury service, and 4) legal penalties for citizens who ignore a summons to report for jury duty.

The Master Jury List

The first step in the juror qualification and summoning process is the creation of the master jury list. This list includes the names and mailing addresses of people who are potentially eligible for jury service in the geographic area served by the court. Staff employed by the jury commissioner, who may be a court administrator, the Clerk of Court, or another state or locally appointed official, are responsible for creating the master jury list. This process involves obtaining one or more juror source lists from state and local agencies, merging the lists, identifying and removing duplicate records, and updating name and address records.[2] The list of licensed drivers and state identification cardholders maintained by state motor vehicle departments and the list of registered voters maintained by state election registrars are the two most frequently used juror source lists.[3] Two states employ lists unique to their states: an annual municipal census in Massachusetts[4] and recipients of proceeds from the Alaska Permanent Fund.[5] Box 5.1 features a court administrator and describes the important work courthouse staff do every day related to empaneling citizens for jury service.

Box 5.1: From the Field

Name: Sara Boches

Position: Senior Administrative Specialist—Jury Operations

How long have you been a practitioner in this position?
I have worked in the County of Chester for the last six years in the Court Administration Department.

What are your primary duties and responsibilities as a practitioner in this position?
As the jury supervisor, the staff and I manage questions, concerns, and requests from prospective and current jurors. In addition to assisting jurors, I am responsible for responding to our judges' needs and requests for jurors, providing them with jury panels for voir dire for their jury trials. We are responsible for summoning jurors, ensuring that there are enough jurors to appear for jury trial dates as requested by the judges, and managing the jurors from the start of their check-in process until they are seated for voir dire. We also handle all paperwork and records regarding the outcome of the voir dire process and jury trial verdict. Additionally, I manage the costs associated with jurors and the financials associated with the jury wage account.

What qualities or characteristics are most helpful in this career?
The ability to work under pressure, a cheerful outlook, excellent customer service, diligence, ability to maintain a high level of discretion and confidentiality, public speaking skills, and ability to be empathetic, but firmness and consistency are necessary skills in this position.

What does a typical day for a practitioner in this field look like?
You will be screening prospective jurors by asking them qualification questions to ensure that they are eligible to serve as a juror, as well as dealing with any requests that they make to be excused or disqualified as a juror, or to have their jury duty deferred to a later date. You will be handling end-of-the-day tasks, such as summoning the necessary number of jurors via the jury management system to appear for check-in the following day to ensure there will be enough jurors in the jury panel for voir dire. In the morning you will handle checking jurors in, holding orientation to give them an overview of the process and how their day will look, creating a randomized juror list and seating them accordingly to create the jury panel, collecting

their questionnaires and creating a jury packet for the judge and trial attorneys to use during voir dire, and ensuring that the jury panel is seated in the courtroom for the judge to begin the voir dire process. Each week you will review the financials to pay the jurors and each month you will deposit money into the jury wage account and create a record to balance the account.

What is your advice to someone either wishing to study, or now studying, criminal justice and is interested in becoming a practitioner in this field?
It is important to continue with your education and get your degree—even if course work does not directly apply to this career, you will learn important qualities and characteristics to aid you in succeeding in this career. It is important not to take anything personally when working with the public, as at times you will have to interact with difficult people. You should maintain professionalism and good customer service, while also being firm and fair to create a "jury of your peers."

Each state has its own eligibility requirements and procedures for jury selection. These eligibility requirements related to citizenship, residency, age, English fluency, and criminal history were discussed in Chapter 4. The eligibility criteria are not designed to bias a jury or select jurors who would reach one decision over another. Indeed, the individuals who are identified for jury service using the source lists should be as inclusive as possible. For example, the Superior Court of California—County of San Diego described that no one can be disqualified from jury service due to "occupation, economic status, race, national origin, ethnic group identification, religion, age, sex, sexual orientation, color, disability, or for any other reason."[6] Even judges and lawyers can be summoned to serve as a juror at trial.[7]

Selecting Jurors

The master jury list serves as the sampling frame. A sampling frame is a list of all subjects in the population from which a random sample is drawn.[8] Random (or probability) sampling occurs when each subject in the sample has an equal chance of being selected.[9] This means that no one subject, or prospective juror, has a greater likelihood of being selected than any other. Today, most courts use computerized random selection methods for jury operations, but some still employ manual methods.[10] Box 5.2 provides more details about historical jury selection procedures employed before the use of computers and electronic randomization options.

It is critically important that the master list contain accurate and complete information on as many eligible jurors as possible. However, a U.S. Census Bureau report indicated that in 2021 approximately 12.8 percent of the American population moved to a new residence, which was down slightly from 13.7 percent in 2019.[13] Specifically, 6.7 percent of U.S. residents moved, but stayed within the same state and same county, while 3.3 percent stayed in state, but moved to a different county in 2021.[14] This finding suggests that a court's source lists, compiled primarily from driver's license and voter registration records, can become outdated very quickly. The National Center for State Courts identified this as a significant problem for reaching randomly selected jurors and urged courts to update its master list at least once annually.[15]

Box 5.2: Master Jury Wheel[11]

Today, a master list generates prospective jury pools from computerized searches of voter registration records, driver's license information, etc. This was not always possible, however, as computerized records were not available to randomly select jurors. In the days before computers, court officials wrote the names of community members on slips of paper and inserted them into a large barrel, referred to as a "**Master Jury Wheel**." The wheel was turned to mix or randomize the juror names before a set number was selected.[12]

> I consider trial by jury as the only anchor ever yet imagined by man, by which a government can be held to the principles of its constitution.
>
> —Thomas Jefferson, Founding Father
> Letter to Thomas Paine (1789)

The master list should be as inclusive of the jury-eligible population as possible. The more inclusive the list, the greater the number of community members who are represented. Some courts and legal professionals have recognized the importance of having a complete sampling frame from which a representative jury can be drawn. In response to these concerns, some courts sought additional source lists beyond the traditional driver's license and voter registration records. These other sources include state income tax and local property tax records, and unemployment compensation, public assistance, and public welfare recipients.[16] There are risks associated with using multiple source lists, however. The records from different source list agencies are usually formatted differently, making it difficult to identify and remove duplicate records. People who appear more than once on the master jury list have a greater probability of being selected than people who appear only once, which undermines the basic premise of random selection. Depending on the inclusiveness of the underlying source lists, different demographic groups may be disproportionately reflected in duplicate records, which distorts representation. Also, these source lists include names of community members who are statutorily ineligible for jury service, such as capturing individuals who are underage, noncitizens, nonresidents, or have limited English proficiency or previous felony convictions. This creates more work for the jury commissioner to confirm the eligibility of prospective jurors and ensure that ineligible persons are not mistakenly empaneled as trial or grand jurors.

Finally, a larger master list does not guarantee that all people in a population will be represented on a jury panel. Increasing the number and breadth of the source lists may simply increase the number of jurors who are identified as eligible to serve. It is possible that the larger net cast by an increased number of source lists may capture more eligible jurors from the *same* communities but not extend or expand the pool of jurors from less accessible, more racially diverse regions, neighborhoods, and populations.[17]

The Jury Summons

After creating the master jury list, the jury commissioner selects prospective jurors using a one-step or two-step summoning process. As the name implies, a two-step jury system is characterized by two distinct steps. The first step involves delivering a **juror qualification questionnaire** (JQQ) to prospective jurors randomly selected from the master jury list.

Jury Summons

A court order directing the recipient to appear for jury service at a specific time, date, and location.

Most courts send the JQQ by first-class mail, but some still have a local sheriff deliver the JQQ in person to the juror's home address (personal service of process). Based on responses to the questionnaire, the jury commissioner determines an individual's eligibility for jury service and places them on a **qualified** juror list. The second step is to randomly select names from the qualified juror list; those individuals will be sent a **jury summons**.[18] In contrast, a one-step system combines the JQQ and the jury summons into a single mailing. If the prospective juror is not disqualified, exempt, excused, or deferred from service, they are directed by the jury summons to report for jury service on a specific day and time. The one-step system is preferred due to cost savings associated with printing and postage, staff administration efforts and coordination, and improved jury yield.[19] Regardless of whether the court employs a one-step or two-step jury system, the initial notification instructs prospective jurors to respond within a short period of time (typically 10 days or less). The jury commissioner reviews each response as it arrives at the courthouse and sorts it into one of five categories: undeliverable, disqualified, exempt, excused, or qualified.

Courts have made great strides in recent years to remove some of the mystery from jury service, including posting answers to frequently asked questions on court websites and social media accounts. Individuals who receive a summons for jury service in federal and some state courts are instructed to open a specific website, access the system with a login code (typically their jury identification number) and a password (typically their date of birth), and complete a JQQ.[20] The number of state courts that have fully electronic procedures for recipients to respond to the jury summons and JQQ for has increased in recent years; however, among a sample of 1,249 state trial courts in 45 states and the District of Columbia, only 32 percent reported online qualification portals.[21]

Undeliverable

If a prospective juror's address on the master jury list is inaccurate or out of date, the jury summons or JQQ may be returned marked **undeliverable** by the U.S. Postal Service (USPS). Nationally, 11 percent of jury mailings are undeliverable,[22] which is consistent with the rate at which people move to a new address. If a forwarding address has been filed, the USPS will forward commercial mail, including a jury summons or JQQ, for up to 12 months.[23] From month 13 to 48, the USPS will return the mailing to the courthouse with a sticker indicating the new address. After four years, the mailing is returned to the courthouse simply marked "undeliverable." Courts employ several techniques to minimize the undeliverable rate and ensure that jury mailings are delivered in a timely manner. One technique is to periodically refresh the master jury list with updated juror source lists. Another technique is to verify the accuracy of address records with the National Change of Address database maintained by the USPS before mailing the jury notifications.[24]

Disqualified

Another category of response is **disqualified**. As discussed in Chapter 4, some of the records selected from the master jury list are people who are not qualified for jury service based on the eligibility criteria established for the state or federal court. If so, the jury commissioner will inform the prospective juror that they are ineligible and that they should not appear for service. The jury commissioner also documents the prospective juror's status as disqualified on the master jury list. They are not permanently removed from the master jury list, however, and the person can be reselected and can serve if they meet the eligibility requirements in the future. Noncitizens, for example, can become naturalized citizens and convicted felons can have their civic rights restored in the future.

Questions asked on the JQQ vary from court to court but generally cover several categories of information. For example, the court may require prospective jurors to confirm basic administrative information, including legal name, current address, and contact information, such as telephone numbers and email addresses. Courts recognize such personal information is sensitive and may specify the information will not be shared publicly. The court may also inquire about an individual's physical and mental health conditions and the need for, or the type of accommodation(s) required. All local, county, state, and federal courthouses must be accessible to people with disabilities.[25]

Other information gathered by the courts includes basic demographic and social background characteristics. As mentioned, individuals may be asked to report their age, citizenship, English fluency, prior incarcerations, and criminal history. This category of questions is used by the court to determine whether the individual is statutorily qualified for jury service, and whether they claim an exemption, or request to be excused or defer their service date due to personal dilemmas or **hardships**. Individuals who are excused from service may be randomly sampled for jury service in the future.

Finally, the JQQ may inquire about an individual's military experience, occupational and employment history, marital status, and educational attainment. This information is provided to the trial judge and attorneys for use when empaneling a jury. These responses will only be reviewed if the individual is qualified and available to serve jury duty. Figure 5.2 shows the questions asked of prospective jurors on a standard jury summons and JQQ from the state of Missouri.

Exempt

Some individuals are **exempt** from jury service, which means they have a right to decline to serve, even if they were summoned. Exemptions are created by the state or federal legislature as recognition that some people should be allowed to opt out of jury service based on personal or occupational status. The most common type of exemption is previous jury service for some statutorily prescribed period (typically 12–36 months). If a person who has served as a trial or grand juror is resummoned during this period, it is their prerogative either to serve again or to claim the exemption. Other personal status exemptions include being an elderly person (e.g., over age 70), being a nursing mother, or being the sole caregiver of minor children or an incompetent adult.

Occupational exemptions recognize that some people have full-time employment that makes them essential workers or whose career would pose a conflict of interest with their role as a juror. In many states and in federal courts, active-duty military and national guard members, police and corrections officers, and publicly elected officials are exempt.[26] If the prospective juror indicates that they are exempt from jury service, the jury commissioner will document the exemption on the master jury list. Like being disqualified, the prospective juror can be resummoned in the future and, if the exemption still applies, must reclaim the exemption.

DO NOT MAIL OR RETURN THIS SECTION.
BRING THIS SECTION WITH YOU WHEN YOU REPORT.

DATE AND TIME TO REPORT	REPORT TO
WHERE TO REPORT	TERM OF SERVICE

SUMMONS FOR JURY SERVICE

By order of the Presiding Judge of the Circuit Court of XXX County, Missouri, you are hereby summoned to serve as a juror as indicated above. **IF YOU FAIL TO APPEAR AS DIRECTED BY THIS SUMMONS YOU MAY BE HELD IN CONTEMPT OF COURT AND FINED AS PROVIDED BY SECTION 494.450, RSMo.** Please bring this summons with you when you report for jury service. Do not return this section by mail. If you need an accommodation for disability, please call (XXX) XXX-XXXX at least one week in advance of your report date. You may also use this number in case of an emergency while you are serving. Access to jury service is available to all individuals with a disability as required by the Americans with Disabilities Act of 1990.

PLEASE READ IMPORTANT INFORMATION ON BACK OF FORM

JUROR QUALIFICATION FORM

DETACH HERE *COMPLETE, SIGN AND RETURN THIS BOTTOM SECTION WITHIN 10 DAYS* DETACH HERE

NOTE: Please Print

Last Name First Name Middle Initial Age

Home Address Home Phone Work Phone

Mileage from your home to the XXX County Courthouse in XXX City (round trip)_____

1. Are you a United States citizen? ☐Yes ☐No
2. Do you live in XXX County? ☐Yes ☐No
3. Do you read, speak and understand English? ☐Yes ☐No
   If no, is your inability to read, speak and understand English due to a vision or hearing impairment? ☐Yes ☐No
4. Have you been convicted of a felony and not had your civil rights restored? ☐Yes ☐No
5. Are you on active duty in the armed forces or a member of the Missouri Militia on active duty under order of the Governor? ☐Yes ☐No
6. Are you a judge of a court of record? ☐Yes ☐No
   Please indicate which court _____
7. Do you have a physical or mental disability that would interfere with or prevent you from serving as a juror? If yes, doctor's letter must be provided. ☐Yes ☐No

8. Are you presently employed? ☐Yes ☐No
   If yes, state employer and occupation _____
   If no, state your last employer and occupation _____
   Are you a member of the Missouri General Assembly? ☐Yes ☐No
9. Marital Status: ☐Single ☐Married ☐Widowed ☐Separated ☐Divorced
10. Race: _____
11. Gender: ☐Male ☐Female
12. Spouse's employer and occupation _____
13. Do you have children under the age of 18? ☐Yes ☐No
14. Indicate your highest grade level completed
    Grade School ____ College ____
    High School ____ Post Graduate ____
    Technical/Trade ____
15. Are you related to a law enforcement officer? ☐Yes ☐No
16. Have you been convicted of a crime other than a traffic ticket? ☐Yes ☐No
17. Have you served as a juror before? ☐Yes ☐No
    Type of case? ☐Criminal ☐Civil
    When? _____
    What county? _____
18. Have you ever been a party in a lawsuit (as a plaintiff or defendant, not merely as a witness)? ☐Yes ☐No
19. Have you ever made a claim or had a claim made against you to obtain or recover money, either for physical injuries or for damage to property? ☐Yes ☐No

I swear/affirm under penalty of perjury that these facts are true according to my knowledge and belief.

× _____
Juror's Signature

_____
Date

PLEASE RETURN COMPLETED FORM WITHIN 10 DAYS AS DIRECTED ABOVE.
Additional questions <u>may</u> be continued on a following page.

Figure 5.2: Example of Summons for Jury Service

Excused

Some people who are summoned for jury service have legitimate reasons for not serving but may not have an exemption that they can claim. In those cases, the prospective juror can request to be **excused** from service for hardship. An excusal differs from an exemption insofar that the jury commissioner (or a judge) has discretion to grant or deny the request. Most states and the federal courts recognize three types of hardship that merit excusal: medical hardship, financial hardship, and extreme inconvenience. First, a juror can request to be excused for medical hardship if they have a temporary or permanent healthcare condition that would make it difficult or impossible to serve. For example, they may be recovering from a recent surgery the day of their scheduled jury service. Second, jurors who are employed as hourly workers and whose employers do not compensate for jury service can request to be excused for financial hardship if being away from work would cause a significant economic burden for themselves or their families. Finally, jurors who have preexisting commitments during the time they are required to serve, such as vacation or business travel, can request to be excused due to extreme inconvenience. Increasingly, courts do not excuse jurors outright but instead will postpone their service to a more convenient date.

Responding to the Summons

These categories describe how jury commissioners manage the responses of prospective jurors who answer their jury notification. Not all prospective jurors respond, however, and some respond but then never appear at the courthouse for jury service on their reporting date. Depending on whether the court employs a one-step or two-step jury system, between 16 and 22 percent of prospective jurors fail to respond to the initial jury notification or fail to appear.[27] Although some jurors deliberately shirk their civic responsibility by not responding, there are many other reasons that jurors fail to respond. For example, approximately half of jurors who fail to respond never received the jury notification.[28] Some are ineligible or exempt from jury service and believe they do not need to respond at all. Others are simply confused about how to respond. Empirical research on nonresponsive jurors suggests they are neither intrinsically bad citizens nor hold negative views about jury service itself.[29]

Nonresponse and failure to appear rates have increased significantly over the past two decades, prompting courts to take more proactive steps to address the problem.[30] For example, a Detroit, Michigan news station reported that of the 62,000 residents of Wayne County, Michigan, who received a jury summons in 2016, approximately one-third (22,000 residents) failed to report to the courthouse on their scheduled day for jury service. Typically, residents who fail to report for jury service receive another notification. Residents who fail to respond after repeated attempts by the courts may receive an **Order to Show Cause**, which is a court order demanding they appear in court and explain to the judge why they should not be held in contempt of court for failing to comply with the jury summons. Media coverage of these hearings in Detroit reported that jurors provided the court with a variety of reasons for ignoring their jury service day, including a lack of public transportation in the city making attending jury duty difficult.[31] Box 5.3 describes a growing phenomenon of fraudulent activity impacting the jury selection process. As shown, jury scams are complicating court efforts to enforce compliance with jury summons.

Today, jurors are clearly instructed not to ignore the summons. A notice from the court to report for jury duty is not a suggestion but a legal mandate that all citizens are expected to follow. Jury service is a civic responsibility built into the founding documents that define

Box 5.3: Jury Scams

In recent years, the number of victims falling prey to fraudulent **jury scams** has increased. Individual victims will receive a phone call at their home and will be told they failed to report on the day of their required state or federal jury service.[32] The caller claims to be an employee of a federal, state, or local government agency or a clerk of the courts. The victims are told if they do not pay a specified amount, ranging from hundreds to thousands of dollars, the government will press charges against them, including finding the victim in contempt of court, failing to appear, and subjecting them to arrest. One such scam involved having the victim transfer money directly to a pay-at-kiosk card that the perpetrator had access to.[33]

These scams are elaborate. The perpetrators know details about the victim, including their address, family dynamics, and work phone numbers. The victim's own caller identification software will report the fake name and location that the perpetrator describes. The numbers are spoofed to make it look like the call is being generated from an official source, when the calls could be originating from an offshore account not located in the United States. Government officials report this sophisticated scam makes it difficult to capture perpetrators and to prosecute these offenders who are outside the U.S. government's jurisdiction.

It is unclear how frequently these scams occur. Victims may not report the incident out of embarrassment for being tricked by such false claims. The way to stop such scams from occurring, according to law enforcement, is not to fall victim to them in the first place. State and federal officials want the public to know that law enforcement personnel will never call on the phone and demand cash payments or request sensitive information;[34] they encourage the public to contact the Internet Crime Complaint Center at www.ic3.gov, if they suspect they were the victim of such a fraudulent scam.

Photo: Protect Yourself Against Jury Duty Scams[35]

the laws of this country and the rights of its citizens. In colonial America, individuals refusing to serve on a jury were fined in an amount up to 20 shillings.[36] This was equivalent to about a week's worth of pay for a skilled laborer in the 1800s. The penalties imposed by courts vary by jurisdiction today, but usually include a charge for contempt of court, fines, imprisonment, or a combination of these. A court in Maricopa County, Arizona, notified dozens of jurors for failing to respond to their jury summons. Jurors provided excuses that included: "care responsibilities, medical issues, divorce, identity theft, a death of family member, a soccer match, no reason at all, and I forgot." The excuses did not impede the presiding judge from issuing fines ranging in the amounts from $50 to $300.[37] Accounts like this illustrate that judges have little tolerance or patience for individuals who disregard their jury summons and are swift to apply fines and other punishments for the jurors' negligent actions.[38]

A review of court websites revealed examples of the language and warnings issued by courts for ignoring jury service. These ranged from very broad statements, "may be found in contempt ... and may be placed in custody and/or fined,"[39] to more specific consequences, like the Massachusetts Court System, which indicates the person may be charged with a criminal offense and fined up to $2,000.[40] Still other courts posted details about what the court would do if an individual continuously ignored the original summons and subsequent mailings. Interestingly, an individual judge's pursual of jurors who ignore the summons may correspond to their personality as much as politics. For example, some judges simply may not want to be bothered with going after negligent jurors, while other judges, who serve in elected offices, may fear reprisal during the next election cycle from jurors who were penalized for ducking their civil responsibilities. Overall, this suggests significant discrepancy exists between individual jurisdictions and courtrooms about how negligent prospective jurors are treated.

Frequently Asked Questions

Federal[41] and most state and local court systems[42] have made efforts to make the jury experience as pleasant as possible for prospective jurors. Important information is included in the original summons and may be posted on the court's website (if available) to make the process of jury service transparent. A court's website address will be shown on the summons; the website may contain answers to questions that jurors have about their pending jury service date and responsibilities. Some websites may contain links to high-quality videos and articles that explain specific details about the jury process from the beginning to the end.

Some courts provide answers to the **frequently asked questions** (FAQs) to allay fears of prospective jurors, but also to decrease calls to the courthouse that overload administrative staff and court personnel. It is a good idea to review all the information provided on the jury summons and access the website (if one exists) before calling the courthouse; your specific concerns will likely have been addressed and answered. The following section describes some of the FAQs individuals have after receiving the jury summons.

Selection criteria

A question jurors frequently have is, "Why was I selected?" Selection criteria, as mentioned previously, include source lists like driver's license, voter registration records, and various other sources to identify residents in the community. Jurors are determined eligible based on characteristics including age, citizenship, residency (address), criminal history, and English fluency.

Compensation

Another question jurors have after receiving a jury summons is, "Do I get paid for jury duty?" The answer to this question about **compensation** varies by state and can be somewhat complicated. Jurors are not paid on an hourly basis, but they may receive some monetary amount to compensate for daily expenses incurred during their jury service experience. The American Bar Association was clear on this matter, urging that all jurors should receive a reasonable fee to defray expenses associated with parking, meals, and childcare.[43]

State courts have varying approaches toward juror compensation. One common approach is a **fixed flat rate** where jurors receive a standard daily payment for each day of jury service regardless of the number of days served. Rates vary significantly by state with many states providing only a nominal fee. On the lower end, for example, the minimum required jury fee in Illinois is $4 per day, although most counties add to this amount using local funding. North Dakota was the most generous state in 2025, compensating jurors $100 per full day of jury service.[44] When considering compensation among all states, the average payment for the first day of jury service is $19.87.[45] A juror may be responsible for their own expenses associated with food and parking during the trial. These expenses often exceed the daily compensation provided by the state courts for one's jury service experience.

Large disparities also exist among state courts for providing compensation related to traveling to and from the courthouse. For example, 27 states do not offer any mileage reimbursement for jurors, seven states match current federal reimbursement rates, 14 states provide a range between 7 cents to less than $1.00, while Utah provides $1.00, and the District of Columbia provides $2.00 per mile.[46] After jury service is completed, jurors will be compensated in the specific amount determined by the state's legislative or statutory guidelines.

A second approach for compensating jurors is referred to as a **graduated rate**. This method is more complicated because jurors may be compensated a lower amount for the first several days of service, then compensated in a greater amount if the trial extends beyond a certain number of days. Some states do not offer any compensation for the first day of jury service and only provide compensation starting on the second and subsequent days. See California's Code of Civil Procedure, for example.[47] Comparatively, the range for compensation for the first day of service is $5 in New Jersey, but this increases to $40 per day, while in Indiana jurors are initially compensated $30 but this increases to $100 after five consecutive days of service.[48] The average daily amount compensated among states that practice the graduated rate option is approximately $38.27.[49] Recently, the state of Arizona revised its juror compensation rates and juror facilities. Box 5.4 provides a description of these improvements.

Box 5.4: Juror Improvements in the State of Arizona and Maricopa County Superior Court (Phoenix, AZ)[50]

The Maricopa County Superior Court has implemented changes to juror compensation amounts and has improved the conditions of its courthouse to address problems and criticisms voiced by jurors over the years. Regarding compensation, the Arizona state legislature updated pay standards to allow up to $300 a day to reimburse lost income for jurors serving in the superior courts.[51] The individual must demonstrate that they could have earned that amount from their employment, as demonstrated through pay vouchers, receipts, etc. This is a significant change from the original pay, which only compensated jurors $12 beginning the second day of jury service. This change was implemented because of juror complaints that jury service caused significant financial hardships.

Also, the Maricopa County Superior Court improved the jury gathering area to better accommodate jurors while waiting for jury selection. The facility upgrades included creating quiet rooms and workspaces with desks so jurors could charge laptops and continue to complete work tasks or school assignments.[52] Also, food service stations were installed for refreshments and additional seating was added for jurors to relax while waiting to be called to the courtroom.

Juror compensation in federal courts follows a similar pattern to the graduated rate practices of the states. Jurors who are called to serve on a trial in federal district court or on a grand jury proceeding are paid $50 per day, which increases to $60 for a trial juror who serves more than 10 days or a grand juror who serves more than 45 days.[53] District courts also may require driving farther distances, so jurors may be eligible for additional compensation to account for miles traveled. In 2025, federal jurors were reimbursed at 67 cents per mile, parking reimbursement in some courts, and subsistence needs for overnight stays primarily. Finally, federal government employees who serve on either a trial or grand jury are paid their regular salary during their jury service in lieu of receiving jury pay.[54]

Many criticisms have been made about the current practices for compensating jurors who participate in the American jury system. It is likely that there has been no louder opposition than from the jurors themselves. Jurors have voiced concerns about the small amount they are compensated for their service and the negative impact this has on them. This disapproval is especially true for those jurors who were self-employed.[55] Overall, the amount of compensation is discouragingly low and often does not account for a full day of lost wages. Some employers may still pay their employees for a lost day's work, or they may require them to make up some of the lost time after their jury service is completed. There may be some limitations to the amount of patience an employer has depending upon the duration of the trial.

Some jurors expressed concern and worried about how long-term jury service will impact their employment status in the future. The American Bar Association values jurors and the jury process itself. The organization emphasized that jurors must be protected from adverse reactions in the workplace, stating:

> Employers should be prohibited from discharging, laying off, denying advancement opportunities to, or otherwise penalizing employees who miss work because of jury service … Employers should be prohibited from requiring jurors to use leave or vacation time for the time spent on jury service or be required to make up the time they served.[56]

Federal and state laws also mandate certain protections for anyone who is selected for jury service. For example, the federal Jury Selection and Service Act (1968) states, "No employer shall discharge, threaten to discharge, intimidate, or coerce any permanent employee by reason of such employee's jury service, or the attendance or scheduled attendance in connection with such service, in any court of the United States."[57] Any employer found guilty of violating this Act may be held "liable for damages for any loss of wages or other benefits suffered by an employee by reason of such violation" and may receive a civil penalty that does not exceed $5,000 for each violation.[58]

Time Commitment for Term of Service

Another question jurors may have is, "How long will my jury service last?" This is an important question, but the answer about **time commitment** is complex and depends on several factors, including the type of case on which one is called to serve. More than half of jury trials conclude in three days or less, and 80 percent take five days or less.[59] More complex cases may take longer to present appropriate evidence pertaining to guilt or fault. Cases involving violent behaviors, like capital cases, may take longer to prosecute because of the severity of the crime and the potential punishment including the death penalty. These cases may involve a detailed presentation of evidence, multiple witness testimonials, victim impact statements from family members and friends, etc.

Today, state and county courts may provide jurors with guidelines about what to expect concerning the length of their jury service responsibilities. The Chester County Justice Center of Pennsylvania informs trial jurors their service may "take between one to five days to complete. Because of this do not make any appointments or commitments that would interfere with you serving on a trial that may take up to five days to complete."[60] The judge also may address the jurors' concerns about the length of a trial during the jury selection process. For example, some judges in the Superior Court of California may inform jurors that "most trials last 3–7 days, but some may go longer,"[61] while in the Superior Court in King County, Washington, jurors are informed that their service is a minimum of a one-day commitment, but "the average trial lasts about two weeks."[62] Jurors who report to the courthouse but are not selected to serve on a trial may be dismissed at the close of the business day.

In some courts, jurors are asked to commit to a range of days or weeks when their jury service may be completed. The jurors will be "on call" during this timeframe and may be asked to report on a given day. This is the case in the U.S. District Court for the Northern District of California, where federal jury service follows a "one appearance or one trial" format. In this approach, jurors are "required to make only one appearance in court for jury selections held that day or serve for one trial."[63] If a juror is not selected to serve on a trial the day they report, they are released at the end of the day and their jury service is considered completed. Generally, jurors who are sworn in and serve on a trial, including participating in the deliberation process, may be exempt from serving again for a minimum of two to three years. Jurors who report for jury duty but are not selected for a trial have met their civic obligations. They are dismissed and may be exempt from further service for another one to two years.[64]

Some court websites also provide jurors with specific details about the court's hours of operation. The U.S. District Court for the Northern District of Iowa, for example, informs federal jurors to report to the courthouse between 8:00 and 9:00 AM with an expectation to stay until 2:30 or 5:00 PM. If the juror is selected for a trial, they should be made aware that the deliberation process itself may impact the start and end times on given days.[65] Courthouses may include this level of detail out of respect for jurors who must plan for childcare, guardianship, etc. Table 5.1 lists other FAQs that prospective jurors had after receiving a jury summons in the mail. Box 5.5 provides comments from a court administrator about working in a Jury Services Office.

Table 5.1: FAQs from Individuals Called to Jury Service

Question	*Answer*
What should I wear?	Some courts may prohibit jurors from wearing shorts, tank tops, T-shirts[66] or jeans[67] inside the courtroom, or clothing displaying logos, symbols, or words that may be offensive to others.[68] Other courts may simply leave attire up to the jurors' discretion, indicating "please dress neatly."[69]
What should I bring when I report?	Some courts allow "something to read during waiting periods"[70] or laptops[71] in specified areas of the courthouse. Other courts specifically warn that certain items are strictly prohibited, for example, "weapons, items with any type of blade, scissors, knitting needles, and alcohol."[72]

Box 5.5: From the Field

Name: Elizabeth A. Dumond

Position: Chief Deputy Court Administrator, County of Chester

How long have you been a practitioner in this position? I have worked in the County of Chester for 30 years.

What are your primary duties and responsibilities as a practitioner in this position? In my current role, I provide high-level administrative support to the District Court Administrator and the Chester County Court of Common Pleas. I coordinate all fiscal operations and statistical reports, prepare and administer the budget of the court and court departments, oversee court staff, and manage the jury and law library operations. Additionally, I serve as the court's Language Access Coordinator and 509 Administrator.

What are the qualities or characteristics that are most helpful in this career? It is important to be flexible in this role. With so many continually changing priorities, you must be able to shift directions at a moment's notice. Being able to relate to and work well with others at many different levels is imperative. We interact with judges, other departments and agencies, and the public daily. Assisting people going through difficult processes and allowing them to have their voices heard is extremely satisfying.

What is a typical day for a practitioner in this career? One of the most satisfying aspects about my position is that every day is different and is always filled with variety. We handle matters involving jury, financials, statistics, interpreters, facilities, contracts, litigants, and help resolve any issues that arise within the court system.

What is your advice to someone either wishing to study, or now studying, criminal justice and wanting to become a practitioner in this field? You must possess the desire to help others in this profession. With policies and procedures transforming over time, it is important to be open to constant change. Continuing education plays an important role in this position because of these variations, whether it be in policies, procedures, rules, or laws. As a court employee, we sign a code of conduct, and your behavior, both professionally and personally, represents the judiciary.

Conclusion

Jury service begins with the summoning and qualification process. It is important that all randomly selected jurors respond to their call for service. This is the best way to ensure the jury pool reflects a fair cross-section of the community where the trial is held. There are legitimate reasons why some people cannot serve on a jury trial after being summoned. Some are not eligible or are exempt from service; others can be excused if they suffer significant hardships or inconvenience by serving. However, courts have found the recent trend toward increased nonresponse and failure-to-appear rates alarming.

Jurors who do not respond to a jury summons disrupt the jury process in several ways. First, the representativeness of the jury pool, as determined through a random selection of citizens, is placed in jeopardy. Also, court staff rely on enough jurors to report to the courthouse on their day of service to seat a full jury panel with enough extras to serve as alternates. Ignoring the call to serve goes against the participatory government envisioned by the Founding Fathers in the late 18th century. Moreover, the power and authority granted to jurors to protect common citizens from the abusive and oppressive actions of government are lost. How would the Founding Fathers react today if they learned that Americans are not taking advantage of the opportunities granted to them that were so fiercely fought for 250 years ago?

The jury selection process will be described further in Chapter 6. This material will address what a prospective juror will experience when they arrive in the courthouse on their assigned jury duty day, including where to gather and what preliminary instructions they may hear. The chapter also addresses the importance of the voir dire process where jurors are escorted to a courtroom to first meet the trial judge and attorneys.

Summary

This chapter addressed the earliest stage of the jury process, jury selection. The process for selecting jurors before the advent of computers was through personal knowledge of community members. This was sufficient when communities were smaller, tightly knit, and all residents were recognized and available. Today, the diversity and geographic distances where citizens reside makes knowing all community residents impossible. Government databases, including driver's license and voter registration records, income tax records, unemployment compensation, public assistance, and public welfare recipients, contain the sampling frame from which a random cross-section of the community is selected.

Citizens who are randomly selected receive a jury summons delivered to their homes through first-class mail or personal service. Prospective jurors must follow instructions to complete a juror qualification questionnaire that assists court staff in determining the eligibility of citizens for certain cases. For example, some citizens are exempt from jury service in federal or state courts because of holding an elected office or are on active duty in the military. The questionnaire also allows prospective jurors to request excusal from jury service. The reasons for requesting excusal may vary, including personal health, financial hardships, caretaker responsibilities, or a conflict with a prescheduled commitment.

Citizens may react differently to receiving summons to jury duty. Prospective jurors may feel anxious, especially if they have never served before and they may have questions about the process of jury service. Federal and state courts have created websites and posted answers to frequently asked questions that prospective jurors have about jury duty. Jurors have many questions, including whether they are compensated for jury service and the anticipated time commitment of jury duty. An increasing number of citizens are ignoring the jury summons when they are received. These individuals may receive several mailings of the jury summons before being notified to report to the courthouse for an Order to Show Cause hearing and explain in person to a judge why they did not respond to the summons. Courts do not respond kindly to citizens who ignore their civic responsibility for jury service. Judges have imposed fines and issued contempt of court citations against jurors who failed to report to jury duty.

Discussion Questions

1. The process of selecting prospective jurors from the community has become increasingly technical since the days of the Master Jury Wheel. Do you believe the current practices for selecting jurors from driver's license, voter registration records, income tax records, unemployment compensation filings, public assistance or public welfare recipients, etc. are sufficient for gathering a fair cross-section of the community? Are there any other types of records that may be more representative or inclusive of community residents?
2. What do you think about the improvements made to the jury system in Arizona? Overall, do you think these changes will improve jurors' satisfaction with being called to serve jury duty? Why or why not? Do you see any unintended consequences that these improvements or accommodation could cause?
3. Ethical consideration. Do you think individuals make false excuses or embellish personal hardships to avoid serving jury duty? If you knew someone was intentionally misrepresenting their situation to get out of jury duty, what would you do? What could you do?
4. Research shows that increasing numbers of individuals are being victimized by jury scams. This may put further negative light on jury service for some individuals and add to the angst many prospective jurors already feel when they receive a jury summons in the mail. Does this knowledge of jury scams change your opinion about serving jury duty in the future? Explain. How concerned are you about becoming a victim of a jury scam?

Review Questions

1. Describe the current process for selecting prospective jurors from a community. What instructions are citizens given on the jury summons that they receive through first-class mail?
2. Describe who may be exempt from jury service. Why are they given this exemption?
3. What are some of the legitimate reasons why a prospective juror can request an excusal from jury service?
4. What penalties have been imposed on individual citizens for failing to respond to a jury summons?
5. Search the Web. Conduct a search of a district court website (UScourts.gov) or an individual state or county court website that was not discussed in this chapter. What do these sources tell you about the average length of days and time that jurors should anticipate committing to if they are called to serve on a criminal or civil trial in those jurisdictions?
6. Search the Web. Pick any state in the United States. Explore that state's website about issues related to jury service discussed in this chapter. Answer the following:
   a. What are some of the FAQs and answers posted by the state court? What compensation do jurors get for their time, what are the penalties for ignoring the jury summons, and what concerns seem to be the most pressing for prospective jurors in that state? Make a list of anything interesting and unique that you find.
   b. Conduct a search for a federal district court website (UScourts.gov) or an individual state website. What do these sources tell you about the average number of days and hours that prospective jurors should anticipate committing to, if they were called to serve either a criminal or civil trial in that jurisdiction? (Hint: A general search for "jury information" and your selected state should get you access to the needed source material.)

Answers to Chapter 5 "What Do You Think?" Questions

1. False. Many courthouses throughout the states have their own jury administration offices, referred to as the Jury Services Office, that oversee all aspects of the jury duty prospective jurors.
2. True. The master list compiles information from source lists, including driver's license information, voter registration records, income taxes records, etc. that determines who may be summoned for jury service.
3. True. Public officials currently in office are exempt from federal jury service.
4. False. A jury summons is delivered to a prospective jurors' home address using U.S. first-class mail or personal service.
5. True. The JQQ, completed by a prospective juror, provides details about relevant characteristics and requests for excusal that determines eligibility for jury service.
6. False. A graduated per diem fee increases juror compensation the longer the trial continues. This approach is used in some states and the federal court system.
7. False. Judges may react adversely to citizens who blatantly ignore a jury summons and have imposed contempt of court citations and fees for failing to meet their civic responsibility.

Key Terms

compensation
disqualified
excused
exempt
fixed flat rate
frequently asked questions
graduated rate
hardships
juror qualification questionnaire
jury scams
jury summons
master jury list
Master Jury Wheel
Order to Show Cause
qualified
source lists
time commitment
undeliverable

References

1 Hannaford-Agor, P.L. (2025). *Rebuilding the foundation: Addressing a crisis in juror participation.* Trends in State Courts 2025. https://www.ncsc.org/sites/default/files/media/document/NCSC-Trends-2025.pdf

2 Hannaford-Agor, P.L., Hamilton, M., & Bailey, E. (2022). *Eliminating shadows and ghosts: Findings from a study of inclusiveness, representativeness, and accuracy in master jury lists and juror source lists in three states.* National Center for State Courts. https://ncsc.contentdm.oclc.org/digital/collection/juries/id/349/rec/15

3 Hannaford-Agor, P.L., & Moffett, M. (2024). *2023 State-of-the-states survey of jury improvement efforts: Jury operations in state courts.* National Center for State Courts. https://ncsc.contentdm.oclc.org/digital/collection/juries/id/383/rec/1
4 Mass. Gen. Laws § 223a (10)
5 Ak. Stat. 09.20.050
6 Superior Court of California. (2023, November 20). *Jury service frequently asked questions.* County of San Diego. https://www.sdcourt.ca.gov/sdcourt/jury2/juryfaq#:~:text=Most%20jury%20trials%20last%203,be%20completed%20in%20one%20day
7 U.S. Courts. (2014, August 7). *Court shorts: Jury service* [Video]. YouTube. https://www.youtube.com/watch?v=iKpiwpajm6I
8 Maxfield, M.G., & Babbie, E.R. (2009). *Basics of research methods for criminal justice and criminology* (2nd ed.). Wadsworth.
9 Maxfield, M.G., & Babbie, E.R. (2009). *Basics of research methods for criminal justice and criminology* (2nd ed.). Wadsworth.
10 Maxfield, M.G., & Babbie, E.R. (2009). *Basics of research methods for criminal justice and criminology* (2nd ed.). Wadsworth.
11 Image URL https://encrypted-tbn0.gstatic.com/images?q=tbn:ANd9GcTpxEpWfKnQGrvFv7eZU_GgWT7HObzQwteYSA&s or https://historicimages.com/cdn/shop/products/hca37096_1200x.jpg?v=1617390851
12 Court Historical Society Newsletter. (2024, January 13). *The jury wheel.* The Historical Society of the United States District Court for the Eastern District of Tennessee, Inc. https://www.tned.uscourts.gov/sites/tned/files/0709history.pdf
13 Palarino, J.V., Pugh, J.K., & McKenzie, B. (2023). *Share of Americans who said they moved declined between 2019 and 2021.* U.S. Census Bureau. https://www.census.gov/library/stories/2023/04/fewer-people-moving-between-2019-and-2021.html
14 Palarino, J.V., Pugh, J.K., & McKenzie, B. (2023). *Share of Americans who said they moved declined between 2019 and 2021.* U.S. Census Bureau. https://www.census.gov/library/stories/2023/04/fewer-people-moving-between-2019-and-2021.html
15 Hannaford-Agor, P.L., Hamilton, M., & Bailey, E. (2022). *Eliminating shadows and ghosts: Findings from a study of inclusiveness, representativeness, and accuracy in master jury lists and juror source lists in three states.* National Center for State Courts. https://ncsc.contentdm.oclc.org/digital/collection/juries/id/349/rec/1
16 Mize, G.E., Hannaford-Agor, P.L., & Waters, N.L. (2007). *The state of the state's survey of jury improvements efforts: A compendium report.* National Center for State Courts. https://www.ncsc-jurystudies.org/__data/assets/pdf_file/0016/5623/soscompendiumfinal.pdf
17 Administrative Office of the U.S. Courts. (2023, November 27). *Juror qualifications, exemptions and excuses.* https://www.uscourts.gov/services-forms/jury-service/juror-qualifications-exemptions-and-excuses
18 National Center for State Courts. (2009). *Jury managers' toolbox. Converting from a 2-step to 1-step jury system.* http://www.ncsc-jurystudies.org
19 National Center for State Courts. (2009). *Jury managers' toolbox. Converting from a 2-step to 1-step jury system.* http://www.ncsc-jurystudies.org
20 Administrative Office of the U.S. Courts. (2024, March 17). *Jury service.* https://www.uscourts.gov/services-forms/jury-service
21 Hannaford-Agor, P.L, & Moffett, M. (2024). *2023 State-of-the-states, survey of jury improvement efforts: Jury operations in state courts.* National Center for State Courts. https://www.ncsc-jurystudies.org/__data/assets/pdf_file/0019/103825/2023-SOS-Jury-Ops.pdf
22 Hannaford-Agor, P.L., & Moffett, M. (2024). *2023 State-of-the-states survey of jury improvement efforts: Performance measures for jury operations.* National Center for State Courts. https://ncsc.contentdm.oclc.org/digital/collection/juries/id/366/rec/7
23 United States Postal Service. (2025, July 29). *Extended mail forwarding.* https://faq.usps.com/s/article/Extended-Mail-Forwarding
24 Smith, O.K.H., & Hannaford-Agor, P.L. (2022). *Delivering the jury summons to the correct address: Benefits and costs of NCOA processing.* National Center for State Courts. https://ncsc.contentdm.oclc.org/digital/collection/juries/id/351/rec/1
25 National Center for State Courts. (2024, March 17). *The courthouse.* https://www.ncsc.org/courthouseplanning/needs-of-persons-with-disabilities/accessible-courtrooms

26 Administrative Office of the U.S. Courts. (2023, November 27). *Juror qualifications, exemptions and excuses.* https://www.uscourts.gov/services-forms/jury-service/juror-qualifications-exemptions-and-excuses
27 Hannaford-Agor, P.L. & Moffett, M. (2024). *2023 State-of-the-states survey of jury improvement efforts: Performance measures for jury operations.* National Center for State Courts. https://ncsc.contentdm.oclc.org/digital/collection/juries/id/366/rec/7https://ncsc.contentdm.oclc.org/digital/collection/juries/id/366/rec/7
28 Hannaford-Agor, P.L., Moffett., M., Embry, V., Hustedt, B., Murtch, E., Walker, A., & Modjididi, A. (2023). *Why won't they come? A study of juror nonresponse and failure to appear in Harris County, Texas.* National Center for State Courts. https://ncsc.contentdm.oclc.org/digital/collection/juries/id/388/rec/1
29 Smedley, T.L. (2008). *Beyond failure to appear notices: A reexamination of juror attitudes in the Circuit Court of Jackson County, Missouri and an examination of other techniques to address failure to appear patterns.* Institute for Court Management. https://ncsc.contentdm.oclc.org/digital/collection/juries/id/172/rec/2
30 Hannaford-Agor, P.L. & Moffett, M. (2024). *2023 State-of-the-states survey of jury improvement efforts: Performance measures for jury operations.* National Center for State Courts. https://ncsc.contentdm.oclc.org/digital/collection/juries/id/366/rec/7
31 WXYZ-TV. (2017, March 21). *Warning for skipping jury duty* [Video]. YouTube. https://www.youtube.com/watch?v=Fc0jlz5ZRFY
32 Guercio, G.F. (2016). Scam alert! How to beat jury scammers. *Courts Today*, *3*, 6–10.
33 KPRC 2. (2023, November 19). *Jury duty phone scam warning* [Video]. YouTube. https://www.youtube.com/watch?v=axlToL167d8
34 Administrative Office of the U.S. Courts. (2023, November 19). *Federal court scams.* https://www.uscourts.gov/about-federal-courts/federal-courts-public/federal-court-scams
35 Washington Court. (2025, October 18). *Protect yourself against jury duty scams.* https://www.courts.wa.gov/content/publicUpload/News/JuryDutyScamPSAPoster.pdf
36 Office of Jury Commissioner. (2023, November 14). *The early days of the jury system.* Commonwealth of Massachusetts. https://www.mass.gov/info-details/learn-about-the-history-of-the-jury-system#the-early-days-of-the-jury-system
37 Fox 10 KSAZ. (2023, October 20). *Jury duty crackdown: Scofflaws ordered to report to Maricopa County judge* [Video]. YouTube. https://www.youtube.com/watch?v=v851Pkoi93w
38 Hansen, M. (1993). No excuses allowed: Judge removed for punishing prospective jurors who claimed bias. *American Bar Association Journal*, *79*(3), 40.
39 Superior Court of California. (2023, November 20). *Jury service frequently asked questions.* County of San Diego. https://www.sdcourt.ca.gov/sdcourt/jury2/juryfaq#:~:text=Most%20jury%20trials%20last%203,be%20completed%20in%20one%20day
40 Mass. Gen. Laws ch. 234A, § 42 (n.d.).
41 The Third Branch. (2007). Federal courts aim to make jury service pleasant and informative. *The Third Branch*, *39*(1), 1–12.
42 Tait, T., & Funari, V. (2023). *Maricopa County Superior Court improves juror experience.* Judicial Branch of Arizona. https://superiorcourt.maricopa.gov/posts/press-releases/2023/maricopa-county-superior-court-improves-juror-experience/#:~:text=With%20compensation%20up%20to%20%24300,the%20Court's%20Jury%20Advisory%20Committee
43 American Bar Association. (2005). *Principles for juries and jury trials.* https://www.uscourts.gov/sites/default/files/aba_principles_for_juries_and_jury_trials_2005.pdf
44 Hannaford-Agor, P.L., & Moffett, M. (2024). *2023 State-of-the-states survey of jury improvement efforts: Jury operations in state courts.* National Center for State Courts. https://www.ncsc-jurystudies.org/__data/assets/pdf_file/0019/103825/2023-SOS-Jury-Ops.pdf
45 Hannaford-Agor, P.L., & Moffett, M. (2024). *2023 State-of-the-states, survey of jury improvement efforts: Jury operations in state courts.* National Center for State Courts. https://www.ncsc-jurystudies.org/__data/assets/pdf_file/0019/103825/2023-SOS-Jury-Ops.pdf
46 World Population Review. (2023, November 30). *Jury duty pay by state 2023.* https://worldpopulationreview.com/state-rankings/jury-duty-pay-by-state
47 Judicial Branch of California. (2025, July). *Jury service.* https://courts.ca.gov/courts/jury-service#:~:text=Juror%20Per%20Diems:,about%20your%20court's%20payment%20process

48 Hannaford-Agor, P.L., & Moffett, M. (2024). *2023 State-of-the-states, survey of jury improvement efforts: Jury operations in state courts.* National Center for State Courts. https://www.ncsc-jurystudies.org/__data/assets/pdf_file/0019/103825/2023-SOS-Jury-Ops.pdf
49 Administrative Office of the U.S. Courts. (2023, November 17). *Juror pay.* https://www.uscourts.gov/services-forms/jury-service/juror-pay
50 Fox 10 KSAZ. (2023, November 29). *Juror improvements at Maricopa County Superior Court (Phoenix, AZ).* [Video]. YouTube. https://www.youtube.com/watch?v=K6MMIv5uQiE
51 Tait, T., & Funari, V. (2023). *Maricopa County Superior Court improves juror experience.* Judicial Branch of Arizona. https://superiorcourt.maricopa.gov/posts/press-releases/2023/maricopa-county-superior-court-improves-juror-experience/#:~:text=With%20compensation%20up%20to%20%24300,the%20Court's%20Jury%20Advisory%20Committee
52 Tait, T., & Funari, V. (2023). *Maricopa County Superior Court improves juror experience.* Judicial Branch of Arizona. https://superiorcourt.maricopa.gov/posts/press-releases/2023/maricopa-county-superior-court-improves-juror-experience/#:~:text=With%20compensation%20up%20to%20%24300,the%20Court's%20Jury%20Advisory%20Committee
53 U.S. Code § 1871. (2023). *Fees.* Administrative Office of the U.S. Courts. https://www.uscourts.gov/services-forms/jury-service/juror-pay
54 Administrative Office of the U.S. Courts. (2023, November 17). *Juror pay.* https://www.uscourts.gov/services-forms/jury-service/juror-pay
55 National Center for State Courts (1998). *Through the eyes of the juror: A manual for addressing juror stress.* State Justice Institute. https://www.ncsc-jurystudies.org/data/assets/pdf_file/0022/7438/through-the-eyes-of-the-juror.pdf
56 American Bar Association. (2005). *Principles for juries and jury trials.* https://www.uscourts.gov/sites/default/files/aba_principles_for_juries_and_jury_trials_2005.pdf
57 Jury Selection and Service Act, 28 U.S.C. § 121 (1968).
58 Jury Selection and Service Act, 28 U.S.C. § 121 (1968).
59 Hannaford-Agor, P.L. & Moffett, M. (2024). *2023 State-of-the-states survey of jury improvement efforts: High profile trials.* National Center for State Courts. https://ncsc.contentdm.oclc.org/digital/collection/juries/id/382/rec/4
60 Chester County Justice Center. (2023, November 29). *Jury service information.* County of Chester. https://www.chesco.org/239/Jury-Service-Information
61 Superior Court of California. (2023, November 27). *Frequently asked questions.* County of San Bernardino. https://www.sb-court.org/jury-information/frequently-asked-questions
62 King County Superior Court. (2023, November 27). *Jury service—Frequently asked questions.* King County. https://kingcounty.gov/en/legacy/courts/superior-court/juror-information/faq
63 Northern District of California. (2023, November 27). *Jurors' frequently asked questions.* U.S. District Court. https://www.cand.uscourts.gov/jury-frequently-asked-questions
64 Chester County Justice Center. (2023, November 29). *Jury service information.* County of Chester. https://www.chesco.org/239/Jury-Service-Information
65 Northern District of Iowa. (2023, November 27). *Jurors' frequently asked questions.* U.S. District Court. https://www.iand.uscourts.gov/content/how-long-typical-jury-day-and-will-there-be-breaks
66 Chester County Justice Center. (2023, November 29). *Jury service information.* County of Chester. https://www.chesco.org/faq.aspx?TID=29#:~:text=What%20is%20the%20dress%20code,tee%20shirts%20are%20not%20suitable
67 Delaware Courts. (2023, November 20). *Frequently asked questions.* Delaware Judiciary. https://courts.delaware.gov/superior/jury/jury_faq.aspx
68 West Virginia Judiciary. (2023, November 17). *Jury service in West Virginia* [Video]. YouTube. https://www.youtube.com/watch?v=tIXehANFLP4
69 Southern District of Mississippi. (2023, November 20). *Petit jury information.* United States District Courts. https://www.mssd.uscourts.gov/petit-jury-information
70 Chester County Justice Center. (2023, November 29). *Jury service information.* County of Chester. https://www.chesco.org/faq.aspx?TID=29#:~:text=What%20is%20the%20dress%20code,tee%20shirts%20are%20not%20suitable
71 Fox 10 KSAZ. (2023, November 29). *Juror improvements at Maricopa County Superior Court (Phoenix, AZ)* [Video]. YouTube. https://www.youtube.com/watch?v=K6MMIv5uQiE
72 Pierce County, Washington. (2023, November 29). *Prohibited items while on jury duty.* Pierce County. https://www.piercecountywa.gov/3729/Prohibited-Items-while-on-Jury-Duty

6 Reporting for Jury Duty and Voir Dire

What Do You Think?

Before reviewing the concepts addressed in this chapter, answer True or False to each of the following questions or statements. Correct answers can be found at the end of Chapter 6.

1. Jurors are immediately assigned to a trial when they report to the courthouse for their jury service.
2. Prospective jurors are separated into groups and relocated to a courtroom to be further questioned by the judge and attorneys before a trial.
3. A trial attorney has a limited number of challenges for cause to use during the voir dire process.
4. The U.S. Supreme Court has allowed trial attorneys to use peremptory challenges without restriction.
5. Prospective jurors who object to being sworn in due to religious reasons can affirm their intent to act truthfully during the trial and deliberation without referencing God.

Learning Objectives

After reading this chapter, you will be able to:

1. Explain what occurs when a prospective juror reports to the courthouse for jury service.
2. Describe the voir dire process and its importance to trial outcomes.
3. List examples of challenge for cause and peremptory challenges.
4. Recognize the criticisms of peremptory challenges for empaneling a fair and impartial jury.
5. Understand the controversy associated with the swearing-in process.

Introduction

Summoning and qualifying prospective jurors is a critical first step of the jury selection process; however, it is only the first step. After qualified jurors report to the courthouse, they are questioned by the judge and attorneys in open court to determine whether they can serve fairly and impartially in a specific case. The questions are designed to identify potential conflicts of interest and biases by jurors. As noted in Chapter 2, the Sixth Amendment to the U.S. Constitution guarantees criminal defendants the right to trial "by an impartial jury." This stage of the jury selection process is called "voir dire." This term is most often translated as "to speak the truth" in reference to prospective jurors speaking candidly about their ability to serve impartially.[1]

DOI: 10.4324/9781003677796-8

Voir dire is more than a simple vetting process to identify fair and impartial jurors. Attorneys use voir dire strategically to identify and remove prospective jurors they believe are skeptical of their client's evidence, and to retain jurors who would be persuaded by it. The process is complicated by the mechanics of voir dire, which vary dramatically from state to state, court to court, and even judge to judge. These variations affect jurors' willingness and ability to respond candidly and completely. A major criticism of contemporary voir dire processes is the extent to which attorneys, in the absence of complete information, rely on assumptions and stereotypes to draw conclusions about juror impartiality, especially based on race and gender. The U.S. Supreme Court has ruled that attorneys cannot discriminate against African Americans or women in jury selection, yet critics argue that they continue to do so on a widespread basis.

In This Chapter

This chapter describes specific aspects of the American jury system. Here material will be reviewed related to: 1) what citizens can experience when arriving at the courthouse for jury service; 2) the role of trial attorneys during the voir dire process; 3) the options available for attorneys to strike prospective jurors from being empaneled on a jury; and 4) jurors' concerns about the swearing-in process.

Reporting for Jury Duty

Prospective jurors typically receive their jury summons four to six weeks before the date on which they are told to report for service. This gives jurors enough time to respond to the jury summons and the courts to confirm their eligibility and respond to exemption and excusal requests. The jury summons typically includes additional instructions for prospective jurors to confirm their reporting status before appearing at the courthouse in case the trial for which they were summoned has been postponed or cancelled. Jurors can either call a recorded telephone message or check the court's website. In addition, some courts send email or text messages to update jurors on their reporting instructions. If told to report as instructed in the summons, jurors should promptly arrive at the courthouse at the scheduled time.

Prospective jurors should prepare themselves for what they will see and experience once they arrive at the courthouse. Courthouses are public buildings that serve many functions for the community beyond jury trials and may be filled with busy people bustling about the building. Security is a primary concern in these facilities. Most courthouses will have security personnel monitoring the public entrances to prevent prohibited items from being brought into the courthouse, including weapons and, in some courts, cell phones. These are standard measures for the protection of all citizens as well as courthouse staff and legal professionals, including judges and attorneys. There is no reason to be alarmed by this; however, prospective jurors should realize these safety protocols may delay entry to the building. It is wise to arrive a few minutes early and be patient. Individuals will find that both patience and waiting are a large part of jury service.

Assembly Room

If the courthouse has a jury **assembly room**, prospective jurors are instructed to report to that location upon arriving at the courthouse. Many older courthouses do not have a jury assembly room, and jurors are usually directed to a courtroom for orientation. The area is designated specifically for prospective jurors reporting for jury service on a given day. The room or facility should be well marked in the courthouse and information about its exact location may have been provided with the juror summons material. Staff from the Jury Services

Office will be present in the assembly room to greet individuals as they arrive and will provide them with additional information.

Multiple purposes are served by having prospective jurors gather in a large group. First, each prospective juror will be asked to check in upon arrival, indicating they reported for the required jury service. Second, they will be issued a badge with a **juror identification number** displayed on it. Finally, they may be asked to complete an additional juror questionnaire that will be reviewed by the judge and trial attorneys. Box 6.1 provides an example of questions, adapted from the Chester County Justice Center, West Chester, Pennsylvania, that prospective jurors may be asked once they arrive at the assembly room.[2] Court staff will conduct a brief orientation about jury service in that court, including what to expect throughout the day. Some courts may show a juror orientation video that provides broad information about the courthouse, their role as a juror, and jury service in general. One complaint that jurors made was the extraordinary amount of time spent on this preliminary step of the jury selection process.[3]

While prospective jurors are waiting in the assembly room, staff from the Jury Services Office are quickly and diligently working behind the scenes. The staff are reviewing the list

Box 6.1 Sample Voir Dire questionnaire

Voir Dire Information
(Please Print)

Name ______________ Juror # ___________ Age ______________

City, Township, or Borough ________________
Marital Status _____ No. of Children _____ No. of Children Home _____
Education Level:
high school degree? Y/N
college degree? Y/N
graduate degree? Y/N

Previous Jury Duty? None/civil/criminal Disabilities, if any ___

Name of Employer ________________ Nature of Work ________________
(If retired, please state nature of work):

If spouse is employed, state their nature of work:

Do you drive a car? Y/N
Have you ever been involved in an auto accident? Y/N

If involved in an auto accident which resulted in a lawsuit, were you the plaintiff or the defendant?

Have you or any member of your immediate family been the *victim* of a crime? Y/N
If so, who, and what crime?

Have you, or a member of your immediate family, previously been *convicted* of a crime? Y/N
If so, who and what crime?

of individuals who reported for jury service that day and are randomly separating the pool of prospective jurors into smaller, manageable groups. These groups of prospective jurors are called **venires**.[4] Each venire may be assigned to a specific courtroom. If selected, all prospective jurors will be relocated to the courtroom for the next phase of the jury selection process. Inside the courtroom, traditionally, the trial judge first addresses the prospective jurors. This may vary by jurisdiction where the judge and trial attorneys both ask questions, or the attorneys dominate the questioning.

Voir Dire

The purpose of the voir dire is twofold. First, it is designed to identify jurors who can decide a case in a fair and impartial way.[5] This means that jurors who have a conflict of interest or who express explicit bias against one party would not be selected. The differences and challenges for determining jurors' explicit versus implicit bias against others will be discussed in the next chapter. The second purpose of the voir dire is related to equality for how jurors are selected from the venire. Each prospective juror has a constitutional right to be considered as a juror for the trial and should not be dismissed due to inappropriate practices by trial attorneys. This issue will be discussed further below related to the U.S. Supreme Court's finding in ***Batson v. Kentucky*** (1986).[6] In most jurisdictions, jurors who are not selected to serve on a trial after reporting to the courthouse are dismissed. Those who are selected will serve until the trial is over and a verdict is reached.

Typically, judges provide prospective jurors with information before beginning voir dire. The information shared may be nothing more than the type of case that is to be tried (e.g., criminal or civil). Next, the judge may ask questions to confirm prospective jurors' legal qualifications to serve. These inquiries were discussed in Chapter 4 related to eligibility requirements and may include age, citizenship, residency, English fluency, and criminal history. The judge may also inquire about personal hardships that an individual is experiencing that will make jury service difficult given their circumstances. The type of hardships that judges will accept as legitimate excuses to be released from jury service vary. Some judges are fairly lenient, but others are less accommodating.[7] As mentioned previously, hardships that may be considered as reasons for excusals include personal health–related issues (e.g., medications that impact one's concentration or focus), medical equipment needs, stress-related concerns, or responsibilities for the 24-hour medical care or supervision of a child, parent, or dependent.[8] Other hardships may be found acceptable by a court and are considered on an individual basis.

After the judge completes their preliminary review of jurors' ability to serve impartially, they may allow the attorneys to question prospective jurors.[9] The degree to which attorneys are permitted to question prospective jurors during voir dire varies from state to state, and between state and federal courts. Typically, federal judges provide attorneys much less opportunity to participate in voir dire, while state court judges permit attorneys greater latitude to explore jurors' backgrounds and attitudes.

> The defendant wants to hide the truth because he's generally guilty. The defense attorney's job is to make sure the jury does not arrive at that truth.
>
> —Alan Dershowitz, American Lawyer
> *The Best Defense* (1982)

The questions that trial attorneys ask during the voir dire process are crafted for a specific purpose. Each attorney is trying to empanel individual jurors who will favor their side and remove prospective jurors who have obvious or unconscious bias against their case.[10] This step of the jury selection process is critical for all trial attorneys. Some attorneys believe that cases are won or lost based solely on the jury selection process.[11] This perspective may oversimplify the matter, however. It is true that jurors' characteristics, like race, age, and gender, influence their perspectives about guilt or harm. This is an important reason why juries should be diverse and representative of the community.

Research reveals, however, that demographic characteristics alone are poor predictors of how jurors perceive trial evidence; the strength and clarity of the evidence presented inside the courtroom most influence the decision-making behavior of the average juror.[12] For example, evidence including DNA findings, witness testimony, audio and video recordings, heavily influences jurors' conclusions about guilt or fault.[13] Research findings from a study of 372 felony cases revealed trial evidence that was weak or ambiguous evidence, including conflicting testimony or low police credibility, resulted in hung juries for approximately six percent of cases.[14] When the trial evidence is evenly balanced or highly ambiguous, jurors' demographic characteristics may have a greater impact on their deliberations and the verdict.[15] This is rare however, and research clearly shows that the strength of the evidence is the main factor contributing to case outcomes.

It takes training and practice for trial attorneys to master the voir dire process. Their questions are designed to assess prospective jurors' attitudes, biases, or prejudices about a topic or a litigant. The lines of questioning are typically open-ended to better solicit subtle and nuanced aspects of an individual's psyche.[16] Attorneys may seek jurors who are assertive but not overbearing; who can speak their opinion but also listen to opinions of others; and who can rely on evidence, arguments, and instructions presented during trial without basing their decisions on preconceived and preexisting understanding of the law and legal proceedings.[17] Today, with the overabundance of television legal dramas, many jurors may enter jury service with possibly inaccurate perceptions about the courts and acceptable legal practices. The excerpt below was provided from a trial attorney who has experience working with jurors from civil cases. Box 6.2 describes her experiences and the importance of the jury selection process and how attorneys decide which jurors to empanel from those available in the venire.

The open-ended responses that prospective jurors provide attorneys during the voir dire is one way to determine their overall attitudes, biases, and prejudices. Social psychology

Box 6.2: From the Field

Name: Julie Pfaff

Position: Attorney

How long have you worked as a civil lawyer?
I have been an attorney for 20 years.

How important is the voir dire process for a trial attorney and to the outcome of a case?
Very important. While it is the job of the trial attorney to present facts and evidence in a way that is most favorable to their client, jurors (like everyone) evaluate facts and evidence based on their own experiences and biases. If a juror is prejudiced—against a person or set of circumstances—they are

less likely to apply the law fairly. For example, if a juror believes that a woman should not work outside of the home, their own prejudices may not allow them to impartially consider a case involving a professional woman with an important position in the workplace.

What are the main things you look for when selecting prospective jurors to serve on a jury trial?

To begin, it's important to remember that the job of an attorney is to be a zealous advocate for their client. For that reason, my first objective when evaluating prospective jurors is to remove prospective jurors who may be biased *against* my client. My second objective is to seat jurors who are biased *in favor* of my client. My third objective is to seat jurors who are neutral, showing no bias, one way or another.

In most circumstances, attorneys have only a brief opportunity to evaluate prospective jurors, and so they are often forced to make quick decisions based on a limited amount of information. In this case, the attorney's own biases and stereotypes can affect their decision-making process. For that reason, I have found that it is beneficial to have two attorneys participate in the jury selection process because they can challenge one another's assumptions and biases and engage in a dialogue about prospective jurors.

research on actual jurors, however, showed neither the prosecutors nor defense attorneys selected or rejected jurors based solely on observed personality traits (openness to experience, neuroticism, extraversion, conscientiousness, and agreeableness);[18] rather, trial attorneys are also trained to observe nonverbal behaviors and cues. Examples of nonverbal communication may include facial expressions, body movements, and eyerolling. Attorneys will look for patterns among nonverbal responses as additional indicators to determine conscious or unconscious biases that a prospective juror may have.[19] Other nonverbal factors exist and can provide attorneys with valuable information or a best guess about how an individual may react, if seated in a jury. These include basic demographic characteristics, such as race, age, and gender.

Trial attorneys may believe that jurors' social background characteristics are important nonverbal cues to consider. Social science researchers have recognized for some time that a research subject's characteristics may impact on how they respond to certain stimuli;[20] therefore, juror characteristics may predict how a prospective juror will respond to questions during the voir dire and how they might perceive evidence presented during a trial proceeding. It is imperative that attorneys be familiar with research about the differences among attitudes and beliefs by juror demographic characteristics and other considerations, including education and specialized training, socioeconomic status, religious beliefs, etc.[21] Attorneys who represent powerful law firms may be equipped financially to hire **trial consultants** to aid in the jury selection process.[22] These consultants are trained in the social and behavioral sciences and provide advice to attorneys about how certain jurors might react to specific evidence and the level of influence they might exert over other empaneled jurors. Box 6.3 describes developments in the field of jury consulting and opportunities for citizens to become involved in **mock jury research** trials. Box 6.4 features a trial consultant who shares his experiences related to the voir dire process and conducting mock jury trials.

> There's a lot of money with a lot of big law firms that have a tremendous amount at stake by getting the right language to convince the right jury that my client is either innocent or that the opposition is guilty.
>
> —Frank Luntz, American Politician
> *The Persuaders* (2004)

Box 6.3: Trial Consultant Industry

The earliest accounts of trial consulting were from the 1970s when academics applied social and behavioral research findings to the courtroom and legal profession. They conducted survey research with members of the community to assess attitudes and biases for the purpose of tailoring jury selection in high profile cases.[23] From the 1980s through the 1990s, trial consultants expanded their services beyond conducting simple surveys to inform jury selection to use more sophisticated data collection strategies and services, including one-on-one interviews, paneled focus groups, and witness preparation.[24]

Another technique used by trial consultants is the mock jury trial. These tasks can be performed online or in-person, and the entire process is recorded so that lawyers can see, hear, and study the real-world reactions that mock jurors have to each piece of evidence, testimony, and attorney argument before the case goes to trial. Mock jurors are compensated for their time and the amount provided ranges from a few dollars to several hundred dollars depending on the type of case, length of time commitment, and specific activities they are asked to perform. The popularity of trial consulting expanded from 1980–1990 to include less high-profile criminal and civil cases as social science research became more acceptable and viewed as a viable, data-driven strategy for obtaining a favorable verdict. While consultant services can impact verdicts, their influence is not a guarantee of a specific outcome. As mentioned, verdicts are heavily impacted by the strength and quality of evidence and the clarity of presentation inside the courtroom.

Since 2000, trial consulting has continued to expand. Now, technology allows for more assessments of individual implicit bias and attitudes. Research has revealed trial consultants were involved with

> identifying juror beliefs and attitudes that could be favorable to the case (72 percent); developing the case theme, theory, and messaging (64 percent); assisting in selecting jurors during voir dire (59 percent); conducting mock trials (41 percent); and preparing clients/witnesses for trial (28 percent).[25]

Trial consultants have been criticized for the services they provide. For example, jury-rigging or stacking the jury with individuals assessed to be favoring one side has been perceived as unethical and counter to the notion of an impartial jury, which is a hallmark of the American jury system.[26] Critics advise caution about providing one's client with an advantage inside the courtroom so that they still maintain equity and fairness in the justice system.

Box 6.4: From the Field

Name: Richard Gabriel

Position: President, Decision Analysis, Inc.

Location: California

From your perspective, why is the voir dire process such an important part of a trial? What difference can it make in the outcome of a case?

Jurors are the factfinders in a case. Each juror uses their own life experiences and belief systems to interpret and judge the evidence and the law. Voir dire, if done effectively, is an opportunity for the attorneys and the judge to learn as much as they can about the most important people in the trial. The more the attorneys know about the jurors, the more they can exercise their cause and peremptory strikes wisely and tailor their case presentations to the chosen jurors. The wiser that counsel is in selecting a jury, the more likely they will have an audience that will be receptive to their case.

Attorneys often worry about jurors' hidden biases. What strategies do trial consultants use to help identify when someone might not be truly impartial?

We design questionnaires and voir dire questions to get jurors to disclose personal experiences, opinions, and beliefs that might affect how they listen objectively to a case. We also train attorneys to ask questions in a particular way to prompt candid disclosure. The courts and attorneys do not have a very good understanding about how bias affects decision making, so the design of questions and how you ask them is critical to understanding a juror's thought process. That will give the parties and courts a better idea about whether a juror truly has a bias that would impair their ability to be fair and impartial.

The chapter mentions mock juries and surveys. How do these tools help you and the attorneys you work with better understand how real jurors might react to a case?

Mock trials and surveys help attorneys to understand how lay jurors translate the evidence and legal instructions they are supposed to use to reach a verdict into a story that makes sense to them. These projects tell attorneys about the strengths and weaknesses in their case, as well as confusing issues they need to clarify for the jury. They are also a valuable tool for attorneys and their clients to accurately assess their chances of success at trial. More and more, mock trials, focus groups, and surveys are also used in mediations for settlement purposes.

Trial consultants do not just help with picking jurors. What other services do you provide to attorneys, and how do they affect the way a case is presented?

Trial consultants provide a number of different research and consulting services. We conduct jury research in the form of mock trials, focus groups, and surveys. We assist witnesses to communicate more effectively in deposition and trial. We help attorneys develop case themes and assist them in putting together trial presentations for opening statement and closing arguments, and even mediations. In some instances, we can conduct shadow juries during a trial, as well as monitor the trial to help the attorneys make adjustments to how the jurors may be reacting to the case.

Attorneys have several other options available to them to determine whether a prospective juror is suitable to serve on a particular case. First, if the court administered a voir dire questionnaire with the juror qualification questionnaire (JQQ), they have access to those written responses. These forms may provide attorneys with valuable information about relevant life experiences that occurred in the distant past during jurors' childhood and more recent events and situations they are coping with as adults. Their life experiences could affect their interpretation and opinions about evidence presented at trial and their decision-making during the jury deliberation.

Attorneys must be thorough and mindful to inquire about all incidents of personal physical and emotional abuse that might be relevant to issues likely to arise at trial. In a case involving a physical assault, attorneys are likely to ask whether jurors or their close friends or family have been victims of violent crime, or have been accused of committing assault themselves.[27] Trial attorneys will likely not want to select a juror whose lived experiences could cause bias or prejudice against their side, or whose life experiences could trigger an emotional response during the trial proceedings or during the deliberation with fellow jurors.[28]

Finally, attorneys have another way to screen for suitable prospective jurors. Today, online searches of social media accounts allow attorneys direct access to what prospective jurors have posted or written about related to current events and other issues. These personalized accounts may provide attorneys with information about prospective jurors' personal interests, hobbies, political leanings, family and homelife, and religious beliefs.[29] Information included on publicly accessible websites and accessed through a simple browser search is a contemporary method that trial attorneys could use to learn more about a prospective juror during the voir dire process. These simple searches can provide instant information that can facilitate an attorney's decision to empanel a juror in their trial or to remove them from the venire as quickly as possible. It should be noted that in more than half of jury trials, attorneys do not get the names of prospective jurors until the day of trial or even until the voir dire begins in the courtroom;[30] therefore, attorneys often do not have enough time to do an extensive, or any, social media search on a prospective juror.

Some objections have been made about trial attorneys conducting social media searches of prospective jurors during the jury selection process. Concerns were raised about an individual's right to privacy and the possibility that prospective jurors may feel intimidated or coerced knowing background searches were conducted on them by the trial attorneys. These issues might be brought out later, if there is an appeal of the trial's outcome.[31] In many states, local court rules specify whether internet searches of prospective jurors are permitted and, if so, parameters for what information and sources can be explored.

In most cases, jury selection takes place relatively quickly, so attorneys have limited time in which to draw conclusions about the suitability of prospective jurors. Generally, voir dire accounts for 10–20 percent of the total trial length in criminal trials[32] and less than 10 percent in civil trials.[33] Consequently, the median length of voir dire is three hours in capital felony trials, two hours in noncapital felony and civil trials, and one hour in misdemeanor trials.

Juror (De)Selection

After the judge and attorneys have interviewed the prospective jurors and gathered information about their backgrounds, attitudes, and beliefs, the jury selection process moves into its last phase: removing individual jurors from the venire who the judge or an attorney concludes cannot serve fairly and impartially. At this point in the process, jurors can be removed through a **challenge for cause** or a **peremptory challenge**.

Challenge for Cause

A challenge for cause occurs when either the trial judge determines or an attorney makes a formal motion to remove a prospective juror on grounds that they are statutorily ineligible, they have an impermissible conflict of interest, or they exhibited bias or prejudice against one of the parties in their responses to voir dire questions. The juror can be removed by the trial judge on their own authority, or the judge can grant an attorney's motion to remove the juror for cause. In addition to qualification criteria, most states and the federal courts have statutes or court rules that require the removal of jurors who have significant conflicts of interest that might affect their decision-making, including having a close personal, family, or professional relationship with one of the parties, witnesses, or trial participants. In addition, prospective jurors who have personal knowledge about facts of the case can be removed. Finally, a prospective juror might be removed for cause for expressing overt prejudice or bias in their responses to voir dire questions. The trial judge must remove a prospective juror for cause if they find a reasonable doubt that the juror can serve fairly and impartially. There is no preset limit on the number of jurors who can be removed for cause.[34]

Peremptory Challenge

The second way a trial attorney can remove a prospective juror from the venire is by exercising a peremptory challenge. In federal courts and in all states except Arizona, attorneys are authorized to remove a defined number of prospective jurors without stating a reason.[35] An attorney may remove a juror simply because they question how an individual juror will vote or how they will influence other jurors. If an attorney's original challenge for cause was rejected by the judge, the juror may still be excused through the attorney's use of a peremptory challenge. Ultimately, attorneys will use their limited number of peremptory challenges to remove prospective jurors who they believe will favor the other side.[36] Indeed, legal professionals and academics may instruct attorneys to "reserve peremptory challenges for striking the jurors most hostile to a client's case who cannot successfully be challenged for cause."[37]

The exact number of peremptory challenges trial attorneys are allowed varies between jurisdictions and the type of case that is being considered. For example, in the federal court system, in criminal cases where the crime is punishable by death, 20 peremptory challenges are allowed by both sides; when the maximum sentence exceeds one year, the prosecutor is allowed six challenges and the defense is allowed 10 challenges.[38] If the punishment is less than one year or in a civil trial involving a fine, each side is given three peremptory challenges.[39] Additional challenges may be issued depending upon the nature of the case.[40]

The state court systems have their own variations concerning peremptory challenges. For example, in California each trial attorney may be given up to 10 peremptory challenges in criminal cases. If it is a capital trial or a case where life imprisonment is a possibility, attorneys are given 20 challenges. For civil cases, however, the number of peremptory challenges is far more limited, only six per side.[41] In Pennsylvania, the prosecutor and defense attorney each has seven challenges in noncapital felony cases, while in misdemeanor cases each side has five challenges.[42] Figure 6.3 describes other state variations for the number of peremptory challenges allowed in civil, misdemeanor, and noncapital felony cases.

In many states, the number of challenges also varies depending upon the number of defendants. Unless they are needed in another jury trial, jurors who are removed, either through a challenge for cause or a peremptory challenge, are dismissed from jury service. Although they did not serve on an actual trial, they have successfully completed their civic responsibility

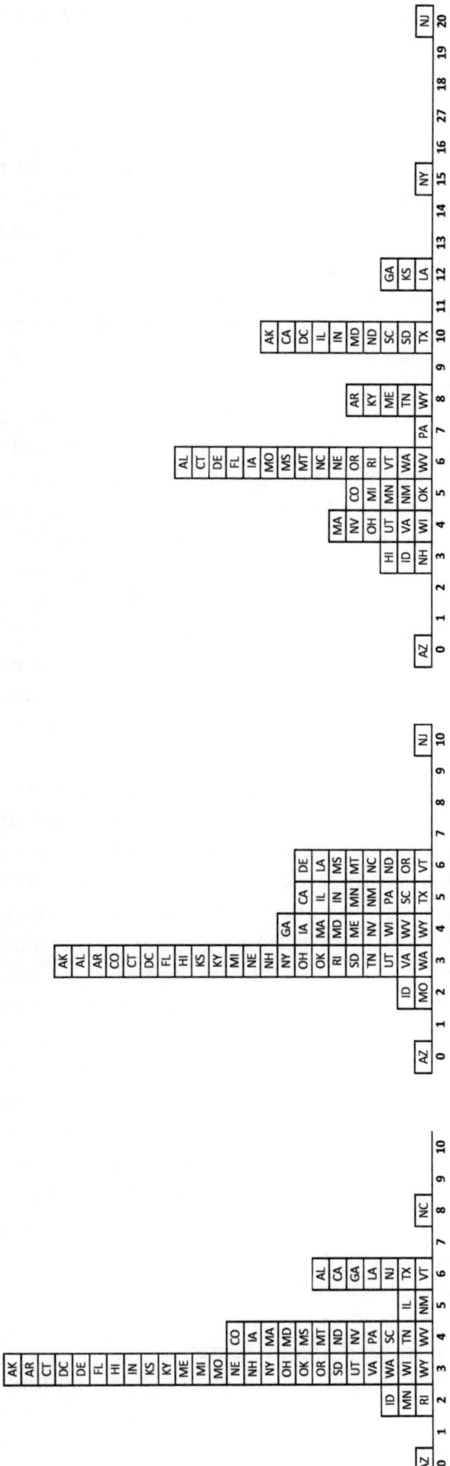

Figure 6.3: Peremptory Challenges

(*Source:* National Center for State Courts.[43])

to the courts and their community. In many jurisdictions, they will not have to serve again for one to two years, or longer.

Criticism of Peremptory Challenges

The use of peremptory challenges in the juror selection process is controversial and has been criticized for some time. The debate relates to an attorney's request to have a prospective juror removed without specifying a clear reason. Critics have argued, and cases have been appealed to the U.S. Supreme Court, that attorneys routinely use their peremptory challenges to exclude people of color from the jury. It should be noted that it is perfectly legal to use peremptory challenges to try to produce a jury that favors the attorney's client; what is impermissible is to use such challenges to exclude jurors on the basis of race or gender, which may or may not produce an unfair jury.

The U.S. Supreme Court considered the discriminatory use of peremptory challenges in *Batson v. Kentucky*.[44] Briefly, James K. Batson, an African American, was arrested and charged with burglary and receipt of stolen goods. He was tried by jury in the Circuit Court of Jefferson County, Kentucky. At Batson's original trial, the trial judge oversaw juror dismissals for cause and allowed the trial attorneys to dismiss other jurors using their peremptory challenges. The prosecuting attorney removed "all four black persons on the venire,"[45] which left an all-White jury to deliberate about Batson's guilt. Despite his defense attorney's objection that the removal of all Black jurors violated the Sixth Amendment right to an impartial jury and the Fourteenth Amendment right to equal protection under the law, the trial judge denied the objection. The jury convicted Batson on both charges. Batson appealed the convictions to the Kentucky Supreme Court, which affirmed the trial court's decision.

The U.S. Supreme Court reviewed Batson's appeal and reached its decision in 1986. In a 7–2 decision, the Court ruled that eliminating jurors from the venire due to race violated the defendant's equal protection rights guaranteed in the Fourteenth Amendment. This decision showed that a defendant's right to an impartial jury required that jury selection be free from racial discrimination. The Court also concluded in *Batson* that intentionally dismissing jurors based on race violated a citizen's equal protection right to serve as a trial juror, undermining public confidence in the justice system, including the legitimacy of jury verdicts.[46]

The *Batson* decision was relatively narrow insofar that it only prohibited prosecutors from using peremptory challenges to exclude Black jurors in cases in which the defendant was Black. In the following years, the U.S. Supreme Court took up a series of cases extending *Batson* to a broader set of circumstances. In *Powers v. Ohio* (1991), for example, the Court clarified that prosecutors could not exclude jurors on the basis of race regardless of the race of the defendant.[47] In *Edmonson v. Leesville Concrete Company* (1991), it extended *Batson*'s prohibition on the discriminatory use of peremptory challenges to civil cases.[48] In *Georgia v. McCollum* (1992), it ruled that criminal defendants were similarly prohibited from using peremptory challenges to exclude jurors on the basis of race.[49]

The impact of having a racially diverse jury is critically important in death penalty cases. Box 6.5 highlights research findings about empaneling only death-qualified jurors in capital cases where the jury may impose a death sentence. Of note, each of these decisions was grounded in the understanding that the Fourteenth Amendment, enacted following the Civil War to guarantee the rights of citizenship to previously enslaved people, was designed to address racial discrimination. In ***J.E.B. v. Alabama***, the Court extended *Batson* to

Box 6.5: Death-Qualified Jurors

Death qualification occurs during the voir dire process in a capital case when trial attorneys assess whether a prospective juror can consider all sentencing options, including imposing the death penalty, for a defendant who was found guilty and convicted of a capital crime. Today, eligibility to serve on a capital trial is based on a jurors' ability to perform their duties without allowing personal views about capital punishment to impair their decision-making behavior. This standard was set by the U.S. Supreme Court in *Wainwright v. Witt* (1985)[50] and was a stricter standard for qualification in death penalty cases than the previous standard set in *Witherspoon v. Illinois* (1968)[51] when only jurors who could not, under any circumstances, impose a death sentence were excused. The current death qualification practice has been criticized for excluding prospective jurors who are opposed to the death penalty. Research has shown that jurors who have fewer qualms about the death penalty are also more likely to convict and impose a death sentence. Critics referred to these individuals as "automatic death penalty" jurors.[52]

Research also addresses concerns about fair representation and reducing bias in capital cases. Selecting only death qualified-jurors disproportionately excludes Black jurors, who disproportionately oppose the death penalty as a sanctioning option. Less diverse juries, comprised predominantly of White jurors, often resulted in a higher rate of conviction and death sentences, especially when the defendants were Black. Moreover, death-qualified jurors are less likely to consider mitigating factors (family background, mental health issues, etc.), while focusing more on aggravating factors.[53] Other research findings showed capital jurors struggled to understand sentencing guidelines. This very well could "impair their decision-making," which was determined to be an essential aspect of a death-qualified juror.[54]

cases involving gender discrimination.[55] The case involved the defendant withholding child support payments from a mother and a minor child. The prosecuting attorney used their peremptory challenges to strike nine of the 10 prospective male jurors during the voir dire process. The defense argued on appeal that the removal of jurors based on gender violated the equal protection guarantee of the Fourteenth Amendment, like dismissing jurors based on race. The Supreme Court agreed and applied the same reasoning as it did in *Batson*. The Justices found that juror strikes based on gender may impede the defendant's right to a fair and impartial trial.

The legitimate use of peremptory challenges regarding race and gender is still debated today. One study with actual jurors found that prosecutors may be more likely to excuse prospective jurors who are young, male, and employed; however, the study also revealed race effects in peremptory challenges. For example, in criminal cases, prosecutors were more likely to strike prospective jurors who were African American, while the defense attorneys removed Caucasian jurors. The findings were extreme, with 47.5 percent of prosecutors' peremptory challenges going to strike African Americans compared to only 9.9 percent from the defense counsel.[56] These findings were consistent with other research findings that showed an association between how trial attorneys use peremptory challenges and the racial characteristics of the juror.

In the late 1990s, one study found that prosecutors in criminal cases from North Carolina used 60 percent of their peremptory challenges on African American jurors compared to only 23 percent from the defense.[57] A second study involving felony cases conducted in North Carolina some 20 years later uncovered similar practices. Specifically, results from the analysis of jury pool data throughout the state showed that each peremptory challenge used by the prosecution was "associated with a 2.4–2.9 percentage point increase in the conviction rate for black defendants."[58] Opponents, like former U.S. Supreme Court Justice Thurgood Marshall, who wrote a concurring opinion in the *Batson* decision, called for eliminating peremptory challenges from the American jury system altogether.[59] Critics have argued that having peremptory challenges in the arsenal for trial attorneys will facilitate discriminatory practices that may exclude certain ethnic groups from a jury panel.[60] Box 6.6 describes efforts taken by the states of Washington and Arizona to radically change the use of peremptory challenges in their state court systems.

> Ending racial discrimination in jury selection can be accomplished only by eliminating peremptory challenges entirely.
>
> —Thurgood Marshall, Former Justice of U.S. Supreme Court (1967–1991)
> *Batson v. Kentucky*, 476 U.S. 79 (1986)

Box 6.6: Changes to Peremptory Challenge Use in Washington and Arizona

Washington

In 2018, Washington State implemented General Rule 37 (GR37) to reduce racial bias in jury selection resulting from trial attorneys' discriminatory use of peremptory challenges. GR 37 did not eliminate peremptory challenges but added a layer of review or scrutiny to identify implicit or explicit biased decision-making.[61] For example, removing jurors based on prior contact with law enforcement; mistrust of law enforcement; relationships with criminally involved persons; residing in a high-crime neighborhood; state benefit recipients; and juror behavior (inattentiveness, poor demeanor) were presumptively invalid reasons to remove jurors because they are linked with racially discriminatory practices.

GR37 also instructed judges to use an objective observer test to assess whether a peremptory challenge was used discriminatorily instead of relying on their subjective assessment of the lawyers' intent. That test specifies that if an objective observer, who is knowledgeable of conscious or unconscious biases, would conclude that race or ethnicity was a factor in the use of a peremptory challenge, it should be disallowed. Washington was the first state to use this objective framework to evaluate the removal of prospective jurors based on racially and ethnically motivated peremptory challenges.

Arizona

In 2021, the Arizona Supreme Court received two petitions to consider reforming that state's peremptory challenge protocols. One petition was to implement a version of Washington's GR 37, while the second petition called for eliminating peremptory challenges altogether. The Arizona Supreme Court voted to eliminate peremptory challenges from the Arizona court system effective January 1, 2022.

Multiple studies are underway to examine the effects of eliminating peremptory challenges. The main research questions are: 1) Will the elimination of peremptory challenges increase the demographic diversity of jury panels? 2) Does increased jury diversity equalize conviction rates for Black and White defendants? 3) Do judges allow more time for lawyers to ask questions and identify potential bias? 4) Do attorneys raise challenges for cause more frequently, and do judges grant those challenges more often or initiate more removals for cause themselves? and 5) What impact, if any, would the rule change have on jury operations, including the size of venire panels?[62]

Changes implemented in Washington and Arizona have caught the attention of advocates and legislatures in other states, including California, Connecticut, and New Jersey, to consider reforming their own jury selection processes to reduce racial and ethnic discriminatory practices.

Table 6.1: Summary of Racial and Gender Equality for Jury Selection

Case	*Decided*	*Opinion*
Batson v. Kentucky 476 U.S. 79	April 30, 1986	Excluding ethnic groups through peremptory challenge violated the Equal Protection Clause of the Fourteenth Amendment; discrimination needs only to be shown in individual cases, not systematically.
J.E.B. v. Alabama **511 U.S. 127**	April 19, 1994	Equal protection under the law prohibits exclusion from jury service based on gender; explicit bias cannot be assumed based on juror gender.

Sworn In

The voir dire process concludes when the appropriate number of jurors and alternates are selected for the trial. In most jurisdictions, after the voir dire, the selected individuals will be **sworn in** as jurors. The purpose of the oath is to emphasize the importance of jury service. In Pennsylvania, the oath includes,

> You do solemnly swear by Almighty God and those of you who affirm do declare and affirm that you will well and truly try the issue joined between the Commonwealth and the defendant(s), and a true verdict render according to the evidence.[63]

In Michigan, jurors serving on criminal trials are asked to take the following oath:

> You shall well and truly try, and true deliverance make, between the people of this state and the prisoner at bar, whom you shall have in charge, according to the evidence and the laws of this state; so help you God.[64]

Like in Pennsylvania, the reference to God is present in Michigan's oath statement. Jurors who object to being sworn in for religious reasons may **affirm** that they will be truthful in both the trial and deliberation processes by substituting the words, "This you do under the pains and penalties of perjury" for the words "so help you God."[65] Many states allow the alternative to affirm without referencing God.[66] Box 6.7 provides another example of swearing-in instructions provided to trial jurors who perform jury service in the state of California, while Box 6.8 describes a case from the state of Texas where a trial juror objected to any statement of oath or affirmation under the right of Free Exercise guarantee in the Bill of Rights.

Box 6.7: Juror's Oath in California

In California, before the oath is given, the judge may emphasize the importance of jury service and that jurors should seriously consider the responsibility they are about to undertake. Swearing the oath "means you give your word to reach your verdict upon only the evidence ... and the court's instructions about the law ... Remember that your role as a juror is as important as the judge's in making sure that justice is done." After this instruction, individual jurors are asked to take the following oath:

Do you, and each of you, understand and agree that you will well and truly try the cause now pending before this court, and a true verdict render according only to the evidence presented to you and to the instructions of the court?[67]

Box 6.8: *Society of Separationists, Inc. v. Herman*[68]

On December 15, 1987, a prospective juror, Robin Murray-O'Hair, was participating in jury selection for a trial court in Texas. During the voir dire process, she was asked to take an oath to be sworn in as a juror. She refused, indicating she was an atheist and objected to the phrase, "so help me God" contained in the oath. The presiding *judge* acknowledged the juror's objection and asked her to make an affirmation that she would be truthful, without mentioning God. She refused, claiming that affirming was still "religious" in nature. The judge held her in civil contempt and jailed her for three days. Upon release she brought a civil rights action lawsuit against both the judge and court alleging her right to the Free Exercise of Religion was violated.[69]

The case was taken to the United States Court of Appeals (Fifth Circuit). The Court found the juror's "right to Free Exercise guaranteed by the First and Fourteenth Amendments" was violated.[70] The Court indicated that, "when a judge is confronted with a prospective juror's refusal, on grounds of constitutionally protected beliefs, to swear or affirm to answer voir dire questions truthfully, the judge should either allow the person to withdraw from jury duty without penalty or allow the prospective juror an alternative that requires him or her to make some form of serious public commitment to answer truthfully that does not transgress the prospect's sincerely held beliefs.[71] Moreover, the *Herman* Court found that a juror (or witness at trial) may be allowed "to draft his own personalized commitment to tell the truth whenever he finds the usual oath of affirmation offensive."[72]

Conclusion

The process for selecting a fair and impartial jury from the community has been a controversial issue in the American jury system since its inception during colonial times. Identifying prospective jurors who are qualified to serve on a jury is simply the first step. As described in this chapter, jurors who meet the qualification criteria still must face questioning from the judge and trial attorneys about their lived experiences, attitudes, values, and beliefs that could signify explicit or implicit prejudice. Trial attorneys themselves want to choose jurors who will be favorable to their side and may rely on instinct, as much as empirical evidence, to decide which juror will be best for them.

The dismissal of individual jurors based on either their race or gender has been particularly problematic. The long history and broad reach of racial discrimination in the U.S. suggests such prejudice would infiltrate the jury system. The use of peremptory challenges allows trial attorneys great discretion for removing jurors and for hiding the true reasons for doing so, including using the race and gender of the individual. The criticisms against the use of peremptory challenges are unlikely to go away, despite the instructions provided by the U.S. Supreme Court that such decisions were unconstitutional. The inherent likelihood of discriminatory practices will facilitate continued criticism and urge some to seek abandoning the practice altogether.

Despite these controversies, eventually some jurors must be empaneled and seated in a jury. The next chapter focuses on those jurors who were selected to serve on a jury trial. The instructions that a judge provides to jurors prior to the voir dire process, if any, and the instructions provided at the time of being sworn in are not the only instructions given to jurors during the trial process. Next, the jury instructions will be described in greater detail, including tracing the history of jury instructions that were used in the past in England to the current practices, controversies, and criticisms of the modern jury instructions used in the American jury system today.

Summary

This chapter addressed the experiences that prospective jurors may have when they report to the courthouse on their assigned jury duty day. Many jurors will gather in the juror assembly room or other gathering space to complete additional questionnaires and receive instructions about the jury selection process. Some individuals are dismissed at this point, while others are relocated to a courtroom for further questioning by a judge and trial attorneys. This process, referred to as the voir dire, involves trial attorneys selecting jurors who may be favorable to their side, while removing jurors who have conscious or unconscious bias against their party. The voir dire is critically important, and some law firms hire jury consultants to assist in the juror selection process, among other trial processes. Research indicates the personality characteristics of the jurors empaneled do not impact the outcome of the case as much as the quality and strength of the evidence presented inside the courtroom during the trial.

Trial attorneys are given opportunities to strike prospective jurors from being empaneled through a series of challenges for cause or through use of a peremptory challenge. Attorneys have an unlimited number of challenges for cause arguments, but only a limited number of peremptory challenges depending upon the jurisdiction where the trial is being held and the type of case that is being tried. Some states, for example, limited or eliminated the practice of peremptory challenges. The U.S. Supreme Court found that trial attorneys may not use an individual's race or gender as a legitimate reason to strike prospective jurors from being empaneled. Critics argue that, despite the Court's decisions, peremptory challenges are still used in discriminatory ways to empanel juries who are not fair and impartial to all defendants. Once all jurors have been selected, they are sworn in to serve on a jury, and the trial begins.

Discussion Questions

1. Ethical consideration. Should trial attorneys be allowed to conduct internet searches, including examining personal social media accounts of prospective jurors during the voir dire process? Is this fair practice? Why or why not? Would having the court's permission to conduct internet searches favor one side or the other (e.g., the prosecutor or defense attorney)? How would you feel if you found out trial attorneys were reviewing your social media accounts during the jury selection process?
2. Ethical consideration. Do you believe all attorneys use peremptory challenges *appropriately* to provide their side with an advantage during the trial and to reach a desired outcome? How do restrictions on the use of peremptory challenges conflict with the goals of an attorney to win their case?
3. Ethical consideration. What do you think about the use of peremptory challenges during the voir dire process? Should the American jury system allow attorneys to use peremptory challenges during the voir dire, or remove that option as suggested by former U.S. Supreme Court Justice Thurgood Marshall?
4. Religious beliefs were used to determine guilt or innocence in trials by ordeal (Chapter 1) and were shown in this chapter related to taking an oath or swearing-in of trial jurors. What concerns (if any) do you have with a requirement to take an oath or to be sworn in to serve on a jury trial? Are you aware of any other aspects of the American jury system that evokes religion or religious beliefs?

Review Questions

1. What should a prospective juror expect to experience when entering a courthouse on their assigned jury duty day? What occurs inside the juror assembly room?
2. What are the roles of the presiding judge and trial attorneys during the voir dire process? What are the benefits and criticisms of the voir dire process?
3. What options does a trial attorney have for striking a prospective juror from being empaneled? What are the advantages and criticisms associated with these options?

Answers to Chapter 6 "What Do You Think?" Questions

1. False. Jurors report to a jury assembly room or other gathering area to sign in, complete additional questionnaires, and are determined eligible for service by courthouse administrators.
2. True. This process for pooling juries is referred to as a venire.
3. False. Attorneys have unlimited use of challenges for cause but have a limited number of peremptory challenges that vary by jurisdiction and case type.
4. False. The Court found that race and gender are not legitimate reasons to strike a prospective juror from a jury panel.
5. True. The Free Exercise guarantee of the First and Fourteenth Amendments allow jurors to affirm their intentions without referencing religious content or mentioning God.

Key Terms

assembly room
affirm
Batson v. Kentucky
challenge for cause
J.E.B. v. Alabama
juror identification number
mock jury research
peremptory challenge
sworn in
trial consultants
venires

References

1 Hannaford-Agor, P.L., & Moffett, M. (2024). *2023 State-of-the-states survey of jury improvement efforts: Voir dire practices in U.S. courts.* National Center for State Courts. https://ncsc.contentdm.oclc.org/digital/collection/juries/id/363/rec/10
2 Chester County Justice Center. (2023, November 29). *Jury service information.* County of Chester. https://www.chesco.org/faq.aspx?TID=29#:~:text=What%20is%20the%20dress%20code,tee%20shirts%20are%20not%20suitable
3 National Center for State Courts. (2009). *Jury managers' toolbox: Best practices for effective juror utilization.* https://www.ncsc-jurystudies.org/__data/assets/pdf_file/0017/7505/juror-utilization-best-practices.pdf
4 Winfree, T.L., Mays, L.G., & Alarid, L.F. (2022). *Introduction to criminal justice: The essentials* (3rd ed., p. 205). Aspen Publishing.
5 Hans, V.P., & Alayna, J. (2003) *Avoid bald men and people with green socks? Other ways to improve the voir dire process in jury selection.* Cornell Law Faculty Publications, paper 298. http://scholarship.law.cornell.edu/facpub/298
6 *Batson v. Kentucky*, 476 U.S. 79 (1986).
7 11Alive. (2023, July 11). *Trump Georgia: Judge explains grand jury selection process to potential grand jurors* [Video]. YouTube. https://www.youtube.com/watch?v=ri6rEEdj1OQ
8 Hans, V.P., & Alayna, J. (2003) *Avoid bald men and people with green socks? Other ways to improve the voir dire process in jury selection.* Cornell Law Faculty Publications, paper 298. http://scholarship.law.cornell.edu/facpub/298
9 Hannaford-Agor, P.L., & Moffett, M. (2024). *2023 State-of-the-states survey of jury improvement efforts: Voir dire practices in U.S. courts.* National Center for State Courts. https://ncsc.contentdm.oclc.org/digital/collection/juries/id/363/rec/10
10 Winfree, T.L., Mays, L.G., & Alarid, L.F. (2022). *Introduction to criminal justice: The essentials* (3rd ed., p. 205). Aspen Publishing.
11 Tam, J.S. (2020). *Jury selection in federal court.* Thomson Reuters. https://www.dechert.com/content/dam/dechert%20files/knowledge/publication/2020/5/Jury-Selection-in-Federal-Court.pdf
12 Courtroom Sciences. (2023, March 22). *Two of the top factors that influence jury decision-making.* www.courtroomsciences.com
13 Vaughan, T.J., Miller, M.K., & Nemeth, R.J. (2018). What evidence matters to jurors? The prevalence and importance of different homicide trial evidence to mock jurors. *PMC*, *39*(3), 247–262.
14 Waters, N.L., Hans, V.P., & Hannaford-Agor, P.L. (2009). A jury of one: Opinion formation, conformity, and dissent on juries. *Journal of Empirical Legal Studies*, *6*(3), 513–540.
15 Sommers, S.R. (2006). On racial diversity and group decision making: Identifying multiple effects of racial composition on jury deliberations. *Journal of Personality and Social Psychology*, *90*(4), 597–612.
16 Zwier, P. (2024, May 8). *The art of voir dire.* Emory School of Law [Video]. YouTube. https://www.youtube.com/watch?v=9czWGtPd2RM

17 Zwier, P. (2024, May 8). *The art of voir dire.* Emory School of Law [Video]. YouTube. https://www.youtube.com/watch?v=9czWGtPd2RM
18 Clark, J., Boccaccini, M.T., Caillouet, B., & Chaplin, W.F. (2007). Five factor model personality traits, jury selection, and case outcomes in criminal and civil cases. *Criminal Justice and Behavior, 34*(5), 641–660. https://doi.org/10.1177/0093854806297555
19 Jingnan, H. (2022, March 18). *To try or not to try—remotely. As jury trials move online, courts see pros and cons.* National Public Radio. https://www.wlrn.org/npr-breaking-news/2022–03–18/to-try-or-not-to-try-remotely-as-jury-trials-move-online-courts-see-pros-and-cons
20 Maxfield, M.G., & Babbie, E.R. (2009). *Basics of research methods for criminal justice and criminology* (2nd ed.). Wadsworth.
21 American Bar Association. (2019, March). *11 must-dos from a voir dire master.* https://www.americanbar.org/news/abanews/publications/youraba/2019/march-2019/11-tips-for-effectively-conducting-voir-dire
22 Yarbrough, S.L. (2001). The jury consultant: Friend or foe of justice. *SMU Law Review, 54*(5), 1885–1902.
23 Kressel, N.J., & Kressel, D.F. (2002). *Stack and sway: The new science of jury consulting.* Westview Press.
24 Greene, E. (2002). How effective? Review of stack and away: The new science of jury consulting. *Judicature, 85*(5), 1–3.
25 Hannaford-Agor, P.L., & Moffett, M. (2024). *2023 State-of-the-states survey of jury improvement efforts: High-profile trials.* National Center for State Courts. https://ncsc.contentdm.oclc.org/digital/collection/juries/id/382/rec/4
26 Greene, E. (2002). How effective? Review of stack and away: The new science of jury consulting. *Judicature, 85*(5), 1–3.
27 Hecht, P. (2016, October 24). *5 things to look for in the jury selection process.* Magna Legal Service. https://magnals.com/jury-selection-process-warning-signs
28 Hecht, P. (2016, October 24). *5 things to look for in the jury selection process.* Magna Legal Service. https://magnals.com/jury-selection-process-warning-signs
29 New York Courts. (2023, December 19). *Voir dire questions.* New York State Unified Court System. https://www.nycourts.gov/judges/cji/8-Colloquies/Voir%20Dire%20QUESTIONS.pdf
30 Hannaford-Agor, P.L., & Moffett, M. (2024). *2023 State-of-the-states survey of jury improvement efforts: Voir dire practices in U.S. courts.* National Center for State Courts. https://ncsc.contentdm.oclc.org/digital/collection/juries/id/363/rec/10
31 New York Courts. (2023, December 19). *Voir dire questions.* New York State Unified Court System. https://www.nycourts.gov/judges/cji/8-Colloquies/Voir%20Dire%20QUESTIONS.pdf
32 Hannaford-Agor, P.L., & Moffett, M. (2024). *2023 State-of-the-states survey of jury improvement efforts: Criminal jury trials.* National Center for State Courts. https://ncsc.contentdm.oclc.org/digital/collection/juries/id/384/rec/2
33 Hannaford-Agor, P.L., & Moffett, M. (2024). *2023 State-of-the-states survey of jury improvement efforts: Civil jury trials.* https://ncsc.contentdm.oclc.org/digital/collection/juries/id/393/rec/5
34 Winfree, T.L., Mays, L.G., & Alarid, L.F. (2022). *Introduction to criminal justice: The essentials* (3rd ed., p. 206). Aspen Publishing.
35 Winfree, T.L., Mays, L.G., & Alarid, L.F. (2022). *Introduction to criminal justice: The essentials* (3rd ed., p. 206). Aspen Publishing.
36 Winfree, T.L., Mays, L.G., & Alarid, L.F. (2022). *Introduction to criminal justice: The essentials* (3rd ed., p. 206). Aspen Publishing.
37 Tam, J.S. (2020). *Jury selection in federal court.* Thomson Reuters. https://www.dechert.com/content/dam/dechert%20files/knowledge/publication/2020/5/Jury-Selection-in-Federal-Court.pdf
38 Federal Rules of Criminal Procedure. (2023, December 18). *Rule 24: Trial jurors.* https://uscode.house.gov/view.xhtml?req=granuleid:USC-1999-title18a-node36-node75-rule24&num=0&edition=1999
39 28 U.S.C. § 1870
40 Tam, J.S. (2020). *Jury selection in federal court.* Thomson Reuters. https://www.dechert.com/content/dam/dechert%20files/knowledge/publication/2020/5/Jury-Selection-in-Federal-Court.pdf
41 Cal. CCP § 231

42 234 Pa. Code Rule 634. (2023, December 18). *Number of peremptory challenges.* https://www.pacodeandbulletin.gov/Display/pacode?file=/secure/pacode/data/234/chapter6/s634.html&d=reduce
43 Center for Jury Studies. (2023). *Jury data dashboard.* National Center for State Courts. https://www.ncsc.org/resources-courts/jury-data-dashboard
44 *Batson v. Kentucky*, 476 U.S. 79 (1986).
45 *Batson v. Kentucky*, 476 U.S. 79, 83 (1986).
46 *Batson v. Kentucky*, 476 U. S. 79, 85–88 (1986).
47 *Powers v. Ohio*, 499 U.S. 400 (1991).
48 *Edmonson v. Leesville Concrete Co.*, 500 U.S. 614 (1991).
49 *Georgia v. McCollum*, 112 S. Ct. 2348 (1992).
50 *Wainwright v. Witt*, 469 U.S. 412 (1985).
51 *Witherspoon v. Illinois*, 391 U.S. 510 (1968).
52 Sandys, M., & Dillehay, R.C. (1996). Life under *Wainwright v. Witt*: Juror dispositions and death qualification. *Law and Human Behavior*, *20*(2), 147–165. https://doi.org/10.1007/BF01499352
53 Bowers, W.J., Steiner, B.D., & Sandys, M. (2001). Death sentencing in Black and White: An empirical analysis of the role of jurors' race and jury racial composition. *University of Pennsylvania Journal of Constitutional Law*, *3*(1), 171–274.
54 Sandys, M. (2014). Misunderstanding of capital instructions: Clarification is possible. *The Advocate*, *36*(8), 14–18.
55 *J.E.B. v. Alabama*, 511 U.S. 127 (1994).
56 Clark, J., Boccaccini, M.T., Caillouet, B., & Chaplin, W.F. (2007). Five factor model personality traits, jury selection, and case outcomes in criminal and civil cases. *Criminal Justice and Behavior*, *34*(5), 641–660. https://doi.org/10.1177/0093854806297555
57 Rose, M.R. (1999). The peremptory challenge accused of race and gender discrimination? Some data from one county. *Law and Human Behavior*, *23*(6), 695–702. https://doi.org/10.1023/A:1022393506784
58 Flanagan, F.X. (2018). Race, gender, and juries: Evidence from North Carolina. *The Journal of Law & Economics*, *61*(2), 189–214. https://doi.org/10.1086/698193
59 *Batson v. Kentucky*, 476 U.S. 79 (1986).
60 Flanagan, F.X. (2018). Race, gender, and juries: Evidence from North Carolina. *The Journal of Law & Economics*, *61*(2), 189–214. https://doi.org/10.1086/698193
61 Washington State General Rule 37. (2025, July). *Jury selection.* https://www.courts.wa.gov/content/publicUpload/Supreme%20Court%20Orders/GR37.pdf
62 Paula Hannaford-Agor, P.L., & Diamond, S. (forthcoming). *Studying voir dire: Cautionary guidance on research methods.*
63 Pennsylvania Code. (2001) *Rule 640. Swearing the trial jury to hear the cause.* Commonwealth of Pennsylvania. https://www.pacodeandbulletin.gov/Display/pacode?file=/secure/pacode/data/234/chapter6/s640.html&d=reduce
64 Michigan Compiled Laws. (2024, May 8). *768.14 jurors; form of oath.* Michigan Legislature. https://legislature.mi.gov/Laws/MCL?objectName=MCL-768-14
65 South Dakota Codified Law. (2024, May 8). 23A-20–7.1. *Affirmation permitted in lieu of oath.* South Dakota Legislature. https://sdlegislature.gov/Statutes/23A-20–7.1
66 Federal Rules of Evidence. (2011). *Rule 603. Oath or affirmation to testify truthfully.* Cornell School of Law. https://www.law.cornell.edu/rules/fre/rule_603
67 California Courts. (2023, December 18). *About the trial process.* https://www.courts.ca.gov/2240.htm?print=1#:~:text=the%20following%20oath%3A-,%22Do%20you%2C%20and%20each%20of%20you%2C%20understand%20and%20agree,the%20oath%20before%20taking%20it
68 *Society of Separationists, Inc. v. Herman*, 959 F.2d 1207 (1991).
69 *Society of Separationists, Inc. v. Herman*, 959 F.2d 1207 (1991).
70 *Society of Separationists, Inc. v. Herman*, 959 F.2d 1207 (1991).
71 *Society of Separationists, Inc. v. Herman*, 959 F.2d 1207 (1991).
72 Belcher, J. (1992). Religion-plus speech: The constitutionality of juror oaths and affirmations under the first amendment. *William & Mary Law Review*, *34*(1), 287–331.

7 Juror Comprehension and Decision-Making

What Do You Think?

Before reviewing the concepts addressed in this chapter, answer True or False to each of the following questions or statements. Correct answers can be found at the end of Chapter 7.

1. A Bayesian decision-making model describes how jurors construct plausible narratives of events and legal standards that help them reach a verdict about guilt and liability.
2. The instructions used in the American jury system today are the same instructions used in colonial America during the 18th century.
3. A criticism of jury instructions is that they are written using language unfamiliar to ordinary citizens.
4. Explicit bias is expressed through one's personal preference to associate with others who have the same characteristics.
5. Jurors may be trained in race switching techniques to identify unconscious bias.
6. Jurors are encouraged to use social media sources to learn additional details about the case during the deliberation process.

Learning Objectives

After reading this chapter, you will be able to:

1. Compare and contrast the Bayesian and story-based models related to jury decision-making at trial.
2. Describe research findings related to judge-jury agreement and the meaning of the leniency effect.
3. Explain the history associated with creating jury instructions in colonial America.
4. List examples of revised language in jury instructions that were designed to improve clarity and reduce confusion.
5. Describe juror instructions some courts have implemented to reduce biased decision-making.
6. Explain the dangers associated with jurors using social media sources during the trial and deliberation.

Introduction

After jurors have been selected during voir dire and sworn as trial jurors, the trial can begin. Before jurors hear witness testimony or are presented with tangible evidence, such as documents, photographs, or physical items, the trial judge briefly educates jurors about their role

DOI: 10.4324/9781003677796-9

and responsibilities. The judge actively manages the trial process, making decisions about the admissibility of evidence and supervising attorneys to ensure their compliance with court rules, while the jurors have a largely passive role during the evidentiary portion of the trial. Their primary job is to listen carefully to the witnesses, evaluate the credibility and importance of their testimony, and draw informed conclusions about the facts. Only after the parties have presented all their evidence and the judge has instructed the jurors on the law do jurors begin deliberating to reach a collective verdict.

The voir dire process discussed in Chapter 6 is designed to ensure that jurors can fulfill this role. They were vetted to confirm their objectivity and impartiality, and they are now presumed to be competent decision-makers, including having the intellectual and emotional maturity to draw logical conclusions from the evidence and to fairly apply the law. But how do jurors make sense of the evidence and law, especially in cases involving greater complexity? This chapter describes different theories explaining juror decision-making processes and provides some background about the development of both procedural and substantive jury instructions. It also describes factors that often challenge juror comprehension as well as techniques to address these challenges. This chapter focuses on jurors as individuals, while the next chapter will focus on how jurors collectively deliberate to render a verdict.

In This Chapter

This chapter addresses an important and often criticized aspect of the American jury system. This material focuses on: 1) how jurors reach their final decisions at trial; 2) jurors' understanding of jury instructions; 3) jury instruction guidelines and language use; and 4) instructions about implicit racial bias and use of technology inside the courtroom and during the deliberation.

Contemporary Models of Juror Decision-Making

From time immemorial, judges and lawyers have advanced idealized notions of how jurors should approach their role as factfinders within the adversarial process of a jury trial. In this system, attorneys present evidence favorable to their clients in a highly stylized and formal manner, governed by specific rules of evidence and procedure. Former Maricopa County Superior Court Judge B. Michael Dann described the attributes of this ideal juror. These included enforced passivity, silent observation, complete and accurate comprehension and recall of the evidence, and the ability to consider all evidence presented at trial.[1] Ideally, jurors also begin their task as blank slates, with no prior knowledge or expectations about the evidence they will hear, ensuring that their verdict reflects only the evidence and the law. Many of the restrictions imposed on jurors' conduct during trial proceedings are predicated on the validity of these assumptions.

As a practical matter, however, this ideal juror does not exist. Instead, scholars from the fields of social science, cognitive psychology, and behavioral science offer alternative theories of juror decision-making.[2] These approaches typically fall into two main categories: quantitative "decision-rule" models and qualitative "explanation" or "story-based" models. Decision-rule models, such as threshold models or **Bayesian** inference, assume jurors evaluate evidence by assigning numerical weights (e.g., probabilities) to facts and then apply formal decision rules (like "guilty if $p > 0.5$"). These models offer clarity and precision but often fall short in capturing the complexity of real juror reasoning and the narrative nature with which laypeople approach evidence. Opposing this, explanationist or story-based models suggest jurors construct plausible narratives that integrate events, motivations, context, and legal standards, which they then test against the evidence. These models emphasize qualitative coherence, plausibility, coverage, and the ability to discriminate from alternative stories. Box 7.1 describes various research methods used by social scientists and legal professionals when studying jurors and juror decision-making behavior.

Among the explanation-based frameworks, the **Story Model**—developed by Pennington and Hastie—is the most widely accepted and empirically supported theory in legal psychology. It proposes that jurors engage in three interrelated cognitive processes: story-building, story-evaluation, and verdict-rendering.[5] Initially, jurors construct a narrative out of trial evidence, aligning facts into coherent causal sequences involving actors, goals, and outcomes. Next, they evaluate each potential narrative by assessing how well it explains the evidence (coherence), whether it covers all key facts (coverage), and whether it markedly distinguishes itself from competing narratives (uniqueness). Finally, jurors apply legal standards, as a separate

Box 7.1: Common Research Methods for Studying Juror Decision-Making[3]

- *Archival studies* collect data on juror and case characteristics and verdicts as documented in court files to analyze and predict verdict patterns. Because this method uses real cases and verdicts, it provides high external validity without interfering with trial proceedings. It is limited to existing records, however, and cannot control for exogenous variables or probe into juror reasoning.
- *Mock jury experiments* assign research subjects (mock jurors) to different trial simulations or scenarios in which discrete variables are manipulated to assess their impact on juror decision making. This method can isolate causal factors affecting juror decision-making. Depending on the realism of the trial simulations, especially the sophistication of the stimulus materials (e.g., videotaped trial proceeding versus written description), this method may lack complete emotional buy-in from subjects because they know their decision-making about guilt or fault will not directly impact an actual trial litigant.
- *Post-trial surveys* and interviews with trial jurors provide direct insights from real jurors with case-specific reflections and high ecological relevance. Depending on the length of time between the trial and the survey or interview, jurors' memories about relevant details may degrade or become distorted, especially due to 20/20 hindsight or social desirability bias.
- *Public opinion surveys* can reach large, diverse samples and are useful for measuring general attitudes; however, those attitudes may not predict respondents' behaviors in the context of real jury trials.[4]
- *Direct observation* of jurors during trial and deliberations provides rich, real-time data on actual juror behavior and offers high ecological validity. While juror reasoning can sometimes be inferred from behavior, especially from verbal statements and body language, it risks the introduction of subjective interpretations on the part of observers. This method is also extremely labor-intensive and expensive. It may also be difficult to secure permission from judges, lawyers, and jurors for researchers to directly observe jurors during trial and deliberations.

"verdict classification" layer,[6] to decide which story meets the burden of proof (e.g., beyond a reasonable doubt or preponderance of the evidence). Numerous empirical studies find that jurors rely more on coherence judgments about stories than on formal probabilistic reasoning, supporting the dominance of the Story Model.[7]

Underlying this narrative process is the use of **cognitive schemas**; that is, mental frameworks that help jurors categorize and interpret information. Schemas are organized structures of prior knowledge. For example, a "domestic-violence" schema may include typical roles, settings, behaviors, and motives of the assailant and victim. During the trial when jurors hear evidence, they match it to relevant schemas to extract meaning efficiently by filtering, organizing, and evaluating facts within those structures. This schema-based processing is what makes the Story Model so psychologically plausible; it reflects how everyday cognition works. Jurors do not simply compute likelihood ratios; instead, they interpret evidence through familiar story frames, filling gaps, inferring unstated motivations, and rejecting details that do not fit the mental framework. Thus, cognitive schemas are central to juror comprehension, anchoring narrative construction and guiding verdict decisions.

Assessments of Juror Comprehension and Performance

Jurors are not formally tested on their comprehension of the evidence or the law presented at trial. Instead, their decision-making is typically evaluated through the binary verdicts they render—guilty or not guilty in criminal cases, and liable or not liable in civil cases. As such, assessments of jury performance often focus on whether the verdict itself can be justified as a factually and legally reasonable outcome. One widely used measure of juror performance is **judge-jury agreement**, an approach developed by Harry Kalven and Hans Zeisel in their landmark 1966 study *The American Jury.* The origins of this project were described in Chapter 1 and remain a foundational work in the field of jury research.

Kalven and Zeisel conducted extensive surveys of trial judges, gathering data from 3,576 criminal trials and a similarly large number of civil trials. Each judge was asked to "indicate how you would have decided this case if you had tried it without a jury." Their responses were then compared with the actual jury verdicts, allowing the researchers to calculate agreement rates. While the level of judge-jury agreement varied across case types, the overall agreement was remarkably high at 78 percent in criminal cases and 79 percent in civil cases.[8] The rate of overall agreement versus disagreement remained constant regardless of evidentiary complexity.

Despite this overall alignment, Kalven and Zeisel identified a consistent pattern of divergence they termed the **"leniency effect."** Specifically, they found that judges were significantly more likely to convict in cases where juries acquitted (19 percent of trials) than they were to acquit in cases where juries convicted (only 3 percent of trials).[9] This suggested that juries, as a collective body of laypeople, tended to be more lenient than judges when assessing guilt.

To further understand the reasons for these disagreements, Kalven and Zeisel asked judges to explain why they believed the jury had reached a different conclusion. From these responses, five primary factors emerged:

1. Differing assessments about the weight of the evidence (accounting for 52 percent of disagreements)
2. Jurors' views about the law they were instructed to apply (30 percent)
3. Jurors' impressions of the defendant (11 percent)

4. Perceived differences in the quality of the attorneys (4 percent)
5. Information known to the judge but withheld from the jury due to evidentiary rules (3 percent)

> The overall performance of the jury is such as to produce a high degree of conformity to that of the judge, but with elbow room left for the jury to perform a distinctive function. Or, as we have put it on other occasions, the jury agrees with the judge often enough to be reassuring, yet disagrees often enough to keep it interesting.
>
> —Harry S. Kalven
> *The Dignity of the Civil Jury* (1964)

Subsequent research has repeatedly replicated this basic pattern of judge-jury agreement and disagreement in both criminal and civil contexts, reinforcing Kalven and Zeisel's original findings. See, for example, research findings from Sentell (1991),[10] Eisenberg et al. (2005),[11] and Hannaford-Agor et al. (2000).[12] In addition, scholars and legal professionals tend to grade juror comprehension of evidence quite well, including highly complex testimony by expert witnesses. For example, one study found that jurors made decisions by weighing the totality of the evidence, not simply adopting expert views.[13] Findings showed if the facts shared by an expert during the trial did not fit into the cognitive schemas of the jurors, they tended to ignore the evidence or give it less weight. Even when complexity was increased (e.g., via technical jargon), jurors still exhibited meaningful engagement with the material. Another study concluded that jurors rely on sensible criteria such as expert credentials, consistency, reasoning quality, and impartiality when reaching a final verdict in a case.[14] Box 7.2 describes the impact of Hollywood crime dramas on the behavior and decisions reached by real jurors at trial. This phenomenon, known as the CSI Effect, was coined after the franchise that bears its name.

Box 7.2: Crime Scene Investigation (CSI) Effect

Research has examined the effects of social media and television viewership on jury deliberation practices. Forensic crime dramas and programs that portray federal law enforcement tactics have remained popular among television viewers for several decades. This popularity spawned the notion of the **CSI Effect**. These shows have caused some concern among legal professionals. For example, trial attorneys have wondered how viewing such television dramas would impact the average jurors' perceptions of trial evidence, especially forensic evidence involving the collection and analysis of suspects DNA. Specifically, prosecuting attorneys were concerned that jurors may expect DNA evidence to be submitted at trial to prove a defendant's guilt. If no such evidence were presented, jurors might decide that the evidence did not prove guilt beyond a reasonable doubt.[15] Likewise, defense attorneys expressed concern that jurors would unshakingly believe analyses based on DNA, despite other types of exonerating evidence submitted at trial indicating a defendant was innocent of the crime.[16]

Researchers examined the impact of forensic DNA evidence and crime drama viewership on a sample of subjects who participated in mock jury trials. Findings from mock jury trial scenarios revealed that television viewing habits of forensic crime dramas did not impact jurors' perceptions or influence of DNA evidence when determining a final verdict (guilt versus innocence).[17] Moreover, subjects who regularly watched such programming only minimally mentioned during the deliberation that the prosecutor failed to admit DNA evidence during the trial.[18] Overall, research findings indicated forensic crime dramas may not influence jurors' perceptions about trial evidence in ways that impact the verdict; however, the influence of such shows may be more impactful for increasing an individual's career path and interest in the field of forensic sciences and legal practices.[19]

While juror comprehension of evidence receives generally high marks, juror comprehension of the law has been more problematic. The legal standards jurors are tasked with applying are often conveyed in language that is difficult for laypersons to understand. Research over several decades has consistently highlighted the challenges jurors face in comprehending jury instructions, which are intended to guide their decision-making.

Early empirical research on juror comprehension assessed how well jurors understood legal standards based on standard courtroom practices, in which instructions were delivered orally by the trial judge at the end of the trial. These studies often found that jurors who received instructions performed only marginally better than those who received no instructions at all. One of the earliest studies revealed that even among jurors who received instructions, many struggled with basic legal concepts, including due process.[20] A later study found that jury instructions modestly improved juror understanding of unfamiliar legal concepts, but jurors still failed to grasp many essential points.[21]

As these findings accumulated, researchers began exploring how modifications to the delivery of jury instructions might improve comprehension. A major development was the use of written instructions alongside oral delivery. Later studies, including Shari Diamond et al.'s "Kettleful of Law" (2012), observed that providing written copies of instructions led to improved performance. In real jury deliberations, jurors with access to written instructions were better able to refer to legal definitions, clarify misunderstandings among group members, and anchor their deliberations in legal standards. In Diamond's study, 79 percent of statements of law made during deliberations were correct, suggesting a more optimistic assessment of juror understanding—although comprehension errors still occurred in 16 percent of cases.[22]

Despite such gains, structural challenges remain in the way jury instructions are composed. As the phrase "Kettleful of Law" suggests, jurors often feel inundated or doused with an abundance of laws and legal jargon by which they are to reach a decision at trial. Much like being doused with a kettle of water, helpless jurors feel like legal standards and instructions dumped on them. Admirably, jurors do their best to make sense of the instructions and develop an understanding of the law.

Jury instructions typically attempt to achieve two core objectives: ensuring that the instructions are legally accurate and ensuring that they are comprehensible to laypersons. These objectives, however, are often at odds with one another. Instructions must be complete and precise enough to withstand appellate scrutiny, yet accessible enough to be understood by individuals with no legal training.[23] This dual demand can result in instructions that are technically correct but linguistically impenetrable.

Diamond et al.'s "Kettleful of Law" study offers a particularly insightful look into the barriers that persist even when jurors are performing at relatively high levels. Based on extensive observations of real jury deliberations, Diamond identified three main sources of difficulty in jury instructions. First, unfamiliar terminology or **legal jargon** often obscures key legal concepts. Second, structural inconsistencies or misleading relationships between provisions create confusion about how different parts of the instructions relate to one another. This means that sometimes judges and attorneys piece together jury instructions from multiple sources of legal code. Sometimes the codes defined terms and procedures similarly, other times not. This inconsistency further complicates the clarity of jury instructions. Third, omission errors, in which essential elements of the law are either underemphasized or missing entirely, leave jurors without the full tools needed to apply the law correctly.

These comprehension issues are not merely academic. They carry significant implications for the fairness and accuracy of jury verdicts. If jurors misunderstand the law, they may fall back on intuitive reasoning or "commonsense justice," which may conflict with the legal standards they are supposed to apply. To address these challenges, judges and lawyers have begun efforts to improve pattern jury instructions by simplifying language, restructuring content, and ensuring that written versions are provided. Box 7.3 features a trial judge's perspective on juror comprehension and performance.

Box 7.3: From the Field

Name: Pamela Gates

Position: Presiding Judge, Superior Court of Arizona in Maricopa County

How long have you been a trial judge?
I was appointed to the bench in 2009.

Some researchers say jurors use math-like formulas (Bayesian models), while others say jurors build stories to make sense of a case. From your perspective on the bench, do you see jurors working more like "storytellers" than "calculators"?

In Arizona, the jury instructions explain that their duty is to determine what the facts are in the case by deciding what actually happened. We encourage the jurors to use the tests for determining truthfulness in matters of importance in everyday life, including a witness's ability to see or hear the things the witness testified to, the quality of the witness's memory, the witness's manner while testifying, whether the witness had any motive or bias or prejudice, whether the witness was contradicted by other testimony or evidence or something they said or wrote before trial, and the reasonableness of the testimony when considered in the light of the other evidence. The instructions invite jurors to consider what testimony to accept and what to reject, offering them the option of accepting everything a witness says, part of it, or none of it. Although jurors are not asked to memorialize how they reached a verdict, in my experience the jurors work very hard to assess what really happened and to piece everything together based on the facts and evidence they find credible.

Studies show that judges and juries agree on verdicts about 80% of the time, but juries are often more lenient. Why do you think juries sometimes see a case differently than judges?

In criminal cases in Arizona, we explain that proof beyond a reasonable doubt is proof that leaves you "firmly convinced" of the defendant's guilt. We remind the jurors that there are very few things in this world that we know with absolute certainty and the law, in a criminal case, does not require proof that overcomes every doubt. The law requires that the jurors are firmly convinced that the defendant is guilty of the crime charged and if there is a real possibility that the defendant is not guilty, the jurors are instructed to give the defendant the benefit of the doubt and find the person not guilty. As judicial officers, we consider evidence and testimony every day and apply the facts to the law. Although we understand the importance of the decisions we make and we often question our decisions and how we arrived at the result, we typically have years of experience making these incredibly important, life-altering decisions. When I retire, I will have made decisions of whether the burden of proof was satisfied thousands of times. For individuals called to jury service, this may be the only time in their lives they make a decision that could deprive another person of their freedom, and in a capital case, of their life. There is no uniformity in whether a person feels "firmly convinced" that a defendant is guilty. Perhaps feeling "firmly convinced" feels different when it is the first time you are asked to make this type of life-altering decision.

Research shows jurors often struggle with legal jargon and complex instructions. As a judge, how do you try to make sure jurors understand the instructions you give them?

We work hard to simplify the instructions but ensure that the instructions are legally accurate. Some instructions, like the definition of money laundering or the distinction between second-degree murder and manslaughter can be legally complex. In Arizona, jurors have the right to ask questions during their deliberation, and they frequently request help when they do not understand the law. As judicial officers, I believe that it is our job to respond to their call for assistance. We should challenge ourselves to not simply refer the jurors back to the instructions they just told us they do not understand, and instead confer with the parties to provide an answer to the question or ask the jury whether supplemental argument from the lawyers would be helpful. It is the jurors' job to determine the facts, and it is the court's job to instruct the jury on the law. If the jury does not understand the law, it is the court's responsibility to assist the jury without commenting on the evidence and within the parameters of the law.

History of Jury Instructions

Jury instructions used in colonial America have evolved over the generations. The earliest courts of the American colonies modeled their standard practices from the English legal system in many ways. For example, English judges did not instruct jurors about how they were to reach a decision in a particular case. The jurors were given the freedom to decide on their own what the law was and whether it was broken. This tradition, honorable on its face, may have contributed to arbitrariness[24] for how similar cases were decided and resolved.

The American colonists originally adopted the English legal traditions where juries were not instructed about the law when reaching a decision in a case. Indeed, the Founding Fathers wanted juries to decide cases based on their own common sense. Although English common law was well settled in the old country, it did not always work well in the colonies where settlers had to develop new laws and practices to address novel legal issues as they arose. The success of the United States and its fast development made expansion of the judicial system and reformation of the jury as necessary as it was inevitable. The nation was evolving and with it there was a need to standardize and apply the rules of law to similar cases consistently.

The need to apply laws consistently demanded a change to jury practices and responsibilities. The tradition of allowing jurors to decide the legal grounds of a case was gradually replaced with the trial judge instructing jurors about the law. In the late 1800s, the United States Supreme Court found it was the trial judge's responsibility to determine the law and the jury's responsibility to determine whether the facts of the case showed there a violation of the law(s).[25] This change in the roles of the judge and the jury at trial, necessitated other changes including the need for the judge to clearly instruct a **layperson jury** about the relevant laws.

In the early part of the 20th century, judges throughout America began providing instructions to juries to aid their decision making. Writing such instructions was found to be a time-consuming matter that involved contributions from the judge and attorneys.[26] Trial attorneys would also try to frame the jury instructions to favor their side.[27] Jury instructions that incorrectly state the law can serve as grounds for an appeal for the party that loses at trial.[28] It was apparent that changes to the jury system, including clearer jury instructions, were needed.

History of Jury Instructions in California

In the 1930s, a committee consisting of judges and trial attorneys was formed in California to address the complex issue of jury instructions. The committee was tasked with developing a standard set of jury instructions that could be used by multiple counties within the state. The original document the committee produced, and its subsequent revisions, is known as the **Book of Approved Jury Instructions (BAJI)** for civil cases. There were several advantages to developing standard jury instructions. For example, standardizing jury instructions could: 1) save valuable time and resources of judges and attorneys in individual jurisdictions from having to develop their own instructions; 2) reduce the number of cases being overturned upon appeal; and 3) improve jurors' comprehension of the legal issues in disputes and their role as finders of fact.[29]

The California committee revised the jury instructions based on previously published juror guidelines. For example, specific language was taken from legislation or statutes and from previous judicial opinions that survived appellate review. This logic was sound; specifically, if the instructions were not overturned in the past for instructional errors or misinformation, the language was deemed to be acceptable. Other states found this approach useful and began drafting pattern jury instructions for their own courts.

These standard or pattern instructions were widely used in California for decades. Judges and attorneys supported their use, but critics pointed out that the instructions were developed for attorneys.[30] Specific complaints voiced were that the average juror struggled to understand the meaning of the law being conveyed. Researchers and legal professionals were eager to assess jurors' understanding of specific jury instructions. In one study, researchers played a recording of juror instructions from the BAJI to determine research subjects' level of comprehension. Only 50 percent of respondents could correctly paraphrase the meaning of the original BAJI jury instructions.[31] Generally, researchers found confusion developed over the use of complex words, double negatives, and passive voice.[32] Critics called for reforming the BAJI, including using clearer language to increase juror comprehension and understanding. The Judicial Council of California assigned a committee to revise the BAJI. In 2003, the **California Civil Jury Instructions (CACI)** were introduced to address issues of poor comprehension among jurors.

While many states have been influenced by the early efforts of California and borrowed the revised jury instructions for their own jurisdictions, both the federal courts and other state court systems have addressed this issue on their own and have implemented other strategies to facilitate jurors' understanding and comprehension of jury instructions. By the late 1980s, there were approximately 100 established **Pattern Jury Instruction (PJI) committees** at work in the federal and state court systems.[33] Like California, many of the PJI committees were comprised of judges and attorneys who labored to develop jury instructions for the purposes of: 1) increasing the accuracy and improving the comprehension of the instructions: 2) saving courts time from developing instructions individually on a case-by-case basis; and 3) removing combative and argumentative language.[34] It was believed that revised PJIs could reduce the number of cases that would be reversed upon appeal.

Change in society is inevitable. Societies tend to grow more sophisticated, technologically and industrially, over time. For example, the pharmaceutical, healthcare, and medical fields have developed into greater specialization now more than at any other point in history. Given the fast-paced development of society, cases are brought to trial that require specific, not general, descriptions of the law. Some PJI committees have addressed this reality by developing specialized instructions for distinct areas of law, including juvenile and family, business and insurance, product liability, etc.[35] Critics of trial by jury argued that such highly specialized laws go beyond the comprehension of the average juror, and they used this to justify the need for professional or specialized juries to decide complex cases. This is a controversial topic that is discussed in Chapter 10.

Guidelines for Jury Instructions

Researchers and legal scholars alike have spent decades studying jury instructions. The results of their findings provided guidelines to the PJI committees as the judges and attorneys underwent the task of writing or revising individual instructions for jurors. Many of the guiding principles related to how instructions are communicated to jurors. For example, PJI committees must keep in mind that jurors are selected, or at least should be selected, from a fair cross-section of the community. This may include a diverse population of various backgrounds and education levels; therefore, jurors may be representative of various blue-collar and white-collar professions. Obviously, it will be impossible to write one set of jury instructions that is understandable to all jurors, but the goal should be to write instructions for the common or ordinary citizen. This may include high school graduates who do not have a legal background.[36] When the committees recognize who the jurors are, they can better focus on the language or terms to include in the instructions.

Jury instructions should strike a balance between formal and informal language. For example, juror instructions should not include informal slang or street language, which might not be understandable to a set of diverse individuals gathered from a cross-section of the community. Conversely, PJI committees must not use overly formal language, which might impact comprehension and make individual jurors feel isolated from the trial process.[37] This

Table 7.1: Examples of Technical Legal Terms[38]

Mala Fide	A behavior committed with an intent to deceive.
Ipso Facto	A decision based strictly on the facts alone.
Preponderance of the Evidence	The legal burden of proof in civil cases, which is often explained as the evidence showed that it is "more likely than not" that the defendant caused the plaintiff's injury.
Proximate Cause	The direct cause that sets in motion a chain of events leading to injury or damage in a civil case.
Malice Aforethought	The intent to commit a crime, often murder, without justification of cause.

is an important but difficult task, as many of the terms used in jury instructions are content specific and not part of the daily vernacular of an average layperson. This has been referred to by some researchers as **legalese**. For example, many jurors are unlikely to hear the words or terms *mala fide* or *ipso facto* spoken in their ordinary life outside of the courtroom. Today's judges and trial attorneys recognize that using such terms in court may confuse the average juror, and doing so may even be grounds for appealing the trial outcome after it is delivered by the jury. As such, judges and trial attorneys closely monitor themselves and each other in terms of the legal language used at trial. Table 7.1 lists several examples of legalese terms and their meaning that may be included in standard jury instructions or be overheard by jurors inside the courtroom.

When such terms are used, the trial judge should clearly explain the meaning of the term to the jury using language that an ordinary citizen can understand. Previous research has showed that jurors have consulted dictionaries during the deliberation process to determine the meaning of the instructions judges provided during a trial.[39] In a study of 50 civil trials in Arizona, juries were provided with a copy of the instructions during their deliberation. Findings showed that the juries referred to the instructions, reading some of them out loud to the group, but still found the language confusing.[40] Research findings such as these provided clear evidence that jurors are often confused by the legal terms contained in many instructions.

Alternatively, some legal terms that are used during jury trials are common to ordinary citizens. Some legal terms constitute violations of law that are spoken in ordinary, everyday life. Jurors may recognize these terms and immediately understand the instructions being described. A problem arises, however, when a term used in ordinary life does not correspond with the legal meaning or definition of the term. For example, this occurs when crimes are **legal homonyms**.[41] Many jurors may believe that a burglary involves an individual breaking into another's home and stealing items like televisions, jewelry, or money. From a legal perspective, however, the crime of burglary has four distinct elements: 1) breaking and entering through force and without authorization; 2) a domicile—that is, a house where people are living; 3) at night; and 4) with the intent to commit a felony. A specific item does not need to be stolen for a burglary to have occurred. Judges and attorneys should clearly describe these differences between such terms that are viewed one way in common language and differently by legal standards.

Much of the confusion and comprehension problems that jurors experience can be remedied and overcome by simplifying the word selection and sentence structure. Generally, PJI committees should strive to write jury instructions in short sentences, especially if the issue at hand is complex in nature. Longer sentences are difficult for jurors to comprehend if the

Box 7.4: Recommendations Beyond Changes to Jury Instructions

Some PJI committees comprised of judges, attorneys, and other legal professions have made suggestions beyond simple improvements to the language of jury instructions and encouraged other changes to the trial process that could improve jurors' experiences, understanding of evidence, and quality of interactions with their fellow jurors. For example, in 1994, an Arizona committee made sweeping recommendations to the operations of its court system for the purposes of making the jury more effective. The recommendations were published in a report titled *Jurors: The Power of 12*, and were revolutionary for its time.[43] Overall, 55 recommendations were made relating to improving jury service,[44] including providing jurors with the written and oral instructions related to the case, allowing note-taking during the trial, and allowing jurors to ask witnesses questions.[45]

Another recommendation was that jurors be allowed to discuss evidence in the jury room during court recesses at trial. In 1996, the Arizona Supreme Court approved this request for jurors serving on civil trials only. This change is referred to as Rule 39(f).[46] Research was conducted to examine the impact of this change on jury dynamics. Several findings were uncovered. First, jurors made use of the opportunity to discuss the trial with fellow jurors by asking about their opinions, sharing differing viewpoints, and discussing missing or confusing evidence.[47] Also, the discussions helped jurors "reconstruct evidence," especially in complex trials, and facilitated the development of inferences about individual witnesses, the timeline of different events, and the personal motives of those involved in the case.[48] Other states began to examine the new approaches implemented in the Arizona courts to determine whether such changes could be implemented in their own jury systems. In 2023, the Arizona court system made other changes, as discussed previously, by significantly increasing monetary compensation for those who are called to jury service.[49]

topic itself is already challenging. Instructions written in active voice and following a traditional subject-verb-object order are preferred over sentences written in passive voice or that include double negative terms or statements.[42] Simple word choices and sentence structure can significantly aid jurors' comprehension levels. Box 7.4 provides additional information about PJI committee guidelines for improving jury instructions and other changes suggested to improve the jury service experience, in general.

Types and Timing of Procedural and Substantive Jury Instructions

Most jury instructions are designed to educate jurors about the precise legal elements that must be proven for a party to prevail at trial. In criminal cases, these elements will be statutorily set out in state statutes that classify the seriousness of the criminal offense, the act or omission that constitutes a crime (actus reas), the required mental state or intent of the person committing the crime (mens rea), the requirement that the act and intent occur simultaneously, and the relationship between the act and the harm or injury. In civil cases alleging negligence, these elements require evidence that the defendant owed duty of care toward the plaintiff; that the defendant violated their duty of care; that the violation caused the plaintiff's injury; and a determination of damages quantified in monetary terms. Substantive jury instructions also include instructions about the applicable burden of proof (beyond a reasonable doubt in criminal trials and by a preponderance of the evidence in civil trials) as well as fundamental legal principles, such as the presumption of innocence, the defendant's right not to testify, and guidance on assessing witness credibility.

Traditionally, these instructions were imparted to jurors at the end of the trial after the parties presented all their evidence and gave their closing arguments. The judge gave the jury instructions immediately before directing jurors to begin final deliberations, ostensibly so the guidelines would be fresh in the jurors' memory as they began deliberating. It is only recently that judges have also begun providing substantive jury instructions at the beginning of trial, so that jurors have a legal framework to help them understand the significance of trial testimony as it is presented.[50] In 2007, jurors were pre-instructed on the law in only 18 percent of jury trials in state courts.[51] By 2023, pre-instruction rates had increased to 30 percent in civil cases and 45 percent in criminal cases.[52]

In addition to substantive jury instructions, judges also instruct juries on procedural matters, especially on how jurors are to conduct themselves during the trial. These procedural instructions are uniformly delivered at the very beginning of trial, immediately after the jurors are sworn in. Many of these instructions are designed to ensure that jurors remain independent and impartial during the evidentiary portion of the trial and are not swayed by outside influences. For example, jurors are told not to discuss the case with friends, family members, or coworkers until after they have returned a verdict at the end of the trial. In most states, civil juries in Arizona being an exception, the jury is not allowed to discuss the case among themselves until they are formally sent into deliberations. Jurors are also instructed not to attempt to investigate the facts of the case themselves, but instead to rely exclusively on the evidence presented at trial. This includes avoiding news reports about the case as well as visiting the scene of the crime or accident unless the judge specifically authorizes the trip for the entire jury.

Instructions about Technology Use

Historically, these types of general prohibitions were sufficient to keep jurors isolated from outside influences that might bias jurors' decision-making. However, the introduction of contemporary internet technologies, including social media, has greatly complicated things by making it possible for jurors to access virtually any piece of published information about pending cases in minutes. A large portion of the American public now uses these technologies to complete routine daily tasks (e.g., shopping, banking, getting directions to unfamiliar locations). Jurors have become highly reliant on these tools for daily living and are thus often confused when judges instruct them that they cannot use their devices to make informed decisions related to jury service.[53]

In 2021, the National Center for State Courts surveyed over 800 judges and trial lawyers from across the country about their experience with juror use of internet technologies during trial. Only one-quarter of survey respondents reported any personal experience with inappropriate juror use of these technologies, the vast majority of whom recounted only one incident over the course of their professional careers. The highest risk of inappropriate juror use of news media occurred in criminal trials involving serious charges (e.g., homicide, assault/battery, and sex offenses); trials lasting longer than five days; complex trials involving unfamiliar terms or concepts; and trials in which jurors believed they may find information to assist their decision-making on reputable websites or news media.[54] In the *2023 State-of-the-states survey of jury improvement efforts*, allegations of juror misconduct involving internet technologies occurred only 35 times in nearly 6,000 trials (less than 1 percent). A similar study by the **Federal Judicial Center** reported only 30 out of 508 federal judges believed jurors used social media during the trial or deliberation process.[55]

In spite of the relative infrequency of known incidents, both state and federal courts increasingly provide detailed jury instructions about appropriate and inappropriate use of internet technologies. Box 7.5 illustrates the basic contours of these jury instructions, including explicit descriptions of prohibited conduct, an explanation of the underlying rationale for the prohibition, a description of the consequences of noncompliance for both the parties and jurors themselves, and a request that jurors report concerns about juror use of new media to the judge. To minimize the risk that jurors might forget or misunderstand the importance of the instructions, many judges give the instruction at the beginning of the trial and then repeat it periodically during the trial, especially before court recesses.

Federal Judicial Center[56]

The Federal Judicial Center was established by Congress in 1967 to conduct research and inform the public about issues related to the judicial branch of the U.S. government. The Center's mission, in part, is to educate and train federal employees, including judges and public defenders. It also records the history of the federal courts and "conducts empirical studies and exploratory research … such as case management, alternative dispute resolution, and proposed amendments to the federal rules."[57]

Box 7.5: Warnings about Social Media Use

A committee of the U.S. Judicial Conference developed modeled instructions for federal judges to share with jurors about social media use at each stage of the trial proceeding. This included juror selection at the voir dire, before the trial begins, at the beginning and ending of each day of the trial, and after closing arguments. The following is a portion of the instructions that the committee developed to be shared with jurors at the close of the case and before the deliberation began:

> Throughout your deliberations, you may discuss with each other the evidence and the law that has been presented in this case, but you must not communicate with anyone else by any means about the case … you may not use any electronic device or media (such as a phone, computer, or tablet), the internet, any text or instant messaging service, or any social media apps (such as Twitter, Facebook, Instagram, LinkedIn, YouTube, WhatsApp, and Snapchat) to research or communicate about what you've seen and heard in this courtroom … Information you find on the internet or through social media might be incomplete, misleading, or inaccurate. And, as I noted in my instructions at the start of the trial, even using your smartphones, tablets, and computers—and the news and social media apps on those devices—may inadvertently expose you to certain notices, such as pop-ups or advertisements, that could influence your consideration of the matters you've heard about in this courtroom.[58]

Implicit Bias

Another recent development in jury instructions is the introduction in many courts of instructions about implicit racial bias. Racial prejudice has impacted the American criminal justice system for generations, including the function, composition, and operation of trial juries. **Explicit bias** occurs when an individual is fully aware of their beliefs and preferences for judging others differently because of skin color, ethnic background, sexual preference, or other characteristics. The U.S. Supreme Court has shown intolerance for juror decision-making and trial verdicts based on such racial discriminatory thinking.[59]

Social science research has explored other aspects of jurors' biased and prejudiced thinking. For example, **implicit bias** relates to one's personal preferences and perceived associations that link group members together. Individuals acting under implicit bias may not be consciously aware of their preferences or stereotyped thinking.[60] Research has shown that implicit bias can be transferred through watching or listening to media outlets, where a person's thinking can be influenced without them even realizing it;[61] however, individuals who demonstrate implicit bias often do not harbor ill will for another group (outgroup) but rather focus on helping members of groups like themselves (ingroup).[62] Implicit bias has significant implications for the court system, including the jury deliberation process and the verdict reached at trial.

Bringing attention to issues of race can educate jurors about the dangers of unconscious or implicit bias, facilitating jury deliberations that are based solely on the law and evidence presented at trial.[63] Judges in courtrooms throughout America are experimenting with implicit racial bias instructions. It is not known, however, what effect these instructions have on jurors' perceptions of race or how deliberations differ among jurors after these instructions are given. Research findings about making race salient during a trial proceeding are mixed. Some research showed White jurors provide more socially desirable responses when attention to a defendant's race was made salient, and they showed more bias when race was not emphasized.[64] Another study showed that White and Asian jurors reported significant bias against Black defendants, while younger jurors and jurors identifying as liberal showed less racial bias.[65] Social psychologists have developed tools for assessing implicit bias on a number of dimensions. Box 7.6 provides more details about the Implicit Association Tests (IATs).

Impartial Jury

Social scientists and legal professionals have inquired about providing jurors with **implicit bias instructions** about race.[67] For example, judges in courtrooms throughout America have

Box 7.6: Implicit Association Test (IAT)

Social psychologists have developed a series of assessment tools to measure an individual's implicit attitudes and beliefs about people and topics of interest. Among the earliest work conducted on the concept of implicit bias was performed by Project Implicit.[66] The tests are designed to uncover an individual's hidden attitudes that they might not be interested or willing to discuss openly or publicly. Specific IATs have been designed to assess implicit bias for race, age, gender, religion, weight, sexuality, and disabilities. These are publicly available tests and can be taken online. The assessments may take approximately 10–15 minutes to complete. The participant will be provided with an overall implicit bias score once completing the test.

intervened to address the concerns about implicit bias. Their intent was to mitigate the effects of implicit bias during the trial and inside the jury deliberation room, and to educate jurors about their potential unconscious bias and to focus their attention on the facts and evidence presented at the trial when reaching a verdict.[68] Consider the instructions that were drafted by Judge Mark W. Bennett of the United States District Court for the Northern District of Iowa:[69]

> Do not decide the case based on "implicit biases" … These hidden thoughts can impact what we see and hear, how we remember what we see and hear, and how we make important decisions. Because you are making very important decisions in this case, I strongly encourage you to evaluate the evidence carefully and to resist jumping to conclusions based on personal likes or dislikes, generalizations, gut feelings, prejudices, sympathies, stereotypes, or biases. The law demands that you return a just verdict, based solely on the evidence, your individual evaluation of that evidence, your reason and common sense, and these instructions. Our system of justice is counting on you to render a fair decision based on the evidence, not on biases.

Other variations of implicit bias instructions have been used with jurors to reduce racially biased decision-making at trial and when reaching a verdict. One example is "race switching" instructions. **Race switching** is based on the assumption that people use racial stereotypes to make decisions every day, even if they are unaware that they are doing it. Jurors, therefore, may be susceptible to making racially stereotyped decisions about defendants or witnesses at trial or during the deliberation process on a conscience or unconscious level. To draw attention to such tendencies, trial attorneys or willing judges may ask the jurors to engage in an informal test or assessment before reaching a final verdict. The jurors may be asked to imagine the facts presented at trial, including the actual events, circumstances, and people, but switch the racial characteristics of the parties. If their decision about guilt or innocence remained the same, implicit racial bias may not have impacted their verdict.

The American Bar Association (ABA) recognized the importance for providing the jury with implicit bias instructions and provided a review of relevant research findings and additional example instructions for legal professionals and the public's review.[70] Box 7.7 provides more details about the ABA's **"Achieving an Impartial Jury Project"** and toolbox.

Box 7.7: Achieving an Impartial Jury (AIJ) Project

The ABA was founded in 1878. The organization has evolved over time. Initially, the ABA "set the legal and ethical foundation for the American nation" and currently is "committed to its mission of defending liberty and pursuing justice."[71] One of the main goals of the ABA is to "eliminate bias in the legal profession and the justice system."[72] For example, the ABA has examined and shared social science evidence about implicit bias for the purposes of reducing bias and adhering to the ideals that the American jury is fair and impartial.

The ABA designed the AIJ project to provide practitioners with useful tools and best practices for identifying sources of implicit bias and remedies for removing it from the legal process. These materials include literature that define and describe implicit bias and a checklist that could remove implicit bias from the courtroom, displaying, for example, pictures that only depicted former judges who were White. Visual images inside the courtroom should be representative of all community members who are served by the court. The AIJ toolbox also provides suggestions for patterned jury instructions that could be used throughout the trial process, including during voir dire (the jury selection process) and when the judge explains pre-deliberation instructions after the presentation of evidence during the trial proceedings.

Box 7.8: From the Field

Name: Stella M. Tsai, J.

Position: Judge, Court of Common Pleas, Orphans' Court Division Philadelphia, PA

How long have you been a trial judge?
I was appointed to the bench in 2016 and won election in my own right to a 10-year term in 2017.

Do you think jurors have an appreciation for the role implicit bias might play throughout the trial, including the deliberation process?
As a legal professional, I have long been aware of the scientific literature showing that implicit biases affect our understanding, decision-making, and behavior. Because of this history, I am open to the notion that implicit biases inform human behavior. Not all jurors come to court with the same exposure to decades of studies demonstrating that our gut instincts about other people, which may be born out of basic survival instincts, might be based on irrational, unconsidered biases.

The judicial system asks a lot of jurors when we instruct them to shed their implicit biases in making their decisions, especially if they have never before confronted the issue of implicit bias. It's not easy for anyone to admit that they might be acting on a bias that they did not realize they had. Such revelations about human nature take time to absorb, and we often do not have the luxury of time.

The good news is that de-biasing agents are built into the jury deliberation process itself. In Philadelphia, the jury pool is diverse in many ways: race, gender, income level, zip code, and profession, to name a few. With this broad set of perspectives to work from, the jurors, who usually bond as a group as the trial proceeds, can help each other see their respective blind spots with respect and civility, which inevitably leads to better factfinding.

Do you believe implicit bias instructions should be a standard policy in all courtrooms today?
The use of jury instructions is generally left to the discretion of each judge. I think we should encourage judges to use standard instructions that address implicit bias, but I would advise against a mandate given the wide variety of matters and procedural postures we each have to deal with. In my experience, Pennsylvania's Suggested Standard Civil Jury Instruction 1.140 on bias is

generally well received by jurors. In stating that "we may not be fully aware" of some biases, the instruction does not get pedantic about implicit bias. Rather, the instruction provides the juror with an analytical framework for guarding against any form of bias in evaluating the testimony and other evidence that they must consider in rendering a verdict. I often refer back to these metrics to guide my own factfinding in a bench trial or hearing.

Several research studies have assessed the effectiveness of implicit bias instructions. One research study showed that the instructions had little effect on jury verdicts.[73] Another study "showed no differences between those who had heard the standard instructions and those who had heard the implicit bias instructions." This study revealed that jurors who were exposed to implicit bias instructions "were more attuned to the prohibition against bias ... and they were more likely to discuss the issue of bias." However, their deliberations "showed no differences" with those jurors who had heard standard jury instructions.[74] Moreover, jurors who heard implicit bias instructions invoked concerns about bias that "shut down ... critical inquiry" into trial evidence and witness credibility. Finally, research showed that jurors used accusations of racially biased decision-making as a "weapon" during deliberations to counter fellow jurors with whom they disagreed.[75] Clearly, these studies revealed mixed results about the effectiveness of implicit bias instructions. Additional research is needed to determine whether such instructions can be used in a manner to educate and remove racial biasing effects during a jury deliberation.

Despite the attention to addressing the issues of implicit bias inside the courtroom, many judges are reluctant to identify or even acknowledge it. For example, the Supreme Court of Kansas upheld a judge's decision not to allow race switching instructions in a case where a Black defendant was charged with the assault, rape, and murder of a White, elderly victim. The Court found that the judge, who oversaw the petitioner's original trial, was not obligated to allow such instructions and further claimed that doing so might inject racial bias into the jury's decision-making, where it might not otherwise have existed.[76] Overall, courts have held that "there is no constitutional right to an implicit bias jury instruction."[77] Box 7.8 features a trial judge who shares her observations about levels of implicit bias present in the court system today.

Grounds for Appeal

Jurors' misunderstanding of instructions may have a significant impact on the verdict reached and the outcome of the case. Yet juror misunderstanding is not a legally valid basis for overturning a verdict on appeal. Rather, the only legal grounds for challenging the jury instructions are when the judge materially misstated the applicable law. The losing party in approximately 11 percent of civil cases ultimately files an appeal,[78] and roughly one-quarter of losing parties allege a substantive error in the jury instructions as the grounds for reversing the verdict.[79] Yet only 20 percent of civil cases are ultimately reversed for this reason (approximately 4 percent of civil appeals). Criminal cases tend to have higher appeal rates, mainly because criminal defendants in most states have a statutory right to have their conviction reviewed on appeal. The success rate for appeals in criminal cases, however, is much lower (only 8.5 percent cases reversed) for this reason.[80]

This is a particular problem among capital cases where jurors are called upon to make the ultimate decision about whether a defendant should be sentenced to death because of the crime that was committed. Jurors from capital cases were asked to discuss their understanding of trial evidence and to determine what factors contributed to the verdict they reached. Research findings have revealed that many jurors reached decisions in murder trials without understanding critical statutes regarding punishment guidelines.[81] Medoff (2021) provided a review of published research findings that revealed how jurors misunderstood the jury instructions about the meaning and examples of mitigating and aggravating circumstances.[82] This knowledge is essential for imposing a death sentence in many states.

Weeks v. Angelone provides a stark illustration of the dilemma in these cases.[83] During the sentencing phase of Weeks' capital murder trial, the jury was instructed in accordance with Virginia law, which required jurors to decide whether the defendant posed a future danger or whether the crime was particularly vile. Only if the jury unanimously found one of these factors could it impose a death sentence. If not, a life sentence would result. However, the instructions did not include a separate directive about how jurors should consider mitigating evidence in their decision-making. The jury sent a question to the judge during their deliberation. Specifically, they inquired that if they found aggravating factors present, could they still consider mercy for the defendant? The judge responded by directing them back to the written jury instructions. The defense argued that this response failed to clarify the jury's duty to consider mitigating evidence, potentially causing jurors to believe they had no discretion to recommend a life sentence if one of the aggravating factors was found. The primary concern was that the jury may have misunderstood the role of mitigating evidence, believing they were required to impose a death sentence once they found the statutory aggravating factors, even if they believed mitigating circumstances warranted mercy. Weeks argued this violated the Eighth Amendment, referring to excessive bail, fines, or punishment by preventing jurors from giving full effect to mitigating evidence.

Eighth Amendment

Excessive bail shall not be required, nor excessive fines imposed, ***nor cruel and unusual punishments inflicted.*** (emphasis added)

The Supreme Court ruled against Weeks. In a 5–4 decision, the Court held that the trial judge's reference to the original instructions was constitutionally sufficient. The majority reasoned that the instructions were not misleading and that jurors were presumed to follow them as given. The Court emphasized that although clearer instructions might have been preferable, the Constitution did not require a separate instruction explicitly stating jurors could impose a life sentence based on mitigating evidence, even after finding aggravating factors.

Trial attorneys may try to speak with jurors after a verdict has been reached. During some of these discussions, the jurors may reveal their misunderstanding about the instructions provided to them despite having reached a decision. Trial attorneys may include this information in an appeal to justify a mistrial. Traditionally, even with signed testimonies from actual jurors verifying their misunderstanding of the jury instructions, appellate courts are unwilling to invalidate a jury verdict.[84] Overturning a capital jury's decision to impose a death sentence based on an attorney's argument that the jurors misunderstood the instructions would surely go against dozens of appellate decisions that such evidence is inadmissible.[85] Also, if an appellate court overturned one death penalty case on these grounds, surely other defendants on death row would raise similar claims that juror misunderstanding contributed to their death sentence verdict. What judge or appellate court do you think would be the first to open that Pandora's box?

Conclusion

Juries consistently find ways to navigate trial evidence and reach decisions consistent with those of experienced trial judges. This is impressive given that some jurors are confused by the very instructions informing them about their roles and responsibilities as finders of fact. The instructions juries are provided throughout the trial process should be clear and understandable for all citizens to comprehend and to use when reaching a decision about guilt of criminal wrongdoing or harm caused to another person(s). Jury verdicts that are reached based on a misunderstanding of legal principles and misuse of evidence are counterproductive for all. First, it may facilitate a general distrust among the public for the legal system and the jury's role in it. Second, it may detract from the original purpose of juries to shield the public against the oppressive and abusive practices of a central government.

The presentation of evidence is an essential part of the trial proceeding where jurors determine the facts of the case being tried. After both sides present their case and the judge fully informs the jury about the relevant laws, the members of the jury relocate to a secure room to begin their deliberation about the defendant's criminal wrongdoing. The ability of a jury to reach a decision that runs counter to outdated laws or traditions, or a decision based on the special circumstances faced by a defendant, illustrates the power of the American jury and demonstrates the meaning of the conscience of the community. The next chapter describes the jury deliberation process and factors that may impact the final verdict rendered by a jury.

Summary

How jurors make decisions during a deliberation is somewhat a mystery. Some experts believe jurors use a calculated approach (Bayesian) by assigning values to facts and then applying formal decision rules. Increasing evidence suggests, however, that jurors make decisions following a story-based approach by creating a narrative of the events, motivations, and legal standards. Cognitive schemas help jurors fill in the gaps among trial evidence, familiar story frames, and unstated motivations to reach a verdict in the case.

Research shows that juries reach decisions that align with trial judges in approximately 80 percent of criminal and civil cases, regardless of case complexity. When judges and jurors disagree on the trial outcome, jurors appear to be more lenient than judges. Differences in how judges and jurors assess the weight of the evidence, the nondisclosure of facts at trial, misunderstanding of the law, and emotional impressions about the defendant and trial attorneys may also be factors. Also, jurors often struggle to comprehend the instructions given to them by the judge. Unfamiliar terms of the law or legal jargon negatively impact the fairness and accuracy of jury verdicts.

Jurors have a very specific role in the decision-making process and therefore require clear instructions about their duties and responsibilities. Several attempts have been made to develop clearer jury instructions. Standard instructions improve juror comprehension, save courts time and resources, and remove argumentative language. Overall, legal professionals agree that jury instructions should be written in short, clear sentences, with a simple sentence structure, and in active voice. Double negatives and passive voice should be avoided. Many courts provide jurors with instructions about avoiding using technology and social media accounts during the trial and deliberation; however, some courts include instructions about implicit racial bias and race switching techniques, while other courts do not.

Discussion Questions

1. Think of a time when you were asked to reach a decision but did not have all the facts. This could be related to a family situation, circumstances with your friends, or a work-related matter. What did you do or use to reach a decision in that situation? How did your knowledge of the people involved, their personality traits, the specific environment, etc., come into play in your decision-making and the outcome you reached? Is this any different than what jurors do when they try to decide whether someone is guilty or at fault? Explain why or why not.
2. If you had to design a research study to examine jurors' understanding of jury instructions, what methodology or methodologies would you use? How could you be sure that the findings you were gathering with your chosen method were not subject to error or that the jurors were not simply telling you something they thought you wanted to hear?
3. If you had to write your own jury instructions, what would you consider an essential instruction for jurors to understand? How would you specifically phrase the instruction to minimize misunderstanding? Is there a certain type of case or a trial outcome where a misunderstanding of jury instructions is more concerning? Explain.
4. Ethical consideration. What are your thoughts about an appellate court not invalidating a jury's decision that may have been based on a misunderstanding of jury instructions? Should the courts be responsible for assessing an individual's understanding of jury instructions about trial evidence and the deliberation process? Why or why not? Does the importance of a trial outcome, resulting in a monetary award (civil), long-term imprisonment (criminal), or a death sentence (capital), impact your answer?

Review Questions

1. What are the differences between Bayesian and story-based models related to juror decision-making practices? How do cognitive schemas utilize one's prior knowledge and experiences?
2. How often do trial judges report agreement with the verdicts reached by jurors in civil and criminal cases? What factors contribute to the different verdicts being reached?
3. What was the original role of the jury at a trial proceeding? How did changes in the jury's role impact the development of jury instructions?
4. What were some problems identified with early jury instructions? What are some of the problems today?
5. What do jury instructions mention about implicit bias during the deliberation process and final verdict? What instructions are provided about the use of electronic devices and social media sources during the trial or the deliberation?

Answers to Chapter 7 "What Do You Think?" Questions

1. False. An explanationist or story-based model describes how jurors use event, motivations, and context cues when reaching decisions at trial and during deliberation.
2. False. Standard jury instructions have been revised multiple times over the centuries in both the federal and state court systems.
3. True. Jury instructions should avoid using complex words, formal legal language, double negatives, passive voice, etc.

4. False. Implicit bias occurs when one expresses a desire to associate with an "ingroup" over an "outgroup." Explicit bias occurs when one is fully aware of their prejudiced beliefs.
5. True. Race switching is a technique used to determine whether racial characteristics negatively impact juror decision-making.
6. False. Jurors are repeatedly informed to disconnect from all social media sources during the trial proceeding and during the jury deliberation process.

Key Terms

Achieving an Impartial Jury Project
Bayesian
Book of Approved Jury Instructions
California Civil Jury Instructions
cognitive schemas
explicit bias
Federal Judicial Center
implicit bias
implicit bias instructions
judge-jury agreement
jury instructions
layperson jury
legal homonyms
legal jargon
legalese
leniency effect
Pattern Jury Instruction committees
race switching
Story Model

References

1 Dann, B.M. (1993). "Learning lessons" and "speaking rights": Creating educated and democratic juries. *Indiana Law Review*, *68*, 1229–1279. https://www.repository.law.indiana.edu/cgi/viewcontent.cgi?article=1565&context=ilj
2 Winter, R.J., & Greene, E. (2007). Juror decision-making. In F.T. Durso, R.S. Nickerson, S.T. Dumais, S. Lewandowsky, & T.J. Perfect (Eds.), *Handbook of applied cognition* (2nd ed., pp. 739–761). John Wiley & Sons. https://www.researchgate.net/profile/edie-greene/publication/227992167_juror_decision-making/links/5b7efdd9299bf1d5a723b821/juror-decision-making.pdf)
3 Diamond, S.S. (2003). Truth, justice, and the jury. *Harvard Journal of Law & Public Policy*, *26*(1), 143–155.
4 Hans, V.P. (2000). *Business on trial.* Yale University Press.
5 Hastie, R., Penrod, S.D., & Pennington, N. (1983). *Inside the jury.* Harvard University Press.
6 Hastie, R., Penrod, S.D., & Pennington, N. (1983). *Inside the jury.* Harvard University Press.
7 Hastie, R., Penrod, S.D., & Pennington, N. (1983). *Inside the jury.* Harvard University Press.
8 Kalven, H., & Zeisel, H. (1966). *The American Jury.* Little, Brown.
9 Kalven, H., & Zeisel, H. (1966). *The American Jury.* Little, Brown.
10 Sentell, R.P., Jr. (1991). The Georgia jury and negligence: The view from the bench. *Georgia Law Review*, *26*, 85–99.
11 Eisenberg, T., Hannaford-Agor, P., Hans, V.P., Waters, N.L., Munsterman, G.T., Schwab, S.J., & Wells, M.T. (2005). Judge-jury agreement in criminal cases: A partial replication of Kalven & Zeisel's *The American Jury*. *Journal of Empirical Legal Studies*, *2*(1), 171–207.

12 Hannaford-Agor, P.L., Hans, V.P., & Munsterman, G.T. (2000). Permitting juror discussions during trial: Impact of the Arizona reform. *Law & Human Behavior*, *24*(3), 359–382. https://core.ac.uk/download/pdf/189460412.pdf
13 Horowitz, I.A., ForsterLee, L., & Brolly, I. (1996). Effects of trial complexity on decision making. *Journal of Applied Psychology*, *81*(6), 757–768.
14 Shuman, D., Champagne, A., & Whitaker, E. (1996). Assessing the believability of expert witnesses: Science in the jury box. *Jurimetrics Journal*, *37*, 23–33.
15 Durnal, E.W. (2010). Crime scene investigation (as seen on TV). *Forensic Science International*, *199*(1), 1–5. https://doi.org/10.1016/j.forsciint.2010.02.015
16 Durnal, E.W. (2010). Crime scene investigation (as seen on TV). *Forensic Science International*, *199*(1), 1–5. https://doi.org/10.1016/j.forsciint.2010.02.015
17 Klentz, B.A., Winters, G.M., & Chapman, J.E. (2020). The CSI effect and the impact of DNA evidence on mock jurors and jury deliberations. *Psychology, Crime & Law*, *26*(6), 552–570. https://doi.org/10.1080/1068316X.2019.1708353
18 Klentz, B.A., Winters, G.M., & Chapman, J.E. (2020). The CSI Effect and the impact of DNA evidence on mock jurors and jury deliberations. *Psychology, Crime & Law*, *26*(6), 552–570. https://doi.org/10.1080/1068316X.2019.1708353
19 Christoloukas, N., & Mitsea, A. (2022). The CSI effect in forensic odontology. A systematic review. *The Journal of Forensic Odonto-Stomatology*, *40*(2), 38–43.
20 Strawn, D.J., & Buchanan, R.W. (1976). Jury confusion: A threat to justice. *Judicature*, *59*, 478–483. https://www.ojp.gov/ncjrs/virtual-library/abstracts/jury-confusion-threat-justice
21 Reifman, A., Gusick, S.M., & Ellsworth, P.C. (1992). Real jurors' understanding of the law in real cases. *Law and Human Behavior*, *16*(5), 539–554. https://doi.org/10.1007/BF01044622
22 Diamond, S.S., Murphy, B., & Rose, M.R. (2012). The "Kettleful of Law" in real jury deliberations: Successes, failures, and next steps. *Northwestern University Law Review*, *106*(4), 1537–1568.
23 Kramer, G., & Koenig, D. (1990). Do jurors understand criminal jury instructions? Analyzing the results of the Michigan Juror Comprehension Project. *University of Michigan Journal of Law Reform*, *23*(3), 401–437. https://repository.law.umich.edu/mjlr/vol23/iss3/2/
24 Butler, S.M. (2006). Degrees of culpability: Suicide verdicts, mercy, and the jury in medieval England. *Journal of Medieval and Early Modern Studies*, *36*(2), 263.
25 Tiersma, P. (2001). The rocky road to legal reform: Improving the language of jury instructions. *Brooklyn Law Review*, *66*(4), 1081–1118.
26 Tiersma, P. (2001). The rocky road to legal reform: Improving the language of jury instructions. *Brooklyn Law Review*, *66*(4), 1081–1118.
27 Brown, D.K. (1999). Regulating decision effects of legally sufficient jury instructions. *Southern California Law Review*, *73*(5), 1105–1132.
28 Tiersma, P. (2001). The rocky road to legal reform: Improving the language of jury instructions. *Brooklyn Law Review*, *66*(4), 1081–1118.
29 McCord, D. (2005). The jury revisited. *Judicature*, *88*(6), 284–299.
30 Tiersma, P. (2001). The rocky road to legal reform: Improving the language of jury instructions. *Brooklyn Law Review*, *66*(4), 1081–1118.
31 Charrow, R.P., & Charrow, V.R. (1979). Making legal language understandable: A psycholinguistic study of jury instructions. *Columbia Law Review*, *79*(7), 1306–1374.
32 McCord, D. (2005). The jury revisited. *Judicature*, *88*(6), 284–299.
33 Hannaford-Agor, P.L., & Lassiter, S.N. (2008). *Contemporary pattern jury instruction committees: A snapshot of current operations and possible future directions*. National Center of State Courts. https://www.ncsc-jurystudies.org/__data/assets/pdf_file/0021/6537/contemporary-pattern.pdf
34 Hannaford-Agor, P.L., & Lassiter, S.N. (2008). *Contemporary pattern jury instruction committees: A snapshot of current operations and possible future directions*. National Center of State Courts. https://www.ncsc-jurystudies.org/__data/assets/pdf_file/0021/6537/contemporary-pattern.pdf
35 Hannaford-Agor, P.L., & Lassiter, S.N. (2008). *Contemporary pattern jury instruction committees: A snapshot of current operations and possible future directions*. National Center of State Courts. https://www.ncsc-jurystudies.org/__data/assets/pdf_file/0021/6537/contemporary-pattern.pdf
36 Tiersma, P.M. (2005). Communicating with juries: How to draft more understandable instructions. *The Scribes Journal of Legal Writing*, *10*, 1–32.

37 Tiersma, P.M. (2005). Communicating with juries: How to draft more understandable instructions. *The Scribes Journal of Legal Writing*, *10*, 1–32.
38 State of Connecticut Judicial Branch. (2024, November 2024). *Common Legal Terms*. https://www.jud.ct.gov/legalterms.htm#T
39 Tiersma, P.M. (2005). Communicating with juries: How to draft more understandable instructions. *The Scribes Journal of Legal Writing*, *10*, 1–32.
40 Diamond, S.S., Vidmar, N., Rose, M., Ellis, L., & Murphy, B. (2003). Juror discussions during civil trials: Studying an Arizona innovation. *Arizona Law Review*, *45*(1), 1–81.
41 Tiersma, P.M. (2005). Communicating with juries: How to draft more understandable instructions. *The Scribes Journal of Legal Writing*, *10*, 1–32.
42 Tiersma, P.M. (2005). Communicating with juries: How to draft more understandable instructions. *The Scribes Journal of Legal Writing*, *10*, 1–32.
43 Arizona Supreme Court. (1994). *Jurors, the power of 12*. The Committee on more Effective Use of Juries. https://www.azcourts.gov/Portals/0/15/Jury/Jury12.1.pdf
44 Diamond, S.S., Vidmar, N., Rose, M., Ellis, L., & Murphy, B. (2003). Juror discussions during civil trials: Studying an Arizona innovation. *Arizona Law Review*, *45*(1), 1–81.
45 Brutinel, R., & Thumma, S.A. (2023). Preliminary instructions can boost participation. In Perfecting Jury Trials. *Judicature*, *107*(1), 12–21.
46 Arizona Rules of Civil Procedure 39(f).
47 Diamond, S.S., Vidmar, N., Rose, M., Ellis, L., & Murphy, B. (2003). Juror discussions during civil trials: Studying an Arizona innovation. *Arizona Law Review*, *45*(1), 1–81.
48 Diamond, S.S., Vidmar, N., Rose, M., Ellis, L., & Murphy, B. (2003). Juror discussions during civil trials: Studying an Arizona innovation. *Arizona Law Review*, *45*(1), 1–81.
49 Fox 10 KSAZ. (2023, November 29). *Juror improvements at Maricopa County Superior Court (Phoenix, AZ)* [Video]. YouTube. https://www.youtube.com/watch?v=K6MMIv5uQiE
50 Munsterman, G.T., Hannaford-Agor, P.L., & Whitehead, M.G. (1997). *Jury trial innovations*. National Center for State Courts. https://ncsc.contentdm.oclc.org/digital/collection/juries/id/78/rec/1
51 Mize, G.E., Hannaford-Agor, P.L., & Mott, N.L. (2007). *State-of the-states survey of jury improvement efforts: A compendium report*. National Center for State Courts. https://ncsc.contentdm.oclc.org/digital/collection/juries/id/112/rec/3
52 Hannaford-Agor, P.L., & Moffett, M. (2024). *2023 State-of-the-states survey of jury improvement efforts: Criminal jury trials*. National Center for State Courts. https://ncsc.contentdm.oclc.org/digital/collection/juries/id/384/rec/2;
Hannaford-Agor, P.L., & Moffett, M. (2024). *2023 State-of-the-states survey of jury improvement efforts: Civil jury trials*. National Center for State Courts. https://ncsc.contentdm.oclc.org/digital/collection/juries/id/393/rec/5
53 Hannaford-Agor, P.L., Trochessett, A., Bailey, E., & Kelliher, C. (April 2021). *Jurors and new media: Filling knowledge gaps for judicial and legal policymakers*. National Center for State Courts. https://ncsc.contentdm.oclc.org/digital/collection/juries/id/385/rec/1
54 Hannaford-Agor, P.L., Trochessett, A., Bailey, E., & Kelliher, C. (April 2021). *Jurors and new media: Filling knowledge gaps for judicial and legal policymakers*. National Center for State Courts. https://ncsc.contentdm.oclc.org/digital/collection/juries/id/385/rec/1
55 Administrative Office of the U.S. Courts. (2023, December 8). *Most federal judges warned jurors about social media*. https://www.uscourts.gov/news/2012/01/24/most-federal-judges-warn-jurors-about-social-media
56 Federal Judicial Center. (2023, December 8). *About the FJC*. https://www.fjc.gov/about
57 Federal Judicial Center. (2023, December 8). *The Federal Judicial Center: Education and research for the U.S. federal courts*. https://www.fjc.gov/sites/default/files/2015/About-FJC-English-2014-10-07.pdf
58 Administrative Office of the U.S. Courts. (June 2020). *Proposed model jury instructions: The use of electronic technology to learn or communicate about a case*. https://www.uscourts.gov/sites/default/files/proposed_model_jury_instructions.pdf
59 *Pena-Rodriguez v. Colorado*, 137 S. Ct. 855 (2017).
60 Neitz, M.B. (2019). Pulling back the curtain: Implicit bias in the law school dean search process. *Seton Hall Law Review*, *49*(3), 629–678.
61 Levinson, J.D., Cai, H., & Young, D. (2010). Guilty by implicit racial bias: The guilty/not guilty implicit association test. *Ohio State Journal of Criminal Law*, *8*(1), 187–208.

62 Greenwald, A.G., & Pettigrew, T.F. (2014). With malice toward none and charity for some: In-group favoritism enables discrimination. *The American Psychologist*, *69*(7), 669–684. https://doi.org/10.1037/a0036056
63 Doyle, T. (2017, April). U.S. District Court produces video, drafts jury instructions on implicit bias. *Bar Bulletin*, *1*, 1–2. https://www.courts.wa.gov/content/publicupload/eclips/2017%2004%2006%20US%20District%20Court%20Produces%20Video%20Drafts%20Jury%20Instructions%20on%20Implicit%20Bias.pdf
64 Sommers, S.R., & Ellsworth, P.C. (2001). White juror bias: An investigation of prejudice against Black defendants in the American courtroom. *Psychology, Public Policy, and Law*, *7*(1), 201–229. https://doi.org/10.1037/1076–8971.7.1.201
65 Cardi, J., Hans, V.P. & Parks, G. (2020). Do Black injuries matter? Implicit bias and jury decision making in tort cases. *Southern California Law Review*, *93*(3), 507–570.
66 Greenwald, A.G., McGhee, D.E., & Schwartz, J.L.K. (1998). Measuring individual differences in implicit cognition: The implicit association test. *Journal of Personality and Social Psychology*, *74*(6), 1464–1480. https://doi.org/10.1037/0022–3514.74.6.1464
67 Miller, C. (2022). The constitutional right to an implicit bias jury instruction. *The American Criminal Law Review*, *59*(2), 349–391.
68 Lynch, M., Kidd, T., & Shaw, E. (2022). The subtle effects of implicit bias instructions. *Law & Policy*, *44*(1), 98–124. https://doi.org/10.1111/lapo.12
69 American Bar Association. (2017). *Achieving an Impartial Jury (AIJ) toolbox*. https://www.americanbar.org/content/dam/aba/publications/criminaljustice/voirdire_toolchest.pdf
70 American Bar Association. (2017). *Achieving an Impartial Jury (AIJ) toolbox*. https://www.americanbar.org/content/dam/aba/publications/criminaljustice/voirdire_toolchest.pdf
71 American Bar Association. (2024, January 4). *About the American Bar Association*. https://www.americanbar.org/about_the_aba
72 American Bar Association. (2024, January 4). *ABA mission and goals*. https://www.americanbar.org/about_the_aba/aba-mission-goals
73 Elek, J.K., & Hannaford-Agor, P. (2014). *Can explicit instructions reduce expressions of implicit bias? New questions following a test of a specialized jury instruction* [Conference session]. 2014 National Center for State Courts Conference, National Center for State Courts. https://papers.ssrn.com/sol3/papers.cfm?abstract_id=2430438
74 Lynch, M., Kidd, T., & Shaw, E. (2022). The subtle effects of implicit bias instructions. *Law & Policy*, *44*(1), 98–124. https://doi.org/10.1111/lapo.12181
75 Lynch, M., Kidd, T., & Shaw, E. (2022). The subtle effects of implicit bias instructions. *Law & Policy*, *44*(1), 98–124. https://doi.org/10.1111/lapo.12181
76 *State v. Nesbitt*, 417 P.3d 1058, 1068 (2018).
77 Miller, C. (2022). The constitutional right to an implicit bias jury instruction. *The American Criminal Law Review*, *59*(2), 349–391.
78 Waters, N.L. (2007). *Civil trials on appeal, Part 1*. National Center for State Courts. https://ncsc.contentdm.oclc.org/digital/collection/appellate/id/87/rec/1
79 Waters, N.L., & Sohoni, T. (2007). *Civil trials on appeal, Part 2*. National Center for State Courts. https://ncsc.contentdm.oclc.org/digital/collection/appellate/id/94/rec/1
80 Waters, N.L., Gallegos, A., Green, J., & Rozsi, M. (2015). *Criminal appeals in state courts*. Bureau of Justice Statistics. https://bjs.ojp.gov/content/pub/pdf/casc.pdf
81 Bentele, U., & Bowers, W.J. (2001). How jurors decide on death: Guilt is overwhelming; aggravation requires death; and mitigation is no excuse. *Brooklyn Law Review*, *66*(4), 1011–1080.
82 Medoff, M. (2021). The confusing nature of jury instructions in capital cases. *University of Central Florida Department of Legal Studies Law Journal*, *4*, 35–52.
83 *Weeks v. Angelone*, 528 U.S. 225 (2000).
84 Tiersma, P. (2001). The rocky road to legal reform: Improving the language of jury instructions. *Brooklyn Law Review*, *66*(4), 1081–1118.
85 Tiersma, P. (2001). The rocky road to legal reform: Improving the language of jury instructions. *Brooklyn Law Review*, *66*(4), 1081–1118.

8 Jury Deliberation and Trial Outcome

What Do You Think?

Before reviewing the concepts addressed in this chapter, answer True or False to each of the following questions or statements. Correct answers can be found at the end of Chapter 8.

1. The typical jury foreperson is a female, blue-collar, and introverted.
2. Evidence-driven juries place an importance on determining a verdict at the beginning of the deliberation.
3. The Solomon Asch study addressed issues of race and gender related to juror decision-making.
4. The racial and gender composition of the jury can influence the verdict reached in capital cases.
5. Jurors can be arrested if their final verdict does not correspond with the evidence presented at trial.
6. The John Peter Zenger case related to jury nullification and committing seditious libel.

Learning Objectives

After reading this chapter, you will be able to:

1. List the typical characteristics associated with the jury foreperson.
2. Compare two strategies for how jurors review trial evidence during deliberations.
3. Describe the Solomon Ashe conformity experiment.
4. Describe how the racial and gender composition of a jury impacts trial outcomes in capital cases.
5. Define jury nullification and describe reasons why juries engage in such practices.
6. Explain examples of jury nullification in practice.

Introduction

As discussed in Chapter 6, many lawyers regard voir dire as the decisive stage of the trial proceedings. Some go so far as to assert that the trial's outcome is effectively determined once the jury is empaneled, with the remainder of the trial unfolding as little more than the working out of an inevitable conclusion. Kalven and Zeisel did not view voir dire as the defining phase of a jury trial but did argue that the verdict is largely fixed by the end of the evidentiary phase, leaving deliberations as a procedural formality rather than a meaningful forum for decision-making.[1] Chapter 7 introduced a related skepticism of the role of deliberations in

DOI: 10.4324/9781003677796-10

group decision-making, grounded in cognitive psychology—namely, that jurors begin the trial with preexisting cognitive schema that influence how they interpret and organize trial evidence. These mental frameworks, shaped by prior knowledge, experiences, and beliefs, filter the testimony and exhibits presented in court. If jurors' interpretations of the evidence are essentially locked in by these schemas before deliberations begin, then, as some have argued, there may be little opportunity for post-evidentiary discussion to shift perspectives in any meaningful way.

Such perspectives diminish the importance of deliberation, portraying it as an administrative step rather than a substantive one. Findings from empirical research challenge these views. One study employed post-trial juror surveys to examine the timing of juror opinion formation in civil trials. More than 20 percent of jurors reported that they began deliberations with no personal preference for a verdict, and 40 percent of jurors reported they changed their minds about their verdict preference during deliberations.[2] Far from being perfunctory, deliberations play a critical role in shaping verdicts. Group discussion can correct misunderstandings, fill evidentiary gaps in memory, reframe legal concepts, and raise minority viewpoints that ultimately influence the majority. The deliberation room is not where a foregone conclusion is formalized, but rather a dynamic environment in which jurors actively test, revise, and sometimes overturn their initial impressions. These findings invite a reexamination of deliberations—not as an afterthought to the evidentiary phase but as a vital component of the jury's truth-seeking process.

In This Chapter

This chapter reviews material related to: 1) how jurors begin the deliberation process; 2) factors that impact jury deliberation practices; 3) the influence of juror race and gender on verdicts in capital cases; and 4) why jury nullification occurs.

Jury Deliberation

Deliberations begin once all the evidence has been presented and the judge has instructed the jury on the applicable law. The final jury instructions may include guidance about conducting deliberations. Consider, for example, the instructions provided to jurors serving in the Missouri Courts about how jurors should approach and interact with one another:

> Each of you should respect the opinions of your fellow jurors as you would have them respect yours, and in a spirit of tolerance and understanding endeavor to bring the deliberations of the whole jury to an agreement upon a verdict. Do not be afraid to change your opinion if the discussion persuades you that you should. But a juror should not agree to a verdict that violates the instructions of the court. Nor in a criminal case should a juror agree to a verdict of guilty unless the juror is convinced of the defendant's guilt beyond a reasonable doubt.[3]

With very rare exceptions, jury deliberations take place secretly, and the resulting verdict reflects only the binary choice between conviction and acquittal, or liability and no liability in civil cases. Thus, most empirical studies rely on post-trial surveys and interviews and on mock jury experiments to understand how interpersonal dynamics affect decision-making during this stage of the jury trial. Findings from these studies, however, show that jury deliberations are focused on trial facts and that jurors tend to self-correct when issues or discussions go off topic.[4]

Box 8.1: The Arizona Jury Project[5]

In 1998, the Arizona Supreme Court allowed social science researchers and legal scholars a unique opportunity to study the American jury system. The Court approved a research request to study civil jury trials in the Pima County Superior Court (Tucson, AZ). The project was funded jointly by the American Bar Association and the National Science Foundation. Between 1998 and 2001, a total of 50 civil juries were examined, while employing multiple methods of data collection. Findings were gathered through post-trial questionnaires with judges, trial attorneys, and jurors. Also, unique to this project was that researchers were granted permission to videotape jury discussions during trial and jury deliberations.[6]

The goals of the project were diverse, but focused on the impact of **Rule 39(f)**, a change made by the Arizona Supreme Court to the Arizona Rules of Civil Procedure that allowed jurors to discuss the evidence presented at trial in the jury room during recesses or breaks in the trial proceeding.[7] Researchers examined whether jurors took the opportunity to talk with one another during the trial proceedings, what was discussed during the trial deliberations, when their final judgment was reached, and how allowing discussions during the trial affected juror morale, cohesiveness, and "perceived legitimacy of the trial process."[8] These findings are discussed throughout this text.

In addition to mock jury trial experiments, several research studies have recorded the actual deliberations and interviewed actual jurors about their jury selection and deliberation experiences. Box 8.1 describes the **Arizona Jury Project** and researchers' unprecedented access to the deliberation process with actual jurors in civil cases. The information described in the next section of this chapter will focus on jury deliberation practices. The research findings will be separated into specific themes or categories. Research gathered about what jurors do upon entering the deliberation room and how they begin their discussion will be addressed first.

Foreperson

There are few guidelines for how a jury proceeds once it enters the deliberation room. In some jurisdictions, the **foreperson** is appointed by the judge or randomly selected by lot. In most jurisdictions, however, the jury's first task is to name or elect a foreperson. Research from mock jury trials shows the process for selecting a foreperson is informal and resulted from either self-nominating or from being nominated by another juror(s).[9] The foreperson has unique responsibilities on the jury. These duties may include contributing to and monitoring the flow of the discussion and ensuring everyone has an opportunity to speak and to be heard. Research on real juries revealed the foreperson talked more frequently than any other jury member,[10] including twice as much as the average juror in some mock jury research studies.[11] The foreperson may also be responsible for describing how and when a vote will be taken during the deliberation, periodically summarizing the issue(s) being discussed by jurors, signing the verdict form, and sharing the final verdict in the courtroom, if the courtroom clerk does not do so.[12]

Several research studies have documented the social background characteristics of the jury foreperson. Research gathered through actual trials and mock jury simulations of the

American jury system revealed the juror selected to serve as the group leader or foreperson typically was White,[13] male,[14] and a working professional.[15] An individual may be chosen for the position of foreperson because they have had prior jury experience(s) or because they took the most extensive notes during a trial.[16] Findings from social psychological research studies with real jurors showed that forepersons were extraverted, measured as being "very active and social people from those who are more subdued … prefer contact with others, enjoy a high level of activity, and tend to be happy."[17] Other findings revealed juries with an extrovert foreperson deliberated longer and that fellow jurors perceived the foreperson to be influential when reaching a verdict in criminal cases.[18]

Verdict-Driven vs Evidence-Driven Deliberations

Jurors' attention will quickly turn back to the trial after the foreperson has been selected. How an individual jury begins the deliberation process varies, however. Traditionally, two approaches have been identified. One format for beginning a jury deliberation has an **evidence-driven** focus.[19] Juries using this approach reserve the initial vote about a trial verdict until the evidence has been sufficiently discussed. Individual jurors do not share their opinion about a verdict until the jury has reviewed the relevant facts or evidence presented during the trial. A first vote about a verdict on these juries may not come until the end of the deliberation process when all the facts and evidence have been reviewed.[20]

The second approach has a **verdict-driven** focus.[21] Juries that use this format place an importance on determining the verdict or the outcome of the case at the beginning of the deliberation.[22] Individual jurors who approach the deliberation from this viewpoint will cite specific trial evidence that supports their opinions or reasoning; if all are in agreement, jurors see little need to spend time discussing issues not in dispute by others.[23] Also, verdict-driven juries are characterized by frequent polling throughout the deliberation process to determine whether a decision has been reached. Juries that follow the verdict-driven approach have a public vote about an outcome early during the deliberation process to determine where the jury stands overall.[24] Research gathered with 50 civil juries from Arizona found in 60 percent of cases a juror called for a vote within the first 10 minutes of the deliberation, but the request was denied two-thirds of the time because some jurors wanted to continue discussing the trial evidence.[25] Research findings are mixed about which approach is more commonly used among juries, or whether there is a blending of both approaches.

Research indicates that a jury's leaning on the first vote is highly associated with the jury's final verdict and the trial outcome. For example, one study examined the leanings of jurors at the beginning of the deliberation process and compared those findings with the final verdict reached after deliberating with fellow jurors.[26] In that study, 90 percent of the cases were rendered in the manner that corresponded with the initial jurors' leanings. However, the degree of consensus among jurors on the first vote is extremely significant. In 2002, research findings were published from a study of hung juries in four urban courts.[27] Findings from the report, shown in Figure 8.1 below, revealed that as the size of the minority faction increased, the probability of persuading the majority faction to their position also increased. Thus, out of 91 cases in which the first vote leaned slightly (e.g., eight or nine jurors out of 12) towards conviction or acquittal, more than one-third of the cases either resulted in the verdict favored by the minority faction on the first vote or the jury deadlocked. The study also found that the scenario in *12 Angry Men*,[28] in which a single holdout juror can change the minds of his fellow jurors, is not just Hollywood fiction. When one or two jurors favored acquittal when the first vote strongly leaned toward conviction (10 to 12 jurors out of 12), they were able to change the minds of other jurors in one out of eight cases.

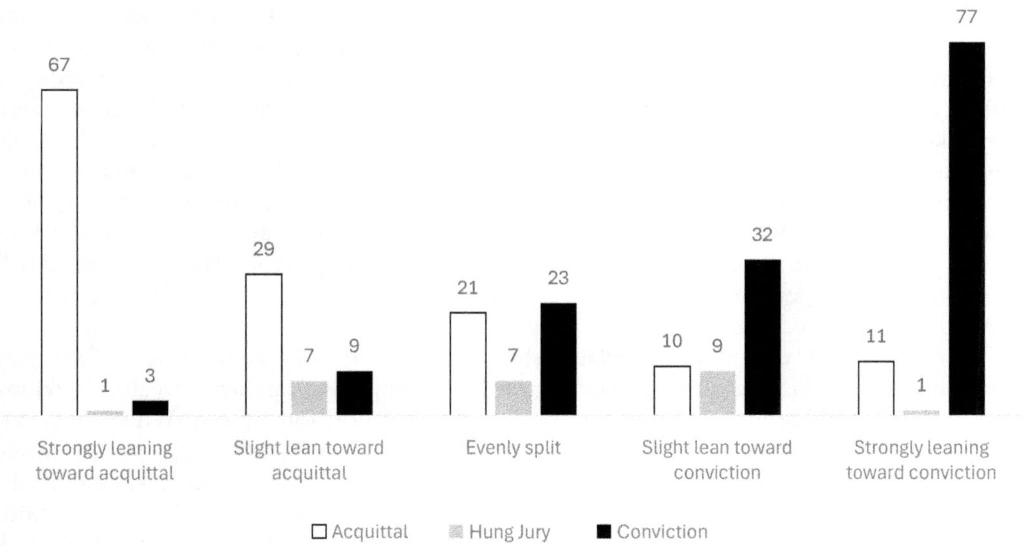

Figure 8.1: First Vote and Final Jury Verdicts
(*Source:* National Center for State Courts.[29])

Length of Jury Deliberations

One of the few aspects of jury deliberations that can be objectively measured is the length of time jurors engage in deliberations. In 2023, the National Center for State Courts collected information about deliberation length in nearly 6,000 jury trials. The median deliberation length for capital felony trials was four hours compared to three hours for noncapital and civil trials, one hour for misdemeanor trials, and two hours for other case types (e.g., domestic relations, juvenile, probate and mental health).[30] In addition to case type, deliberation length was also highly correlated with trial length and with legal complexity, but not with evidentiary complexity.

Deliberation Practices

What shapes jury deliberation practices, and the verdict juries reach? The Administrative Office of the United States Courts described how jurors should behave during the trial deliberation process: "To decide cases correctly, jurors must be honest and intelligent. They must have both integrity and good judgment."[31] Empirical studies repeatedly confirm that the weight of the evidence presented at trial is the single biggest predictor of trial outcomes. Nevertheless, some factors impact the quality and substance of the jury deliberation process, including juror characteristics and the degree to which jurors feel pressured to conform their beliefs to those of other jurors.

Juror Characteristics

Juror social background characteristics have been examined over the decades related to deliberation practices, individual participation levels, and the verdicts reached. For example, traditionally research about **juror characteristics** showed that male jurors,[32] jurors who were employed in professional jobs,[33] and those who had higher socioeconomic status (education and income)[34] spoke more frequently during the jury deliberation. Jurors who were employed as professionals tended to render higher damage awards for victims in civil cases than did clerical or blue-collar workers,[35] while female jurors were more likely than male jurors to acquit the defendant in rape trials.[36] The changing role of women in American society in recent years has been observed inside the jury, as some research showed participation levels between male and female jurors were the same.[37] Finally, mock jurors who had a religious affiliation (Protestant) and who espoused fundamentalist views of the Bible were more likely to show support for the death penalty,[38] while prior jury experience did not greatly impact or predict a juror's verdict in either a criminal or civil case.[39]

The research also examined the relationship between the racial composition of the jury with deliberation practices and trial outcomes. For example, researchers revealed in felony cases from North Carolina how increasing the jury composition by one White, male juror "increased the conviction rate for a Black defendant by 3.8 percentage points," while increasing the jury composition by one Black male juror "would decrease the probability of conviction for a Black defendant by 7.8 percentage points."[40] Similar findings were made in Florida where it was found that "when there are no potential Black jurors in the pool, Black defendants are significantly more likely than Whites to be convicted of at least one crime" (81 percent for Black defendants versus 66 percent for White defendants).[41]

Other findings from a computer-based study revealed participants' behavior during mock jury deliberations using mixed-race groups. The findings showed racially diverse juries produced discomfort and "social anxiety among a sample of predominantly White participants" as measured by "reduced word count, more self-monitored responses, and fewer social words."[42] Rather than viewing this finding in a negative light, the researchers suggested that the jurors' better self-control, self-monitoring, and greater cognitive efforts enhanced the deliberation process that should focus on important features like case facts and the law.[43] Other research revealed similar findings that White jurors engaged in more substantial discussions of trial evidence in mixed-race juries.[44]

The impact of demographic diversity on jury deliberations extends beyond self-monitoring by White jurors when interacting with Black jurors. Professors Shari Diamond and Valerie Hans pointed to the laudable impact of diversity on the quality of deliberations.[45] For example, deliberations with diverse juries tend to be longer and involve a more thorough discussion of case facts. They also noted that the probability of a diverse jury increases as the size of the jury increases and that jurors engage in more vigorous deliberations when required to render a unanimous verdict.

Conformity

Conformity is another factor that could impact the jury deliberation process, and the verdict reached. For example, findings from a renowned social science research study revealed how individuals conformed to group pressure and coercion. The Solomon Asch conformity experiment illustrated this point when non-coerced research subjects selected clearly incorrect answers during an experiment related to conformity.[46] Box 8.2 provides more details about the study and its findings. Overall, researchers found one-third of subjects provided answers that conformed with the other confederate subjects' answers even when their response was clearly incorrect.

Box 8.2: Solomon Asch Conformity Experiment

In 1951, Solomon Asch designed and conducted his classic experiment on conformity. The research involved six subjects, five who were confederates of Asch and were pre-instructed to provide specific answers during the experiment. There was only one true research subject in the group. Variations in the experiments altered the number of participants, sometimes eight in total, but there was only one true research subject being assessed.

The research subjects (n=50) were male, college students. During the experiment, the confederates provided clearly wrong answers when asked to match a target line with a line of similar length from a board of options. Asch was interested in determining whether the subject would conform to the group, even when the answers given by the confederates were obviously wrong. The experiment was designed to include 18 trials or rounds. Overall, the findings were startling. One-third of the subjects conformed with the confederates in each of the rounds that a wrong response was given, 75 percent conformed in at least one of the rounds, while only 25 percent of subjects never conformed.

The findings from Asch's social psychology experiment about conformity is important for jury deliberations. If there is a lone holdout or dissenter on the jury, that juror may, sooner or later, simply adopt the majority opinion rather than retain their own viewpoint and reach a verdict according to their own conscience. Conformity under these circumstances may reflect the normative influence of juries on dissenting jurors. For example, a dissenting juror may privately retain their belief about the guilt or innocence of a defendant or the level of culpability for criminal wrongdoing; however, they may still confirm to the majority viewpoint to avoid feeling pressured, being alienated, or viewed as disruptive. A juror who is motivated to conform for these reasons does so because of an emotional response.[47]

Alternatively, a dissenting juror's decision to conform may be related to the informational influence of the jury. For example, a juror might be undecided or confused about the evidence presented at the trial. The deliberation discussion with fellow jurors may guide a dissenting juror's decision to rethink or analyze information in a new way. When a dissenting juror is motivated to change their decision based on these reasons, they do so because of a cognitive response.[48] This was the question that researchers investigated in response to a puzzling finding from a hung jury study—namely, that 13 percent of jurors reported that, if it were entirely up to them, they would have reached a different verdict, and 8 percent of jurors reported still being undecided about their personal verdict preference at the conclusion of jury deliberations.[49] Moreover, over one half of the cases had at least one juror who disagreed with other jurors about the verdict. While group conformity likely contributed to their assent to the majority verdict preference, the researchers found that jurors' views of the evidence, jurors' sense of fairness, and deliberation procedures were related to the likelihood they would dissent.

It should be noted, however, that conforming to the group is not the intended purpose of the deliberation process. Indeed, the pre-deliberation instructions provided to Missouri jurors that were shared at the beginning of this chapter echoed this point. Research showed that jurors, who hold differing opinions than the majority, are more able to maintain their contradicting viewpoint, if at least one other juror shares their opinion.[50] These findings are consistent with those uncovered in the Asch conformity experiment.[51] Pressure for changing one's own opinion may be exacerbated in smaller juries of six compared to 12 members, where smaller groups may be more homogeneous and may not reflect the full conscience of the community. Box 8.3 describes the experiences one of the coauthors of this textbook had while serving as a trial juror in 2024 in Virginia.

Box 8.3: From the Field

Name: Paula Hannaford-Agor

Position: National Center for State Courts (1993–2025) (Director, Center for Jury Studies, 2006–2025)

Describe your experience during the jury deliberation.

Jury deliberations were much more chaotic than I expected. They were not at all as they are depicted in juror orientation videos in which jurors calmly take turns discussing their views around the table. The acoustics in the room were not great. The table was long and narrow, making it difficult to see everyone. And it is more difficult than you would expect for 12 people to engage in sustained discussion without talking over each other or engaging in side conversations. Nevertheless, after 30 minutes or so, it became apparent that most of us harbored some doubts about the defendant's guilt.

This was perhaps the most significant insight from my experience as a trial juror. Most criminal jury trials result in a guilty verdict in which jurors reach a unanimous consensus that the defendant committed the crime of which they were accused beyond a reasonable doubt. Substantial empirical research has shown that most jurors are profoundly satisfied with their jury deliberations and confident in their verdict. Voting to convict the defendant involves a certain moral clarity in which jurors may ultimately find comfort.

In our case, however, we had concluded only that the Commonwealth had not proved the defendant guilty beyond a reasonable doubt. But there was no consensus about whether the defendant had committed the crime. Instead, our views covered the gamut, from the defendant's complete exoneration (the victim was lying or was coerced by her mother) to the defendant probably committed the crime, but the collective testimony of witnesses was too equivocal to support a conviction. I found the lack of a consensus about that underlying issue to be profoundly disquieting—we had done our duty as trial jurors with respect to the conclusion of guilt versus acquittal, but we had failed to find the truth of the allegations. In this respect, I was surprised and unhappy at how unsatisfying the process was. In 20/20 hindsight, this may be a more common sentiment for jurors than is generally recognized.

Note: The above was an excerpt from a longer essay published about the coauthor's personal experience serving as a trial juror.[52]

Trial Outcomes

A verdict based on the evidence presented at trial and the law as instructed by the trial judge is the desired outcome of every jury trial. Findings revealed this is the result in most cases. For example, a 2024 report from the National Center for State Courts of approximately 6,000 cases revealed 95 percent of criminal trials resulted in convictions, acquittals, or mixed verdicts; only 5 percent of trials resulted in a hung jury or a mistrial.[53] These results are shown in Figure 8.3. Juries reached verdicts in nearly as many civil trials, with only 8 percent of cases resulting in non-verdicts due to hung juries, mistrials, settlements, or dismissals.[54]

Capital Juries

One type of criminal case involved capital offenses in which the potential sentence is life imprisonment or the death penalty. Thus, unbiased and impartial jury deliberations in capital trials are of utmost importance. After determining someone is guilty of a capital crime, the jury may be asked to consider reasons for imposing the ultimate punishment, including a death sentence. How do jurors reach such decisions in capital cases? How does the racial and gender composition of an individual jury shape the deliberation discussion and trial outcome? Box 8.4 describes the **Capital Jury Project (CJP)**, a research initiative that examined jurors' decision-making in capital cases, including their decision about finding someone guilty of a capital crime and their decision to impose a death sentence.

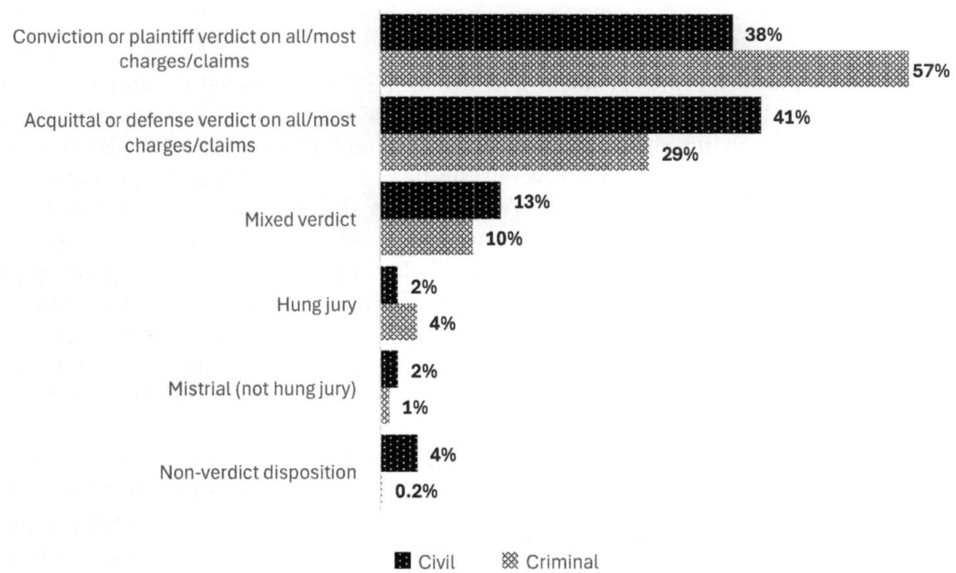

Figure 8.3: Jury Trial Outcomes

(*Source:* Hannaford-Agor & Moffett, 2024. *2023 State-of-the-states survey of jury improvement efforts: Criminal jury trials*; Hannaford-Agor & Moffett, 2024. *2023 State-of-the-states survey of jury improvement efforts: Civil jury trials.*)

Box 8.4: Capital Jury Project

The Capital Jury Project (Phase 1) was a National Science Foundation funded study that began in 1990. The purpose of the CJP was to "examine and systematically describe jurors' exercise of capital-sentencing discretion; identify the sources and assess the extent of arbitrariness in jurors' exercise of capital discretion; and assess the efficacy of the principal forms of capital statutes in controlling arbitrariness in capital sentencing."[55] Fourteen death penalty states were included in the research: Alabama, California, Florida, Georgia, Indiana, Kentucky, Louisiana, Missouri, North Carolina, Pennsylvania, South Carolina, Tennessee, Texas, and Virginia. These states were selected, in part, because of the large number of executions conducted in the 1980s and 1990s. Also, these states represented the principal variations in guided discretion capital statutes (e.g., threshold, weighing, and directed).[56]

Jurors who served on the guilt and punishment phases of a capital trial were randomly selected to participate in three-to-four-hour interviews about their experiences serving on a capital case. The total sample consisted of 1,198 jurors from 353 capital trials. Approximately four jurors from each case were interviewed by researchers. The interview consisted of open- and closed-ended questions designed to uncover factors impacting jurors' decision-making during the guilt and punishment phases of the trial. Jurors were asked about the main factors that influenced their decisions about punishment and the dynamics of the deliberation with other jurors. The extensive interview contained 700 closed-ended questions and provided multiple opportunities for respondents to provide additional open-ended narratives.

Findings published by the CJP, starting in the mid-1990s, revealed the impact that race and gender had on trial outcomes of capital cases. The impact was dramatic, especially in interracial killings involving either a White defendant and Black victim (W/B) or a Black defendant and White victim (B/W). Overall, findings revealed that a death sentence was three times more likely to result in a B/W case when the jury consisted of five or more White male jurors, while a life sentence was two times more likely to result if the jury consisted of one Black male juror.[57] Other race-specific findings showed the divergent opinions that jurors expressed during their deliberation about punishment in these capital cases. For example, White jurors openly struggled to recognize mitigating circumstances such as "the defendant's background and upbringing," while Black jurors thought about the defendant's homelife and childhood and what they perceived as remorse shown by Black defendants during the trial.[58]

The potential risk that racial characteristics of a defendant and victim may have on a jury's decision-making and trial outcome was addressed by the U.S. Supreme Court in the mid-1980s. In *Turner v. Murray*, the Court found that jurors could be questioned during the voir dire about racial bias, and they could be informed about any race-based characteristics that are relevant to the case where they will be empaneled. The Court opined that providing jurors with this information is minimally intrusive.[59] One year later, however, the Court found in *McCleskey v. Kemp* that evidence of racial discrimination, in general, does not negate certain statutory regulations or violate a defendant's constitutional protections.[60] For example, allowing juries to impose the death penalty as the ultimate punishment in capital cases is permissible, even though social science research findings clearly demonstrated that the death penalty is imposed in a racially discriminatory manner. Box 8.5 provides more details about these trials and the Court's opinion. Box 8.6 features comments from a judge about jurors' experiences in serious criminal cases, including homicide.

Box 8.5: U.S. Supreme Court Rulings on Race and the Capital Jury

Turner v. Murray (1986)[61]

The decision reached by the Supreme Court in *Turner* originated from the defendant's appeal of his death sentence imposed by a jury in Virginia. The defendant, an African America male, was accused of killing a White store owner during an armed robbery. The guilt of the defendant was not in dispute; however, during the voir dire process at Turner's original trial, the judge refused the defense attorney's request to question the jury about racial bias or prejudice. Specifically, the attorney wanted to ask jurors the following question:

> The defendant, Willie Lloyd Turner, is a member of the [African] race. The victim, W. Jack Smith, Jr., was a White Caucasian. Will these facts prejudice you against Willie Lloyd Turner or affect your ability to render a fair and impartial verdict based solely on the evidence?[62]

The Supreme Court wrote a lengthy opinion noting three factors for overturning the defendant's death sentence, including "the crime charged involved interracial violence, the broad discretion given the jury under Virginia law at the sentencing hearing, and the special seriousness of the risk of improper sentencing in a capital case."[63]

McCleskey v. Kemp (1987)[64]

The defendant, Warren McCleskey, an African American male, was sentenced to death by a jury in Georgia for the killing of a White police officer during an armed robbery. The defendant appealed the verdict based on findings from social science research conducted in Georgia during the 1970s that included 2,000 murder cases.[65] The research, referred to as the Baldus study, revealed that Black defendants accused of killing White victims were more likely to receive the death penalty. The defendant argued that Georgia's capital sentencing statutes allowed for racially discriminatory decisions that violated the Eighth and Fourteenth Amendments.

The U.S. Supreme Court found in *McCleskey* that the defendant's rights were not violated and affirmed the jury's sentencing decision. In 1987, Justice Lewis F. Powell, writing the opinion for the Court, stated the defendant needed to show that the jurors acted in discriminatory ways in his specific case to demonstrate a violation of Constitutional rights; the results of a research study do not show biased decision-making related to his specific sentencing outcome. Moreover, Powell added,

> The Constitution does not require that a State eliminate any demonstrable disparity that correlates with a potentially irrelevant factor in order to operate a criminal justice system that includes capital punishment. Petitioner's arguments are best presented to the legislative bodies, not the courts."[66]

Box 8.6: From the Field

Name: Giovanni O. Campbell

Position: Judge, Court of Common Pleas, Philadelphia, Pennsylvania

How long have you worked in this position?
I have worked in this position for 12 ½ years.

Jurors sometimes express concerns about their physical safety and confidentiality, how their verdict will affect the defendant, and experiencing personal trauma from serving. What measures are taken to ensure the wellbeing of jurors?
We employ several measures to protect jurors and the confidentiality of their communications. The movements of prospective jurors and selected jurors are closely managed by court officers. They are sequestered within the courthouse upon arrival, are kept together in the same rooms throughout the day and are escorted out of the building at the end of the day. They are also required to wear yellow badges to publicly identify them as jurors. All of this is done to prevent any contact with the defendant, attorneys, witnesses, or anything that may prejudice them.

Part of the selection process requires prospective jurors to complete a questionnaire regarding beliefs and attitudes that may affect their impartiality as jurors. These forms are captioned with general biographical information about them, like what part of the city they live in, their educational level, marital status, present and past occupations, their spouse's occupation, and whether they have children. This information is available to the attorneys and the defendant as part of jury selection. However, once jury selection is complete, the parties' copies are collected and destroyed to protect the jurors' privacy.

Jurors are often concerned about the future consequences of their verdict, so much so that many jurors agree to serve only after being assured that the case they are about to hear does not involve the death penalty. They are informed that capital cases are no longer brought in Philadelphia and are rarely brought in Pennsylvania. Even still, some jurors are aware that a first-degree murder conviction in Pennsylvania triggers a mandatory sentence of life without parole, which is also a concern for them.

To address these concerns, jurors are reminded that their role is to determine culpability, and that it would be the judge's role (not theirs) to determine the appropriate sentence, if they find the defendant guilty. Additionally, the attorneys are prohibited from focusing on the legal consequences of conviction when they present their arguments to the jury. Sometimes, after delivering a guilty verdict, jurors inquire what the defendant's sentence will be. A succinct explanation of the sentencing process, without encouraging discussion about the defendant's particular fate, respects their role as jurors and helps minimize the risk of tainting their future service.

Finally, jurors sometimes experience trauma from hearing and deciding serious cases. The nature of the allegations, explicit photographs, and the testimony of victims can be dramatic presentations that could affect a juror's wellbeing. Our courthouse makes psychological/social services available to jurors who are negatively impacted by the process.

During your years on the bench, what are the highs and lows of being a judge overseeing serious crimes, like homicide?

The best thing about presiding over homicide cases and other serious criminal trials is working with juries. It is truly rewarding to help citizens from outside the legal field play such a critical role in our system of justice. Before and after their participation, we emphatically express our gratitude to jurors for their time and service. It is gratifying to see the sense of fulfillment in their eyes once they have completed their work. Jurors overwhelmingly describe their service as a positive experience.

Sometimes jurors ask if my decision would have been the same as theirs. This is always an opportunity to stress that since they were the ultimate factfinders, their decision is the only one that matters. Also, while jurors are the sincere evaluators of the facts presented, the judge's role is to ensure due process and serve as the referee between the parties.

The downside to presiding over serious criminal trials is the victim impact phase of sentencing proceedings. At that time, affected persons have the right to share with the court how their lives have been changed by the loss of life and/or serious bodily injury to their loved ones. This type of testimony is offered in most cases by parents, siblings, friends, and others who cared for the decedent. It is also common to hear testimony from the defendant's loved ones at sentencing. This testimony is often very emotional and can be personally taxing.

Jury Nullification

Consistent with previous studies of judge-jury agreement, judges reported agreement with the jury's verdict in 78 percent of criminal trials and 68 percent of civil trials. As discussed in Chapter 7, Kalven and Zeisel identified differences in perceptions of the weight of the evidence as the primary factor explaining disagreements with the juries' verdicts. But they also noted that jury sentiments about the law contributed to judge-jury disagreement, too.[67] **Jury nullification** describes instances when the jury renders a verdict contrary to the evidence and the law. In most instances, it refers to criminal cases in which the jury intentionally acquits when the evidence and law strongly support a conviction.[68] The term is sometimes used more broadly to describe verdicts contrary to the evidence and law in civil cases or criminal cases in which the jury convicts when the evidence and law supports an acquittal. The intent to nullify is key. When a jury misinterprets the law and reaches a decision not corresponding with what the law indicates, the jury does not engage in nullification.[69]

> The trial by jury might safely be introduced into a despotic government, if the jury were to exercise no right of judging of the law, or the justice of the law.
>
> —Lysander Spooner, American lawyer

Someone who is studying the American jury system for the first time may find the concept of jury nullification confusing. Indeed, some seasoned legal professionals who have practiced law for their entire careers may feel the same way. One may wonder: why would a jury intentionally avoid prosecuting an individual who broke the law? There are multiple reasons why a jury may act this way. One reason is the jury might simply disagree with the law itself.[70] Even though the evidence presented at trial determined the defendant's guilt beyond a reasonable doubt, a jury may still acquit. Consider the following example.

The United States in the mid-1900s was highly segregated along racial lines. Jim Crow laws existed in many southern states that prohibited people of color from entering establishments like private businesses, community restaurants, and public restrooms.[71] If a person of color violated these restrictions by entering a White-only establishment, the individual may have been arrested and prosecuted for breaking the law. A jury would be responsible for reviewing evidence presented during the trial that the individual did enter the restricted facility and thereby violated the law. Concerning the concept of nullification, however, the jury could review the facts presented at trial and still vote not guilty. A jury's reason to nullify the verdict in this example could be because it simply disagreed with the law. This is the awesome power given to a jury.

A key function of the jury is to interject the conscience of the community in court decisions. Each juror is given an equal opportunity to determine whether a law is fair, reasonable, or appropriate. Enacting a new law or revising an existing law may take years of legislative negotiations. Often the changing norms of society, including shifting attitudes, values, beliefs, and the sense of fairness about social issues, facilitate changes in the laws themselves. Jury nullification, therefore, is a way that the jury can protect defendants from unjust laws that have not been revised to reflect contemporary views of society.[72] Another reason juries might nullify a verdict is to send a message that it disapproves of restrictive, oppressive, or discriminatory laws, thus spurring political or social change.[73]

A jury may also nullify a verdict in response to the specific circumstances faced by the defendant. For example, consider a case of domestic violence between a wife and husband, where the wife may have endured prolonged suffering and physical abuse. If the wife suddenly retaliated and caused physical harm to her husband (even death) after years of abuse, a jury may decide to acquit the wife, even though evidence of guilt was established beyond a reasonable doubt. Jurors may understand the law, including capital statutes, as described by the judge during trial, but may decide that the law does not apply to the defendant in that case.[74] Jury verdicts are strictly protected under the law, even if the decision reached does not follow the law itself. Jurors cannot be prosecuted for engaging in jury nullification.

Some purported instances of nullification include cases when jurors perceived the police or prosecution engaging in unfair practices. Even if jurors believe the law itself is fair and is being fairly applied to the defendant, jurors may still be reluctant to award the prosecution with a conviction if they believed the prosecution engaged in some form of misconduct. Jury deliberations featured in a 1986 Public Broadcasting Service episode of *Frontline* are widely portrayed as jury nullification.[75] The case involved a defendant charged with possession of a firearm by a person previously convicted of a felony. Although jurors voiced their beliefs that the law preventing convicted persons from possessing firearms was fair, several jurors appeared visibly angry that police tricked the defendant, who was intellectually disabled, into incriminating himself, including turning over the handgun.

Professor Darryl Brown argued that all three of these examples of jury nullification reflect the legitimate exercise of jurors' power within the American legal system.[76] But he also identified a fourth example that is not within jurors' legitimate authority, that is, bias against the government or for the defendant. A common illustration of this illegitimate form of jury nullification is White jurors in the South who routinely acquitted White defendants for crimes involving violence against African Americans following the Civil War and up to the Civil Rights Era. Others, however, disagreed with Brown's characterization of these cases as jury nullification, noting that federal prosecutors often secured convictions of the same defendants for civil rights violations based on the same alleged crimes. While some acquittals may be due to racial prejudice, they could also be the result of police and prosecutors who intentionally presented weak evidence to juries to prevent a conviction.

There are two ways that a jury can nullify a verdict. First, all the jurors can individually, and intentionally, decide that the defendant is not guilty of the crime(s) for which they are being charged. This is referred to as an acquittal. This is the best scenario for a defendant, because under these circumstances the defendant cannot be retried for the alleged crime or wrongdoing. Forcing another trial would violate the double jeopardy clause of the Fifth Amendment of the U.S. Constitution, which states, in part, "nor shall any person be subject for the same offence to be twice put in jeopardy of life or limb."[77] This guarantee indicates that the jury's vote to acquit is final.

A second way to nullify a verdict is through a hung jury. This occurs when one or more of the jurors votes to acquit the defendant (find them not guilty) for the crime(s) being charged. When nullification occurs in this manner, the defendant is not convicted in that trial but is subject to being tried again by a different jury. Judges are wary of jurors who enter the deliberation process with a specific intent to nullify the verdict. While the deliberation process is secret, judges do receive notes from jury members about fellow jurors who seem intent on causing a hung jury. Federal appellate courts have ruled that it is the prerogative of a judge to remove jurors who intentionally engage in nullification, but they cannot remove jurors who legitimately harbor doubts about the weight of the evidence.[78]

The concept of jury nullification has been a source of debate among legal professionals for centuries. It may come as no surprise that support or opposition for jury nullification is split down the middle of the courtroom. For example, nullification clearly provides benefits for the defense attorneys and their clients. Their argument in support of nullification is that it provides the defendant with an extra line of protection against abuse and wrongful imprisonment at the hands of a powerful government. Jury nullification is an important tool for juries, if used properly. Several classic examples of jury nullification will be described at the end of this chapter.

> The jury has the right to determine both the law and the facts.
>
> —Samuel Chase
> U.S. Supreme Court Justice (1796–1811)

A few judges, although certainly not the majority, believe jurors should be told they have the power to nullify a verdict;[79] while many prosecutors and other legal professionals, who represent the State, oppose the concept of jury nullification. Opponents have argued that nullification violates the ideals of a trial by jury. Jurors are "factfinders, not arbiters of the morality of the law."[80] Opponents have warned this kind of decision-making is problematic and can weaken a jury system if the law is applied differently to certain individuals.[81] For example, jury nullification in one case does not mean other trial juries will reach the same verdict in a similar case. Also, the arbitrariness of jury nullification makes that power subject to abuse and misuse. For example, one jury might conclude that the government abused its power and vote to acquit a defendant while another jury might convict the same defendant rather than use its power to nullify.

Many jurors who completed their jury service reported not knowing they had the right to nullify a verdict. This may be because judges do not include this information in the jury instructions.[82] Judges may want to ensure that the law is a guiding factor when reaching a verdict, fearing that chaos could result if jurors were told about their power to nullify.[83] Also, some judges believe nullification runs counter to the sworn oath that jurors took during the voir dire process to follow the law and complete their civic responsibilities.[84] Opponents of nullification argue it violates a juror's agreement to render an impartial verdict based solely on the facts presented at trial.

Jury Nullification in Practice

Edward Bushel (1670)

Several examples of jury nullification are worth mentioning here. For example, the Penn and Mead case is a classic example of jury nullification that occurred in England. Briefly, 17th century England was engulfed in religious conflict between the ruling authorities and their subjects. In 1664, the British Parliament passed the Conventicle Act, which established the Church of England as the only recognized church. The Act further prohibited religious assemblies of four or more people who were not members of the authorized Church of England. Anyone caught violating the Act would be arrested and subject to trial by a jury. In August 1670, two Quaker preachers, **William Penn** and **William Mead**, were locked out of their usual meeting place and decided to preach to a crowd of believers in an area known as Gracechurch Street. Authorities arrested Penn and Mead for violating the Conventicle Act by preaching to an unlawful assembly and disturbing the peace.

Edward Bushel, a common English citizen, served as a trial juror in the case against Penn and Mead. In England at that time, many citizens were unhappy with the restrictions placed on civil liberties and one's right to practice a religion of their choosing. After deliberating over the case, Bushel and his fellow jurors found Penn and Mead guilty of preaching at Gracechurch Street but refused to find them guilty of unlawful assembly as specified in the Conventicle Act. The jury's decision infuriated the judge who refused to accept the outcome and sent the jury back to the deliberation chamber. When the jury was reconvened in the courtroom, they reported the same outcome, that Penn and Mead were not guilty of unlawful assembly. The judge refused to release the jury until it changed its verdict and imprisoned all jury members overnight, denying them access to "meat, drink, fire, and tobacco."[85]

Writ of Habeas Corpus (pronounced ha·be·as cor·pus)

A petition to a court requesting a review of a perceived unlawful detention or imprisonment.

The jury returned the next day steadfast in their decision that Penn and Mead were not guilty of unlawful assembly. After three days, the court had to accept the jury's decision but imposed a penalty (40 marks) on the jurors for their misbehavior. Bushel refused to pay the fine and was imprisoned for three months for his actions. During his imprisonment he sent the Chief Justice of the English Court of Common Pleas, Sir John Vaughan, a writ of habeas corpus. Vaughan, under pressure from his fellow justices, eventually released Bushel and reversed the fine. Moreover, Vaughan issued a declaration that no jury may in the future be coerced by the court to reach a verdict that runs counter to its own conscience or free will.[86]

John Peter Zenger (1735)

Libel (pronounced lī-bəl)

Defamatory statements are published through any manner or media. If intended to simply bring contempt, disrespect, hatred, or ridicule to a person or entity, it is likely a civil breach of law.[87]

In the early part of the 18th century, the American colonies were growing rapidly. British loyalists were heavily involved in all aspects of social and political life. In New York City, William Cosby was Governor. By many accounts, Cosby was controlling and greedy. He would remove people from positions of power who challenged his decisions and replaced them with individuals who were loyal to him and the Crown.

The American colonists were angered by Cosby's oppressive and abusive behavior. James Alexander, in opposition to the Governor, formed an independent, politically focused newspaper called the *New York Weekly*. He intended to bring public attention to Cosby's questionable practices. Alexander asked **John Peter Zenger**, a known New York City publisher, to print the newspaper. Alexander and others contributed to the paper, but did not include their names or identities, as their writings could lead to charges of **seditious libel** for criticizing Cosby and his administration. When Cosby read the article that was printed against him, he charged Zenger with seditious libel, as his was the only name that appeared in the publication. Two separate grand juries held in New York City refused to issue indictments against Zenger, as he was only the printer and not the author of the content written in the article. Outraged Cosby had Zenger arrested and tried for seditious libel anyway.

Zenger selected a renowned trial attorney, Andrew Hamilton, to defend him against the charge of seditious libel. Under Hamilton's representation, Zenger admitted to printing and publishing the paper; however, he claimed those actions were not enough to show seditious libel. Such a charge required evidence that the words printed were false claims or seditious. The judge disagreed that the words had to be proven incorrect to show libel. Hamilton skillfully pleaded to the jury of 12 men and encouraged them to vote what they believed the true outcome should be for a person who was only involved in printing and publishing, but not the actual writing of the article. He also emphasized how their decision may affect all colonists who lived under a British rule in the American colonies. Hamilton's strategy worked and the jury returned a not guilty vote for Zenger in 1735. This verdict is widely perceived as the earliest example of jury nullification in America. Box 8.7 describes how the ideals for freedom of speech and the right to a trial by jury (in both civil and criminal cases) are associated with one another in the Bill of Rights through the First Amendment.

Box 8.7: Freedom of Speech and Trial by Jury

Freedom of speech was one of the fundamental rights that the Founding Fathers guaranteed in the Constitution. Indeed, it was enshrined in the First Amendment. The Framer's insistence for freedom of speech may have developed from attempts by the English monarchy to control expressions of speech.[88] Juries, however, had the power to punish or withhold sanctions from individuals accused of criticizing the crown. The earliest juries in the colonies retained this power, even while under the control of England. In this sense, American juries were already protecting freedom of speech. Legal scholars have argued that the jury's role for determining "free speech" today has largely been given to judges, however.

The ideal for protecting free speech reflects the principles of the jury itself.[89] For example, individual jurors are encouraged and expected to share their ideas and perspectives during a jury deliberation.[90] Discussion and debate among jurors provides for better decision-making and presumably increased accuracy in verdicts. Also, as mentioned previously, jury trials allow the citizens to actively participate in their government. This participation and decision-making power are only allowable because of rights guaranteed in the First Amendment.[91]

First Amendment[92]

Congress shall make no law respecting an establishment of religion or prohibiting the free exercise thereof; or abridging the freedom of speech, or of the press; or the right of the people peaceably to assemble, and to petition the Government for a redress of grievances.

Conclusion

The jury deliberation and unguided discussions about the evidence presented at trial among common citizens is an important part of the American jury system. The deliberation is secret and happens behind closed doors. A few research opportunities existed, however, to assess what happens during deliberations. The hallmarks of the jury system still exist today as they did in the 18th century. Citizens who are called to jury service in the 21st century have the same civic responsibility to share their unique perspectives with their fellow jurors while listening to and considering another's point of view as well as the evidence presented at trial.

The next chapter addresses issues that occur after a jury reaches a trial verdict. Specifically, this material will explain the legal procedures that are available to invalidate a jury's verdict and will describe the U.S. Supreme Court's finding that expands the exceptions to the no-impeachment rule. Also, the chapter will describe research findings about jurors' emotional reactions to the jury service experience and actions taken by some jurisdictions to identify and improve jurors' physical and mental wellbeing after the trial proceeding has ended.

Summary

This chapter discussed multiple issues related to the jury deliberation and final verdict reached at trial. All jurors should approach the deliberation with an open mind and willingness to work with their fellow jurors. Traditionally, juries begin the deliberation process by selecting a jury foreperson, reviewing the jury instructions, and determining a strategy for reviewing evidence presented at trial. Research findings indicate the weight of the evidence presented at trial is the most significant factor that influences group discussions, but certain demographic characteristics of the jury, including racial and gender composition, can impact the length of the deliberation and attention to certain details. Jury composition was cited as a significant contributor to trial outcomes in capital cases. The likelihood of individual jurors conforming to the majority decision also impacts deliberation times and trials resulting in a hung jury.

Jury nullification is an important issue related to trial outcomes. Juries can choose to nullify for multiple reasons, including perceived fairness of the law, to send a message of disapproval, or in response to specific circumstances of the case. Nullification typically favors criminal defendants, but critics claim that jurors who agreed to render an impartial verdict based on the facts violate their oath when they nullify the law. The Edward Bushel case from England was provided as an example of nullification related to religious freedoms, while the John Peter Zenger case from colonial American was described in relation to rights to free speech.

Discussion Questions

1. If you were selected for a jury trial, what characteristics would you look for when selecting a jury foreperson? Is this a leadership role that you would agree to serve in, if your fellow jurors selected you to be the foreperson? Why or why not? What characteristics do you have that make you an ideal candidate for the position? What characteristics might serve you better?
2. How do the findings gathered from the Asch experiment on conformity relate to jury deliberations and verdicts? What instructions would you provide to jurors about conformity before they entered the deliberation room? How would nonunanimous trial verdicts impact this? Do the findings of the Asch conformity experiments support or undermine your confidence in jury decision-making in the American jury system? Explain your decision.
3. Why do you think the foreman and his fellow jurors were so unyielding in their decision not to find Preachers William Penn and William Mead guilty of unlawful assembly? Would you have been this steadfast in your decision when faced with the punishment imposed by the trial judge? What are some pressures juries face today when reaching a verdict in a sensational or highly publicized case?
4. The cases shown in this chapter describe two examples of jury nullification. One was set in England in the 17th century and the other in the American colonies in 18th century. Now review two more contemporary cases of jury nullification from the U.S. in the 20th century. The two cases are Dr. Jack Kevorkian and The Camden 28. Answer the following: What crimes were the defendants being accused of committing? What evidence were individual juries asked to review and what laws were claimed to have been broken in each case? Finally, what was the jury's decision, and how did the American public react after the decision was made known?

Review Questions

1. What responsibilities does the jury foreperson typically perform during deliberations, and what social or personality characteristics have studies commonly associated with individuals selected for this role?
2. Compare evidence-driven and verdict-driven deliberation approaches. How does each structure discussion, voting behavior, and juror participation?
3. Why is the jury's initial vote significant? Summarize research findings on how first-ballot leanings and minority faction size influence final verdicts or the likelihood of a hung jury.
4. Explain how the Solomon Asch conformity experiment relates to jury behavior. Distinguish between normative and informational conformity in the context of juror decision-making.
5. Define jury nullification. Identify at least two reasons why juries may nullify and explain the difference between intentional nullification and a verdict based on misunderstanding the law.

Answers to Chapter 8 "What Do You Think?" Questions

1. False. The jury foreperson if often a male, working professional, and high socioeconomic status.
2. False. *Verdict-driven* juries emphasize finding a verdict at the beginning of the deliberation, while *evidence-driven* juries delay an initial vote about a verdict until trial evidence has been discussed.
3. False. The Solomon Asch experiment addressed issues of conformity related to juror decision-making.
4. True. The presence of even one female and/or racial minority juror significantly reduces the likelihood a jury will impose the death sentence.
5. False. American courts follow the rule established in the Bushel case that jurors cannot be punished for their verdicts.
6. True. The Zenger case was an example for freedom of speech guaranteed under the First Amendment.

Key Terms

Arizona Jury Project
Bushel, Edward
Capital Jury Project
conformity
evidence-driven
foreperson
juror characteristics
jury nullification
Mead, William
Penn, William
Rule 39(f)
seditious libel
verdict-driven
Zenger, John Peter

References

1 Kalven, H., & Zeisel, H. (1966). *The American Jury*. Little, Brown.
2 Hannaford-Agor, P., Hans, V.P., Mott, N.L., & Munsterman, G.T. (2000). The timing of opinion formation by jurors in civil cases: An empirical examination. *Tennessee Law Review*, *67*(3), 627–652. https://scholarship.law.cornell.edu/facpub/405
3 Price, W.R. (2023, December 12). *Step 4: Jury deliberations*. Missouri Courts: Judicial Branch of Government. https://www.courts.mo.gov/page.jsp?id=1015
4 Bornstein, B.H., & Greene, E. (2011). Jury decision making: Implications for and from psychology. *Current Directions in Psychological Science: A Journal of the American Psychological Society*, *20*(1), 63–67. https://doi.org/10.1177/0963721410397282
5 Diamond, S.S., Vidmar, N., Rose, M., Ellis, L., & Murphy, B. (2003). Juror discussions during civil trials: Studying an Arizona innovation. *Arizona Law Review*, *45*(1), 1–81.
6 Supreme Court of Arizona. (2024, January 3). *Administrative order 98–10 (198)* (authorizing the civil jury filming project). https://www.azcourts.gov/portals/22/admorder/orders99/pdf98/9810.pdf
7 Arizona Rules of Civil Procedure 39(f).

8 Diamond, S.S., Vidmar, N., Rose, M., Ellis, L., & Murphy, B. (2003). Juror discussions during civil trials: Studying an Arizona innovation. *Arizona Law Review*, *45*(1), 1–81.
9 Devine, D.J., Olafson, K.M., Jarvis, L., Bott, J.L., Clayton, L.D., & Wolfe, J.T. (2004). Explaining jury verdicts: Is leniency bias for real? *Journal of Applied Social Psychology*, *34*(10), 2069–2098.
10 Sannito, T., & Arnolds, E.B. (1982). Jury study results: The factors at work. *Trial Diplomacy Journal*, *1*, 6–11.
11 Diamond, S.S., & Casper, J.D. (1992). Blindfolding the jury to verdict consequences: Damages, experts, and the civil jury. *Law and Society Review*, *26*(3), 513–557.
12 American Bar Association. (2019). *How courts work: Steps in a trial.* Division for Public Education. https://www.americanbar.org/groups/public_education/resources/law_related_education_network/how_courts_work/jurydeliberate
13 Lynch, M., & Haney, C. (2011). Mapping the racial bias of the white male juror: Jury composition and the "empathic divide." *Law and Society Review*, *45*(1), 69–101.
14 Devine, D.J., Buddenbaum, J., Houp, S., Stolle, D.P., & Studebaker, N. (2007). Deliberation quality: A preliminary examination in criminal juries. *Journal of Empirical Legal Studies*, *4*(2), 273–303.
15 York, E., & Cornwell, B. (2006). Status on trial: Social characteristics and influence in the jury room. *Social Forces*, *85*(1), 455–477.
16 Diamond, S.S., Vidmar, N., Rose, M., Ellis, L., & Murphy, B. (2003). Juror discussions during civil trials: Studying an Arizona innovation. *Arizona Law Review*, *45*(1), 1–81.
17 Clark, J., Boccaccini, M.T., Caillouet, B., & Chaplin, W.F. (2007). Five factor model personality traits, jury selection, and case outcomes in criminal and civil cases. *Criminal Justice and Behavior*, *34*(5), 641–660. https://doi.org/10.1177/0093854806297555
18 Clark, J., Boccaccini, M.T., Caillouet, B., & Chaplin, W.F. (2007). Five factor model personality traits, jury selection, and case outcomes in criminal and civil cases. *Criminal Justice and Behavior*, *34*(5), 641–660. https://doi.org/10.1177/0093854806297555
19 Hastie, R., Penrod, S.D., & Pennington, N. (1983). *Inside the jury.* Harvard University Press.
20 Lieberman, J., & Krauss, D. (2009). *Jury psychology: Social aspects of the trial process.* Ashgate.
21 Hastie, R., Penrod, S.D., & Pennington, N. (1983). *Inside the jury.* Harvard University Press.
22 Lieberman, J., & Krauss, D. (2009). *Jury psychology: Social aspects of the trial process.* Ashgate.
23 Winfree, T.L., Mays, L.G., & Alarid, L.F. (2022). *Introduction to criminal justice: The essentials* (3rd ed., p. 209). Aspen Publishing.
24 Devine, D.J. (2012). *Jury decision making. The state of the science.* New York University Press.
25 Diamond, S.S., Vidmar, N., Rose, M., Ellis, L., & Murphy, B. (2003). Juror discussions during civil trials: Studying an Arizona innovation. *Arizona Law Review*, *45*(1), 1–81.
26 Bornstein, B.H., & Greene, E. (2011). Jury decision making: Implications for and from psychology. *Current Directions in Psychological Science: A Journal of the American Psychological Society*, *20*(1), 63–67. https://doi.org/10.1177/0963721410397282
27 Hannaford-Agor, P., Hans, V.P., Mott, N.L., & Munsterman, G.T. (2002). *Are hung juries a problem?* National Center for State Courts. https://ncsc.contentdm.oclc.org/digital/collection/juries/id/27/rec/1
28 Lumet, S. (Director). (1957). *12 Angry Men* [Film]. Orion-Nova Productions.
29 Hannaford-Agor, P., Hans, V.P., Mott, N.L., & Munsterman, G.T. (2002). *Are hung juries a problem?* National Center for State Courts. https://ncsc.contentdm.oclc.org/digital/collection/juries/id/27/rec/1
30 Hannaford-Agor, P.L., & Moffett, M. (2024). *2023 State-of-the-states survey of jury improvement efforts: Criminal jury trials.* https://ncsc.contentdm.oclc.org/digital/collection/juries/id/384/rec/2; Hannaford-Agor, P.L., & Moffett, M. (2024). *2023 State-of-the-states survey of jury improvement efforts: Civil jury trials.* https://ncsc.contentdm.oclc.org/digital/collection/juries/id/393/rec/5
31 Administrative Office of the U.S. Courts. (2024, February 21). *Handbook for trial jurors serving in the United States District Courts* (p. 15). https://www.uscourts.gov/sites/default/files/trial-handbook.pdf

32 Strodtbeck, F.L., & Mann, R.D. (1956). Sex-role differentiation in jury deliberations. *Sociometry, 19*(1), 3–11.
33 Devine, D.J. (2012). *Jury decision making. The state of the science.* New York University Press.
34 Hastie, R., Penrod, S., & Pennington, N. (1983). *Inside the jury.* Harvard University Press.
35 Goodman, J., Loftus, E.F., & Greene, E.L. (1990). Matters of money: Voir dire in civil cases. *Forensic Reports, 3*(3), 303–329.
36 Batchelder, J.S., Koski, D.D., & Byxbe, F.R. (2004). Women's hostility toward women in rape trials: Testing the intra-female gender hostility thesis. *American Journal of Criminal Justice, 28*(2), 181–200. https://doi.org/10.1007/BF02885871
37 Rose, M.R., Diamond, S.S., & Murphy, B. (2006). He said/she said: An analysis of gender and participation in real jury deliberations. In *Annual Meeting of the American Sociological Association*, Montreal, Quebec.
38 Miller, M., & Hayward, R.D. (2007). Religious characteristics and the death penalty. *Law & Human Behavior, 32*(2), 113–123. https://doi.org/10.1007/s10979-007-9090-z
39 Werner, C.M., Strube, M.J., Cole, A.M., & Kagehiro, D.K. (1985). The impact of case characteristics and prior jury experience on jury verdicts. *Journal of Applied Social Psychology, 15*(7), 409–427. https://doi.org/10.1111/j.1559–1816.1985.tb02262.x
40 Flanagan, F.X. (2018). Race, gender, and juries: Evidence from North Carolina. *The Journal of Law & Economics, 61*(2), 189–214. https://doi.org/10.1086/698193
41 Anwar, S., Bayer, P., & Hjalmarsson, R. (2012). The impact of jury race in criminal trials. *The Quarterly Journal of Economics, 127*(2), 1017–1055. https://doi.org/10.1093/qje/qjs014
42 Stevenson, M.C., Lytle, B.L., Baumholser, B.J., & McCracken, E.W. (2017). Racially diverse juries promote self-monitoring efforts during jury deliberation. *Translational Issues in Psychological Science, 3*(2), 187–201. https://doi.org/10.1037/tps0000113
43 Stevenson, M.C., Lytle, B.L., Baumholser, B.J., & McCracken, E.W. (2017). Racially diverse juries promote self-monitoring efforts during jury deliberation. *Translational Issues in Psychological Science, 3*(2), 187–201. https://doi.org/10.1037/tps0000113
44 Sommers, S.R. (2006). On racial diversity and group decision making: Identifying multiple effects of racial composition on jury deliberations. *Journal of Personality and Social Psychology, 90*(4), 597–612. https://doi.org/10.1037/0022–3514.90.4.597
45 Diamond, S.S., & Hans, V.P. (2023). Fair juries. *University of Illinois Law Review, 2023*(3), 881–954. https://www.scholars.northwestern.edu/en/publications/fair-juries
46 Asch, S.E. (1955). Opinions and social pressure. *Scientific American, 193*(5), 31–35. https://doi.org/10.1038/scientificamerican1155-31
47 Wattal, S., Racherla, P., & Mandviwalla, M. (2010). Network externalities and technology use: A quantitative analysis of intraorganizational blogs. *Journal of Management Information Systems, 27*(1), 145–174.
48 Wattal, S., Racherla, P., & Mandviwalla, M. (2010). Network externalities and technology use: A quantitative analysis of intraorganizational blogs. *Journal of Management Information Systems, 27*(1), 145–174.
49 Waters, N.L., & Hans, V.P. (2009). A jury of one: Opinion formation, conformity, and dissent on juries. *Journal of Empirical Legal Studies, 6*(3), 513–540. https://scholarship.law.cornell.edu/cgi/viewcontent.cgi?article=1113&context=lsrp_papers
50 Saks, M.J. (1996). The smaller the jury, the greater the unpredictability. *Judicature, 79*(5), 263–265.
51 Asch, S.E. (1955). Opinions and social pressure. *Scientific American, 193*(5), 31–35. https://doi.org/10.1038/scientificamerican1155-31
52 Hannaford-Agor, P.L. (2024). *What were they thinking? Musings from the director of the NCSC Center for Jury Studies on her stint in the jury box.* National Center for State Courts. https://ncsc.contentdm.oclc.org/digital/collection/juries/id/361/rec/1
53 Hannaford-Agor, P.L., & Moffett, M. (2024). *2023 State-of-the-states survey of jury improvement efforts: Criminal jury trials.* National Center for State Courts. https://ncsc.contentdm.oclc.org/digital/collection/juries/id/393/rec/5
54 Hannaford-Agor, P.L., & Moffett, M. (2024). *2023 State-of-the-states survey of jury improvement efforts: Civil jury trials.* National Center for State Courts. https://ncsc.contentdm.oclc.org/digital/collection/juries/id/393/rec/5

55 Antonio, M.E. (2008). Stress and the capital jury: How male and female jurors react to serving on a murder trial. *The Justice System Journal*, *29*(3), 396–407. https://doi.org/10.1080/0098261X.2008.10767903
56 Antonio, M.E. (2008). Stress and the capital jury: How male and female jurors react to serving on a murder trial. *The Justice System Journal*, *29*(3), 396–407. https://doi.org/10.1080/0098261X.2008.10767903
57 Bowers, W.J., Steiner, B.D., & Sandys, M. (2001). Death sentencing in black and white: An empirical analysis of the role of jurors' race and jury racial composition. *University of Pennsylvania Journal of Constitutional Law*, *3*, 171–275.
58 Bowers, W.J., Steiner, B.D., & Sandys, M. (2001). Death sentencing in black and white: An empirical analysis of the role of jurors' race and jury racial composition. *University of Pennsylvania Journal of Constitutional Law*, *3*, 171–275.
59 *Turner v. Murray*, 476 U.S. 28 (1986).
60 *McCleskey v. Kemp*, 481 U.S. 279 (1987).
61 *Turner v. Murray*, 476 U.S. 28 (1986).
62 *Turner v. Commonwealth*, 221 Va. 513, 522 (1980).
63 *Turner v. Murray*, 476 U.S. 28 at 37 (1986).
64 *McCleskey v. Kemp*, 481 U.S. 279 (1987).
65 *McCleskey v. State*, 245 Ga. 108 (1980).
66 *McCleskey v. Kemp*, 481 U.S. 282 at 314–319 (1987).
67 Kalven, H., & Zeisel, H. (1966). *The American Jury*. Little, Brown.
68 Hannaford-Agor, P., & Hans, V.P. (2003). Nullification at work? A glimpse from the National Center for State Courts' study of hung juries. *Chicago-Kent Law Review*, *78*(3), 1249–1277. http://scholarship.law.cornell.edu/facpub/397
69 McCord, D. (2005). The jury revisited. *Judicature*, *88*(6), 284–299.
70 Marder, N.S. (2021). Jury nullification: Don't ask, don't tell? *Law, Culture and the Humanities*, *17*(3), 404–413. https://doi.org/10.1177/1743872117721986
71 Frampton, T.W. (2018). The Jim Crow Jury. *Vanderbilt Law Review*, *71*(5), 1593–1654.
72 Frampton, T.W. (2018). The Jim Crow Jury. *Vanderbilt Law Review*, *71*(5), 1593–1654.
73 Frampton, T.W. (2018). The Jim Crow Jury. *Vanderbilt Law Review*, *71*(5), 1593–1654.
74 Marder, N.S. (2021). Jury nullification: Don't ask, don't tell? *Law, Culture and the Humanities*, *17*(3), 404–413. https://doi.org/10.1177/1743872117721986
75 Frontline. (1986, April 8). *Inside the jury room*. [Video]. YouTube. https://www.youtube.com/watch?v=Enkf4OXZa0A&t=44s
76 Brown, D.K. (1997). Jury nullification within the rule of law. *Minnesota Law Review*, *81*(5), 1149–1200. https://scholarship.law.umn.edu/mlr/1095/
77 U.S. Const., amend. V
78 *United States v. Thomas*, 116 F.3d 606 (2nd Cir.) (1997).
79 Simson, G.J. (1975). Jury nullification in the American system: A skeptical view. *Texas Law Review*, *54*(3), 488–525.
80 Peters, R. (2023). The rule of law and jury trials. *Stance (Muncie, Ind.)*, *16*(1), 72–83. https://doi.org/10.33043/S.16.1.72-83
81 Marder, N.S. (2021). Jury nullification: Don't ask, don't tell? *Law, Culture and the Humanities*, *17*(3), 404–413. https://doi.org/10.1177/1743872117721986
82 Yorke, S. (2020). Jury nullification instructions as structural error. *Washington Law Review*, *95*, 1441.
83 Marder, N.S. (2021). Jury nullification: Don't ask, don't tell? *Law, Culture and the Humanities*, *17*(3), 404–413. https://doi.org/10.1177/1743872117721986
84 Marder, N.S. (2021). Jury nullification: Don't ask, don't tell? *Law, Culture and the Humanities*, *17*(3), 404–413. https://doi.org/10.1177/1743872117721986
85 Hacking, D. (1975). The verdict of the jury: An English perspective. *Litigation*, *2*(2), 21–50.
86 Hacking, D. (1975). The verdict of the jury: An English perspective. *Litigation*, *2*(2), 21–50.
87 Black's Law Dictionary. (2024, May 8). Libel. In *Black's Law Dictionary* (2nd ed.). https://thelawdictionary.org/libel
88 Barth, J. (2023). "Liberty of conscience is every man's natural right": Historical background of the First Amendment. *Journal of Policy History*, *35*(4), 435–453. https://doi.org/10.1017/S0898030623000234

89 Gibson, M.T. (1986). The Supreme Court and freedom of expression from 1791 to 1917. *Fordham Law Review*, *55*(3), 263–333.
90 Ferguson, A.G. (2012). *Why jury duty matters: A citizen's guide to constitutional action*. New York University Press.
91 Stembridge, P.M. (2000). Adjusting absolutism: First amendment protection for the fringe. *Boston University Law Review*, *80*(3), 907–938.
92 U.S. Const., amend. I

PART III

Future—Reaction and Projection

Chapters in this section examine critical aspects of the American jury system, focusing on post-verdict issues and systemic adaptability. The Federal Rules of Evidence, Rule 606(b), known as the no-impeachment rule, protects jury verdict finality by limiting jurors' testimony about deliberations, with rare exceptions for external influences, verdict errors, or racial bias, as upheld by the U.S. Supreme Court. Jurors often find service rewarding but face significant stress in high-profile or complex cases, prompting some courts to offer post-trial debriefing and mental health support. The COVID-19 pandemic forced adaptations like remote voir dire, virtual trials, and socially distanced jury selection, addressing disruptions while highlighting the system's flexibility. However, declining jury trials, driven by institutional constraints and alternative dispute resolution methods like mediation, have reduced attorney expertise and citizen participation, risking public confidence. Emerging trends, including technology use and mental health support, aim to enhance juror diversity, reduce costs, and improve satisfaction, ensuring the jury system's resilience and future vitality.

DOI: 10.4324/9781003677796-11

9 Verdict Rendered and the Jury Experience

What Do You Think?

Before reviewing the concepts addressed in this chapter, answer True or False to each of the following questions or statements. Correct answers can be found at the end of Chapter 9.

1. Juries must inform the court-appointed bailiff of the verdict that was reached before leaving the deliberation room.
2. High-profile trials involve cases on a national level.
3. A jury verdict cannot be invalidated for any reason.
4. The type of trial that jurors observe impacts their overall jury service experience.
5. Trial jurors are forever prohibited from discussing with the media any events that occurred during the jury deliberation.
6. Jurors are provided with access to psychological counseling services, if requested, after being dismissed from jury duty.

Learning Objectives

After reading this chapter, you will be able to:

1. Explain the Federal Rules of Evidence 606(b) and the exceptions to the no-impeachment rule.
2. Discuss the main findings and implications of *Tanner v. United States* and *Peña-Rodriguez v. Colorado.*
3. Describe how the average juror reacts to serving on a jury.
4. List the symptoms and identify the sources of juror stress.
5. Describe the purpose and effectiveness of juror debriefing sessions.

Introduction

The phrase "all good things must come to an end" may be a facetious way to describe the final verdict reached by a trial jury; however, there is some truth in this phrase. When the jury reaches a decision and shares that decision with the court, their jury service responsibilities are complete. Many are humbled by the experience, and almost all are excited to get back to the routines of their normal lives. Jurors may reflect on the experience, including the evidence they heard during the trial, how fellow jurors treated them during the deliberation, and how their discussions led them to the verdict. These reflections could occur immediately

DOI: 10.4324/9781003677796-12

upon leaving the courthouse, or in the days or weeks following the trial. Many jurors reflect favorably about the jury experience; however, some jurors are more negatively impacted by it.

There is much uncertainty for prospective jurors when they report for jury duty. They may be uncertain about the type of case they will hear, anxious about interacting with other jurors, and unclear whether the court is prepared to address emotional duress after the trial. As will be described in this chapter, these dynamics significantly affect jurors' overall satisfaction with jury service. Court rules restrict what courts can do if a juror complains, after the trial, that inappropriate juror behaviors contributed to the final verdict that was reached. Courts also have little guidance concerning the steps they can take to alleviate juror stress after a traumatic trial. As will be shown in this chapter, jurors' emotional and physical needs are increasingly being addressed; however, proponents argue that more can be done.

In This Chapter

This chapter describes juror experiences after the verdict has been delivered in the courtroom. Here material addresses: 1) the likelihood of invalidating a verdict; 2) the Court's findings about the Rule 606(b) (no-impeachment rule); 3) jurors' physical and emotional reactions to their jury service experience; and 4) resources made available to jurors after the trial proceedings.

Delivering the Jury Verdict

The jury is instructed to notify the bailiff once they have reached their verdict; however, the jury does not share the decision with the bailiff. Instead, the bailiff informs the judge about the jury's status, and all parties reassemble inside the courtroom where the verdict is read publicly for the first time. Typically, the courtroom clerk, or sometimes the jury foreperson, will read the charge(s) and the verdict that the jury reached. Jurors may also be polled individually to confirm their vote.[1] Box 9.1 describes an example of these polling procedures. Once the verdict is given, the jurors' responsibilities are over.

Box 9.1: Delivering the Verdict

The guidelines for delivering the verdict reached by a jury vary by jurisdiction. For example, in the state of Iowa, the rules of criminal procedure state that when the jury has been reassembled in the courtroom, the verdict will be read aloud, and "inquiry made of the jurors if it is their verdict."[2] The trial attorneys (either prosecutor or defense counsel) may then request each juror be polled to inquire about whether the verdict given was their vote. The verdict must be unanimous. If a juror disagrees with the verdict, the entire jury will be sent back to the deliberation room to continue its discussion. If all jurors indicate their agreement with the verdict, the trial is complete, and the jury is dismissed. The procedure is similar in civil trials.

Iowa statutes also allow the jury, in misdemeanor cases, to deliver the verdict to the court in a sealed envelope, if both parties agree to such a format. All jurors sign the verdict while in the deliberation room, seal the document in an envelope, and hand it to the court. The envelope will be opened in court and the verdict read aloud. The process is equivalent to stating the verdict aloud. However, in this process the jury cannot be polled to inquire about agreement with the verdict reached.

The purpose of jury deliberation is to decide, based on the evidence and law presented at trial, whether the prosecution or plaintiff has met the burden of proof to secure a conviction in a criminal trial or a plaintiff verdict in a civil trial. The decision the jury reaches is called the verdict. Juries must reach a unanimous decision in criminal cases. In many states, a verdict in a civil case only requires a supermajority of jurors. But what are the consequences—positive or negative—of a verdict for the jurors themselves? Research has revealed jurors' experiences during the trial and how the deliberation process has had profound effects on their physical and emotional wellbeing.

Some jurors have reported to trial attorneys, judges, and news media outlets after the trial rather outlandish behavior and discussions that occurred during the deliberation process itself. Some jurors have wanted to testify after the verdict to invalidate the jury's decision. Jurors have tried to do this in instances when the deliberation discussion included prejudicial or discriminatory decision-making practices by jury members. However, how typical are these responses among jurors? Research indicates that most jurors enjoy their experience, feel proud about completing their civic responsibility to society, and learn more about the American justice system during the process.

Invalidating a Jury Verdict

Secrecy is a key characteristic of jury deliberations. No one other than the empaneled jurors are allowed in the jury deliberation room and no recordings are made of their discussions. Their decision as memorialized on the verdict form consists of a binary choice for each criminal charge or civil claim (guilty/not guilty, liable/not liable) and possibly a monetary award following a plaintiff verdict in a civil case. The **verdict form** does not include an explanation of how the jurors reached their decision, the evidence they considered most persuasive, or whether they believed the verdict reflects the fairest possible outcome. The only way for judges, lawyers, the parties, or the public to learn these details is if one or more jurors choose to disclose what happened in the deliberation room.[3] Even then, most jurors restrict their comments to their personal views without ascribing those views to other jurors. Box 9.2 shows an example of a verdict form adapted from Massachusetts.

> I believe in people. Human beings, deep down, are essentially good. Any jury can filter through whatever bull might be thrown their way and use common sense to get to the truth of a case. Juries make the right decisions, almost unfailingly, because people know right from wrong.
>
> —Chris Christie, Former Governor of New Jersey (2010–2018)
> *Republican Rescue: Saving the Party from the Truth Deniers* (2021)

One reason for the secrecy of jury deliberations is to ensure jurors feel free to discuss their views candidly with one another. A second reason is to promote the finality of the verdict and prevent parties from contesting trial outcomes on grounds that jurors misunderstood, or even deliberately disregarded the evidence or law.[4] Lawyers have few legal bases for invalidating the jury's verdict and typically have very limited time in which to do so.

The first opportunity to challenge the verdict takes place at the trial court level after the jury announces its verdict and is released from service. Defendants who were convicted in a criminal trial or either the plaintiff or defendant who lost in a civil trial can file a motion for a

Box 9.2: Sample Verdict Form

Commonwealth of Massachusetts

County of Middlesex at Lowell

The Superior Court

CRIMINAL DOCKET #1981CRY/Z

Commonwealth
vs.
Defendant Z

VERDICT SLIP

Choose Only One Verdict Among 1, 2, 3, or 4.
The Jury finds the Defendant:

1. ____ Not Guilty
2. ____ Guilty of Murder in the First Degree (choose either theory)
   A. () With Deliberate Premeditation
   B. () With Extreme Atrocity or Cruelty
3. ____ Guilty of Murder in the Second Degree
4. ____ Guilty of Voluntary Manslaughter

And this is our unanimous verdict.

____
Foreperson of the Jury

Dated: _______

new trial or for a judgment notwithstanding the verdict (JNOV). In these motions, attorneys typically argue that:

1. the judge made a legal error during the trial proceeding (e.g., concerning the admissibility of evidence or the jury instructions) that affected the trial outcome,
2. the parties discovered new evidence that was not available at the time of the trial
3. jurors engaged in misconduct that prevented a fair trial,
4. there was insufficient evidence to support the jury's verdict, or
5. the jury's damage award in civil trials was so disproportionate that it suggests prejudice or a fundamental misapplication of law.

For the most part, trial judges are disinclined to admit that their own rulings deprived the parties of a fair trial; they generally defer to jurors' assessments of the evidence, and they are skeptical of post-trial claims about "new" evidence. For these reasons, motions for a new trial or a JNOV are rarely granted. Once a judge denies such a motion, the losing party's only option is to pursue an appeal. As explained in Chapter 7, the only legally recognized basis for overturning a jury verdict is a materially significant legal or procedural error.

Invalidate[5]

The action of proving that an opinion, argument, etc. is wrong.

There is one significant exception: claims of juror misconduct. Occasionally, trial attorneys or judges learn about juror misconduct after the trial is over. Sometimes it is the jurors themselves who alert the judge or lawyers about the language or behavior of other jurors and how those actions affected the final verdict. These complaints go beyond describing incidents where their fellow jurors simply displayed rude behavior or minimized dissenting jurors' opinions. Sometimes jurors report serious problems that occurred during the deliberation, including claims that one or more jurors lied during the voir dire process,[6] concerns about the mental competence of fellow jurors,[7] and jurors openly engaged in misconduct that compromised the fairness of the trial.[8] Under these circumstances, the judge is required to hold a hearing to investigate. Still, the law places strict limits on what qualifies as misconduct that warrants **invalidating** a verdict.

No-Impeachment Rule

To challenge a jury verdict based on juror misconduct, attorneys must overcome restrictions under the jurisdiction's "**no-impeachment rule**." In federal courts, this is **Rule 606(b)** of the Federal Rules of Evidence. Most states have a state-specific equivalent of Rule 606(b) that applies to jury trials in state courts. Federal Rule of Evidence 606(b)(1) states:

Affidavit

A written statement, made without coercion or while under pressure, that one claims is truthful and correct.

> During an inquiry into the validity of a verdict or indictment, a juror may not testify about any statement made or incident that occurred during the jury's deliberations; the effect of anything on that juror's or another juror's vote; or any juror's mental processes concerning the verdict or indictment. The court may not receive a juror's affidavit or evidence of a juror's statement on these matters.[9]

Rule 606(b)(1) protects the secrecy of jury deliberations and the finality of jury verdicts. The reasons for this might seem obvious. First, juries play an essential role in the American jury system for guarding against an oppressive government.[10] Justice Anthony M. Kennedy of the U.S. Supreme Court described the no-impeachment rule as having "substantial merit" and

> promotes full and vigorous discussion by providing jurors with considerable assurance that after being discharged they will not be summoned to recount their deliberations, and they will not otherwise be harassed or annoyed by litigants seeking to challenge the verdict. The rule gives stability and finality to verdicts.[11]

He further noted that the rule "has evolved to give substantial protection to verdict finality and to assure jurors that, once their verdict has been entered, it will not later be called

Box 9.3: Evolution of the No-Impeachment Rule

Justice Kennedy described the evolution of the no-impeachment rule in ***Peña-Rodriguez v. Colorado*** (2017). Kennedy traced the history of the rule back to English common law and the Mansfield Rule. Under Mansfield, jurors were barred from testifying, after the verdict was rendered, about their "subjective mental processes" or about behaviors that occurred during the trial deliberation.[13] In the U.S., certain jurisdictions adopted less strict versions of the Mansfield Rule. For example, under the Iowa Rule, jurors could not testify about their personal beliefs and motives but could testify, and corroborate with other jurors, about events and specific behaviors that occurred during the deliberation.[14]

Another version of the no-impeachment rule was used in the U.S. along with the Iowa Rule. Referred to as the Federal Approach, jurors could not provide testimony about circumstances of the deliberation process, except when extraneous events occurred; for example, a juror relied on outside evidence to aid the jury when reaching a verdict. The U.S. Supreme Court considered versions of the rule over the decades. In 1975, Congress adopted the Federal Rules of Evidence, Rule 606(b), which endorsed a broad no-impeachment rule with only limited exceptions.

Table 9.1: Exceptions to Rule 606(b), the No-Impeachment Rule

Exception	*Meaning*	*Example*
Extraneous prejudicial information was improperly brought to the jury's attention.	Information was acquired by a juror(s) during the deliberation process that was not introduced as evidence during the trial proceeding.	News broadcasts, social media accounts, conversations with family members, friends
An outside influence was improperly brought to bear on any juror.	Outside source(s) coerced, pressured, or harassed a juror(s) to elicit specific verdict or outcome.	Mafia threatens the safety of family members to elicit specific outcome
A mistake was made in entering the verdict on the verdict form.	In civil jury trials, when juries are required to deliberate and award damages, then record the amount of the award on an official document.	Jury intended to award plaintiff $50,000 for pain and suffering but recorded $500,000 on the court paperwork

into question based on the comments or conclusions they expressed during deliberations."[12] Box 9.3 briefly describes the origin and the evolution of the no-impeachment rule practiced in the United States.

Rule 606(b)(1) prohibits testimony about the jury's deliberations; however, there are exceptions when a juror may offer testimony that a court could use to invalidate a jury verdict. For example, Rule 606(b)(2) allows for jury testimony when "(A) extraneous prejudicial information was improperly brought to the jury's attention; (B) an outside influence was improperly brought to bear on any juror; or (C) a mistake was made in entering the verdict on the verdict form."[15] Table 9.1 provides examples of the exceptions described in Rule 606(b) related to the no-impeachment rule.

Historically, it has been difficult for a petitioner to make a claim for impeachment that meets the standards for an exception under Rule 606(b). As mentioned, the U.S. Supreme Court has previously rejected claims for exceptions to the rule based on inferences about jurors' mental competencies[16] and for jurors caught lying during the jury selection process.[17] Indeed, the Court has refused to allow juror testimony that may invalidate a verdict even when faced with outrageous claims of juror misbehavior. Consider the petitioner's claim in ***Tanner v. United States.***[18] In the late 1980s, Tanner claimed jurors were engaging in drinking and illicit drug use during lunch breaks and were sleeping inside the courtroom while the trial proceeding was in session. Despite such claims and multiple jurors' willingness to testify about such behaviors, the Court rejected the petitioner's request for exception under Rule 606(b). Box 9.4 describes the findings from *Tanner v. United States* in more detail, including

Box 9.4: *Tanner v. United States*

In 1987, the U.S. Supreme Court found in *Tanner v. United States* that jury testimony cannot be used to reverse a jury verdict, except if an outside influence coerced the jurors and the trial outcome was impacted as a result. The petitioner, Anthony R. Tanner, was convicted of conspiring to defraud the United States and to commit mail fraud.[19] During the original trial, Tanner filed two motions (both denied) requesting a new trial due to a reasoned belief of jury misconduct during the trial. The motions, based on jurors' claims, alleged that multiple jurors engaged in drinking and used illicit drugs (marijuana and cocaine) during lunch breaks and were sleeping in the afternoons during the trial.

The 11th Circuit Court upheld the conviction, stating "appellants' motion for new trial does not allege that prejudicial information was brought to the jury's attention. Similarly, it does not allege that any outside influence was brought to bear upon any juror."[20] Essentially, the District Court concluded juror testimony that revealed intoxication and drug use among fellow jurors was not grounds for an exception allowable under Federal Rules of Evidence 606(b) because the claims did not meet with any of the allowable reasons.[21]

On further appeal, the U.S. Supreme Court affirmed the District Court's decision, indicating that Rule 606(b)

> is supported by substantial policy considerations, including the need to assure full and frank discussion in the privacy of the jury room, to prevent the harassment of jurors by losing parties, and to preserve the community's trust in a system that relies on the decisions of laypeople.[22]

Moreover, the Court found that the petitioner's constitutional right to an impartial jury was "adequately protected by other procedural safeguards" through the voir dire process, staff and judicial observations of jurors' behaviors during trial, and other non-juror testimonials.[23]

the original conviction, subsequent appeal, and the U.S. Supreme Court's reasons not to invalidate the jury's verdict based on the exceptions allowable under Rule 606(b).

To fit within the Rule 606(b) exception, trial judges must find extraneous prejudicial information, an outside influence, or a mistake. However, the definition of extraneous prejudicial information or "extra judicial contact"[24] can differ between state and federal courts, and across different states. Black's Law Dictionary defines extraneous evidence as, "any evidence that comes from outside the court."[25] The U.S. District Court for the Middle District of Alabama defines extraneous information as "exposure of jurors to prejudicial information not admitted into evidence, such as media reports or the fruits of independent juror investigations of facts relating to the case … or other prejudicial contacts between jurors and third parties."[26] Other courts use different terms, such as "outside influence." In 2011 the Texas Appeals Court concluded that for information to be considered an outside influence, it must come from someone who is outside the jury.[27] Therefore, "information gathered by a juror and introduced to the other jurors by that juror" does not constitute an outside influence. Conversely, in 2010 the Florida Court of Appeals reversed and remanded a trial court's denial of a motion for a new trial because a juror used his smartphone to look up the definition of the word "prudent" during deliberations.[28]

What Fits the Exception

If a trial judge was unwilling to find the jurors' behaviors described in *Tanner*, including alcohol and drug use, as an exception provided under Rule 606(b), what behavior(s) rises to the standard where an exception will be granted? The U.S. Supreme Court found such an exception in the petitioner's claim of racial discrimination in *Peña-Rodriguez v. Colorado* (2017), where Justice Kennedy stated

> The instant case presents the question whether there is an exception to the no-impeachment rule when, after the jury is discharged, a juror comes forward with compelling evidence that another juror made clear and explicit statements indicating that **racial animus** was a significant motivating factor in his or her vote to convict.[29]

Consider the details of the case and jurors' claims that the verdict was based on overt racially discriminatory statements and behaviors. Briefly, the defendant, Miguel Angel Peña-Rodriguez, was convicted in 2017 by a Colorado jury for unlawful sexual contact and harassment of two teenage sisters. After the jury's verdict was rendered inside the courtroom and the jury was dismissed, two jurors approached the defense attorney and raised concerns that the deliberation and subsequent verdict was made under the cloud of overt racial discrimination.

The two jurors described multiple instances of racial discriminatory statements voiced by another juror during the deliberation. These jurors claimed the juror determined guilt based on his beliefs and statements that "Mexican men had a bravado that caused them to believe they could do whatever they wanted with

> **Racial Animus**
>
> Referring to behaviors that are motivated by racial discrimination, including overt negative attitudes toward, harboring ill will or mistrust for, or acting out against a cultural minority group.

women," "Mexican men are physically controlling of women," and that "nine times out of ten Mexican men were guilty of being aggressive toward women and young girls."[30] The trial judge reviewed the jurors' affidavits describing the language of their fellow juror but denied the motion for a new trial under the Colorado Rules of Evidence 606(b) that stated a juror cannot testify about statements made during deliberations for the purposes of impeaching a verdict.

The petitioner appealed the conviction to the U.S. Supreme Court. Justice Kennedy wrote that the case "lies at the intersection of the Court's decisions endorsing the no-impeachment rule and its decisions seeking to eliminate racial bias in the jury system. The two lines of precedent, however, need not conflict."[31] Upon review of the claims of racially discriminatory language voiced by a juror during the deliberation, the Court found:

> where a juror makes a clear statement that indicates he or she relied on racial stereotypes or animus to convict a criminal defendant, the Sixth Amendment requires that the no-impeachment rule give way in order to permit the trial court to consider the evidence of the juror's statement and any resulting denial of the jury trial guarantee.[32]

The Court's decision in *Peña-Rodriguez* meant that a juror's claim of racially discriminatory statements or behaviors may be reviewed upon appeal as violating a defendant's Sixth Amendment right to an impartial jury. The Court qualified its findings, however, by noting that "not every offhand comment" will fall under an exception to the no-impeachment rule.[33] It must be shown that one or more jurors expressed overtly racial and discriminatory statements that impacted the fairness and impartiality of the deliberation and verdict. The U.S. Supreme Court's finding in *Pena-Rodriguez* was praised by proponents who believed the decision "extended the no-impeachment rule to move beyond the mere survival of the jury system and toward a more effective system of ensuring the quality of justice."[34] Box 9.5 features comments from a judge about the importance of jury decisions as a measure of the conscience of the community.

Table 9.2: Summary of Court Decisions

Case	*Decided*	*Opinion*
Tanner v. United States 483 U.S. 107	June 22, 1987	The U.S. Supreme Court considered whether a district court was in error when it refused to find claims that jurors were under the influence of drugs and alcohol during the original trial of the defendant. The Court found other safeguards were rightfully in place to determine whether juror misconduct was committed.
Peña-Rodriguez v. Colorado **508 U.S. (2017)**	March 6, 2017	Jurors claimed racial bias and discrimination contributed to the jury verdict. The U.S. Supreme Court extended the no-impeachment rule exceptions to include overt racially discriminatory statements that deny one's Sixth Amendment guarantee to a fair and impartial jury.

Box 9.5: From the Field

Name: Barbara A. McDermott

Position: Pennsylvania Court of Common Pleas, First Judicial District

How long have you worked in this position?
I worked 12 years in the Criminal Division, Homicide Program.

A jury's verdict can only be invalidated under extreme circumstances. Why is it so important to protect the decision reached by a jury?
While a judge may, on occasion disagree with a jury's verdict, it is exceedingly rare that the judge will overturn the verdict because a citizen's right to a jury trial is guaranteed by our constitution. A jury is meant to represent the community's conscience (or moral code). Accepting its verdict ensures that ordinary citizens have a substantial role in delivering justice. To quote Abraham Lincoln, "The greatest duty of citizenship is jury duty."

Courts are cautious but will intervene in extreme cases and invalidate a jury verdict if there is significant evidence of racial bias, which can be based upon discriminatory jury selection or expressed during deliberations (there can be other factors, but not really related to the jury). The bias must have impacted the fairness or impartiality of the trial.

Racial animus was identified in *Pena-Rodriguez v. Colorado* as a factor that should be considered for invalidating a jury's decision. Are there any other groups or social issues that should be considered?
While race is the most common type of prejudice that is discussed, there are other types of prejudices that may invalidate a jury's verdict, since our legal system requires jurors to decide cases solely on the evidence presented at trial, without improper influence or personal bias. The following types of biases have been held to either invalidate a jury verdict, contribute to an invalidation, or been raised as issues: religious (e.g. Muslim, Jewish, atheist), gender or sexual orientation (women, men, LGBTQ+ individuals, or non-conforming gender people), ethnic or national origin (immigrant, undocumented, or from a specific country), socioeconomic/class bias (poor, homeless, low-income background), disability bias (mental or physical), victim bias/sympathy (children, elderly victims, high-profile), and political or ideological (Black Lives Matter movement, pro-life, climate activism).

Reactions to Jury Service

The no-impeachment rule may cause some readers to wonder how often jurors claim inappropriate behavior occurred or whether discriminatory language was spoken during the deliberation process. Fortunately, legal research indicates that such occurrences are rare. Jurors typically react to ending their jury service experience with a feeling of satisfaction, pride, and relief. This reaction is for good and well-deserved reasons.

Overall, jurors take their assigned duties and responsibilities seriously. One individual who served on a federal jury commented,

> Our country asks very little of us. The responsibility of serving on a jury, initially, was overwhelming. Your judgment is critical. I kept in mind that if I were on trial and I depended on the fairness of jurors, I would want the best person possible for me or my family.[35]

Another federal juror reported a better understanding about the justice system and the jury's role in it. ("I came away with a better sense of understanding the system, trust and comfort in the selection process, but, above all, an appreciation for the need of ordinary citizens, like myself, to serve when given the opportunity."[36]) Box 9.6 illustrates the feelings of satisfaction most individuals have after serving on jury duty and describes how most Americans meet their civil responsibilities to society when given an opportunity to do so.

Box 9.6: Happy Jurors Give Back

A previous chapter described the discouragingly low amounts jurors are compensated when serving jury duty. Court administrators noticed, nonetheless, that many of the compensation checks mailed to jurors' homes after the trial go uncashed.[37] Creative courthouse staff saw an opportunity. Approximately half of all state courts permit jurors to waive their juror fee or donate them to charity.[38] Waived fees are returned to the courts' general operating funds. Donated fees are overwhelmingly allocated for state or local social service agencies or court-approved nonprofit organizations serving disadvantaged children (e.g., Court Appointed Special Advocates (CASA) programs, foster care, and juvenile treatment programs) or victims of crime. Approximately 5 percent of donated fees are used for court improvement programs or juror services.

Several counties in Pennsylvania developed a **Jury-Fee Donation Program** that allowed jurors to donate their compensation to local charities or nonprofit organizations in the community. Allegheny County started the program in the late 1990s with tremendous success. The program grew every year it was active. From 2010 to 2015, jurors of Allegheny County donated approximately $307,000 for projects that improved the jury assembly and jury deliberation rooms and allowed local charities to purchase gifts and clothing for community children in need.[39]

From 2003 through 2015, the fee-donation program in Delaware County, PA, collected $750,000 in donated jury fees for five organizations: Children and Youth Services, Domestic Abuse Project, Hero Scholarship Fund, Operation Warm, and CASA Youth Advocates.[40] In 2010, jurors were given an opportunity to donate their juror fee to an emergency relief effort for the people of Haiti who suffered a devastation earthquake. A total of 470 jurors donated $6,100 to provide emergency supplies, including water and food.[41] Chester County, PA initiated its program in 2015 and collected $10,000 in jury-fee donations in its first year. Jurors choose where their fees would be allocated: the county parks and recreation office, the county library system, or the local long-term healthcare facility.[42]

The jury office in Ada County, Idaho, created a Jury Assistance Fund that pays for transportation (Uber/Lyft) for jurors who do not have access to public transportation, reimbursement for childcare costs, and mental health counseling for jurors experiencing posttraumatic stress symptoms due to their jury service. It also covers drinks and snacks in the café, which are free for all jurors, and meals for jurors who are empaneled on a trial. In 2023, more than half of jurors summoned in Ada County donated their fee.[43]

The success of these county jury-fee donation programs is attributed to jurors' perceptions that their small fee can be reallocated for the benefit of the local community, including organizations and people in need.[44] Jurors who participate in these programs truly give back in many ways. They fulfill their civic responsibilities to jury service by representing their local community in resolving criminal or civil disputes, and they donate their small compensation to various county organizations to assist others in their communities who are in need.

Other jurors reported that jury duty was a learning experience. Some capital jurors reported their jury service was "exciting and really enjoyed it" and "very rewarding, educational."[45] Jurors also noted the experience made jury duty real, not something they heard about or saw on television crime dramas. ("I felt like I was part of it, it wasn't like watching TV or reading about it, I was actually involved in it."[46]) Other research found that jury service changed individuals' perceptions about their responsibilities to the legal process in America and about their level of enthusiasm for being called again to serve in the future. For example, 60 percent of jurors in a sample of 1,184 who were summoned to jury duty or who served on an actual trial believed that jury service should be mandatory for all Americans, while 80 percent of former or prospective jurors indicated they would reach a verdict based on the law, even if the decision went against their personal morals.[47]

Other studies and public opinion polls confirm the impact of jury service on public confidence in the courts. One study conducted focus groups with a variety of individuals representing different political, demographic, and professional groups.[48] It found that former jurors had positive views, not only about their own experiences as jurors but also about the justice system. A 2023 study compared responses of 781 citizens who served as jurors since 2013, with a sample of 1,017 people drawn randomly from the general population in the United States.[49] It found that nearly three-quarters of former jurors expressed trust in state court judges compared to less than half in the general public survey. Even more significant, respondents from both samples trusted citizens serving on juries (76 percent former jurors, 58 percent general public) more than they trusted other justice system participants, including state and federal judges, civil and criminal trial lawyers, and court staff.

The impact of previous jury service extends beyond citizens' opinions about government. It actively promotes greater civic engagement in the form of more frequent voting behavior, more attention paid to community news, and increased participation in civic and community organizations.[50] Jury deliberation teaches critical thinking and problem-solving skills as jurors work together to reach a unanimous verdict. Reaching consensus across diverse perspectives in a single court case increases their confidence in tackling other community problems and creates a virtuous cycle toward increased engagement with government. This finding demonstrates the Founding Fathers' intentions for American citizens to become actively involved, and to shape their own government rather than have a centralized government that oppresses individuals' rights and liberties.

Juror Stress

The experiences that individual jurors have during their jury service vary. Some juries reach a verdict quickly, while other juries require days of deliberation before reaching a verdict. Some juries are asked to review facts and evidence that are clear and easy to understand, while other juries have complex, technical information, and struggle to make sense about the evidence presented during the trial. Finally, some juries allocate monetary awards, while other juries decide whether a defendant deserves a life sentence or should be sentenced to death. Indeed, the experiences jurors have differ significantly depending upon the case.[51] The differences among cases contribute to differences in reactions and adverse side effects during and after the trial.[52]

Jury service can be stressful not only because of the evidence or decisions involved in a trial, but also because it disrupts daily life and often involves unpleasant conditions.[53] Jurors may spend long hours waiting in cramped, poorly maintained courthouses, face public questioning during voir dire, or endure conflicts with fellow jurors. Frustrations about low juror pay, unclear instructions, and poor facilities further add to the stress. Courts have sought to reduce these pressures by offering orientation videos, improving jury assembly rooms, increasing compensation, and adopting "one day/one trial" policies that respect jurors' time.

Routine levels of stress experienced by jurors dissipate quickly after jurors are released from service following the trial. Sometimes, however, what they observe and experience during the trial and the deliberation process stays with them for prolonged periods after being dismissed from their jury service responsibilities. Some jurors may be left with adverse effects from their jury service experience, including persistent and debilitating **stress**.

Secondary Traumatic Stress[54]

A form of stress that occurs when one hears about the suffering of another person through some traumatic event(s) and feels a compelling desire to help alleviate that person's suffering.

Today, the media, medical research organizations, and public health agencies frequently share findings about mental wellbeing, incidents of trauma, and posttraumatic stress disorder (PTSD). For example, PTSD can develop in an individual after exposure to a traumatic life event and symptoms may include flashbacks or nightmares about the event, avoidance of similar situations, temperament changes, withdrawing from family or social events, and decreased productivity at work.[55] Jurors' experiences during the trial may expose them to disturbing images (e.g., photos of crime scenes and victim injuries) and witness testimony about incidents where innocent people were severely injured or killed. Jurors who are well intentioned and sympathetic to another's suffering may experience **secondary trauma**[56] simply by listening to evidence presented in the courtroom and when diligently considering such information during jury deliberation.[57]

Jurors react differently to their jury experience. What some jurors find stressful and burdensome may not adversely affect others. Today, some courts provide jurors with information about symptoms and descriptions of emotional stress that might occur after their jury service experience.

Generally, jurors should recognize that **symptoms of stress** may include:

> anxiety, sleep or appetite changes, moodiness, physical problems (e.g. headaches, stomachaches, no energy, and the like), second guessing your verdict, feeling guilty, fear, trouble dealing with issues or topics related to the case, a desire to be by yourself, or decreased concentration or memory problems.[58]

Box 9.7: After-Service Support for Jurors

West Chester University-Community Mental Health Services (WCU-CMHS) provides after-trial support for jurors and those completing voir dire who are experiencing emotional distress from their trial participation or lingering stress from the jury selection process. The program offers three free 30-minute phone consultations with either a clinically trained doctoral student or a licensed psychologist. These one-on-one phone calls aim to assess the individual's emotional wellbeing and available internal and external resources using Psychological First Aid (PFA). Psychological First Aid is an evidence-informed approach developed to help individuals in the immediate aftermath of traumatic or stressful events. Confidentiality is ensured for all participants seeking support. Facilitators are trained to address juror stress and emotional challenges arising from jury service in civil or criminal cases. For jurors requiring additional counseling beyond the three sessions, WCU-CMHS provides referrals to mental health professionals in their local community. Upon completion of jury duty, jurors are provided with a QR code to access a website and online request form. After completing the request form, jury service is verified and CMHS staff contact the individual within 48 hours to schedule an initial phone call. There is no charge to jurors to use this service.

These symptoms coincide with those representing PTSD. One capital juror referred to this stress as the "**post jury blues**,"[59] while other jurors reported that "negative emotions" resulting from jury service lingered with them for years after the trial.[60] Box 9.7 describes community services immediately available to jurors who experience distress from their trial experience with opportunities to continue treatment with licensed clinical therapists due to prolonged stress.

> It takes courage to sit on a jury. How many of us want to decide the fate of another person's life or freedom? How many of us want to hold that kind of power in our hands?
>
> —Regina Brett, American Journalist
> Public statement

High-Profile Trials

The level of stress jurors experience may depend upon the type of trial they are called to serve. Trials that are widely known in the local community or on a national level, those that are high-profile in nature,[61] may be associated with a different level of stress than routine trials. For example, high-profile cases may involve more complex evidence. Research has revealed that jurors in **high-profile trials** were "four times more likely to exhibit symptoms of stress" compared to jurors in routine trials.[62] High-profile cases involving video evidence, such as the death of George Floyd by police officer Derek Chauvin while kneeling on his neck, spawned outrage and public protests throughout the country.[63] Some research suggests that the names of the jurors who serve on highly publicized cases should remain anonymous to further protect them from post-trial scrutiny that could contribute to stress and anxiety during the trial and after the verdict was reached.[64] In general, jurors reported more stress when the trial involved a high-profile case,[65] complex evidence, detailed witness testimonials, and difficult-to-understand legal principles.[66] Box 9.8 describes how the public's reaction can impact jurors during the deliberation about a trial outcome.

Box 9.8: Public Reaction in High-Profile Trials

Trials bring varying levels of public attention and media coverage. Incidents of police-involved shootings and racially motivated killings may elicit significant national and global attention.[67] Often protesters will gather outside the courthouse where the high-profile trials are held. National protests may occur during the trial proceedings and continue during jury deliberation that vocalize support for one side or the other. Sometimes protests turn violent[68] as tempers and opinions of the public are polarized on many social issues and beliefs about an appropriate case outcome and the administration of fair and impartial justice.

The protests and public reaction during and after a trial often headline printed and online news sources and lead nightly news broadcasts.[69] These media sources have reported on violent and destructive rioting throughout the country after the acquittals of George Zimmerman,[70] Kyle Rittenhouse,[71] policer officer Jason Stockley,[72] and the four police officers involved in the beating of Rodney King in 1992.[73] Jurors serving on these trials understandably may be concerned about public reaction to unpopular verdicts. In 2001, Casey Anthony was acquitted of murdering her 2-year-old daughter by jurors empaneled from Pinellas County, Florida. Several jurors moved out of state or quit their jobs due to the hostility they encountered in their community.

> Putting pressure on grand juries to indict in my view is un-American. A grand jury should be allowed to be fair and impartial. They shouldn't have people yelling and screaming.
>
> —Rudy Giuliani, Mayor of New York City (1994–2001)
> Public statement

Also, jurors who served on a capital case may experience heightened levels of stress due to their decision to impose the ultimate punishment, including the death penalty. Research has revealed that capital jurors experienced "severe emotional and psychological duress"[74] after serving on a death penalty case. Overall, 63 percent of jurors who imposed a death sentence reported the experience was emotionally upsetting, compared to 58 percent of jurors in trials that resulted in a life sentence.[75] Gender differences and perceived stress were also uncovered among capital jurors. Specifically, a greater percentage of female jurors (71 percent) compared to male jurors (50 percent) reported the experience was upsetting, while 48 percent of female jurors reported trouble sleeping, bad dreams or nightmares, and loss of appetite compared to only 24 percent of male jurors.[76] Other research uncovered similar gender-specific effects where female jurors exhibited more symptoms of trauma after the trial proceedings than did male jurors.[77]

Sources of Stress

Jurors reported numerous sources of stress during their jury service experience. Often, these sources of stress were associated with the specific case they were asked to serve. In cases involving credible threats of jury intimidation or jury tampering, some courts will take the increasingly rare step of **sequestering** jurors—keeping them locked in the deliberation room during the day and providing meals and hotel accommodations overnight—during deliberations or even for the entire trial.[78] The act of being sequestered itself can cause jurors stress related to missed time with family, work responsibilities and loss of wages, canceled medical appointments, and general concerns about lodging accommodations and dietary restrictions.[79] Also, jurors from murder trials reported the evidence and witness testimony presented during the trial was troubling, "just to see the grave, hearing the testimony of the family, and how the bullets went in his head and came out."[80] Jurors also reported being fearful of retaliation[81] by litigants and their families, friends, and associates.[82] This is especially true for cases involving defendants charged with serious crimes or crimes that have been sensationalized and are well known in the local community or nationally.[83]

Another source of stress for jurors comes from contact by the media after the verdict has been reached and been made public. After jurors are dismissed from the courthouse, they are allowed to speak publicly about their experiences. Some former jurors have written books about their jury experiences.[84] Judges may address jurors' concerns about interacting with media after the trial has concluded. The Model Criminal Jury Instructions Committee of the Colorado Supreme Court composed the following language for judges to use with jurors during such discussions:

> You have now completed your duties as jurors in this case and are discharged with the thanks of the court. The question may arise whether you may now discuss this case with the lawyers, the defendant, or other persons involved in the case. For your guidance the Court instructs you that whether you talk to anyone is entirely your own decision. It is proper for others to discuss the case with you, and you may talk with them, but you need not. If you talk to them, you may tell them as much or as little as you like about your deliberations or the facts that influenced your decision. If any person persists in discussing the case over your objection or becomes critical of your service either before or after any discussion has begun, please report it to me.[85]

Judges who choose to read such instructions to jurors may be keenly aware of the level of stress jury service puts on the average juror. Research with judges, who had broad legal backgrounds and experiences on the bench, agreed that jurors can experience significant stress from different aspects of the trial proceeding, including not understanding what is expected of them and having to reach a verdict among fellow jurors who may not get along.[86]

Jurors may also experience stress related to questions they have about the trial proceeding, evidence presented during the trial, and even the accuracy of their verdict.[87] Some judges meet with jurors after the trial.[88] This meeting allows judges to address questions and concerns jurors have and is a good opportunity for judges to focus on the accomplishments of the jury and the good work they performed while fulfilling their civic responsibilities to the community.[89]

> There may sometimes be a mistake, but I think that the citizens who are sworn to uphold their duty in a jury setting are going to try to do their best to do that regardless of the consequences.
>
> —Janet Reno, Former United States Attorney General (1993–2001)

Remedies for Addressing Juror Stress

Courts increasingly recognize the need to address jurors' wellbeing and to identify coping mechanisms to help jurors relieve symptoms of stress resulting from their jury service. The

Tips for Coping After Jury Duty

From the Superior Court of Arizona, Maricopa County, Jury Service Website at http://www.superiorcourt.maricopa.gov/JuryServices/GeneralInformation/coping.asp

The Jury Duty Experience

Thank you for serving your community. Being on a jury is a rewarding experience which in some cases may be quite demanding. You were asked to listen to testimony and to examine facts and evidence. Coming to decisions is often not easy, but your participation is appreciated.

Serving on a jury is not a common experience and may cause some jurors to have temporary symptoms of distress.

Not everyone feels anxiety or increased stress after jury duty. However, it may be helpful to be aware of the symptoms if they arise.

Some temporary signs of distress following jury duty include: anxiety, sleep or appetite changes, moodiness, physical problems (e.g. headaches, stomach aches, no energy, and the like), second guessing your verdict, feeling guilty, fear, trouble dealing with issues or topics related to the case, a desire to be by yourself, or decreased concentration or memory problems.

Symptoms may come and go, but will eventually go away. To help yourself, it is important to admit any symptoms you may have and deal with any unpleasant reactions.

Coping Techniques After Serving On A Jury

- Talk to family members and friends. One of the best ways to put your jury duty experience in perspective is to discuss your feelings and reactions with loved ones and friends. You may also want to talk with your family physician or a member of the clergy.
- Stick to your normal, daily routines. It is important to return to your normal schedule. Don't isolate yourself.
- Before you leave the court, you may wish to get the names and numbers of at least two of your fellow jurors. Sometimes it is helpful to talk to people who went through the experience with you. This can help you to remember that you were part of a group (jury) and are not alone.
- Remember that you are having normal responses to an unusual experience.
- You can deal with signs of distress by cutting down on alcohol, caffeine, and nicotine. These substances can increase anxiety, fatigue and make sleep problems worse.
- Relax with deep breathing.
- Breathe in slowly through your nose.
- Breathe out through your mouth.
- Slow your thoughts down and think about a relaxing scene.
- Continue deep breathing until you feel more relaxed.
- Cope with sleep problems.
- Increase your daily exercise, but do not exercise just before bedtime.
- Decrease your caffeine consumption, especially in the afternoon or evening.
- Do "boring" activities before bedtime.
- Listen to relaxation tapes or relaxing music before bedtime.

Final Thoughts

- Remember that jury service is the responsibility of good citizens.
- Resist negative thoughts about verdict.
- No matter what others think about the verdict, your opinion is the only one that matters.
- You don't have to prove yourself to anyone.
- Sometimes it takes a lot of courage to serve on a jury. Some cases are very violent and brutal and hard to deal with. The case is now over and it is important for you to get on with your life.
- If you are fearful of retaliation or if you are threatened after the trial, tell the court and/or law enforcement immediately.

If signs of distress persist for two weeks after the jury service has ended consider contacting your physician.

Figure 9.2: Tips for Coping after Jury Duty

first involves alerting jurors that they might experience higher levels of stress, providing them with techniques to manage stress, and encouraging them to seek additional support or counseling if their symptoms persist. Many courthouses distribute brochures to jurors when they report to the courthouse or post the documents on their court websites. Figure 9.2 shows the brochure provided by the Superior Court of Arizona in Maricopa County, which is typical of the type of information included in these brochures.[90]

Although not specifically designed to address heightened juror stress, many trial judges make it a practice to meet privately with jurors after they have completed their jury service to thank them for their participation, to answer questions that jurors might have that could not be addressed during the trial, to solicit feedback about their experience, and to listen to suggestions for improving jury service in the future.[91] During these meetings, judges can address any concerns jurors raise and help provide them a sense of closure research revealed many jurors enjoyed speaking with judges and attorneys after the trial and deliberations were finished.[92]

In the 1990s, some jurisdictions began holding **debriefing sessions** for jurors who served on trials in which the evidence was particularly sensitive and emotionally taxing.[93] These cases included criminal trials where graphic crime scene evidence was presented, or medical malpractice trials where a patient was horribly disfigured or permanently injured. The debriefing sessions are modeled after **Critical Incident Stress Management** programs that are used with law enforcement officers and other first responders to traumatic incidents as part of their profession.[94] The option to attend a debriefing session is voluntary. One juror in a capital case who completed jury service in a jurisdiction where a debriefing session was not practiced commented about the court's apparent lack of concern for jurors' wellbeing:

> I also think it sucks that they do not offer counseling to the jury for all this bullshit, you know. But if it was offered, I definitely would of [sic] taken them up on it. In fact, this [the juror interview] has been therapeutic to go through and work through some of this. This really gives me better closure to it. That's another thing the system is lacking in it. It's like okay, thank you, goodbye. You know. I've just given you four months of my life and now you're just kicking me out.[95]

Debriefing procedures differ by jurisdiction. The topics of the discussion depend upon the case being tried and the concerns addressed by the individual jurors who decided to attend the debriefing session. Jurors may be encouraged during the debriefing session to talk about their feelings and the jury service experience with their family members and friends, and to maintain contact with fellow jurors after the trial as an additional source of support, if needed.[96] Overall, debriefing sessions were reported to be helpful by jurors and judges largely supported this post-trial discussion.[97] Box 9.9 provides comments from a practitioner about the importance of debriefing sessions from a courthouse administrator. This single debriefing session may be all that is required for some jurors after the trial. This small window provided what they needed to hear, share, and communicate with the court and their fellow jurors about their experiences and the impact it had on their psyche and perspective of the jury system.

Research, however, reveals little about the overall effectiveness of debriefing sessions for reducing long-term stress among jurors. It may be that a single session with courtroom staff and a mental health professional after the trial does not adequately address all aspects of stress and trauma experienced during the trial. Proponents urge conducting additional empirical research studies that use more strict controls, including treatment and control group membership to determine the true and lasting effects of a post-trial debriefing session.[98] In addition,

Box 9.9: From the Field

Name: Patrick Martin

Position: Jury Commissioner for the First Judicial District of Pennsylvania

How long have you worked in this courthouse?
I have worked here for 21 years.

What reactions do jurors typically have to their jury service experience?
Initially, there is a mixed reaction to jurors serving. Most of them do not mind being here, and some are excited. It is important to respect their time here and to utilize their services as quickly as possible. The last thing we want is for delays in the courtroom to cause the jurors to sit around for extended periods of time. Those who are selected to a trial understandably have a very favorable view of jury duty. Those who sit through the process of selection but do not get selected sometimes feel disappointed because they either were not selected or because they felt their time was wasted.

What services are jurors provided after the trial to address issues of emotional stress that resulted from their jury service?
Currently, we are offering post-trial support for jurors in two ways. First, we provide a coping pamphlet that describes signs and symptoms of stress, self-care tips, and behavioral health web resources. Second, we have partnered with West Chester University (WCU) of Pennsylvania to offer "Post Trial Support" to jurors. WCU will offer Psychological First Aid to jurors who may have suffered vicarious trauma from hearing testimony, seeing evidence, or struggling with the fact that their decision may have sent someone to jail for a part of their life. Stress for jurors could also occur during heated deliberations, or from the disruptions of normal day to day things such as childcare concerns.

In 2025, the Mid-Atlantic Association for Court Management (MAACM) recognized Martin's leadership and innovation, honoring him with the John Neufeld Court Achievement Award for his work on the Post Trial Support Program for Jurors. The program has been featured on *CBS Evening News* and reported on in *The New York Times*.

many jurors are exhausted by the end of the trial and simply want to go home to rest rather than spend several more hours at the courthouse for a debriefing session. They may not fully realize the extent of stress they experienced until days or weeks after the trial has concluded.

Concerns about the timing and effectiveness of debriefing sessions led some courts to offer individual counseling to jurors. Since the early 2000s, federal courts use the Federal **Employee Assistance Program** (EAP) to provide up to six no-cost counseling sessions to jurors who served on high-stress trials.[99] To make the services available, the trial judge must first enter an order that extends the jurors' service for up to six months, thereby making them eligible to receive federal EAP benefits. Next, the juror can make individual arrangements for counseling sessions as needed. The primary downside to this approach is that it is entirely dependent on the trial judge recognizing that jurors have experienced stress during service and are aware of the existence of the EAP program.

Some states also offer individual counseling to jurors. In Alaska, jurors serving in cases involving murder, manslaughter, criminally negligent homicide, felonious assault, or sexual assault are eligible for individual counseling. The Alaska Code of Criminal Procedure (Title 12) specifies that

> [t]he trial judge may offer not more than 10 hours of post-trial psychological counseling, without charge, to a juror or an alternate juror who serves on a trial jury in a trial involving extraordinarily graphic, gruesome, or emotional evidence or testimony.[100]

If seeking counseling under this statute, the juror is required to do so within 180 days after the jury is dismissed. Jurors may choose either group or individual counseling, and individual counselors may be "provided by the court system, by a state agency, or by contract."[101]

In 2023, Massachusetts started offering mental health counseling to all jurors, regardless of whether they served in a particularly traumatic trial.[102] Massachusetts provides a brochure to all jurors when they complete their jury service informing them about available services, which are provided by a private mental health provider under a contract with the Office of the Massachusetts Jury Commissioner. The counseling sessions are confidential, but the court receives regular reports about the number of jurors who are accessing services. The court also conducts an exit survey with all jurors following their service. Many jurors reported that, although they themselves did not feel they needed counseling, they were thankful the services existed.

Conclusion

Stress is part of everyday life. The American jury system is not immune to these effects. The verdict a jury reaches is unlikely to be invalidated because of jury behavior during the deliberation process; therefore, jurors will have to be comfortable with the trial outcome. Jurors, pending the case assigned to them, may experience varying levels of stress from the trial evidence they are exposed to and their interactions with fellow jurors. Research findings from the social and natural sciences, including psychology and biology, have publicized the dangerous effects of stress on the mental and physical wellbeing of individuals who are exposed to traumatic events. These findings are important and are applicable to jurors who may be exposed to gruesome evidence or testimony about injuries to others for days or weeks on end.

Prospective jurors should be made aware of what they may experience during their jury service. This may include gathering in the assembly room, voir dire process, purpose of jury instructions, and potential deliberation dynamics. Each trial has subtle differences, as do the jurors who are called to serve. Jurors have their own lived experience and will react to similar situations differently. Research findings overwhelmingly report that jurors are satisfied with their jury experience and there is collegiality among the jury members; therefore, to emphasize the potential negative side effects over the favorable reactions may do prospective and future jurors a disservice.

The next chapter will discuss the future of the American jury system. The material will re-address some of the criticisms of the current system, including jurors' inability to understand complex evidence and proponents' arguments for moving toward professional juries. The chapter will conclude with a summary of the major points addressed throughout the text and what the future may hold for the American jury system over the next 250 years.

Summary

This chapter addressed issues of the American jury system that occurred after the verdict was reached and the jurors were dismissed from their jury service responsibilities. The Federal Rules of Evidence, Rule 606(b), referred to as the no-impeachment rule, protects the secrecy of jury deliberations and the finality of jury verdicts. The reasons for this are obvious and reflect the Founding Fathers' insistence on a trial by jury, not a centralized government, to resolve criminal and civil matters. The U.S. Supreme Court has been unwilling to invalidate a jury's verdict even when faced with claims of jurors' mental incompetence, intoxication, and other drug use during the trial proceeding. There are exceptions to Rule 606(b), however, which stipulate a verdict can be invalidated if the jury's decision is based on extraneous prejudice, outside influences, or a mistake on a verdict form. These exceptions have been extended to invalidate verdicts where prejudiced decision-making and racially discriminatory comments were made during the deliberation discussion.

This chapter also addressed jurors' reactions to their jury service experience. Many jurors reported enjoying the jury service experience. The type of trial an individual served on, however, impacted this reaction, and their experience of side-effects, including anxiety and post-traumatic stress symptoms such as nightmares, withdrawal, and reduced focus. Jurors who reported the most stress served on high-profile cases, cases that involved complex and graphic evidence, and long trials that required sequestration. Also, capital jurors, who were required to impose the ultimate punishment, including the death penalty, reported heightened levels and more persistent stress.

Both the federal and state court systems have been receptive to issues of jury stress. Many jurisdictions have created post-trial debriefing sessions where jurors meet with the judge, and possibly the trial attorneys and other courtroom personnel, after the verdict was read and the jury was dismissed from service. The debriefing sessions are designed to allow jurors to ask questions about the trial and to inform them about the mental health services available to them, should they experience any symptoms in the days after leaving the courtroom. Federal funding, and funding in many states, has been allocated to courts to provide mental health counseling, and other services to jurors who experience anxiety and stress resulting from their jury service.

Discussion Questions

1. The U.S. Supreme Court's finding in ***Peña-Rodriguez v. Colorado*** (2017) extended the exceptions to the no-impeachment rule to include racially discriminatory statements made during the jury deliberation. What is the next step in the evolutionary process of the no-impeachment rule? What other exceptions, if any, should be made to Rule 606(b) to address overt discriminatory actions, speech, or attitudes today?
2. Do you think the public reaction to a jury verdict in highly publicized and high-profile cases impacts the deliberation process? If a jury is worried about the public's reaction, what concerns or issues could the jurors be struggling with specifically? What are some safeguards that the courts could implement to lessen the impact of the public's reaction on jury decision-making and the trial verdict?
3. Think of a recent trial that has received a lot of national publicity. The trial could be criminal or civil. Be specific. What stands out to you in this trial? If you were a juror in that case, what would cause you the most stress and why? What options would be available for you to cope with that stressful experience?

4. Ethical consideration. Research shown in this chapter indicates there is a real possibility that a juror may be adversely impacted from their jury service experience. What responsibilities do the courts have for telling prospective jurors about the physical and emotional harm they may endure during and after the trial, and what effect do you think sharing this information would have on their psyche going into a trial? How could the court best approach this issue with prospective jurors and how would this impact their willingness to participate in a jury trial? Does this information change your mind about serving as a juror in the future?

Review Questions

1. Can a jury verdict be invalidated? If so, how? Why does Rule 606(b) of the Federal Rules of Evidence make invalidating a jury verdict so difficult?
2. Generally, how do individuals react to serving on a trial jury? What have they reported learning from their experience?
3. What adverse side-effects have jurors reported after a trial proceeding and jury deliberation? What were the sources or causes of these adverse effects?
4. What is the purpose of a post-trial debriefing session? What specific information may be shared with jurors during a debriefing session?

Answers to Chapter 9 "What Do You Think?" Questions

1. True. Juries inform the bailiff a verdict was reached, then the judge reassembles all parties in the courtroom to read the verdict for the first time.
2. False. High-profile trials can be on a national level, state level, or local level.
3. False. Rule 606(b) permits jury verdicts to be invalidated in rare circumstances, as the term "high profile" generally refers to cases that are well known and discussed.
4. True. Jurors reported greater stress and dissatisfaction in cases involving complex evidence, gruesome photographs, and graphic testimonials.
5. False. Trial jurors are allowed to speak about any events that occurred during the trial proceeding; however, stricter guidelines are placed on grand jurors.
6. False. The number of courthouses that provide information about accessing psychological counseling services is increasing, but many jurisdictions still do not provide any information beyond a brochure about coping strategies.

Key Terms

Critical Incident Stress Management
debriefing session
Employee Assistance Program
high-profile trials
invalidating
jury-fee donation program
no-impeachment rule
Peña-Rodriguez v. Colorado
post jury blues
racial animus

Rule 606(b)
secondary trauma
sequestering
stress
symptoms of stress
Tanner v. United States
verdict form

References

1 Peak, K.J., Madensen-Herold, T.D. (2019). *Introduction to criminal justice: Practice and process* (p. 239) Sage Publications.
2 Iowa Rules of Criminal Procedure 2.22(5)(a). (2024, May 10). *Return of jury and verdict: Return and polling of unanimous verdict.* https://www.legis.iowa.gov/docs/ACO/CourtRulesChapter/2.pdf
3 Marder, N.S. (2022). *The power of the jury.* Cambridge University Press.
4 Markovitz, A. (2001). Jury secrecy during deliberations. *The Yale Law Journal, 110*(8), 1493–1530.
5 Cambridge Dictionary. (2024, April 10). Invalidate. In *Cambridge Dictionary Online.* https://dictionary.cambridge.org/us/dictionary/english/invalidation
6 *Warger v. Shauers*, 574 U.S. 40 (2014).
7 *United States v. Dioguardi*, 361 F. Supp. 954, 957 (1973).
8 Hannaford-Agor, P.L., Trochessett, A., Bailey, E., & Kelliher, C. (2021). *Jurors and new media: Filling knowledge gaps for judicial and legal policymakers.* National Center for State Courts. https://ncsc.contentdm.oclc.org/digital/collection/juries/id/328/rec/3
9 Federal Rules of Evidence 606(b)(1).
10 *Duncan v. Louisiana*, 391 U. S. 145.
11 *Peña-Rodriguez v. Colorado*, 137 S. Ct. 855, 865 (2017).
12 *Peña-Rodriguez v. Colorado*, 137 S. Ct. 855, 861 (2017).
13 *Vaise v. Delaval*, 1 T. R. 11, 99 Eng. Rep. 944 (K. B. 1785).
14 *Wright v. Illinois & Miss. Tel. Co.*, 20 Iowa 195 (1866).
15 Federal Rules of Evidence 606(b)(2).
16 *United States v. Dioguardi*, 361 F. Supp. 954, 957 (1973).
17 *Warger v. Shauers*, 574 U.S. 40 (2014).
18 *Tanner v. United States* 483 U.S. 107, 136 (1987).
19 *United States v. William M. Conover and Anthony R. Tanner*, 772 F.2d 765 (11th Cir. 1985).
20 *United States v. William M. Conover and Anthony R. Tanner*, 772 F.2d 765, 770 (11th Cir. 1985).
21 *United States v. William M. Conover and Anthony R. Tanner*, 772 F.2d 765, 770 (11th Cir. 1985).
22 *Tanner v. United States*, 483 U.S. 107, 120 (1987).
23 *Tanner v. United States*, 483 U.S. 107, 141 (1987).
24 Hannaford-Agor, P.L., Trochessett, A., Bailey, E., & Kelliher, C. (2021). *Jurors and new media: Filling knowledge gaps for judicial and legal policymakers.* National Center for State Courts. https://ncsc.contentdm.oclc.org/digital/collection/juries/id/328/rec/3
25 Black's Law Dictionary. (2020). Extraneous evidence. In *Black's Law Dictionary* (2nd ed.). https://thelawdictionary.org/extraneous-evidence/
26 *United States v. Siegelman*, 2007 U.S. Dist. LEXIS 45648 (M.D. Ala. June 22, 2007).
27 *McQuarrie v. State*, 380 S.W.3d 145 (Tex. Crim. App. 2012) (citing *Soliz v. Saenz*, 779 S.W.2d 929 (Tex. App.—Corpus Christi 1989, pet. denied)).
28 *Tapenes v. State*, 43 So. 3d 159 (Fla. Dist. Ct. App. 2010).
29 *Peña-Rodriguez v. Colorado*, 137 S. Ct. 855 (2017).
30 *Peña-Rodriguez v. Colorado*, 137 S. Ct. 855, 862 (2017).
31 *Peña-Rodriguez v. Colorado*, 137 S. Ct. 855, 868 (2017).

32 *Peña-Rodriguez v. Colorado*, 137 S. Ct. 855, 869 (2017).
33 *Peña-Rodriguez v. Colorado*, 137 S. Ct. 855, 869 (2017).
34 Grant, C.A. (2022). Holding juries accountable: Assessing the right to a competent and unimpaired jury in light of Tanner and Federal Rule of Evidence 606. *The Georgetown Journal of Legal Ethics*, *35*(4), 773–804.
35 Administrative Office of the U.S. Courts. (2024, January 15). *Juror experiences*. https://www.uscourts.gov/services-forms/jury-service/learn-about-jury-service/juror-experiences
36 Administrative Office of the U.S. Courts. (2024, January 15). *Letter to editor: Jury duty*. https://www.uscourts.gov/services-forms/jury-service/learn-about-jury-service/letter-editor-jury-duty
37 Administrative Office of PA Courts. (2016). Giving back. *AOPC Connected*, *1*, 1–3.
38 Hannaford-Agor, P.L., & Moffett, M. (2024). *2023 State-of-the-states survey of jury improvement efforts: Jury operations in state courts*. National Center for State Courts. https://ncsc.contentdm.oclc.org/digital/collection/juries/id/383/rec/1
39 Administrative Office of PA Courts. (2016). Giving back. *AOPC Connected*, *1*, 1–3.
40 Schaefer, M.A. (2015, December 7). *Jury-fee donation program is a hit in suburbs*. The Philadelphia Inquirer. https://www.inquirer.com/philly/news/20151207_Jury-fee_donation_program_is_a_hit_in_suburbs.html
41 Schaefer, M.A. (2015, December 7). *Jury-fee donation program is a hit in suburbs*. The Philadelphia Inquirer. https://www.inquirer.com/philly/news/20151207_Jury-fee_donation_program_is_a_hit_in_suburbs.html
42 Chester County Justice Center. (2023, November 29). *Jury service information*. https://www.chesco.org/faq.aspx?TID=29#:~:text=What%20is%20the%20dress%20code,tee%20shirts%20are%20not%20suitable
43 State of Idaho Judicial Branch. (2024). *Ada County receives national jury innovation award*. https://isc.idaho.gov/sites/default/files/press-release-documents/20241010-ada-jury-award.pdf
44 Administrative Office of PA Courts. (2016). Giving back. *AOPC Connected*, *1*, 1–3.
45 Antonio, M.E. (2006). "I didn't know it'd be so hard": Jurors' emotional reactions to serving on a capital trial. *Judicature*, *89*(5), 282–288.
46 Antonio, M.E. (2006). "I didn't know it'd be so hard": Jurors' emotional reactions to serving on a capital trial. *Judicature*, *89*(5), 282–288.
47 Keller, J. (2023) (2024, January 15). *Confessions of a juror: How mandatory jury duty impacts Americans*. BarPrephero. https://barprephero.com/confessions-of-a-juror
48 Trust in Justice Project (2024). Phase 2: *Why the public is losing trust in justice and what to do about it*. https://perma.cc/5MDY-4HY7.
49 Jackson, C., & Lohr, A.A. (2023). *Ipsos survey: Jury service and the legal system*. Ipsos. https://www.ipsos.com/en-us/ipsos-survey-jury-service-and-legal-system
50 Gastil, J., Deess, E.P., Weiser, P.J., & Simmons, C. (2010). *The jury and democracy: How jury deliberation promotes civic engagement and political participation* (1st ed.). Oxford University Press.
51 Miller, M.K., & Bornstein, B.H. (2013). The experience of jurors: Reducing stress and enhancing satisfaction. In M.K. Miller & B.H. Bornstein (Eds.), *Stress, trauma, and wellbeing in the legal system*. Oxford University Press. https://doi.org/10.1093/acprof:oso/9780199829996.003.0011
52 Antonio, M.E. (2006). "I didn't know it'd be so hard": Jurors' emotional reactions to serving on a capital trial. *Judicature*, *89*(5), 282–288.
53 National Center for State Courts. (1998). *Through the eyes of the juror: A manual for addressing juror stress*. https://ncsc.contentdm.oclc.org/digital/collection/juries/id/310/rec/1
54 Shalabi, K.M., Alshraif, Z.A., Ismail, R.I., Almubarak, K., Mohmoud, N., & Shaik, S.A. (2023). Secondary traumatic stress disorder among physiotherapists working in high morbidity departments: A cross-sectional study. *Journal of Multidisciplinary Healthcare*, *16*, 3287–3297. https://doi.org/10.2147/JMDH.S428034
55 American Psychiatric Association. (2013). *Diagnostic and statistical manual of mental disorders* (5th ed.). American Psychiatric Association.
56 Beck, C.T. (2011). Secondary traumatic stress in nurses: A systematic review. *Archives of Psychiatric Nursing*, *25*(1), 1–10. https://doi.org/10.1016/j.apnu.2010.05.005
57 Rabil, M., McQuiston, D., & Wiseman, K.D. (2021). Secondary trauma in lawyering: Stories, studies, and strategies. *Wake Forest Law Review*, *56*(4), 825–857.

58 Chester County Justice Center. (2024, January 15). *Coping techniques after serving on a jury.* https://www.chesco.org/DocumentCenter/View/42023/Coping-jury-service-brochure?bidId=

59 Antonio, M.E. (2006). "I didn't know it'd be so hard": Jurors' emotional reactions to serving on a capital trial. *Judicature, 89*(5), 282–288.

60 Keller, J. (2024, January 15). *Confessions of a juror: How mandatory jury duty impacts Americans.* BarPrephero. https://barprephero.com/confessions-of-a-juror

61 Hannaford-Agor, P.L. (2008). When all eyes are watching: Trial characteristics and practices in notorious trials. *Judicature, 91*(4), 197–201.

62 Hannaford-Agor, P.L. (2008). When all eyes are watching: Trial characteristics and practices in notorious trials. *Judicature, 91*(4), 197–201.

63 Heaney, M.T. (2020). *The George Floyd protests generated more media coverage than any protest in 50 years.* The Washington Post Online. https://www.washingtonpost.com/politics/2020/07/06/george-floyd-protests-generated-more-media-coverage-than-any-protest-50-years

64 Carrie, J. (2015, November 30). *Why courts use anonymous juries, like in Freddie Gray case.* National Public Radio. https://www.npr.org/sections/thetwo-way/2015/11/30/457905697/why-courts-use-anonymous-juries-like-in-freddie-gray-case

65 Blackmon, S.M., Neville, H.A., & Jones Thomas, A. (2019). Ideology matters: College students' emotional reactions to the killing of Trayvon Martin. *The Counseling Psychologist, 47*(6), 909–937. https://doi.org/10.1177/0011000019893089

66 Bornstein, B.H., Miller, M.K., Nemeth, R.J., Page, G.L., & Musil, S. (2005). Juror reactions to jury duty: Perceptions of the system and potential stressors. *Behavioral Sciences & the Law, 23*(3), 321–346. https://doi.org/10.1002/bsl.635

67 Poon, L., & Patino, M. (2023, January 30). *Rodney King to Tyre Nichols: A timeline of U.S. police protests.* Bloomberg. https://www.bloomberg.com/news/articles/2020–06–09/a-history-of-protests-against-police-brutality

68 Enos, R.D., Kaufman, A.R., & Sands, M.L. (2019). Can violent protest change local policy support? Evidence from the aftermath of the 1992 Los Angeles riot. *The American Political Science Review, 113*(4), 1012–1028. https://doi.org/10.1017/S0003055419000340

69 Mudde, C. (2021, November 19). *Kyle Rittenhouse has walked free. Now it's open season on protesters.* The Guardian. https://www.theguardian.com/us-news/commentisfree/2021/nov/19/kyle-rittenhouse-verdict-acquitted-protest

70 Castellano, A. (2013, July 15). *George Zimmerman protesters take to the streets with anger over acquittal.* ABC News. https://abcnews.go.com/US/george-zimmerman-protesters-streets-anger-acquittal/story?id=19665990

71 Delisio, M. (2021, November 20). *Kyle Rittenhouse acquittal sparks protests across U.S.* ABC News. https://abcnews.go.com/US/kyle-rittenhouse-acquittal-sparks-protests-us/story?id=81299021

72 Associated Press. (2017, September 17). *St. Louis protests over police officer's acquittal turn violent for second night.* The Wall Street Journal. https://www.wsj.com/articles/st-louis-police-officers-acquittal-triggers-second-day-of-protests-1505612388

73 Lichfield, J. (1992, May 4). *LA riots: How The Independent covered the events on this day in history.* The Independent. https://www.independent.co.uk/news/world/americas/los-angeles-riots-anniversary-rodney-king-white-officers-black-race-relations-a9496011.html

74 Antonio, M.E. (2006). "I didn't know it'd be so hard": Jurors' emotional reactions to serving on a capital trial. *Judicature, 89*(5), 282–288.

75 Antonio, M.E. (2008). Stress and the capital jury: How male and female jurors react to serving on a murder trial. *The Justice System Journal, 29*(3), 396–407. https://doi.org/10.1080/0098261X.2008.10767903

76 Antonio, M.E. (2008). Stress and the capital jury: How male and female jurors react to serving on a murder trial. *The Justice System Journal, 29*(3), 396–407. https://doi.org/10.1080/0098261X.2008.10767903

77 Lonergan, M., Leclerc, M.È., Descamps, M., Pigeon, S., & Brunet, A. (2016). Prevalence and severity of trauma- and stressor-related symptoms among jurors: A review. *Journal of Criminal Justice, 47*, 51–61. https://doi.org/10.1016/j.jcrimjus.2016.07.003

78 Hannaford-Agor, P.L., & Moffett, M. (2024). *2023 State-of-the-states survey of jury improvement efforts: High-profile trials.* National Center for State Courts. https://ncsc.contentdm.oclc.org/digital/collection/juries/id/382/rec/4
79 National Center for State Courts. (1998). *Through the eyes of the juror: A manual for addressing juror stress.* https://www.ncsc-jurystudies.org/__data/assets/pdf_file/0022/7438/through-the-eyes-of-the-juror.pdf
80 Antonio, M.E. (2008). Stress and the capital jury: How male and female jurors react to serving on a murder trial. *The Justice System Journal, 29*(3), 396–407. https://doi.org/10.1080/0098261X.2008.10767903
81 Bornstein, B.H., Miller, M.K., Nemeth, R.J., Page, G.L., & Musil, S. (2005). Juror reactions to jury duty: Perceptions of the system and potential stressors. *Behavioral Sciences & the Law, 23*(3), 321–346. https://doi.org/10.1002/bsl.635
82 *Until the end, Gotti plotted to bribe jurors, documents show.* Tampa Bay Times (March 27, 2005). https://www.tampabay.com/archive/2005/03/27/until-the-end-gotti-plotted-to-bribe-jurors-documents-show
83 National Center for State Courts. (1998). *Through the eyes of the juror: A manual for addressing juror stress.* https://www.ncsc-jurystudies.org/__data/assets/pdf_file/0022/7438/through-the-eyes-of-the-juror.pdf
84 Thornton, J. (1996). A review of hung jury: The diary of a Menendez juror. *Journal of Forensic Sciences, 41*(5), 899–899. https://doi.org/10.1520/JFS14022J
85 Supreme Court of Colorado. (2024, January 17). *Colorado jury instructions, criminal (2022).* Model Criminal Jury Instructions Committee. https://www.courts.state.co.us/userfiles/file/Court_Probation/Supreme_Court/Committees/Criminal_Jury_Instructions/2022/COLJI-Crim%202022%20-%20Final.pdf
86 McQuiston, D.E., Hooper, M.D., & Brasington, A.E. (2019). Vicarious trauma in the courtroom: Judicial perceptions of juror distress. *The Judges' Journal, 58*(2), 32–35.
87 Robertson, N., Davies, G., & Nettleingham, A. (2009). Vicarious traumatization as a consequence of jury service. *Howard Journal, 48*(1), 1–12.
88 Miller, M.K., & Bornstein, B.H. (2004). Juror stress: Causes and interventions. *Thurgood Marshall Law Review, 30,* 237–269.
89 National Center for State Courts. (1998). *Through the eyes of the juror: A manual for addressing juror stress.* https://www.ncsc-jurystudies.org/__data/assets/pdf_file/0022/7438/through-the-eyes-of-the-juror.pdf
90 Superior Court of Arizona. (2025, August 22). *Tips for coping after jury duty.* https://www.courts.oregon.gov/courts/washington/jury/Documents/Tips_for_Coping_After_Jury_Service.pdf
91 Munsterman, G.T., Hannaford-Agor, P.L., & Whitehead, M. (2006). *Jury trial innovations* (2nd ed.). https://ncsc.contentdm.oclc.org/digital/collection/juries/id/77/rec/9.
92 Bienen, L.B. (1993). Helping jurors out: Post-verdict debriefing for jurors in emotionally disturbing trials. *Indiana Law Journal (Bloomington), 68*(4), 1333–1355.
93 Dabbs, M.O. (1992). Jury traumatization in high profile criminal trials: A case for crisis debriefing? *Law & Psychology Review, 16,* 201–216.
94 Finn, P. (1998). Correctional officer stress: A cause for concern and additional help. *Federal Probation, 62*(2), 65–74.
95 Antonio, M.E. (2006). "I didn't know it'd be so hard": Jurors' emotional reactions to serving on a capital trial. *Judicature, 89*(5), 282–288.
96 Chester County Justice Center. (2024, January 15). *Coping techniques after serving on a jury.* https://www.chesco.org/DocumentCenter/View/42023/Coping-jury-service-brochure?bidId=
97 McQuiston, D.E., Hooper, M.D., & Brasington, A.E. (2019). Vicarious trauma in the courtroom: Judicial perceptions of juror distress. *The Judges' Journal, 58*(2), 32–35.
98 Bornstein, B.H., Miller, M.K., Nemeth, R.J., Page, G.L., & Musil, S. (2005). Juror reactions to jury duty: Perceptions of the system and potential stressors. *Behavioral Sciences & the Law, 23*(3), 321–346. https://doi.org/10.1002/bsl.635
99 Hannaford-Agor, P.L. (2007). Jury news: A new option for addressing juror stress? *Court Manager, 26*(2), 50–52.

100 Alaska Code of Criminal Procedures. AK Stat § 12.45.018 (2023). *Juror counseling following graphic evidence or testimony.*
101 Alaska Code of Criminal Procedures. AK Stat § 12.45.018 (2023). *Juror counseling following graphic evidence or testimony.*
102 Center for Jury Studies. (2024). *The juror counseling program with Pam Wood* (Season 1, Episode 3) [Audio podcast episode]. In Jury talk. Apple Podcasts. https://podcasts.apple.com/us/podcast/s1-ep3-the-juror-counseling-program-with-pam-wood/id1754242793?i=1000660363718

10 A Jury in Jeopardy

What Do You Think?

Before reviewing the concepts addressed in this chapter, answer True or False to each of the following questions or statements. Correct answers can be found at the end of Chapter 10.

1. Courthouses were required to remain open, and jurors were required to report for jury service as usual during the COVID-19 pandemic.
2. Prospective jurors who did not have the technology to participate in jury service remotely were automatically exempt from jury service.
3. Trial attorneys encourage defendants to seek a jury trial to resolve most disputes.
4. The number of jury trials conducted today are decreasing because fewer attorneys know how to conduct jury trials.
5. Arbitration involves a neutral third party who works with disputing parties to identify areas of agreement and reach a consensus about a case outcome.

Learning Objectives

After reading this chapter, you will be able to:

1. Describe how courthouses adapted to COVID-19 pandemic restrictions, including jury selection procedures and social distancing.
2. Explain the hybrid approach courthouses used for trial proceedings during the global pandemic.
3. Compare the advantages and disadvantages of a fully virtual jury trial from the perspective of trial attorneys and jurors.
4. List structural and operational reasons why the number of jury trials are decreasing in recent years.
5. Describe current alternatives to jury trials to resolve disputes.
6. List and explain important issues that the American jury system will face in the future.

Introduction

Juries have evolved into sophisticated entities since the use of trials by ordeal in the Middle Ages.[1] The American jury system was built on the early English model but has been molded and evolved from its origins penned by the Founding Fathers 250 years ago. Critics of the jury system today have pointed to the problems juries have for reaching verdicts that are impartial and just. Indeed, the previous chapter addressed issues about invalidating a jury

DOI: 10.4324/9781003677796-13

verdict if the jury's decision-making was tampered with, hindered, or influenced in some way. Also addressed were concerns about the complexity of a case and the emotional stress some jurors suffered because of their jury service. This led some critics to seek reforming the jury system. Specific issues related to reform have been addressed throughout the text, including misunderstanding of jury instructions, reaching nonunanimous jury verdicts, and making decisions using implicit (or explicit) racial bias.

Research shows these criticisms are valid; however, juries comprised of ordinary citizens have no real power to change the system in which they serve. Rather, it is the judges, lawyers, court administrators, and legislators, as directed by voters during regular elections, who are the ones that make the jury system function and flourish. Natural disasters, including the global pandemic, threatened all aspects of human society and forced legal professionals and courthouse administrators to get creative and think innovatively. Thanks to the tireless efforts of many individuals, courts throughout America implemented changes to make the jury experience more inclusive and enjoyable for all. This finding provides clear evidence that the jury system is adaptable. Moreover, these changes should help to quiet the outspoken critics, while simultaneously encouraging every American to look toward the future of trial by jury with a renewed sense of hope and excitement.

In This Chapter

This chapter describes the adaptability of the American jury system and the challenges it faces now and in the future. Here material will be reviewed related to: 1) the effects of the COVID-19 pandemic on trial juries; 2) measures federal and state court systems employed amid social distancing restrictions and mandatory shutdowns; 3) reasons for decreasing trends in the number of jury trials; and 4) considerations and predictions about the future of the American jury system.

Juries and Adaptation

Global Pandemic

The onset and spread of COVID-19 throughout the world had a ripple effect that eventually touched every aspect of life. Hospitals and medical centers were flooded with sick and dying patients, supply chains were disrupted causing shortages of common household goods, national economies suffered, and general fear and anxiety gripped individuals across the globe. Courts and juries were not immune to the effects of the pandemic. Court officials and administrators faced difficult decisions about how to continue jury trials while keeping average citizens, litigants, and court staff safe.

In the spring and summer months of 2020, many courthouses were closed to the public under mandatory shutdowns, canceling in-person hearings, including jury trials.[2] The most dramatic impact of COVID-19 on juries and jury trials was the sudden decrease in jury trials in 2020 and continuing into 2021. In 2019, state courts conducted an estimated 125,222 jury trials, but only 33,880 in 2020.[3] Moreover, nearly three-quarters of jury trials conducted by state courts in 2020 likely took place on or before March 13, the date on which COVID-19 was declared a federal emergency. After COVID-19 vaccines became broadly available in 2021, the number of jury trials rebounded to an estimated 48,764, a

44 percent increase over 2020, but still less than half the number of 2019 jury trials. As a result of the courthouse closures, courts experienced significant backlogs of older cases that previously were scheduled for trial and a delay of new cases recently filed after the pandemic began.[4] The delays for rescheduling trial dates were especially problematic for criminal defendants who may have been detained for months longer than usual after their arrest.[5] This issue was raised by many attorneys and their clients as a violation of the right to a speedy trial.[6]

Scheduling delays were only the beginning of practical and legal challenges for jury trials. Most court proceedings in the United States are required to be open to the public. But even after courthouses opened for in-person hearings, allowing attorneys and their clients to enter those facilities, **social distancing** requirements restricted members of the public from coming to court to observe those proceedings.[7] Both criminal defense attorneys and media representatives protested that these restrictions violated the Sixth Amendment right to a public trial. The same social distancing requirements limited the number of people who could safely gather in smaller courtrooms as well as jury deliberation rooms. The Administrative Office of the New Jersey Courts conducted a statewide review and concluded that none of the courtrooms were large enough to hold 23 people simultaneously, the minimum number of people who would ordinarily be present for a jury trial (12 jurors, two alternate jurors, trial judge, two attorneys, court clerk, court reporter, bailiff, two party representatives, and a witness). Accommodating the number of grand jurors necessary to satisfy quorum requirements in federal and in many state courts was similarly challenging.

Finally, it became clear early during the pandemic that elderly people, people of color, and people with underlying health conditions were disproportionately at risk for severe illness or death. Understandably, many of these individuals were reluctant to appear for jury service due to the potential risk of exposure to the virus. Indeed, news reports encouraged people to stay at home and to avoid physical contact with other people whenever possible.[8] In addition, many parents of school-aged children who could not afford childcare also requested to be excused. In a public opinion survey conducted in 2020, 55 percent of respondents reported at least one barrier that would prevent them from jury service if summoned.[9] Many courts relaxed their criteria for granting requests to be excused for hardship or extended the timeframe for jurors to defer service.[10] The result, however, was a less diverse jury pool that skewed more White, male, and younger, raising concerns about whether the jury pool reflected a fair cross-section of the community.[11]

Despite the pandemic, many courts remained open for business, including for jury trials, throughout 2020 and 2021. Figure 10.1, featured in a 2024 report from the National Center for State Courts (NCSC), reveals many courts adjusted their jury practices to minimize the risk of transmitting the virus.[12] In addition to liberalizing excusal and deferral criteria, 43 percent of courts reduced the size of venire panels sent to courtrooms for jury selection and 42 percent staggered the reporting times for jurors appearing at the courthouse to accommodate social distancing requirements. Thirty-eight percent conducted jury selection in a larger venue within the courthouse (e.g., ceremonial courtroom or large conference room) and 19 percent moved jury trials to a venue outside the courthouse, including public school auditoriums or hotel conference rooms. Most courts implemented medical screening protocols at public entrances to the courthouse, barring entry to individuals showing COVID-19 symptoms. They also provided facemasks to all

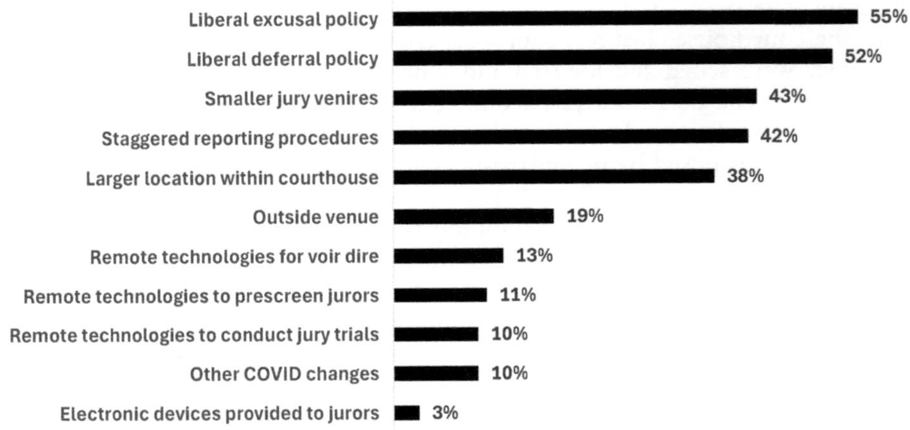

Figure 10.1: Jury Trial Practices during COVID-19
(*Source:* National Center for State Courts.[13])

court users, and many courts mandated facemask use. Some courts reconfigured their courtrooms with plexiglass barriers and replaced seating pews in the courtroom gallery with individual chairs placed six feet apart, so jurors could be assigned a specific seat for the duration of the trial.

Perhaps the most dramatic impact of the pandemic on court operations was the widespread introduction of remote technologies to conduct court hearings, including jury selection and jury trials. Funding from the **Coronavirus Aid Relief and Economic Security (CARES) Act** made it possible for many courts to purchase video conferencing technologies during the pandemic.[14] In 2020, an estimated 7 percent of courts across at least 16 states employed remote technologies to conduct voir dire.[15] Instead of reporting to the courthouse in person, prospective jurors would log into the court's remote meeting platform from their laptop, tablet, or smartphone and answer questions posed by the judge and attorneys to determine whether they could serve impartially. Only those who were selected were instructed to appear in person at the courthouse for trial; the remaining jurors were released from service. The process has been referred to as the **hybrid approach**.[16]

Remote voir dire involved a steep learning curve for judges, courthouse staff, and lawyers to adjust to the online environment. Moreover, the process involved educating prospective jurors, many of whom were less familiar with the remote meeting software and needed help to troubleshoot technology and other operational glitches.[17] Many lawyers were particularly concerned that remote voir dire did not allow them to observe jurors' body language and that jurors would be distracted by personal or work tasks if they were not required to appear at the courthouse in person.[18] Other lawyers, however, found that remote voir dire allowed lawyers to observe jurors' facial expressions much better online than they could possibly do from across the room in a courtroom, especially given that most courts required jurors to be masked during trial. Many judges directed court staff to monitor jurors' behavior during voir dire and to alert the judge if a juror appeared distracted, relieving lawyers about those concerns.

Although courts expressed early concerns about the accessibility of remote voir dire for prospective jurors, research found the overwhelming majority of Americans had both suitable devices (e.g., smartphones, tablets, or personal computers) and reliable home internet service; less than 3 percent had neither suitable devices nor internet access.[19] Moreover, prospective jurors reported they would be more comfortable with the option of remote voir dire than with in-person voir dire by a two to one margin. In addition to assuaging health safety concerns, remote voir dire was considerably more convenient than in-person voir dire. For example, remote voir dire removed traditional barriers to jury service, such as transportation and lost income. For jurors who could not participate remotely, courts partnered with local government agencies, libraries, and nonprofit organizations and equipped their own courthouses with dedicated space and computer access for this purpose.[20] Some courts even purchased internet-enabled tablets that could be lent out to prospective jurors for jury selection. Although pandemic conditions have dissipated since 2020, 38 percent of courts that used remote technologies for voir dire reported that they intended to continue doing so. As of 2025, for example, the Salt Lake County District Court in Utah conducts all voir dire proceedings for jury trials remotely.

A handful of intrepid courts also expanded the use of remote court proceedings to full jury trials. A study from the NCSC about jury improvement efforts found judges and trial attorneys estimated 2 percent of jury trials were conducted entirely online in 2020.[21] Most of these trials were civil cases, which were not as severely constrained by constitutional and statutory requirements. Judges and lawyers were less receptive to the use of remote technology for the entire jury trial than they were for the voir dire exclusively, however. One problem associated with virtual jury trials was trial length, some of which lasted for days or weeks, contributing to "**Zoom fatigue**."[22] Teachers and educators who were forced into delivering lesson plans online and struggled to keep students actively engaged can relate to these problems. The mechanics of admitting evidence and presenting it to jurors, especially physical evidence, in an online environment was very challenging. Also, some judges and lawyers raised concerns about how jurors would deliberate together online, especially given ongoing concerns about external distractions.

Finally, lawyers found that traditional methods of trial advocacy did not translate well to remote trials. Forceful speaking voices and grand theatrical gestures in the courtroom, for example, came across as unnaturally aggressive to jurors.[23] Inventive judges and lawyers developed workarounds to address all of these concerns, and some courts have continued to conduct civil jury trials online. The King County Superior Court in Seattle, Washington, for example, has now conducted hundreds of civil jury trials remotely and has made it the default mode for the foreseeable future.[24] The court's website features an extensive array of educational resources for lawyers and jurors conducting remote jury trials. In most other jurisdictions, however, judges and lawyers concluded that remote jury trials presented more problems than they had solved and were happy to return to in-person jury trials as soon as the pandemic receded enough to do so safely.[25] Box 10.1 features a former judge who shares his insights about the importance of juries, understanding jury instructions, and the predictability of jury verdicts.

Box 10.1: From the Field

Name: Paul Wilson

Position: Superior Court of Massachusetts (ret.); Current Chair of the American Bar Association Commission on the American Jury

How long were you a trial judge in Massachusetts?
I retired in June 2025 after nearly 12 years as a Massachusetts Superior Court judge.

Should juries be asked to decide more cases, fewer cases, or just different types of cases?
The more cases juries decide, the better off we are as a society, for two reasons. First, serving on a jury permits citizens to participate quite directly in our system of democratic self-government, by actually serving as the government decision-maker. Second, juries are particularly well suited to serve as the conscience of the community, because the jurors decide cases in which they have no personal interests that might influence the decision (in contrast, for example, to an arbitrator who may want to be hired by one party for future cases, or a government agency that might have its own political agenda).

What changes could help jurors better understand the evidence and the judge's instructions?
To help jurors understand the evidence, all courts should allow jurors to take notes and to ask questions as suggested in this chapter (although juror questions must be vetted by the judge with the advice of the attorneys, to ensure that the answers will be admissible under the rules of evidence). And jurors pay more attention to the evidence if they believe that they will be asked to decide the case, so alternate jurors should not be designated until just before the jury deliberates—or, better yet, there should be no alternates, because all jurors who remain at the end of the evidence should be allowed to participate in deciding on the verdict (unless there is a constitutional or statutory reason that non-deliberating alternate jurors must be designated).

To help jurors understand the law, a judge should briefly describe the relevant law to the jurors at the beginning of the trial, to give them some legal context for the evidence they will hear. Throughout the trial, the judge should explain legal concepts as they become relevant. Most important, the jury instructions at the end of the trial should be as short as possible and in plain English. For example, rather than telling juries that they must decide a civil case based on the "preponderance of the evidence," a judge could instead say that the jury must decide whether the plaintiff's evidence has "tipped the scale" in favor of the plaintiff's view of the facts. To better hold the jurors' interest, and to juxtapose the elements of the claims or crimes and the lawyers' arguments about whether these elements are satisfied, a judge could also "split the jury charge" at the end of the trial. That is, first the judge would explain what the plaintiff or prosecutor has to prove in this specific case; then the lawyers would deliver closing arguments; and then the judge would deliver the more general jury instructions that apply in all cases, for example about credibility, or about how to conduct the deliberations.

Some people say juries are too slow, too expensive, or too unpredictable. How would you respond to those criticisms?

Some juries are "slow," but that is a feature, not a bug. Because juries are intended to serve as the conscience of the community, they are randomly drawn from a cross-section of the local population. Thus it is likely—and in fact ideal—that the jurors will have different life experiences and different viewpoints. Deliberations can be slow because the jurors are taking the time necessary to apply those differing life experiences and viewpoints to reach unanimity. At a criminal trial the jurors also must wrestle with the concept of "reasonable doubt," a standard for decision-making that is largely foreign to lay jurors. Because jurors almost always take these tasks so seriously, jury verdicts are actually not "unpredictable." In a dozen years of judging, I was seldom surprised by a jury's verdict.

Vanishing Jury Trials

> I certainly believe it's over for the jury system, but we won't admit it for a while.
>
> —Joseph Wambaugh, American Writer
> Public interview (2002)

The number of jury trials conducted in state and federal courts fell precipitously in 2020 due to COVID-19 disruptions to court operations, and the rate of jury trials has not yet returned to pre-pandemic levels. Yet the trend toward decreased numbers of jury trials has been apparent for decades. Judges, lawyers, and justice system scholars first became aware of the **"vanishing trials"** phenomenon in the early 1990s.[26] In 2001, the American Bar Association hosted the Vanishing Trials Symposium to explore the causes of declining trial rates and their implications for the American justice system.[27]

The declining rate of jury trials has continued unabated ever since. Figure 10.3 shows the number of civil and criminal jury trials conducted in federal district courts from 2005 to 2023, which shows a steady decline, especially in criminal jury trials.[28] In 2005, there were approximately 6,000 criminal trials and 2,500 civil trials in the U.S. District Courts; however, that number dropped to 4,200 and 1,500, respectively, by 2023. Data on the number of jury trials conducted in state courts is more difficult to collect, but studies published by the NCSC suggest a similar decline in state courts.[29] In 2007, for example, the estimated number of jury trials conducted in state courts was 148,558; by 2019, the number had dropped to 125,222. A closer examination of jury trial rates shows an even more dramatic picture. In 2007, the rate of jury trials per 100,000 population was 58.6, but this rate fell to 37.7 in 2019, a 26 percent decrease. It was only because the U.S. population grew 9 percent during the same period that the decrease in the raw number of jury trials fell by just 17 percent.

Scholars have proposed multiple factors that contribute to this downward trend in the number of jury trials. The most common reasons include insufficient **institutional capacity** and a lack of **incentives** for jury trials.[31] First, jury trials are the single most time-consuming and labor-intensive event that can occur in the life of a case, which makes them extremely expensive for both litigants and taxpayers. They also compete for judges' and lawyers' time and attention on large caseloads, which have increased substantially without commensurate

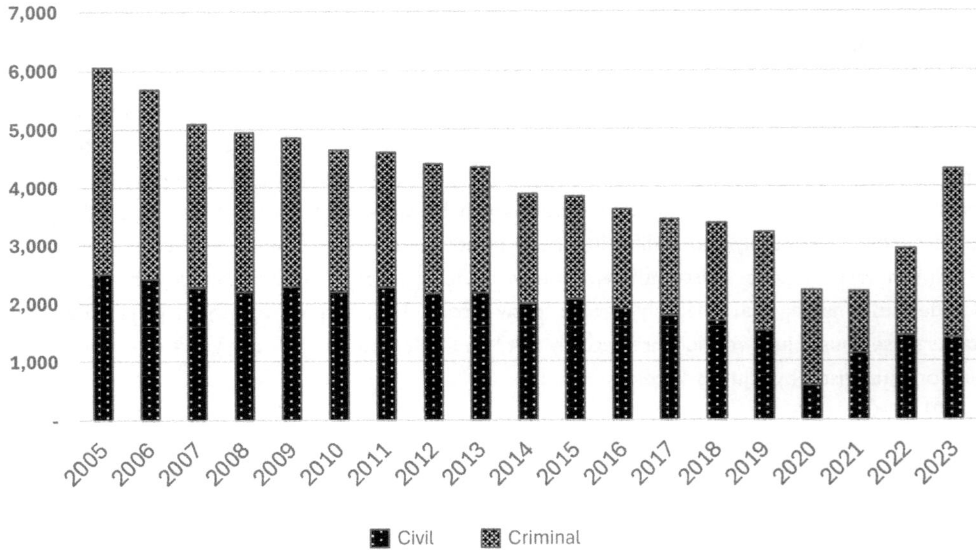

Figure 10.3: Total Jury Trials Held in U.S. District Courts
(*Source:* Administrative Office of the U.S. Courts.[30])

increases in the number of judges, prosecutors and criminal defense attorneys, or even the number of courtrooms.[32] The resulting shift to plea agreements, settlements, and other non-trial dispositions is viewed as necessary to keep the justice system from grinding to a complete halt.

Changes to state and federal rules of civil procedure introduced pretrial barriers that litigants had to overcome before proceeding to trial, including summary judgment, motions to dismiss for lack of legal sufficiency, and restrictions on expert testimony.[33] Contractual requirements for binding arbitration in standard consumer agreements prevent many civil disputes from being filed in court at all.[34] For example, consumers are often required to agree to binding arbitration in contracts for cellphone and internet service, banking and credit card accounts, employment, and healthcare delivery. By doing so, the individual agrees to waive their rights to sue in court in the future. In criminal cases, many states have implemented diversion programs and "problem-solving courts" designed to address underlying social and behavioral circumstances that led defendants to commit crimes.[35] These programs allow defendants to avoid imprisonment, provided they participate in a court-supervised treatment program to address substance abuse, mental illness, or other conditions. But to be eligible for these programs, defendants must waive their right to trial.

In criminal cases, the disincentives for pursuing a jury trial are even more stark. Defendants who choose to go to trial often face the prospect of much harsher sentences if convicted—a phenomenon known as the "**trial penalty**." This can be a powerful deterrent, particularly when coupled with the financial burdens associated with a trial, such as court fees, fines, and the costs of legal representation. For many defendants, pleading guilty to a lesser charge, even if they believe themselves to be innocent, is seen as the safer and more practical option. Box 10.2 addresses the disparities in sentencing outcomes between defendant cases resolved through a negotiated resolution or plea bargaining versus a decision reached by a trial jury.

Box 10.2: Trial Penalty

Defendants may look at trends among sentencing outcomes when deciding whether to proceed with a jury trial or agree to a plea bargain. This issue has been referred to as a trial penalty. For example, among level cases in 2012, drug offenders whose case went to trial received, on average, a 16-year sentence compared to approximately a five-year sentence among drug offenders who plead guilty.[36] Other findings showed federal defendants received trial sentences that were 64 percent higher than defendants who chose to plead guilty to similar crimes.[37] Although there was variation within the state court systems, overall, findings showed sentences imposed following a jury trial were significantly longer than those that were resolved with a guilty plea.[38]

Generally, legal professionals agreed that litigants preferred taking plea bargains rather than risking going to trial; this finding was uncovered from survey results among 89 percent of judges (in a sample of 109) and 63.6 percent of trial attorneys (in a sample 955).[39] These findings may better explain why so many cases in the American jury system result in plea bargaining. Criminal defense attorneys emphasize the disparities in sentencing outcomes for cases going to jury trial versus the outcome resulting from accepting a plea bargain negotiated with the opposing counsel. In this sense, defendants are coerced into taking a plea bargain rather than risking going to trial, where they likely will be penalized with a harsher and longer sentence.

More fundamentally, the legal profession itself is facing a **capacity crisis**. Many newer attorneys have little to no experience in jury trials, and opportunities for young lawyers to gain trial experience have become increasingly rare. Without this foundational experience, fewer attorneys feel comfortable taking cases to trial, further perpetuating the decline in jury trials.[40] The implications of this trend are profound. As fewer cases go to trial, the skills and experience necessary to conduct jury trials are eroding within the legal profession. This creates a feedback loop where the lack of experience leads to fewer trials, which in turn reduces opportunities for gaining that experience.[41] Additionally, the lack of trial experience among lawyers means that when cases do go to trial, they may not be handled as effectively, potentially leading to less favorable outcomes for clients and, at least indirectly, undermining public confidence in the jury system.

What do these trends tell you? Most cases are resolved through plea bargaining or settlement and are never considered by a fair and impartial jury where the conscience of the community determines whether the facts of a case determine the verdict. Voting and jury service, as described in Chapter 2, are the main avenues that most Americans utilize for influencing and defining a community's interest and the conscience of the community itself. Box 10.3 features a trial judge who discusses improving jury instructions and the impact of improved instructions for jurors and plea bargaining.

> You ought to be extremely cautious, watchful, jealous of your liberty; for instead of securing your rights, you may lose them forever.
>
> —Patrick Henry, Founding Father
> First Speech at the Virginia Ratifying Convention (1788)

Box 10.3: From the Field

Name: Lucretia C. Clemons

Position: Judge, Philadelphia Court of Common Pleas, First Judicial District

How long have you been in this position?
I have been a sitting judge for nine years.

Former jurors have reported confusion understanding the instructions provided to them at trial. In your experience as a judge, what instructions do jurors struggle with the most? What changes could be implemented to reduce confusion and frustration among jurors?
In my experience, jurors most often struggle with instructions regarding the elements of criminal offenses. To address this, I make it a practice to provide jurors with written copies of the criminal elements for each charged offense to use during deliberations. Not all individuals process information most effectively through oral communication; some comprehend best when they can read and refer back to the material. Therefore, supplementing the traditional oral delivery of instructions with written copies helps promote comprehension and reduces confusion among jurors.

Judges will review instructions with a jury prior to the deliberation about the law that was allegedly violated. Are there times when you felt jurors were confused at the instructions you provided them? What did or could you do in that situation?
Yes. On occasion, jurors seek clarification because they find certain instructions confusing. When this occurs, I typically solicit proposed responses from both parties to determine whether they can agree on an appropriate answer. If no consensus is reached, I will independently assess the request and provide a clarifying instruction if I believe it is both necessary and consistent with the law. This approach ensures fairness while addressing the jury's need for greater understanding.

Empaneling a professional jury is controversial topic. Critics argue such juries move away from the notion of a fair cross section of the community. Are there any advantages to a professional jury that could sustain or improve the American jury system?
The cornerstone of our criminal justice system is the right to a jury composed of one's peers—a representative cross section of the community. A professional jury would undermine that foundational principle and erode public confidence in the fairness and legitimacy of the jury system.

Most cases are resolved through plea bargaining rather than going to a jury trial. Would better jury instructions contribute to more defendants seeking a jury trial rather than accepting a plea?
I do not believe that improved jury instructions would significantly increase the number of defendants demanding jury trials. The decision to accept a plea bargain is often driven by a desire for certainty and finality, given the inherent unpredictability and risk of a jury trial. While clearer jury instructions may enhance the fairness of the trial process, they are unlikely to alter the calculus that leads most defendants to resolve their cases through plea agreements.

Alternatives to Juries and Jury Trials

Despite the uniqueness of the American jury system for putting the power and authority of decision-making into the hands of its people, commentators have criticized the jury system for years. Juries are comprised of laypersons from the community, typically non-lawyers, who may struggle to sort through complex evidence and legal principles or who may be swayed by emotional considerations that contribute to inflated damage awards in civil cases.[42] Over the past half century, a variety of legal professionals and scholars have suggested alternative methods of dispute resolution, mainly for civil cases.

Throughout the 20th century, for example, state and federal legislatures created administrative agencies both to regulate industry and provide a forum to resolve disputes that arise. At the federal level, the Occupational Safety and Health Administration (OSHA) was created by Congress in 1971 to ensure American workers have safe and healthy working conditions.[43] Instead of filing complaints about working conditions in court, workers now file complaints with OSHA, which is authorized to investigate violations of federal labor standards and impose financial penalties on employers. OSHA works collaboratively with federal and state agencies that provide Workman's Compensation Insurance, which reimburse workers who are injured by unsafe employment conditions.[44] These agencies provide a mechanism for preventing workplace injuries and a more efficient and consistent process for injured employees to receive compensation than would be possible by filing a tort claim in state or federal courts. Similar federal and state agencies perform the same role with respect to worker compensation, race, gender, or age discrimination in employment, consumer safety, financial services, and disputes concerning local zoning regulations and ordinances.

While some types of civil cases are diverted from state and federal courts to administrative agencies, hundreds of thousands of cases are still filed in court each year. To address the volume of cases, courts developed a variety of procedures in the mid-1980s to encourage effective settlement negotiations, including the use of both court-sponsored and private **alternative dispute resolution** (ADR).[45] ADR refers to methods used to resolve disputes between civil parties without resorting to litigation, including mediation and arbitration. In mediation, a neutral third party who is trained in facilitating settlement negotiations works with the parties to identify areas of agreement and reach a consensus about a case outcome perceived as fair and acceptable to all parties. Arbitration, in contrast, offers a quasi-adversarial process in which litigants present information about their respective positions to a privately retained expert, who decides the case based on established legal principles. Many states now require civil cases involving lower monetary stakes to participate in mandatory mediation or arbitration before they can proceed through formal litigation. In Arizona, for example, all civil cases alleging damages less than $50,000 are required to participate in compulsory arbitration with a court-appointed arbitrator.[46] Parties can object to the arbitrator's decision and seek a new trial before a judge or jury. But unless they improve their outcome in the new trial by at least 25 percent, they will be assessed the legal costs, including attorney fees, incurred by the other side, which is generally a strong incentive to accept the arbitrator's decision.

Although nearly all civil cases are resolved through settlement, some ultimately go to trial. As discussed in previous chapters, however, parties in both civil and criminal trials can elect to have their case decided by the trial judge, referred to as a bench trial, without a jury.[47] Jury trials tend to take longer than bench trials, so some lawyers encourage their clients to opt for a bench trial to secure a faster resolution or to reduce litigation costs.[48] Others raise concerns that the evidence and law are too complex for lay jurors to understand, reasoning that judges are specially trained in the law and often acquire expertise about the evidence likely to be presented in these types of cases, even if they are unfamiliar with the details of a particular case. In a bench trial, however, the decision rests with a single judge rather than the collective judgment of a diverse group. Given that most courts assign cases to judges randomly as they are filed, there is no guarantee that the assigned trial judge will have any greater expertise or be less influenced by personal and professional biases than a jury.

As an alternative to the potential downsides of a bench trial, a few commentators have suggested that courts employ **professional juries**, especially in complicated, highly technical cases.[49] A professional jury would consist of trained and certified jurors who are paid for their work and held to strict standards, with the possibility of losing certification for misconduct or bias.[50] Supporters argue that such jurors would be more motivated and impartial than ordinary citizens and would be better equipped to handle complex or lengthy cases involving technical evidence or multiple parties.[51] Professional jurors could also make trials more efficient by eliminating costly jury selection and reducing the need for extensive instructions from judges, since they would already understand courtroom procedures.[52]

Critics, however, note that decisions reached by a professional jury would likely be indistinguishable from a trial judge or from a specially trained arbitrator, both of whom are already available to resolve cases. Professional jurors, therefore, are merely redundant, and offer no increased benefit to parties than options that already exist. Critics of professional juries also argue that identifying potential jurors based on education level and training violates the Sixth Amendment and the due process clause of the Fourteenth Amendment, which guarantees the accused a jury drawn impartially from a cross-section of the community.[53] Although the idea for professional juries has been circulating since the mid-1980s, no state or federal court has seriously contemplated implementing this approach.

The Future of Juries and Jury Trials

Whenever the people are well informed they can be trusted with own government; that whenever things get so far wrong as to attract their notice, they may be relied on to set them to rights.

—Thomas Jefferson, Founding Father
Letter to Richard Price (1789)

In the late 18th century, the Founding Fathers vigorously debated about the structure, power, and authority that should be given to American juries. The past two-and-a-half centuries have seen many revisions and controversial decisions about the practices of juries in the federal and state court systems. While the allure of being summoned to jury duty may have diminished from what the original Framers of the Constitution intended, the jury system is still a vital and unique part of the judicial branch. What does the future hold for the American jury system?

Lawyers with little trial experience express skepticism about juries. Structural characteristics of jury trials exacerbate distrust.

Justice system stakeholders have identified several overarching trends that are likely to affect the continued viability of grand juries, trial juries, and jury trials. The previous discussion about vanishing trials was one trend, especially the erosion of trial experience by lawyers. One consequence of their unfamiliarity with juries and jury trials is decreased trust that jury verdicts are the product of well-informed decision-making and reflect objectively fair outcomes. Recall from Chapter 4 that 12-person juries operating under unanimous verdict rules perform better than smaller juries and juries who are not required to reach unanimity to render a verdict. Thus, lawyers' sense of distrust may be exacerbated by greater unpredictability of jury verdicts in states that employ smaller juries and nonunanimous verdict rules for civil cases. When the U.S. Supreme Court decided *Ramos v. Louisiana* in 2019, it restored the requirement that criminal verdicts be unanimous, but it did not extend its ruling to civil verdicts. Nonunanimous verdicts are permitted in more than half the states, which may contribute to lawyers' skepticism of juries.

Operational and procedural barriers continue to impede citizens' ability to participate in jury service and to make informed decisions as trial jurors.

Another factor affecting the future of juries and jury trials is the extent to which courts facilitate the ability of citizens to serve and to provide appropriate support to the jurors who are ultimately selected for trial. As noted in Chapter 2, the United States has made great progress in expanding eligibility criteria for jury service since its founding, when only White, male property owners were permitted to serve. Following the Civil War, ratification of the Thirteen, Fourteenth, and Fifteenth Amendments extended the franchise to formerly enslaved men. In 1975, the U.S. Supreme Court ruled in *Taylor v. Louisiana* that the exclusion of women from jury service violated the Sixth Amendment right to impartial jury. Today, the right to serve as a trial juror is generally available to adult citizens who are legal residents of the geographic community in which they are summoned. Not only have historical legal restrictions on eligibility been repealed over time but operational practices that erected barriers to jury service for large segments of the population have also been reformed. The "key-man" system in which local jury commissioners individually vetted prospective jurors based on highly subjective criteria, such as public stature, was replaced by a system of random selection from broad-based juror source lists. These reforms have been rightly lauded as promoting the broadest possible participation in jury service.

Yet, for all the rhetorical praise of juries and jury trials, the justice system too often fails to prioritize jurors' ability to serve. Not only is juror compensation a fraction of the average daily income in most jurisdictions; it does not even cover out-of-pocket expenses for transportation, parking, meals, or childcare in many urban areas. Jurors who can afford to appear for jury service often find themselves languishing in crowded jury assembly rooms for long periods before being sent to a courtroom for jury selection—assuming they are sent at all. Procedures implemented to conduct jury trials during the COVID-19 pandemic, especially the use of remote voir dire proceedings, greatly increased the convenience of jury service for many jurors. Other reforms, including increased compensation, shorter terms of service, and liberal excusal and deferral policies, have also reduced the burden of jury service. A great deal of progress in these areas took place in the latter half of the 20th century, but the forward momentum has slowed in recent years.

Also, greater attention should be placed on meeting jurors' needs. The comparatively few individuals empaneled as trial jurors receive little support from judges and attorneys to aid their decision-making during trial and deliberations. Although the evidence and law in most jury trials are described by judges and lawyers as moderately complex, decision-making aids, such as allowing jurors to submit questions to witnesses, providing written copies of jury instructions, and even permitting jurors to take notes, are not allowed in many jurisdictions. The mid-1990s saw a great deal of interest and educational programming for judges and attorneys about effective juror decision-making aids.[54] While some reforms are well established in many states, others have languished. Some jurors experience high levels of stress or anxiety due to the nature of the evidence and testimony they heard at trial, but only a handful of courts have resources in place to support jurors' mental health following jury service. Due to increased concern about Americans' overall mental health and wellness, court efforts to improve this problem have received more attention.

The collective failure to focus on the juror-centered experience is a significant vulnerability for the future of jury trials, the consequences of which extend beyond the individual juror. When jurors leave the courthouse with negative impressions, those perceptions can spread through their communities, discouraging others from participating in future jury service. This reduces the pool of willing jurors and risks creating a jury system that is less representative of the community, undermining public trust in the justice system.

Americans today are less informed about the critical role of juries and jury trials in the American justice system.

The extent to which citizens understand and show their support for the institution of trial by jury through their willingness to participate is another trend affecting the future of juries and jury trials. For many people, jury duty is seen as an inconvenience or a burden, something to be avoided rather than a privilege of citizenship and a vital civic responsibility. A major symptom is the dramatic increase in nonresponse and failure-to-appear (FTA) rates reported by courts across the country. While many factors contribute to nonresponse and FTA rates, not the least of which is unreliable postal service delivery, a substantial factor is a fundamental lack of public understanding about jury service and its role in the justice system, which is rooted in a broader decline in civics education.

Historically, jury service has been promoted as a cornerstone of democratic participation—a means by which ordinary citizens directly influence the administration of justice. This view posits that jury duty is not just an obligation but a powerful exercise of democracy in action. Serving on a jury allows citizens to reflect their community's values in the deliberative process, preventing injustice and ensuring that justice reflects the moral and ethical standards of the populace. Yet in recent years, traditional appeals to civic duty appear less persuasive, particularly in the face of rising partisanship and social division. This landscape of citizen disenchantment, amplified by social media, has made it more challenging to convey the importance of jury service in a way that resonates with diverse audiences. Moreover, the decline in funding for civics education in K–12 education has left many citizens ill-prepared to understand the significance of their role as grand or trial jurors.[55]

Engaging the public in a meaningful way requires a nuanced approach that acknowledges the varied experiences and perceptions of young people, communities of color, and working-class individuals, which each have unique concerns about the jury system that need to be addressed in culturally relevant ways. While schools can serve as a conduit for educating youth, outreach to more dispersed groups may require creative strategies, such as public service announcements during commuting hours or more sustained outreach to the business community to support employees who are summoned for jury service. Simple lectures about the importance of jury service and civic duty may not be as impactful as providing real-world examples of how this aspect of the democratic system, and the empowerment of ordinary citizens, benefits the local community.

Effective public education and engagement strategies must also account for the realities of today's technology-based world. Traditional forums for social and educational engagement have largely shifted online. Reaching the public now demands innovative, attention-grabbing content that can compete with the deluge of information available on social media. Outreach efforts need to be inclusive, providing information in multiple formats and languages to engage a wide variety of communities, cultures, and non-English-speaking populations who may be future jurors even if they are not presently qualified for jury service.

Courts, businesses, educators, and others share responsibility for addressing this vulnerability. Courts, with their unique ability to convene diverse audiences, must lead efforts to educate and engage the public about the importance of jury service. However, the task is far too large for courts to accomplish themselves. The civil and criminal bar should convey confidence in juries and jury trials both as a general proposition and as a viable option for clients to fairly resolve cases. The business community, which benefits from a civically engaged workforce, should also play a substantial role in promoting jury service among their employees. Educators, who shape the civic knowledge and attitudes of future generations, must ensure that civics education is not neglected in favor of other subjects. And cultural, civic, religious, and other groups have a voice in addressing these profound issues as well.

Grand juries face criticism for secrecy, prosecutorial control, and failure to indict police.

While knowledge about trial juries and jury trials is woefully lacking among the American public, their knowledge of grand juries and grand jury proceedings is even worse. Grand jury proceedings have received much criticism from the public and some legal professionals. Generally, the concerns revolve around the secrecy of grand jury proceedings and the absolute authority granted to the prosecutor in the process. In recent decades, grand jurors themselves have been scrutinized for their decisions not to indict police officers who were involved in fatal shootings of citizens or other incidents involving use of lethal force. The public's concern needs to be addressed, but given that the right to a grand jury "for a capital, or otherwise infamous crime" is guaranteed by the Fifth Amendment, its existence in federal courts and in states that mandate the use of grand juries for accusatory purposes will continue. Reforms to grand jury procedures have been proposed, including allowing citizens to directly present evidence to grand juries; amending secrecy requirements to permit disclosure of grand jury materials, including witness transcripts and jury instructions; and removing concerns about conflicts of interest by appointing independent prosecutors or special counsel to present evidence to grand juries in cases involving police use of lethal force.

Conclusion

Anyone familiar with the legal system, or even minimally informed about it, probably knows the American jury system is not perfect. Throughout this text, specific problems have been identified, such as confusing jury instructions, implicit or explicit bias, and nonunanimous verdict rules. Also, to meet the standards intended by the Founding Fathers, juries should be comprised of diverse representatives of the communities where trials are held and should be inclusive of all community members. This standard also has been shown to be challenging to meet.

Overshadowing all the information provided in this text, however, was research about the evolution and improvements made to the American jury system since the 18th century when the right to a trial by jury was granted to citizens in the founding documents of this country, including the U.S. Constitution and Bill of Rights. Sadly, the declining number of jury trials in federal and state court systems diminishes citizens' active participation in the government process. However, research shown throughout this text demonstrates that the jury system is adaptive, active, and vibrant. Today, maybe more than ever before in American history, juries who represent the conscience of the community are needed. Encroachment of a centralized government, loss of basic freedoms and liberties, and protection from an abusive and oppressive government were what the Founding Fathers fought against. The right to a trial by jury and the protection of individual jurors were written into the documents of this country and are the last line of defense to ensure that liberties and freedoms of Americans are protected and maintained.

Summary

This chapter addressed issues of importance for the adaptability of the American jury system to function and flourish during periods of global crisis. The COVID-19 pandemic wreaked havoc throughout the world, decimating families, communities, economies, and life in general. The courts and juries were not immune to these effects. Courthouses and administrators had to adapt to social distancing restrictions while continuing to conduct jury trials. Some courts implemented remote trial practices that involved online voir dire and virtual trial proceeding; other jurisdictions adopted a hybrid approach where voir dire was conducted online, but the trial proceeding occurred in person. Still other jurisdictions conducted the jury selection process in large community facilities, where social distancing could be observed, but held the trial proceeding and deliberation inside the courthouse under controlled conditions.

This chapter addressed other concerns about the current state of the American jury—specifically, the diminishing number of cases being resolved by jury trial. The reasons for the declining numbers may be institutional capacity and an intentional disincentive for defendants to seek jury trials. Regardless, fewer attorneys now possess the skills to argue a case effectively and efficiently to a trial jury, and fewer citizens are called to make decisions reflecting the conscience of the community. Critics have argued that this goes against what the Founding Fathers intended, that is, to have average citizens participate in the government process. The declining number of jury trials may further undermine public confidence in the jury system.

The courts themselves have implemented strategies to resolve conflicts faster and without empaneling a jury trial. Courts encourage settlement of disputes that involve either court-sponsored or private negotiators. Alternative dispute resolution methods used to resolve disputes between civil parties without resorting to litigation, including mediation where a third party negotiates a consensus about a case outcome perceived as fair and acceptable to all parties or an arbitration where litigants present information about their position to a privately retained expert, who decides an outcome based on established legal principles.

What does the future hold for the American jury system? Recent years have demonstrated that the jury is alive, active, and vibrant. There is little evidence that this will change in the future. Some traditions concerning jury operations and procedures have been firmly established, including federal and state allowances for jury size and unanimity or nonunanimous verdicts. Other procedures have only recently been discussed and implemented in select jurisdictions. These issues pertain to creating debriefing sessions and providing opportunities for mental health counseling after the trial proceeding to address emotional stress and strain. Society's increasing awareness of mental health issues, and the decreased stigma for such, suggests more courthouses may be addressing this issue in the future. Finally, the newest development for many courts has been to embrace technology because of the restrictions put in place due to the global pandemic. An unintended consequence for using remote modalities for jury selection and trial proceedings may be a more diverse jury pool, decreased court costs, and happier jurors who enjoyed the convenience of virtual jury service and are interested in serving again in the future.

Discussion Questions

1. In the years following the COVID-19 pandemic, courthouses slowly returned to providing in-person jury selection and trial proceedings. What do you think about this decision to return to the traditional format? Should the jury selection process and/or the entire trial proceeding continue in a virtual format that was used in some jurisdictions during the height of the pandemic? Do you think the verdict reached by virtual juries versus in-person juries differs? In what type of cases might you notice a difference and why?
2. Is the American jury system being used to its fullest potential? What would the Founding Fathers think today if they saw the figures about decreasing numbers of jury trials and the overreliance on plea bargaining and settlement? What do you see as the biggest concern(s) with a reduced number of cases being resolved through a trial by a jury that is representative of the community at large?
3. You have reviewed the information shared throughout this text related to the American jury system. Do you believe trial juries are the most fair, efficient, and effective means for reaching verdicts in criminal or civil matters, or should professional juries (or judges) be used exclusively? What specific material shown in the text or learned through discussion with others helped to inform your decision?
4. In the first chapter of this text (The Seeds of Trial by Jury) a question was posed to the reader: what features of the American jury system do you think are the most important remnants of the old English system and why? Much information was shared in the following chapters that may make it easier to answer this question. What resonated with you the most about the American jury system? What are your hopes for the future of the American jury and what role(s) do you see yourself playing to make these hopes a reality?

Review Questions

1. What concerns did the courts and administrators address and overcome regarding the social distancing mandates during the COVID-19 pandemic? How did some courts adapt to this problem?
2. What technology was embraced in some courthouses during the pandemic? What remote or virtual options were implemented? What was the reaction to such changes among trial attorneys, judges, and jurors?
3. What are the reasons for the number of jury trials decreasing in recent decades? What structural or operational changes could the courts implement, if anything, to increase these numbers?
4. What alternatives now exist for resolving conflicts in the work environment or criminal justice system, and how do these options impact the number of cases going to trial?
5. What does the future hold for the American jury system? What is unlikely to change in the future, and where are changes and improvement needed or expected?

Answers to Chapter 10 "What Do You Think?" Questions

1. False. The Coronavirus Aid Relief and Economic Security (CARES) Act allowed jurisdictions to adopt remote alternatives for trial proceedings during the pandemic, including the voir dire and jury deliberation process.

2. False. Some jurisdictions sent tablets to jurors' residences and made internet hot spots available for them to connect remotely for jury service.
3. False. Due to financial burdens and other reasons, many defendants plead guilty to a lesser charge rather than go to trial, even if they believe themselves to be innocent.
4. True. Fewer attorneys feel comfortable taking cases to trial; the skills and experience necessary to conduct jury trials are eroding within the legal profession.
5. False. Mediation involves a neutral third party working with disputing parties to reach a mutual outcome.

Key Terms

alternative dispute resolution
capacity crisis
Coronavirus Aid Relief and Economic Security Act
hybrid approach
incentives
institutional capacity
professional juries
social distancing
trial penalty
vanishing trials
Zoom fatigue

References

1 Andrews, W. (2013). *Medieval punishments: An illustrated history of torture*. Skyhorse Publishing.
2 Raymond, N. (2020, May 18). *Texas tries a pandemic first: A jury trial by Zoom.* Reuters. https://www.reuters.com/article/us-health-coronavirus-courts-texas/texas-tries-a-pandemic-first-a-jury-trial-by-zoom-idUSKBN22U1FE
3 Hannaford-Agor, P.L., & Moffett, M. (2024). *2023 State-of-the-states survey of jury improvement efforts: Jury trials during COVID-19.* National Center for State Courts. https://ncsc.contentdm.oclc.org/digital/collection/juries/id/364/rec/18
4 Henrickson, K.K. (2021). COVID-19 & the courts: The pandemic's impact on the practice of litigation and considerations for future remote proceedings. *The Review of Litigation*, *40*(2), 305–334.
5 Marimow, A.E., & Jouvenal, J. (2020). *Courts dramatically rethink the jury trial in the era of the coronavirus: The most fundamental aspect of the nation's criminal justice system is being re-engineered.* The Washington Post Online. https://www.washingtonpost.com/local/legal-issues/jury-trials-coronavirus/2020/07/31/8c1fd784-c604–11ea-8ffe-372be8d82298_story.html
6 U.S. Const. amend. VI
7 National Center for State Courts. (2021). *Constitutional concerns related to jury trials during the COVID-19 pandemic.* https://ncsc.contentdm.oclc.org/digital/collection/juries/id/337/rec/1
8 Raymond, N. (2020, May 18). *Texas tries a pandemic first: A jury trial by Zoom.* Reuters. https://www.reuters.com/article/us-health-coronavirus-courts-texas/texas-tries-a-pandemic-first-a-jury-trial-by-zoom-idUSKBN22U1FE
9 National Center for State Courts (2020). *State of the state courts in a (post) pandemic world.* https://ncsc.contentdm.oclc.org/digital/collection/ctcomm/id/194/rec/2
10 Hannaford-Agor, P.L, & Moffett, M. (2024). *2023 State-of-the-states survey of jury improvement efforts: Jury trials during COVID-19.* National Center for State Courts. https://ncsc.contentdm.oclc.org/digital/collection/juries/id/364/rec/18
11 National Center for State Courts. (2021). *Constitutional concerns related to jury trials during the COVID-19 pandemic.* https://ncsc.contentdm.oclc.org/digital/collection/juries/id/337/rec/1

12 Hannaford-Agor, P.L, & Moffett, M. (2024). *2023 State-of-the-states survey of jury improvement efforts: Jury trials during COVID-19.* National Center for State Courts. https://ncsc.contentdm.oclc.org/digital/collection/juries/id/364/rec/18
13 Hannaford-Agor, P.L, & Moffett, M. (2024). *2023 State-of-the-states survey of jury improvement efforts: Jury trials during COVID-19.* National Center for State Courts. https://ncsc.contentdm.oclc.org/digital/collection/juries/id/364/rec/18
14 Coronavirus Aid Relief and Economic Security Act, Section 15002(b)(1), H.R. 748
15 Hannaford-Agor, P.L., & Moffett, M. (2024). *2023 State-of-the-states survey of jury improvement efforts: Jury trials during COVID-19.* National Center for State Courts. https://ncsc.contentdm.oclc.org/digital/collection/juries/id/364/rec/18
16 Raymond, N. (2020, May 18). *Texas tries a pandemic first: A jury trial by Zoom.* Reuters. https://www.reuters.com/article/us-health-coronavirus-courts-texas/texas-tries-a-pandemic-first-a-jury-trial-by-zoom-idUSKBN22U1FE
17 National Center for State Courts. (2023). *Remote jury selection: Technology and staffing.* https://cdm16501.contentdm.oclc.org/digital/collection/juries/id/358
18 Bronstad, A. (2020). Mistrial motion says jurors worked out, checked stove, during virtual voir dire in asbestos case. https://www.law.com/2020/07/20/mistrial-motion-says-jurors-worked-out-checked-stove-during-virtual-voir-dire-in-asbestos-case/?slreturn=20250828084459
19 National Center for State Courts. (2021). *Constitutional concerns related to jury trials during the COVID-19 pandemic.* https://ncsc.contentdm.oclc.org/digital/collection/juries/id/337/rec/1
20 Hannaford-Agor, P.L., & Moffett, M. (2024). *2023 State-of-the-states survey of jury improvement efforts: Jury trials during COVID-19.* National Center for State Courts. https://ncsc.contentdm.oclc.org/digital/collection/juries/id/364/rec/18
21 Hannaford-Agor, P.L., & Moffett, M. (2024). *2023 State-of-the-states survey of jury improvement efforts: Jury trials during COVID-19.* National Center for State Courts. https://ncsc.contentdm.oclc.org/digital/collection/juries/id/364/rec/18
22 Bennett, A.A., Campion, E.D., Keeler, K.R., & Keener, S.K. (2021). Videoconference fatigue? Exploring changes in fatigue after videoconference meetings during COVID-19. *Journal of Applied Psychology*, *106*(3), 330–344. https://doi.org/10.1037/apl0000906
23 Online Courtroom Project. (2020). *Online jury trials: OCP's summary and recommendations report.* https://www.onlinecourtroom.org/demonstration-report
24 King County. (2025, September 1). *Online Superior Court jury trial.* https://kingcounty.gov/en/court/superior-court/courts-jails-legal-system/court-calendars-locations-operations/virtual-hearings-trials/virtual-jury-trial
25 Hannaford-Agor, P.L., & Moffett, M. (2024). *2023 State-of-the-states survey of jury improvement efforts: Jury trials during COVID-19.* National Center for State Courts. https://ncsc.contentdm.oclc.org/digital/collection/juries/id/364/rec/18
26 Galanter, M. (2004). The vanishing trial: An examination of trials and related matters in federal and state courts. *Journal of Empirical Legal Studies*, *1*(3), 459–570. https://api.law.wisc.edu/repository-pdf/uwlaw-library-repository-omekav3/original/0b9f361000c04494e8cff30f04b3afeb486193d4.pdf
27 Lande, J. (2006). Introduction to the vanishing trials symposium. *Journal of Dispute Resolution*, *1*, 1–5. https://scholarship.law.missouri.edu/facpubs/266/
28 U.S. Administrative Office of the Courts. (2024). Caseload statistics data tables C-4, D-4 (2005–2023). https://www.uscourts.gov/statistics-reports/caseload-statistics-data-tables
29 Hannaford-Agor, P.L., & Moffett, M. (2024). *2023 State-of-the-states survey of jury improvement efforts: Volume and frequency of jury trials in state courts.* National Center for State Courts. https://ncsc.contentdm.oclc.org/digital/collection/juries/id/365/rec/19
30 Administrative Office of the U.S. Courts, Table T1 (U.S. District Courts—Trials Federal Judicial Caseload Statistics, 2005–2023). https://www.uscourts.gov/data-news/data-tables/2025/03/31/federal-judicial-caseload-statistics/t-1
31 Diamond, S.S., & Salerno, J.M. (2020). Reasons for the disappearing jury trial: Perspectives from attorneys and judges. *Louisiana Law Review*, *81*(1), 119. https://digitalcommons.law.lsu.edu/cgi/viewcontent.cgi?article=6816&context=lalrev
32 Hannaford-Agor, P.L., Forbust, H., Hamilton, M., Johnson, J., & Moffett, M. (2024). *Preserving the future of juries and jury trials.* National Center for State Courts. https://ncsc.contentdm.oclc.org/digital/collection/juries/id/392/rec/1

33 Hannaford-Agor, P.L. (2016). Jury system management in the 21st century: A perfect storm of fiscal necessity and technological opportunity. In P.M. Koelling (Ed.), *The improvement of the administration of justice* (8th ed., pp. 505, 506–511). American Bar Association.
34 Diamond, S.S., & Salerno, J.M. (2020). Reasons for the disappearing jury trial: Perspectives from attorneys and judges. *Louisiana Law Review*, *81*(1), 119–163. https://digitalcommons.law.lsu.edu/cgi/viewcontent.cgi?article=6816&context=lalrev
35 Haskins, P.A. (2019). Problem-solving courts: Fighting crime by treating the offender. *National Institute of Justice Journal*, *281*, 1–9. https://www.ojp.gov/pdffiles1/nij/252735.pdf
36 Appleman, L.I. (2015) *Defending the jury: Crime, community, and the constitution*. Cambridge University Press.
37 Kim, A.C. (2015). Underestimating the trial penalty: An empirical analysis of the federal trial penalty and critique of the Abrams study. *Mississippi Law Journal*, *84*(5), 1195–1256.
38 Subramanian, R., Digard, L., Washington, M., & Sorage, S. (2020). *In the shadows: A review of the research on plea bargaining*. Vera Institute of Justice. https://www.vera.org/downloads/publications/in-the-shadows-plea-bargaining.pdf
39 Diamond, S.S., & Salerno, J.M. (2020). Reasons for the disappearing jury trial: Perspectives from attorneys and judges. *Louisiana Law Review*, *81*(1), 119–163. https://digitalcommons.law.lsu.edu/lalrev/vol81/iss1/9
40 McCormack, T.W., & Bodner, C.J. (2009). *Honesty is the best policy: It's time to disclose lack of jury trial experience*. U. Texas Law, Public Law Research Paper, No. 151. https://www.kleinandwilson.com/wp-content/uploads/sites/1502222/2020/01/HonestyistheBestPolicy.pdf
41 The Marshall Project. (2020). *The system: The truth about trials*. https://www.themarshallproject.org/2020/11/04/the-truth-about-trials.
42 Greene, E. (2009). Psychological issues in civil trials. In J.D. Lieberman & D.A. Krauss (Eds.), *Jury psychology: Social aspects of trial processes* (pp. 183–205). Ashgate.
43 Laihow, A.W. (2025). *About OSHA*. U.S. Department of Labor. https://www.osha.gov/aboutosha
44 U.S. Department of Labor. (2025). *Workers' compensation*. https://www.dol.gov/general/topic/workcomp
45 Hannaford-Agor, P.L. (2016). Jury system management in the 21st century: A perfect storm of fiscal necessity and technological opportunity. In P.M. Koelling (Ed.), *The improvement of the administration of justice* (8th ed., pp. 505, 506–511). American Bar Association.
46 Superior Court of Arizona, (2025). *Compulsory arbitration*. https://superiorcourt.maricopa.gov/departments/superior-court/civil/arbitration/
47 Hannaford-Agor, P.L., Graves, S.E., & Spacek-Miller, S. (2015). *The landscape of civil litigation in state courts*. National Center for State Courts. https://ncsc.contentdm.oclc.org/digital/collection/civil/id/168/rec/2
48 Diamond, S.S., & Salerno, J.M. (2020). Reasons for the disappearing jury trial: Perspectives from attorneys and judges. *Louisiana Law Review*, *81*(1), 119–163. https://digitalcommons.law.lsu.edu/cgi/viewcontent.cgi?article=6816&context=lalrev
49 Shapiro, G. (2023, July 23). *Local opinion: "Professional" jurors would bring more credibility to verdicts*. Arizona Daily Star. https://tucson.com/opinion/column/local-opinion-professional-jurors-would-bring-more-credibility-to-verdicts/article_a8318b7e-24c1-11ee-b28f-ef4356fc182e.html#:~:text=Local%20Opinion%3A%20%22Professional%22%20jurors%20would%20bring%20more%20credibility%20to%20verdicts,-By%20Gil%20Shapiro
50 Drazan, D. (1989). The case for special juries in toxic tort litigation. *Judicature*, *72*(5), 292–298.
51 Bertelsen, K.L. (1998). From specialized courts to specialized juries: Calling for professional juries in complex civil litigation. *Suffolk Journal of Trial and Appellate Advocacy*, *3*, 1–35.
52 Stockwell, C.J. (2018, December 31). *A professional jury*. Medium. https://medium.com/@chris_12585/a-professional-jury-525b21c6551b
53 U.S. Const. amend. XIV
54 Munsterman, G.T. (1997). *Beyond note taking: Innovations in jury reform*. The Free Library. https://www.thefreelibrary.com/Beyond note taking: innovations in jury reform.-a019634472
55 Spaulding, S., Banks, B., & Nair, D. (2022). *Civics at work: Implementation guide for businesses*. Center for Strategic and International Studies. https://www.csis.org/programs/defending-democratic-institutions/civics/civics-work-initiative

Index

For Product Safety Concerns and Information please contact our EU
representative GPSR@taylorandfrancis.com
Taylor & Francis Verlag GmbH, Kaufingerstraße 24, 80331 München, Germany

www.ingramcontent.com/pod-product-compliance
Ingram Content Group UK Ltd.
Pitfield, Milton Keynes, MK11 3LW, UK
UKHW050234200926
475702UK00020B/3029
9781041151111